W9-BJD-958

Now, The Writing Process is in Full Color

...as only Biays and Wershoven can show it !

The Writing Process in Every Chapter...

Known for its dedication to the writing process, **Along These Lines** offers students intensive, thorough, step-by-step direction through the writing process in each chapter:

■ *Thought Lines:* generating ideas
■ *Outlines:* planning and focusing
■ *Rough Lines:* drafting and revising
■ *Final Lines:* polishing and proofreading.

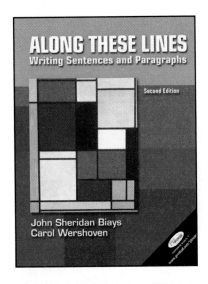

John Sheridan Biays
Broward Community College

Carol Wershoven
Palm Beach Community College

Thought Lines **Gathering Ideas: Illustration**

Suppose your instructor asks you to write a paragraph about some aspect of clothes. You can begin by thinking about your subject, to gather ideas and to find a focus for your paragraph.

Looking through entries in your journal might lead you to the following underlined entry.

Journal Entry About Clothes

I went to the mall yesterday to look for some good shoes. What a crowd! Some big sale was going on, and the stores were packed. Everybody was pushing and shoving. I just left. I'll go when it's not so crowded. I hate buying clothes and shoes. Wish I could just wear jeans and tee shirts all the time. But even then, the jeans

---

Outlines **Devising a Plan: Illustration**

When you plan your outline, keep your topic sentence in mind:

> People of various backgrounds and ages wear all kinds of tee shirts.

Notice the key words, which are underlined, and which lead to three key phrases:

> people of various backgrounds
> people of various ages
> all kinds of tee shirts

Can you put the details together so that they connect to one of these key

---

Rough Lines **Drafting and Revising: Illustration**

Review the outline on tee shirts on page _____. You can create a first draft of this outline in the form of a paragraph. At this point, you can combine some of the short, choppy sentences of the outline, add details, and add transitions to link your ideas. You can revise your draft using the following checklist.

✔ Checklist

A Checklist for Revising an Illustration Paragraph

✔ **Should** some of the sentences be combined?

✔ **Do** I need more or better transitions?

✔ **Should** I add more details to support my points?

✔ **Should** some of the details be more specific?

Final Lines **Proofreading and Polishing: Illustration**

As you prepare the final version of your illustration paragraph, make any changes in word choice or transitions that can refine your writing. Following is the final version of the paragraph on tee shirts. As you read it, you will notice a few more changes: some details have been added, some have been made more specific, and a transition has been added. In addition, a concluding sentence has been added to unify the paragraph. These changes were made as the final version was prepared. (They are underlined for your reference.)

A Final Version of a Paragraph (Changes from the last draft are underlined.)

People of various backgrounds and ages wear all kinds of tee shirts. Athletes and movie stars are seen in them. Musicians often perform in ragged tees, and restaurant workers sometimes work in tee shirts marked with the name of the restaurant. Children, teens, their parents, and elderly people all wear tee shirts. Almost anything can be painted or pictured on a tee shirt. At concerts, for example, fans can buy tee shirts stamped with the name of the group on stage. Col-

...and Now in Full Color!

Writing Your Own Illustration Paragraph

1. Examine the photograph below. After you have looked at it carefully, write a paragraph with this topic sentence:

    Most malls have a variety of stores and eating places. The photograph may help you think of examples to support the topic sentence.

Exercise 8

👥 *Collaborate*

Adding Details to an Outline

Below are three partial outlines. Each has a topic sentence and some details. Working with a partner or group, add more details that support the topic sentence.

1. topic sentence: People caught in the rain find a number of ways to avoid getting wet.

Answers Will Vary.

Possible answers shown at right.

   a. Some cover their heads with newspaper.

   b. Some crouch against the wall of a big building.

   c. Some take off their shoes and race through the puddles.

   d. *Some use their briefcases to cover their heads.*

Name: _____ Section: _____

PEER REVIEW FORM FOR AN ILLUSTRATION PARAGRAPH

After you have written a draft for your illustration paragraph, let a writing partner read it. When your partner has completed the form below, discuss the comments. Then repeat the same process for your partner's paragraph.

The examples in this paragraph relate to this topic sentence: _____

The new full color design allows students to readily recognize the pedagogical features so important to their learning.

Along These Lines offers students exercises!

The Second Edition is characterized by its abundance of exercises. *Connect* exercises link the grammatical principle to practical applications via proofreading and editing exercises.

Collaborative exercises in every chapter have students writing and editing with peers, interviewing classmates, reacting to others' suggestions and building on others' ideas. Working with peers involves each student in completing the task, alleviates the anxiety of working in a vacuum, and promotes critical thinking. *Peer Review Forms* help students organize their thoughts and comments.

Print Components for Students

■ The New American Webster Handy College Dictionary

Available free to students when packaged with **Along These Lines**, this dictionary has over 1.5 million Signet copies in print and over 115,000 definitions, including current phrases, slang, and scientific terms. It offers more than 1,500 new words, with over 200 not found in any other competing dictionary and features boxed inserts on etymologies and language.

Use this ISBN to order **Along These Lines: Writing Sentences and Paragraphs, Second Edition**, with FREE Dictionary: (0-13-105456-2)

■ The Prentice Hall ESL Workbook

Available free to students when packaged with **Along These Lines**, this 138-page workbook is divided into seven major units, providing explanations and exercises in the most challenging grammar topics for non-native speakers. With over 80 exercise sets, this guide provides ample instruction and practice in nouns, articles, verbs, modifiers, pronouns, prepositions, and sentence structure.

Stand-alone ISBN: (0-13-092323-0)

Package ISBN for **Along These Lines: Writing Sentences and Paragraphs, Second Edition**, with FREE ESL Workbook: (0-13-105979-3)

■ The Prentice Hall Grammar Workbook

Available free when packaged with **Along These Lines**, this 21-chapter workbook is a comprehensive source of instruction for students who need additional grammar, punctuation, and mechanics instruction. Each chapter provides ample explanation, examples, and exercise sets. The exercises contain enough variety to ensure a student's mastery of each concept.

Stand-alone ISBN: (0-13-092321-4)

Package ISBN for **Along These Lines: Writing Sentences and Paragraphs, Second Edition**, with FREE Grammar Workbook: (0-13-105981-5)

■ The Prentice Hall TASP Writing Study Guide

Available free to students when packaged with **Along These Lines**, this guide prepares students for the writing portion of the Texas Academic Skills Program test. In addition, it familiarizes the reader with the elements of the test and provides strategies for success. There are exercises for each part of the exam, and then a full-length practice test with answer key so students can gauge their own progress.

Stand-alone ISBN: (0-13-041585-5)

Package ISBN for **Along These Lines: Writing Sentences and Paragraphs, Second Edition**, with FREE TASP Writing Study Guide: (0-13-105983-1)

■ The Prentice Hall Florida Exit Test Study Guide for Writing

Free when packaged with **Along These Lines**, this guide is designed to prepare students for the writing section of the Florida Exit test. It also acquaints readers with the parts of the test and provides strategies for success.

Stand-alone ISBN: (0-13-111652-5)

Package ISBN for **Along These Lines: Writing Sentences and Paragraphs, Second Edition**, with FREE Florida Exit Test Study Guide for Writing: (0-13-105980-7)

■ Research Navigator™

 Research Navigator™ is the one-stop research solution—complete with extensive help on the research process and three exclusive databases including EBSCO's ContentSelect Academic Journal Database, *The New York Times* Search-by-Subject Archive, and *Best of the Web* Link Library. Take a tour on the web at *http://www.researchnavigator.com*. Your students get FREE ACCESS to Research Navigator™ when you package **Along These Lines** with our exclusive EVALUATING ONLINE RESOURCES: ENGLISH 2003 guide. Contact your local Prentice Hall sales representative for ordering details.

Package ISBN for **Along These Lines: Writing Sentences and Paragraphs, Second Edition**, with FREE Research Navigator™: (0-13-143301-6)

Print Components for Instructors

■ Annotated Instructor's Edition

The Annotated Instructor's Edition features the answers to all of the exercises and includes marginal annotations to enhance instruction. Written by John Biays and Carol Wershoven, these annotations are derived from their years of experience teaching developmental writing. (0-13-111606-1)

The annotations include:

■ *Teaching Tips* with practical, proven ideas for getting the most out of each class session. They include specific activities to help students master the material.

■ *Instructor's Discussion Questions* with ideas on promoting class interaction.

■ *Instructor's Notes* providing chapter cross-references and suggestions for helping the class run more smoothly.

■ *Answers Will Vary* features that alert instructors to the exercises with a range of responses.

■ Instructor's Resource Manual

An additional free supplement for instructors, the **Instructor's Resource Manual** provides additional teaching strategies, additional collaborative activities, sample syllabi, chapter summaries, and more. (0-13-111604-5)

■ The Prentice Hall Writing Skills Test Bank

This printed test bank will include hundreds of additional exercises for instructors to give students. Covering many of the basic skills of writing, **The Prentice Hall Writing Skills Test Bank** can be used with any writing text as a source of extra practice or testing. (0-13-111628-2)

To order any of these supplements, please contact your local Prentice Hall sales representative for hard copies or for the user name and password for **English Instruction Central** at *www.prenhall.com/english.*

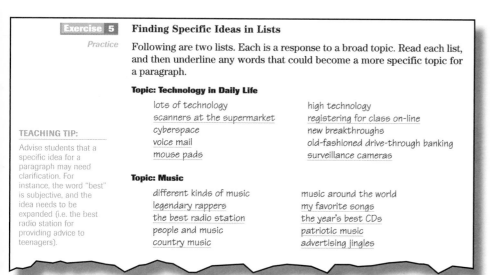

Exercise 5 **Finding Specific Ideas in Lists**

Practice

Following are two lists. Each is a response to a broad topic. Read each list, and then underline any words that could become a more specific topic for a paragraph.

Topic: Technology in Daily Life

lots of technology	high technology
scanners at the supermarket	registering for class on-line
cyberspace	new breakthroughs
voice mail	old-fashioned drive-through banking
mouse pads	surveillance cameras

TEACHING TIP:

Advise students that a specific idea for a paragraph may need clarification. For instance, the word "best" is subjective, and the idea needs to be expanded (i.e. the best radio station for providing advice to teenagers).

Topic: Music

different kinds of music	music around the world
legendary rappers	my favorite songs
the best radio station	the year's best CDs
people and music	patriotic music
country music	advertising jingles

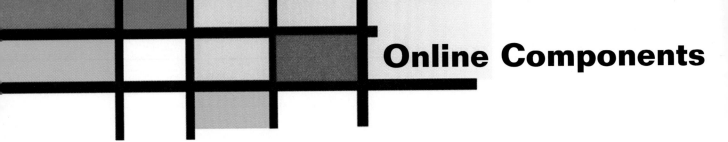

Online Components

The Companion Website™

www.prenhall.com/biays

With FREE access provided, the **Along These Lines Companion Website™** at *www.prenhall.com/biays* is much more than a resource for study or a launching pad for exploration. Its unique tools and support make it easy for you to integrate our online resources into your course, including:

■ **Interactive multiple choice, labeling, and essay exercises** keyed to specific chapters and/or sections of the text allow students the opportunity to take chapter quizzes online with automatic grading.

■ **Writing activities** lead developing writers through the steps of the writing process.

■ **Relevant and informative weblinks** provide students with additional resources on key concepts presented in the text.

■ **A Site Search feature** allows students and instructors to search the Companion Website™ for a particular topic.

The Along These Lines Online Courses

Prentice Hall's online developmental writing course offers you all the advantages of a custom-built program without the hassle of writing it from scratch. Designed specifically for **Along These Lines**, this course supports and augments the text by providing a complete array of writing concepts and exercises at your fingertips—to use just as it is presented or to be customized to your specific course syllabus. Compatible with **BlackBoard™**, **WebCT™**, and **CourseCompass™** platforms, this online course includes the following features: chapter introductions, lecture notes, writing workshops, quizzes, essay questions, and course management. Visit *www.prenhall.com/demo* for more information.

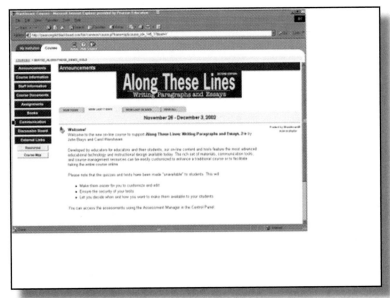

PH WORDS

PH WORDS is an online practice and assessment program covering the entire writing curriculum. Providing instructors the ability to measure and track their students' mastery of all of the elements of writing.

Here's how:

- ONLINE. Available 24/7 on the Web.
- COMPREHENSIVE. **PH WORDS** offers over 130 modules covering the entire writing curriculum and 9000+ exercises, including grammar, writing process, patterns of development, and more. Each module has four parts: *Recall, Apply,* and *Write* exercises, which progress from easy to more difficult, and a *Watch Screen*, which offers a one to two minute audio and visual summary of the concept.
- DIAGNOSTIC. **PH WORDS** offers two ways in which students and instructors can assess individual and overall class areas of weakness:
  - Grammar diagnostic tests assess a baseline of knowledge. Once a student takes a diagnostic test, their **PH WORDS** syllabus indicates which grammar concepts they did not master and provides a customized roadmap for improvement.
  - Gradebook Reports—At any point, an instructor can run several reports that will offer a snapshot of where students need the most work. Three basic types are by Skill, by Class, and by Student.

Visit *www.prenhall.com/phwords* and take the **PH WORDS** virtual tour.
To order **Along These Lines: Writing Sentences and Paragraphs, Second Edition,** with **PH WORDS** for a 50% DISCOUNT, use ISBN: (0-13-105455-4).

Help your students make the grade 24/7 with

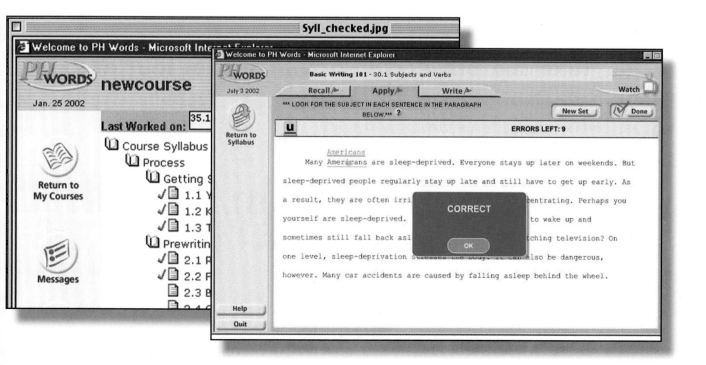

ALONG THESE LINES
Writing Sentences and Paragraphs

Second Edition

John Sheridan Biays
Carol Wershoven

Along These Lines: Writing Sentences and Paragraphs, Second Edition

© 2004, 560 pp., paper (0-13-111221-X)

Annotated Instructor's Edition (0-13-111606-1)

Along These Lines: Writing Paragraphs and Essays, Third Edition

© 2004, 672 pp., paper (0-13-111219-8)

Annotated Instructor's Edition (0-13-111622-3)

Text excerpts are shown approximately 90% of original size. All excerpts and screen shots are accurate as of press time.
© 2004 Prentice Hall/Pearson Education, Upper Saddle River, NJ 07458.

Take the Biays/Wershoven virtual tour at
www.prenhall.com/atl

www.prenhall.com/english
Where words are wired

ALONG THESE LINES

SECOND EDITION

ALONG THESE LINES

Writing Sentences and Paragraphs

Annotated Instructor's Edition

John Sheridan Biays
Broward Community College

Carol Wershoven
Palm Beach Community College

PEARSON

Prentice
Hall

UPPER SADDLE RIVER, NEW JERSEY 07458

Library of Congress Cataloging-in-Publication Data

Biays, John Sheridan.
    Along these lines : writing sentences and paragraphs / John Sheridan Biays and Carol
Wesrhoven. — 2nd ed.
        p. cm.
    Includes index.
    ISBN 0-13-111221-X — ISBN 0-13-111606-1
        1. English language—Sentences. 2. English language—Paragraphs. 3. English
language—Rhetoric. I. Wershoven, Carol. II. Title.
PE1441.B53 2003
808'.042—dc21   2003051702

Editor-in-Chief: Leah Jewell
Senior Acquisitions Editor: Craig Campanella
Assistant Editor: Karen Schultz
Editorial Assistant: Joan Polk
Developmental Editor-in-Chief: Rochelle Diogenes
Marketing Director: Beth Mejia
Senior Marketing Manager: Rachel Falk
Marketing Assistant: Adam Laitman
VP/Director of Production and Manufacturing: Barbara Kittle
Production Editor: Maureen Benicasa
Production Assistant: Marlene Gassler
Copyeditors: Krystyna Budd, Martha Williams
Proofreader: Beatrice Marcks
Permissions Coordinator: Ron Fox
Text Permissions Specialist: Kathleen Karcher
Manufacturing Assistant Manager: Mary Ann Gloriande
Manufacturing Buyer: Brian Mackey
Creative Design Director: Leslie Osher
Art Director: Anne Bonanno Nieglos
Interior and Cover Designer: Carmen DiBartolomeo, C2K, Inc.
Cover Illustration/Photo: Piet Mondrian (1827-1944) Tableau II, 1921-25. Private
Collection, Giraudon/Bridgeman Art Library, New York. © Artists Rights Society (ARS)
New York.
Director, Image Resource Center: Melinda Reo
Manager, Rights and Permissions: Zina Arabia
Interior Image Specialist: Beth Boyd-Brenzel
Image Permission Coordinator: Nancy Seise
Composition: Carlisle Communications, Ltd.
Printer/Binder: Courier Companies, Inc.
Cover Printer: Phoenix Color Corp.

Credits and acknowledgments borrowed from other sources and reproduced, with permission, in this textbook appear on appropriate page within text (or on page 521).

Pearson Education LTD.
Pearson Education Singapore, Pte. Ltd
Pearson Education, Canada, Ltd
Pearson Education–Japan

Pearson Education Australia PTY, Limited
Pearson Education North Asia Ltd
Pearson Educación de Mexico, S.A. de C.V.
Pearson Education Malaysia, Pte. Ltd

10 9 8 7 6 5 4 3 2 1
ISBN 0-13-111221-X (student text)
ISBN 0-13-111606-1 (annotated instructor's edition)

CONTENTS

Chapter 17

Spelling   212

Chapter 18

Words That Sound Alike/Look Alike   223

Chapter 19

Using Prepositions Correctly   241

Part Two: Writing in Steps: The Process Approach   251

Chapter 20

Writing a Paragraph: Generating Ideas—Thought Lines   253

Chapter 25

Writing a Descriptive Paragraph   349

What Is Description?   349

Hints for Writing a Descriptive Paragraph   349

Writing the Descriptive Paragraph in Steps   356

Lines of Detail: A Walk-Through Assignment   370

Writing Your Own Descriptive Paragraph   371

Chapter 26

Writing an Illustration Paragraph   384

What Is Illustration?   384

Hints for Writing an Illustration Paragraph   384

Writing the Illustration Paragraph in Steps   387

TO INSTRUCTORS

This new edition of *Along These Lines: Writing Sentences and Paragraphs* retains the extensive grammar coverage and meticulous process-oriented writing instruction applauded by users of the first edition. Based on encouraging comments from colleagues and conscientious reviewers, we have included more collaborative and individual grammar exercises, and we have incorporated additional chapters and activities that reinforce the stages of the writing process. We have also increased the number of proof-reading and editing exercises to sharpen your students' revision skills.

We believe that an effective text should not only motivate and guide students, but it should also respect their individuality and their innate desire to learn and succeed. We trust that our text's numerous exercises, examples, and activities will work well with any lesson plan or instructional preference. Since each chapter is self-contained, instructors can easily adapt the book's flexible framework to accommodate a formal classroom or a writing lab setting. Ultimately, we hope this book will enable your students to take pride in their work, confidence in their ideas, and responsibility for their own learning.

THE GRAMMAR CHAPTERS

The grammar chapters continue to offer the popular format of **practice** (simple reinforcement), **collaborate** (partner or group work), and **connect** (application of the grammar principle to paragraphs) exercises.

New Features

In response to the suggestions of reviewers, we have incorporated these refinements:

- Expanded paragraph-editing exercises at the end of each grammar chapter
- More sentence-generating exercises requiring students to demonstrate mastery of specific grammar principles
- More exercises on proofreading

Additional Features

Along These Lines: Writing Sentences and Paragraphs continues to offer these features in the grammar chapters:

- Clear, simple steps, as in "Two Steps in Recognizing Sentence Fragments" or "Three Steps in Checking for Sentence Errors with Modifiers"
- Numerous collaborative activities, including exercises that ask students to devise their own examples to illustrate principles just reviewed
- Exercises based on excerpts from powerful writers such as Edgar Allan Poe and Pulitzer Prize-winning Edna Buchanan, along with such historical figures as Martin Luther King, Jr., John F. Kennedy, and Winston Churchill

THE WRITING CHAPTERS

New Features

This edition expands the focus on the writing process and includes these significant enhancements:

- Four new chapters on basic rhetorical patterns: Narration, Description, Illustration, and Process
- A new chapter on moving from writing paragraphs to writing short essays
- New full-color photographs and accompanying topics as writing prompts

Additional Features

Each writing chapter retains these distinctive features:

- A clear and detailed sample of one writing assignment as it progresses through all the stages of the writing process
- Exercises placed immediately after explanatory material
- Collaborative exercises directing students to write with peers, interview classmates, react to others' suggestions, and build on others' ideas
- Numerous writing topics and step-by-step "Walk-Through" assignments providing additional flexibility for instructors
- A Peer Review Form in each chapter so that students can benefit from a classmate's reaction to their drafts

THE READING SECTIONS

New Features

We have made these changes and additions to the reading sections:

- New, accessible reading selections from authors such as Clifton L. Taulbert, Al Roker, Ben Stein, and Amy Dacyczyn (author of *The Tightwad Gazette*).
- New topics in the Writing from Reading sections on everything from saving money to developing self-esteem

Additional Features

Along These Lines: Writing Sentences and Paragraphs continues to offer these popular features in the reading sections:

- A separate and detailed chapter on "Writing From Reading," explaining and illustrating the steps of prereading, reading and rereading, annotating, summarizing, reacting (in writing) to another's ideas, and writing for an essay test
- Vocabulary definitions for each reading selection
- Readings that appeal to working students, returning students, students recently out of high school, and students who are parents
- Readings by authors accessible to a student audience, from Judith Ortiz Cofer to Maya Angelou to John Grisham

- Topics for writing sparked by the content or strategies of the readings – designed to elicit thinking and develop specific writing skills such as unity, coherence, or support

Along These Lines: Writing Sentences and Paragraphs will appeal to instructors, but more importantly, it will work for today's diverse student population. Our years of teaching developmental classes have taught us that beginning writers are more motivated and learn more readily when they are *actively* involved with individual or collaborative tasks. We have designed this text to foster active learning within an atmosphere of respect, encouragement, and meaningful interaction. We trust it will help your classes flourish, and as you and your students work through the writing process, we wish you much success along *all* lines.

ACKNOWLEDGMENTS

Along These Lines: Writing Sentences and Paragraphs reflects the collective wisdom and practical suggestions provided by veteran writing teachers; they have challenged, inspired, and encouraged us over the years. We are indebted to the following professionals for their insightful and comprehensive reviews:

Donald Brotherton	DeVry Institute of Technology
Zoe Ann Cerny	Horry Georgetown Technical College
Keith Coplin	Colby Community College
Janet Cutshall	Sussex County Community College
Kate Gleason	Interborough Institute
Patrick Haas	Glendale Community College
Marian Helms	College of Southern Idaho
Dennis Keen	Spokane Community College
Jill A. Lahnstein	Cape Fear Community College
Susan Nespechal	Kellogg Community College
Keflyn Reed	Bishop State Community College
Maria Villar-Smith	Miami-Dade College
William Yarrow	Joliet Junior College
Holly Young	Arkansas State University at Heber Springs

Joan Polk, editorial assistant, coordinated these valuable reviews and even provided us with a sympathetic ear as we juggled several versions of our manuscript. Thanks for your humor and attention to detail, Joan.

Craig Campanella, senior English editor, continued to impress us with his multi-tasking skills. Whether gently reminding us of deadlines, forwarding questions from sales reps, overseeing the new art design of the *Along These Lines* series, or sharing faculty concerns and suggestions gathered on his numerous school visits, he illustrated why he was named Prentice Hall's Editor of the Year for 2002. Congratulations, Craig!

We were also fortunate to have the sharp eyes and guiding hands of our talented production editor, Maureen Benicasa. She guided us through the extensive revision process, and she provided periodic updates from the many departments involved in this edition. She somehow kept track of both the student version and the annotated instructor's edition in various stages of development, served as our liaison to the permissions editor, made sure we received page proofs promptly, and responded to all of our questions (even the inane ones) with patience and good cheer.

We are also extremely grateful to the many individuals who reshaped and redesigned the *Along These Lines* series. These talented and creative professionals include Krystyna Budd and Martha Williams, copy editors; Brian Mackey, buyer; Carmen DiBartolomeo, designer, and Anne Bonano-Nieglos, art director. Also, many thanks to Bea Marcks for her proofreading skills; Karen Schultz for diligently searching the photo archives to accommodate our suggestions; Jan Williams for providing a detailed index; Kathleen Karcher for securing permissions; and to Rachel Falk and her marketing team for coordinating promotions and providing such attractive mailings. We are also very grateful to Evelyn Kelly for developing the *Along These Lines Online Courses* and for writing the Instructor's Resource Manuals for the series.

Finally, sincere thanks to our colleagues and students at Broward Community College and Palm Beach Community College. You are a constant source of encouragement, friendship, and extraordinary support.

CHAPTER 1

The Simple Sentence

Identifying the crucial parts of a sentence is the first step in many writing decisions: how to punctuate, how to avoid sentence fragments, and how to be sure that subjects and verbs *agree* (match). Moving forward to these decisions requires a few steps backward—to basics.

RECOGNIZING A SENTENCE

Let's start with a few definitions. A basic unit of language is a **word.**

> **examples:** cap, desk, tree

A group of related words can be a **phrase.**

> **examples:** battered baseball cap, on the desk, tall palm tree

When a group of words contains a subject and a verb, it is called a **clause.** When the word group has a subject and a verb and makes sense by itself, it is called a **sentence** or an independent clause.

If you want to check to see whether you have written a sentence and not just a group of related words, you first have to check for a subject and a verb. It's often easier to locate the verbs first.

INSTRUCTOR'S NOTE:

If your students need help understanding the difference between sentences and fragments, refer them to Chapter 6 on sentence fragments.

RECOGNIZING VERBS

Verbs are words that express some kind of action or being. **Action verbs** tell what somebody or something does.

action verbs:
Computers *hold* an amazing amount of information.
We *call* our parents once a month.
The boxer *exercises* at my local gym.
You *missed* the bus yesterday.
David *dented* the back of my car.
He *drives* like a maniac.
They *study* together on weekends.
I *believe* her story.

1

Sometimes a verb tells what something or somebody is. Such verbs are called **being verbs.** Words such as *feels, looks, seems, smells, sounds,* and *tastes* are part of the group called "being verbs". Look at some examples of being verbs and their functions in the following sentences:

being verbs:
Computers *are* a great invention.
The boxer *looks* tired today.
You *sound* happy.
David *is* a good candidate for traffic school.
He *seems* unaware of traffic lights.
They *are* the best students in my class.
I *feel* confident about her story.
Gossip *is* nasty and mean.

Exercise 1

Practice

Recognizing Action Verbs

Underline the action verbs in the following sentences.

1. The box <u>held</u> all my treasures.

2. At night, our dog <u>barks</u> at strange noises.

3. The assignment <u>takes</u> several hours.

4. Aunt Selena <u>changed</u> the flat tire.

5. The mail carrier <u>brought</u> the mail early.

6. Some students <u>register</u> at the last minute.

7. Drunk driving <u>claims</u> many victims each year.

8. An old horror movie <u>kept</u> me awake last night.

9. Mike <u>goes</u> to the mall at least once a week.

10. The dining room table <u>faces</u> the window.

Exercise 2

Practice

Recognizing Being Verbs

Underline the being verbs in the following sentences.

1. Your cologne <u>smells</u> like lemons.

2. Soccer <u>was</u> my father's favorite sport.

3. Alan <u>looks</u> upset about the change of plans.

4. Before the job interview, Lisa <u>seemed</u> nervous.

5. My brother <u>is</u> an expert in martial arts.

6. Your parents <u>were</u> always kind to me.

7. On the phone, Loretta <u>sounded</u> tired.

8. On the weekends, I <u>am</u> relaxed and cheerful.

9. The new quilt <u>feels</u> like a warm cloud over my body.

10. Teenagers <u>are</u> often trendsetters in music and fashion.

Exercise 3

 *Collaborate*

Writing Sentences with Specific Verbs

With a partner or group, write two sentences using each of the verbs listed below. Each sentence must have at least five words. When you have completed the exercise, share your answers with another group or with the class. The first one is done for you.

1. **verb:** removed

   sentence 1: The doctor removed the patient's appendix.

   sentence 2: Yesterday my brother removed that old carpet stain.

Answers Will Vary.

Possible answers shown at right.

2. **verb:** tastes

   sentence 1: That soup tastes like old shoes.

   sentence 2: Your chili always tastes better than mine.

3. **verb:** complains

   sentence 1: Anna constantly complains about the summer heat.

   sentence 2: He complains to the landlord every month.

4. **verb:** sound

   sentence 1: You sound a little unhappy about the decision.

   sentence 2: At night, the frogs on the pond sound strange.

5. **verb:** dreamed

   sentence 1: Last night, I dreamed about my math class.

   sentence 2: They dreamed of moving to California.

6. **verb:** surprises

   sentence 1: Every year, Tom surprises me with a different gift.

   sentence 2: Your lack of computer skills surprises us.

7. **verb:** are

   sentence 1: They are kind and generous people.

   sentence 2: Hot dogs and apple pie are typical American food.

8. verb: is

sentence 1: Mr. Cerullo is the chairman of the company.

sentence 2: A cup of coffee is my only breakfast.

9. verb: crawled

sentence 1: A small green snake crawled under the porch.

sentence 2: Traffic on Sun Boulevard crawled past the accident.

10. verb: controls

sentence 1: In my house, my mother controls the budget.

sentence 2: Keith usually controls his temper around his family.

Helping Verbs

The verb in a sentence can be more than one word. There can be **helping verbs** in front of the main verb (the action verb or being verb). Here is a list of some frequently used helping verbs:

Info BOX

Common Helping Verbs

am	had	should
can	has	was
could	may	were
did	might	will
do	must	would
is	shall	

Here are some examples of sentences with main and helping verbs:

main and helping verbs:
You *should have answered* the question. (The helping verbs are *should* and *have.*)
Laurie *will notify* the lottery winner. (The helping verb is *will.*)
Babies *can recognize* their mothers' voices. (The helping verb is *can.*)
I *am thinking* about a career in medicine. (The helping verb is *am.*)

Exercise   4   **Recognizing the Complete Verb: Main and Helping Verbs**

Practice   Underline the complete verb (both main and helping verbs) in each of the following sentences.

1. I could have driven Luke to the airport.

2. Some of my friends are driving to Tucson tomorrow.

3. My boss <u>will be calling</u> me in an hour.

4. He <u>could have been selected</u> for the Hall of Fame.

5. You and Charlie <u>are taking</u> a chance in that leaky boat.

6. Tamara's dog <u>can perform</u> incredible tricks with a frisbee.

7. Tomorrow, I <u>must finish</u> my paper for social science class.

8. At 8:00 p.m., Dr. Menendez <u>was completing</u> her hospital rounds.

9. The young mother <u>should have been</u> more patient with her children.

10. We <u>may have given</u> you the wrong impression about the college.

Exercise 5

👥 *Collaborate*

Writing Sentences with Helping Verbs

Complete this exercise with a partner or a group. First, ask one person to add at least one helping verb to the verb given. Then, work together to write two sentences using the main verb and the helping verb(s). Appoint a spokesperson for your group to read all of your sentences to the class. Notice how many combinations of main and helping verbs you hear. The first one is done for you.

Answers Will Vary.

Possible answers shown at right.

1. **verb:** complained

   verb with helping verb(s): <u>must have complained</u>

   sentence 1: <u>My supervisor must have complained about me.</u>

   sentence 2: <u>She must have complained twenty times yesterday.</u>

2. **verb:** exaggerating

   verb with helping verb(s): <u>could be exaggerating</u>

   sentence 1: <u>Jeff could be exaggerating the amount of food he ate.</u>

   sentence 2: <u>The men could be exaggerating the size of the fish.</u>

3. **verb:** remember

   verb with helping verb(s): <u>can remember</u>

   sentence 1: <u>My grandmother can remember her Cuban childhood.</u>

   sentence 2: <u>I can remember my first day of school.</u>

4. **verb:** won

   verb with helping verb(s): <u>might have won</u>

   sentence 1: <u>Carl might have won the lottery.</u>

   sentence 2: <u>Our team might have won last night's game.</u>

5. verb: driven

verb with helping verb(s): had driven

sentence 1: Jamie and I had driven three hundred miles.

sentence 2: Luisa had driven me home after work.

6. verb: claiming

verb with helping verb(s): is claiming

sentence 1: The traveler is claiming his lost luggage.

sentence 2: Marisol is claiming her share of the inheritance.

7. verb: stolen

verb with helping verb(s): was stolen

sentence 1: My wallet was stolen yesterday.

sentence 2: That car was stolen from a car dealer in Dallas.

8. verb: support

verb with helping verb(s): should support

sentence 1: You should support your brother's efforts.

sentence 2: We should support the home team in the playoffs.

9. verb: defending

verb with helping verb(s): are defending

sentence 1: Those brave men and women are defending their land.

sentence 2: We are defending our right to free speech.

10. verb: helped

verb with helping verb(s): has helped

sentence 1: My tutor has helped me improve my reading skills.

sentence 2: Swimming has helped my father to stay in shape.

More Than One Main Verb

Helping verbs can make the verb in a sentence more than one word long, but there can also be more than one main verb.

more than one main verb:
Antonio *begged* and *pleaded* for mercy.
I *ran* to the car, *tossed* my books on the back seat, and *jammed* the key in the ignition.
My dog *steals* my shoes and *chews* on them.

Exercise 6

Practice

Recognizing Main Verbs

Some of the sentences below have one main verb; some have more than one main verb. Underline all the main verbs in each sentence.

1. Rude people with cell phones <u>distract</u> moviegoers, <u>interrupt</u> class lectures, and <u>disrupt</u> meetings.

2. Mrs. Kolski and Mr. Fernandez <u>keep</u> the restaurant open from 7:00 a.m. to midnight.

3. Chantal <u>visited</u> my house but never <u>invited</u> me to hers.

4. The newest club in town <u>is</u> an old, remodeled warehouse about ten minutes from campus.

5. I <u>wrapped</u> and <u>tagged</u> about fifty toys for the children's shelter.

6. The rain <u>slipped</u> through a crack in the roof, <u>dripped</u> to the bedroom floor, and eventually <u>soaked</u> the carpet.

7. Nicole <u>bought</u> a gold bracelet at the fair and <u>gave</u> it to her mother on Mother's Day.

8. Most of the furniture in my living room <u>comes</u> from garage sales in the neighborhood and thrift shops in the city.

9. My doctor always <u>examines</u> me carefully, <u>listens</u> to my symptoms, and <u>answers</u> all my questions.

10. Malcolm <u>grew up</u> in Atlanta and <u>returns</u> there every summer.

 Exercise 7

Recognizing Verbs in a Selection from "The Tell-Tale Heart"

Connect

This selection is from "The Tell-Tale Heart," a horror story by Edgar Allan Poe. In it, an insane murderer has killed an old man and buried him under the floor. When the police arrive, they find nothing, but the murderer is convinced that he—and the police—can hear the old man's heart beating under the floor. In this selection, the murderer describes what he feels as he hears the heart beat louder and louder.

Underline all the verbs in the selection. Notice how a careful choice of verbs can make writing exciting and suspenseful.

The officers <u>were</u> satisfied. My manner <u>had convinced</u> them. I <u>was</u> singularly at ease. They <u>sat</u>, and while I <u>answered</u> cheerfully, they <u>chatted</u> familiar things. But, ere* long, I <u>felt</u> myself getting pale and <u>wished</u> them gone. My head <u>ached</u>, and I <u>fancied</u>* a ringing in my ears: but still they <u>sat</u> and still <u>chatted</u>. The ringing became more distinct:—it <u>continued</u> and <u>became</u> more distinct: I <u>talked</u> more freely to get rid of the feeling: but it <u>continued</u> and <u>gained</u> definitiveness—until, at length,* I <u>found</u> that the noise <u>was</u> not within my ears.

No doubt I now <u>grew</u> very pale;—but I <u>talked</u> more fluently, and with a heightened voice. Yet the sound <u>increased</u>—and what <u>could</u> I <u>do</u>? . . . I <u>gasped</u> for breath—and yet the officers <u>heard</u> it not. I <u>talked</u> more quickly, more vehemently;* but the noise steadily <u>increased</u>. I <u>arose</u> and <u>argued</u> about trifles, in a high key and with violent gesticulations,* but the noise steadily <u>increased</u>. Why <u>would</u> they not <u>be</u> gone? I <u>paced</u> the floor to and fro with heavy strides, as if excited to fury by the observation of the men—but the noise steadily <u>increased</u>. Oh God! What <u>could</u> I <u>do</u>? I <u>foamed</u>—I <u>raved</u>—I <u>swore</u>! . . . It <u>grew</u> louder—louder— louder! And still the men <u>chatted</u> pleasantly, and <u>smiled</u>. Was it possible they <u>heard</u> not? Almighty God!— no, no! They <u>heard</u>!—they <u>suspected</u>!—they <u>knew</u>!

* **ere** means before
* **fancied:** imagined
* **at length:** after a time
* **vehemently:** furiously
* **gesticulations:** gestures

RECOGNIZING SUBJECTS

After you learn to recognize verbs, you can easily find the subjects of sentences because subjects and verbs are linked. If the verb is an action verb, for example, the **subject** will be the word or words that answer the question "Who or what is doing that action?" Follow these steps to identify the subject:

sentence with an action verb:

The cat slept on my bed.

Step 1: Identify the verb: *slept*
Step 2: Ask, "Who or what slept?"
Step 3: The answer is the subject: The *cat* slept on my bed. The *cat* is the subject.

If the verb is a being verb, the same steps apply to finding the subject:

sentence with a being verb:

Clarice is his girlfriend.

Step 1: Identify the verb: *is*
Step 2: Ask, "Who or what is his girlfriend?"
Step 3: The answer is the subject: *Clarice* is his girlfriend. *Clarice* is the subject.

Just as there can be more than one word making up a verb, there can be more than one subject.

> **examples:** *Coffee* and a *doughnut* are a typical breakfast for me.
> His *father* and *grandfather* own a landscaping service.

Exercise 8

Practice

Recognizing Subjects in Sentences

Underline the subjects in the following sentences.

1. Mr. Chan should have given the test yesterday.

2. The coaches are picking the teams on Saturday.

3. Sneakers and socks covered the floor of the closet.

4. Anything could have caused the power outage.

5. Anthony and Carla opened a new electronics store on Monroe Street.

6. Running can release stress and relieve muscle tension.

7. Patience and kindness were the dog trainer's best qualities.

8. Chocolate tastes great at any time of the day or night.

9. We watched the game on television last night.

10. The kitchen smells like apples and cinnamon.

Exercise 9

Collaborate

Adding Subjects to Sentences

Working with a partner or a group, complete the paragraph below by adding subjects in the blank lines. Before you fill in the blanks, discuss your answers and try to come to an agreement about the worst movie, the worst album, and so on. When you have completed the paragraph, share your answers with another group or with the class.

Answers Will Vary.

This year has seen many achievements in the arts and entertainment, but it has also seen many creative disasters. On movie screens, there have been some terrible movies. Without a doubt, _____ was the worst movie of the year. It should never have been made. On television, _____ was the worst and also the most irritating show. Every time I see it, I want to turn it off or kick in the television screen. _____ and _____ take the prize for the worst actor and actress of the year. They should consider other careers. In the field of music, _____ ranks as the least successful album of the year. _____ is the most annoying song because the radio played it far too often. Last, _____ is the most annoying singer.

MORE ABOUT RECOGNIZING SUBJECTS AND VERBS

Recognizing the Core Subject

When you look for the subject of a sentence, look for the core word or words; do not include descriptive words around the subject. Look for the subject, not for the words that describe it.

the core subject:

Light blue *paint* will brighten these walls.

Cracked *sidewalks* and rusty *railings* made the old school dangerous for children.

Prepositions and Prepositional Phrases

Prepositions are usually short words that often signal a kind of position or possession, as shown in the following list:

Info BOX

Some Common Prepositions

about	before	by	inside	on	under
above	below	during	into	onto	up
across	behind	except	like	over	upon
after	beneath	for	near	through	with
among	beside	from	of	to	within
around	between	in	off	toward	without
at	beyond				

TEACHING TIP:

Listing (or asking students to list) prepositional phrases that have become clichés can be an amusing way to practice recognizing prepositions (examples: under the weather, down on his luck, up in the air) as well as wordiness.

A **prepositional phrase** is made up of a preposition and its object. Here are some prepositional phrases. In each one, the first word is the preposition; the other words are the object of the preposition.

prepositional phrases:

about the movie   of mice and men
around the corner   off the wall
between the lines   on the mark
during recess   up the chimney
near my house   with my sister and brother

An old memory trick can help you remember prepositions. Think of a chair. Now, think of a series of words you can put *in front of* the chair:

around the chair   *with* the chair
by the chair   *to* the chair
behind the chair   *near* the chair
between the chairs   *under* the chair
of the chair   *on* the chair
off the chair   *from* the chair

INSTRUCTOR'S NOTE:

For additional practice using prepositions, see Chapter 19.

These words are prepositions.

You need to know about prepositions because they can help you identify the subject of a sentence. Here is an important grammar rule about prepositions:

Nothing in a prepositional phrase can ever be the subject of a sentence.

Prepositional phrases describe people, places, or things. They may also describe the subject of a sentence, but they never *include* the subject. Whenever you are looking for the subject of a sentence, begin by putting parentheses around all the prepositional phrases:

parentheses and prepositional phrases:
The park (behind my apartment) has a playground (with swings and slides).

Nothing in the prepositional phrase can be the subject. Once you have eliminated these phrases, you can follow the steps to find the subject of the sentence.

Step 1: Identify the verb: *has*.
Step 2: Ask, "Who or what has?"
Step 3: The answer is the subject: The *park*. The *park* is the subject.

By marking off the prepositional phrases, you are left with the core of the sentence. There is less to look at.

(Across the street) a *child* (with a teddy bear) sat (among the flowers).
subject: *child*
The *student* (from Jamaica) won the contest (with ease).
subject: *student*.

Exercise 10

Practice

Recognizing Prepositional Phrases, Subjects, and Verbs

Put parentheses around the prepositional phrases in the following sentences. Then underline the subjects and verbs, putting *S* above the subject and *V* above the verb.

1. Two of my neighbors work, at the motel across the street.

2. The car skidded off the icy road and stopped between two tall trees.

3. I found a piece of duct tape and stuck it onto the leaky pipe in the kitchen.

4. An oak chair with elaborate carving across the back was the most expensive item at the antiques sale.

5. Mrs. Jensen pulled a tissue from her purse and dabbed at the tears in her eyes.

6. Everyone except my roommate walked behind the tour guide from the museum.

7. A letter inside the old leather trunk had been written to a soldier during the Civil War.

8. In the end, the <u>general</u> <u>was caught</u> between two battalions of
   advancing enemy troops.

9. <u>Steve</u> <u>walked</u> around the campus and finally <u>found</u> a snack bar
   near the back of the science building.

10. <u>Some</u> of the most successful people in my family <u>went</u> to school
    in the daytime), <u>worked</u> at one job at night and <u>held</u> another
    on weekends.

Exercise 11

👥 *Collaborate*

Writing Sentences with Prepositional Phrases

Do this exercise with a partner. First, add one prepositional phrase to the core sentence. Then, ask your partner to add a second prepositional phrase to the same sentence. For the next sentence, switch places. Let your partner add the first phrase, and you add the second. Keep switching places throughout the exercise. When you have completed the exercise, share your sentences (the ones with two prepositional phrases) with the class. The first one is done for you.

1. **core sentence:** Employees are concerned.

   Add one prepositional phrase: <u>Employees are concerned about their</u>
   <u>paychecks.</u>

   Add another prepositional phrase: <u>Employees at the central plant</u>
   <u>are concerned about their paychecks.</u>

2. **core sentence:** The girl saw the monster.

   Add one prepositional phrase: *The girl saw the monster in her*
   bedroom closet.

   Add another prepositional phrase: *The girl saw the monster behind*
   the clothes in her bedroom closet.

3. **core sentence:** The tornado struck.

   Add one prepositional phrase: *The tornado struck with a terrible*
   force.

   Add another prepositional phrase: *During the night, the tornado*
   struck with a terrible force.

4. core sentence: I received a small box.

Add one prepositional phrase: <u>I received a small box of candy.</u>

Add another prepositional phrase: <u>I received a small box of candy for</u>

<u>my birthday.</u>

5. core sentence: Young teenagers must be more aware.

Add one prepositional phrase: <u>Young teenagers must be more aware</u>

<u>of their personal safety.</u>

Add another prepositional phrase: <u>Young teenagers must be more</u>

<u>aware of their personal safety at night.</u>

6. core sentence: A stranger appeared.

Add one prepositional phrase: <u>A stranger appeared in the small</u>

<u>Texas town.</u>

Add another prepositional phrase: <u>A stranger appeared in the small</u>

<u>Texas town near the border.</u>

Word Order

When we speak, we often use a very simple word order: first, the subject; then, the verb. For example, someone would say, "He lost the key." *He* is the subject that begins the sentence; *lost* is the verb that comes after the subject.

However, not all sentences use such a simple word order. Prepositional phrases, for example, can change the word order. To identify the subject and verb, follow these steps:

prepositional phrase and changed subject-verb order:
Behind the cabinet was a box of coins.

Step 1: Mark off the prepositional phrases with parentheses: (Behind the cabinet) was a box (of coins). Remember that nothing in a prepositional phrase can be the subject of a sentence.

Step 2: Find the verb: *was*

Step 3: Who or what was? A box was. The subject of the sentence is *box*.

After you change the word order of this sentence, you can see the subject (*S*) and the verb (*V*) more easily.

       S   **V**
A *box* of coins *was* behind the cabinet.

(Even though *coins* is a plural word, you must use the singular verb *was* because *box* is the singular subject.)

Exercise 12

Practice

Finding Prepositional Phrases, Subjects, and Verbs in Complicated Word Order

Put parentheses around the prepositional phrases in the following sentences. Then underline the subjects and verbs, putting an *S* above each subject and a *V* above each verb.

1. From the back of the classroom came a loud laugh.

2. Behind the counter was a bored clerk with a blank expression.

3. Near the top of the hill are a picnic area and a children's playground.

4. Inside the box was an old, rusty key with a number on it.

5. Beside the entrance to the exclusive club stood a large security guard.

6. Among the papers on the desk is a letter from the head of the FBI.

7. Over the hills soared a flock of geese.

8. Beneath the fancy suits and expensive jewelry hides a man with the heart of a thief.

9. Toward me ran a puppy with a tennis ball in its mouth.

10. Across the lake from my cabin is a famous fishing camp for weekend sports lovers.

TEACHING TIP:

Tell students to (1) identify the prepositional phrases and (2) then to pretend that the phrases do not appear. By doing so, they can easily spot the subjects and verbs.

More on Word Order

The expected word order of a subject followed by a verb will change when a sentence starts with *There is/are*, *There was/were*, *Here is/are*, or *Here was/were*. In such cases, look for the subject after the verb:

S-V order with There is/are, Here is/are:

There *are* a *supermarket* and a *laundromat* near my apartment.

Here *is* my best *friend*.

If it helps you to understand this pattern, change the word order:

A *supermarket* and a *laundromat are* there, near my apartment.

My best *friend is* here.

You should also note that even when the subject comes after the verb, the verb has to *match* the subject. For instance, if the subject refers to more than one thing, the verb must refer to more than one thing:

There are a *supermarket* and a *laundromat* near my apartment. (Two things, a supermarket and a laundromat, *are* near my apartment.)

TEACHING TIP:

Tell students that substituting the appropriate singular or plural pronoun for the complete subject can help them determine the correct verb form.

Word Order in Questions

Questions may have a different word order. The main verb and the helping verb may not be next to each other.

word order in questions:
question: Did you study for the test?
subject: *you*
verbs: *did, study*

If it helps you to understand this concept, think about answering the question. If someone accused you of not studying for the test, you might say, "I *did study* for it." You'd use two words as verbs.

question: Will she call her mother?
subject: *she*
verbs: *will, call*

question: Is Charles making the coffee?
subject: *Charles*
verbs: *is, making*

Practice

Recognizing Subjects and Verbs in Questions and *Here is/are*, *There is/are* Word Order

Underline the subjects and verbs in the following sentences, putting an *S* above each subject and a *V* above the verbs.

           V   S   S
  1. Here <u>are</u> my old <u>sweater</u> and your <u>jacket</u>.

      V   S   V
  2. <u>Has</u> <u>Lonnie</u> <u>returned</u> your photographs of the birthday party?

      V   S   V
  3. <u>Can</u> <u>you</u> <u>imagine</u> the crowds at the beach today?

           V   S
  4. There <u>was</u> a bad <u>accident</u> on Seventh Avenue yesterday.

                          V   S
  5. At the end of the jogging path there <u>is</u> a water <u>fountain</u>.

      V   S   V
  6. <u>Will</u> <u>Mrs. Rosenbloom</u> <u>contact</u> me about the job opening?

         V   S
  7. Here <u>is</u> your <u>ticket</u> for the flight to San Juan.

      V S   V
  8. <u>Do</u> <u>you</u> <u>remember</u> your first day of school?

      V   S   V   V
  9. <u>Have</u> <u>you</u> <u>washed</u> and <u>wiped</u> the windows in the living room?

         V   S
 10. There <u>is</u> <u>nobody</u> at the checkout counter in the convenience store.

Words That Cannot Be Verbs

Sometimes there are words that look like verbs in a sentence but are not verbs. Such words include *adverbs* (words like *always*, *often*, *nearly*, *never*, *ever*) that are placed close to the verb but are not verbs. Another word that is placed between a helping verb and a main verb is *not*. *Not* is not a verb. When you are looking for verbs in a sentence, be careful to eliminate words like *often* and *not*.

They will not accept his apology. (The complete verb is *will accept*.)
Matthew can often repair his truck by himself. (The complete verb is *can repair*.)

Be careful with *contractions*:

He hasn't called me in a long time. (The complete verb is *has called*. *Not* is not a part of the verb, even in contractions.)
Don't you speak Spanish? (The complete verb is *do speak*.)
Won't you come inside? (The complete verb is *will come*.) *Won't* is a contraction for *will not*.)

Recognizing Main Verbs

If you are checking to see if a word is a main verb, try the pronoun test. Combine your word with this simple list of pronouns: *I, you, he, she, it, we, they*. A main verb is a word such as *look* or *pulled* that can be combined with the words on this list. Now try the pronoun test.

For the word *look*: I look, you look, he looks, she looks, it looks, we look, they look
For the word *pulled*: I pulled, you pulled, he pulled, she pulled, it pulled, we pulled, they pulled

But the word *never* can't be used, alone, with the pronouns:

~~I never, you never, he never, she never, it never, we never, they never~~
(Never did what?)

Never is not a verb. *Not* is not a verb, either, as the pronoun test indicates:

~~I not, you not, he not, she not, it not, we not, they not~~ (These combinations don't make sense because *not* is not a verb.)

Verb Forms That Cannot Be Main Verbs

There are forms of verbs that can't be main verbs by themselves, either. An *-ing* verb, by itself, cannot be the main verb, as the pronoun test shows:

For the word *taking*: ~~I taking, you taking, he taking, she taking, it taking, we taking, they taking~~

If you see an *-ing* verb by itself, correct the sentence by adding a helping verb.

He ~~taking~~ his time. (*Taking*, by itself, cannot be a main verb.)
correction: He *is taking* his time.

Another verb form, called an *infinitive*, also cannot be a main verb. An **infinitive** is the form of the verb that has *to* placed in front of it.

Info BOX

Some Common Infinitives

to call	to fall	to run
to care	to give	to smile
to drive	to live	to talk
to eat	to make	to work

Try the pronoun test and you'll see that infinitives can't be main verbs:

> For the infinitive *to live*: ~~I to live, you to live, he to live, she to live,~~
> ~~you to live, we to live, they to live~~

So if you see an infinitive being used as a verb, correct the sentence by adding a main verb.

> He ~~to live~~ in a better house.
> **correction:** He *wants* to live in a better house.

The infinitives and the *-ing* verbs just don't work as main verbs. You must put a verb with them to make a correct sentence.

Exercise 14

Practice

Correcting Problems with Infinitive or *-ing* Verb Forms

Most—but not all—of the following sentences are faulty; an *-ing* verb or an infinitive may be taking the place of a main verb. Rewrite the sentences that have errors.

Answers Will Vary.

Possible answers shown at right.

1. Two of my favorite aunts *are going* to move to the northern part of the state.

2. The long weekend *is* giving Thomas some time for his favorite sport.

3. My son's trips to the doctor are costing me hundreds of dollars.

4. After many disappointments at work, Stedman *is* considering the possibility of changing jobs.

5. Two of the most popular comedians in the country *are going* to perform at our homecoming party next year.

6. The manager of the hotel *was* thinking about a better advertising campaign for out-of-state visitors.

7. Our high school *plans* to raise money for homeless children by holding a carnival and raffle.

8. The people next door want to build a patio in their backyard.

9. Crying toddlers, demanding parents, and overworked colleagues *are* all making me unhappy at my day-care job.

10. A dark-eyed raccoon *was* carefully slinking around my garbage can.

Exercise 15

Practice

Finding Subjects and Verbs: A Comprehensive Exercise

Underline the subjects and verbs in the following sentences, putting an *S* above each subject and a *V* above each verb.

1. <u>Do</u> <u>you</u> ever <u>wonder</u> about the secrets in the old house?

2. <u>They</u> <u>won't</u> <u>buy</u> a car from the used-car dealer on Forest Street.

3. Behind Nathan's bragging <u>was</u> a terrible <u>insecurity</u>. [V S]

4. <u>Mario</u> <u>offered</u> to take the children to a movie. [S V]

5. Isn't the <u>plumber</u> <u>coming</u> today? [V S V]

6. At the end of the day, the <u>bakery</u> often <u>sells</u> cakes and bread at half price. [S V]

7. <u>Whining</u> and <u>worrying</u> <u>will</u> never <u>improve</u> a situation. [S S V V]

8. Here <u>are</u> the <u>guest</u> of honor and her <u>husband</u>. [V S S]

9. <u>Wayne</u> <u>should have told</u> me about the change in plans. [S V]

10. On the highest shelf in the garage <u>is</u> a <u>set</u> of wrenches. [V S]

11. The <u>band</u> <u>played</u> its greatest hits and then <u>took</u> requests from the audience. [S V V]

12. There <u>was</u> an <u>inch</u> of water on the kitchen floor. [V S]

13. The <u>support</u> of my friends and the <u>help</u> of my neighbors <u>have</u> <u>guided</u> me through this difficult time. [S S V V]

14. The mail <u>carrier</u> <u>would</u> <u>like</u> to avoid the house with the angry dog. [S V V]

15. From the top of the Whitney Building <u>you</u> <u>can</u> <u>catch</u> glimpses of three neighborhoods in the city. [S V V]

16. <u>You</u> <u>must</u> <u>have</u> <u>lost</u> your wallet at the grocery store. [S V V V]

17. <u>Melvin</u> <u>called</u> the restaurant and <u>ordered</u> three shrimp dinners. [S V V]

18. The Haitian <u>paintings</u> and Mexican <u>pottery</u> in Eric's house <u>created</u> an open and lively atmosphere in a small space. [S S V]

19. On Saturdays, <u>Alice</u> <u>takes</u> her dog to the park and <u>meets</u> friends at a local restaurant. [S V V]

20. Beneath the stack of crumbling newspapers <u>was</u> an old <u>magazine</u> with a paper bookmark in it. [V S]

Exercise 16

👥 *Collaborate*

Creating Your Own Text

Do this exercise with a partner or a group. Following is a list of rules you have just studied. Write two examples for each rule. When your group has completed the examples for each rule, trade your group's completed exercise with another group's and check its examples while it checks yours. The first rule has been done for you.

Rule 1: The verb in a sentence can express some kind of action.

example 1: My cousin studies biology in college.

example 2: Yesterday the rain destroyed the rose bushes.

Answers Will Vary.

Possible answers shown at right.

Rule 2: The verb in a sentence can express some state of being.

example 1: Your solution to the problem seems practical.

example 2: The room smelled like pine needles.

Rule 3: The verb in a sentence can consist of more than one word.

example 1: The roof must have collapsed under the weight.

example 2: Billy stumbled and fell into the ditch.

Rule 4: There can be more than one subject in a sentence.

example 1: Elena and her mother drove to Jackson.

example 2: The boy and his dog jumped into the pond.

Rule 5: If you take out the prepositional phrases, it is easier to identify the subject of a sentence because nothing in a prepositional phrase can be the subject of a sentence. (Write sentences containing at least one prepositional phrase. Put parentheses around the prepositional phrases.)

example 1: The man (in the restaurant) smiled (at me).

example 2: Nothing (in that box) (of clothes) is worth saving.

Rule 6: Not all sentences have the simple word order of subject first, then verb. (Give examples of sentences with more complicated word order.)

example 1: Here is your money.

example 2: From upstairs came a scream and a thud.

Rule 7: Words like *not, never, often, always, ever* are not verbs. (Write sentences using one of those words, but underline the correct verb.)

example 1: My sister always sets her alarm.

example 2: Stacy will not agree to your plan.

Rule 8: An *-ing* verb form by itself or an infinitive (*to* preceding the verb) cannot be a main verb. (Write sentences with *-ing* verb forms or infinitives, but underline the main verb.)

example 1: Steve hopes to graduate this fall.

example 2: Your sister is thinking of you.

Recognizing Subjects and Verbs in a Paragraph

Underline the subjects and verbs in the following paragraph, putting an *S* above each subject and a *V* above each verb.

        A <u>gift</u> <u>can</u> <u>reveal</u> a great deal about the giver. For instance, a <u>child</u> <u>gives</u> his or her mother a toy. To the child, a <u>toy</u> <u>is</u> the most wonderful present in the world. Therefore, the <u>child</u> <u>shows</u> love with this gift. Similarly, a <u>music-lover</u> <u>buys</u> a CD for a friend. Some <u>gifts</u> <u>can</u> <u>be</u> impersonal or routine. For instance, every year an <u>aunt</u> <u>sends</u> her nephew money for his birthday. Or local <u>businesses</u> or insurance <u>companies</u> <u>mail</u> calendars to their customers each December. <u>These</u> <u>are</u> gifts to fulfill an obligation or to advertise a service. Certain <u>gifts</u> <u>demonstrate</u> the giver's thoughtfulness and care. Among these <u>are</u> handcrafted <u>items</u> like quilts or furni-ture. <u>Someone</u> <u>may</u> <u>have</u> <u>spent</u> months or even years to make these objects. There <u>is</u> also a special <u>love</u> contained in homemade cakes and cookies. A <u>gift</u> <u>can</u> <u>be</u> a message between the giver and the receiver.

CHAPTER 2

Beyond the Simple Sentence: Coordination

A group of words containing a subject and a verb is called a **clause.** When that group makes sense by itself, it is called a sentence or an independent clause. A sentence that has one independent clause is called a **simple sentence.** If you rely too heavily on a sentence pattern of simple sentences, you risk writing paragraphs like this:

> My father never got a chance to go to college. He had to struggle all his life. He struggled to make a good living. He dreamed of sending his children to college. He saved his money for their education. Today, all three of his children are in college. Two of them are working toward degrees in business. My father is very proud of them. His third child has pleased my father the most. The third child, my brother, is majoring in education. My father will be proud of his son the teacher. He thinks a teacher in the family is a great gift.

instead of

> My father never got a chance to go to college, and he had to struggle all his life to make a good living. He dreamed of sending his children to college, so he saved his money for their education. Today, all three of his children are in college. Two of them are working toward degrees in business. My father is very proud of them, yet his third child has pleased my father the most. The third child, my brother, is majoring in education. My father will be proud of his son the teacher, for he thinks a teacher in the family is a great gift.

If you read the two paragraphs aloud, you'll notice how choppy the first one sounds. The second one is smoother. The first one is made up of simple sentences, while the second one combines some simple sentences for a more flowing style.

OPTIONS FOR COMBINING SIMPLE SENTENCES

Good writing involves **sentence variety.** This means mixing a simple sentence with a more complicated one and using both short and long sentences. Sentence variety is easier to achieve if you can combine related, short sentences into one.

Some students avoid such combining because they're not sure how to do it. They don't know how to punctuate the new combinations. It's true that punctuating involves memorizing a few rules, but once you know them, you'll be able to use them automatically and write with more confidence. Here are three options for combining simple sentences, followed by the punctuation rules you need to use in each case.

OPTION 1: USING A COMMA WITH A COORDINATING CONJUNCTION

You can combine two simple sentences with a comma and a coordinating conjunction. The coordinating conjunctions are *and, but, or, nor, for, yet, so.*

To **coordinate** means to *join equals.* When you join two simple sentences with a comma and a coordinating conjunction, each half of the combination remains an **independent clause,** with its own subject (S) and verb (V).

Here are two simple sentences:

    S   V   S   V
Joanne drove the car. *Richard studied* the map.

Here are two simple sentences combined with a comma, and with the word *and,* a coordinating conjunction (CC):

    S   V   , CC   S   V
Joanne drove the car, *and Richard studied* the map.

The combined sentences keep the form they had as separate sentences; that is, they are still both independent clauses, with a subject and verb and with the ability to stand alone.

The word that joins them is the **coordinating conjunction.** It is used to join *equals.* Look at some more examples. These examples use a variety of coordinating conjunctions to join two simple sentences (also called independent clauses).

sentences combined with *but:*

    S   V   , CC S   V
She brought a cake, *but she forgot* a cake slicer.

sentences combined with *or:*

      S   V   , CC S   V
Mr. Chung can call my office, *or he can write* me.

sentences combined with *nor:*

  S   V   V   , CC   V   S   V
We couldn't see the stage, *nor could we hear* the music. (Notice what happens to the word order when you use *nor.*)

sentences combined with *for:*

        S   V   , CC   S   V
My *mother was* furious, *for* the *doctor was* two hours late. (Notice that *for* means *because.*)

sentences combined with *yet:*

S   V   , CC S   V
I loved Botany, *yet I never got* a good grade in it. (Notice that *yet* means *but* or *nevertheless.*)

sentences combined with *so:*

       S   V   , CC S   V
Marshall brought her flowers, *so she forgave* him for his rudeness. (Notice that *so* means *therefore* or *as a result.*)

Where Does the Comma Go?

The comma goes *before* the coordinating conjunction (*and, but, or, nor, for, yet, so*). It comes before the new idea—the second independent clause. It goes where the first independent clause ends. Try this punctuation check. After you've placed the comma, look at the combined sentences. For example:

John saved his money, and he bought a new car.

Now split it into two sentences at the comma:

John saved his money. And he bought a new car.

If you put the comma in the wrong place, after the coordinating conjunction, like this:

comma in wrong place:

~~John saved his money and, he bought a new car.~~

your split sentences would look like this:

John saved his money and. He bought a new car. (The split doesn't make sense.)

This test helps you see whether the comma has been placed correctly—where the first independent clause ends. (Notice that you can also begin a sentence with *and, but, or, nor, for, yet, so*—as long as you've written a complete sentence.)

Caution: Do *not* use a comma every time you use the words *and, but, or, nor, for, yet, so;* use one only when the coordinating conjunction joins independent clauses. Do not use a comma when the coordinating conjunction joins words:

tea or coffee
exhausted but relieved
love and happiness

Do not use a comma when the coordinating conjunction joins phrases:

on the patio or in the garden
in the glove compartment and under the seats
with harsh words but without anger

A comma is used when the coordinating conjunction joins two independent clauses. Another way to say the same rule is to say that a comma is used when the coordinating conjunction joins two simple sentences.

Placing the Comma by Using *S–V* Patterns

An independent clause, or simple sentence, follows this basic pattern:

S (subject)   V (verb)

Here is an example:

S V
He ran.

You can add to the basic pattern in several ways:

S   S V
He and *I ran.*

S   V   V
He ran and *swam.*

S   S V   V
He and *I ran* and *swam.*

Study all the examples above, and you'll notice that you can draw a line separating the subjects on one side and the verbs on the other:

S	V
SS	V
S	VV
SS	VV

So whether the simple sentence has one subject (or more than one), the pattern is subject(s) followed by verb(s).

Compound Sentences

When you combine two simple sentences, the pattern changes:

two simple sentences:

S V
He swam.

S V
I ran.

two simple sentences combined:

S   V   S V
He swam, but *I ran.*

In the new pattern, *SVSV,* you can't draw a line putting all the subjects on one side and all the verbs on the other. The new pattern is called a **compound sentence:** two simple sentences, or independent clauses, combined into one.

Learning the Coordinating Conjunctions

You've just studied one way to combine simple sentences. If you are going to take advantage of this method, you need to memorize the coordinating conjunctions—*and, but, or, nor, for, yet, so*—so that your use of them, with the correct punctuation, will become automatic.

Exercise 1

Practice

Recognizing Compound Sentences and Adding Commas

Add commas only where they are needed in the following sentences.

1. Suzannne gave me a beautiful sweater, but it was too small.

2. A friend of mine waited in line for three hours and got tickets

   for the last game.

3. Before work, Jimmy takes his daughter to preschool and he stops
   at MacDonald's for a big cup of coffee.

4. The students from Panama are spending the summer in Florida
   and studying English at a local community college.

5. The neighbors were having a loud party so I closed my bedroom
   window.

6. Stacey loves to go to the movies yet movies with blood and
   violence make her sick.

7. Georgina talked to her boss about a raise but didn't get much
   of a response.

8. I wanted to meet Enrique for his sister had told me all about him.

9. The flimsy old shack was not built to resist hurricane-force winds
   nor was it able to withstand the pounding rain.

10. You should get to the game early or you won't find a parking space.

 More on Recognizing Compound Sentences and Adding Commas

Practice   Add commas only where they are needed in the following sentences.

1. My brother is considering majoring in computer programming
   or training as a paramedic.

2. The governor's speech was a long yet sincere farewell to the
   people of the state.

3. Lamont forgot to put gas in the car so he left me with a nearly
   empty gas tank.

4. There is a note from your girlfriend on the table for she had
   to leave early.

5. The toddler grabbed at the open box of cereal and I quickly
   moved it beyond his grasp.

6. My dog was barking excitedly so I checked the back yard
   for prowlers.

7. Bernadette and Ryan could have dinner with us on Friday or
   we can meet them in town on Saturday.

8. You can ask Mrs. Gonzalez to watch the twins but she won't keep them overnight.

9. The apartments near campus have neither air conditioning nor central heating.

10. Fred and Roger changed the oil and replaced the windshield wipers in their mother's car.

Exercise 3

 *Collaborate*

Writing and Punctuating Compound Sentences

Working with a partner or a group, write the compound sentences described below. Be sure to punctuate them correctly. When you have completed the exercise, share your answers with another group or with the class.

Answers Will Vary.

Possible answers shown at right.

1. Write a compound sentence using the coordinating conjunction *and*.

   The wind was strong, and the rain beat against the windows.

2. Write a compound sentence using the coordinating conjunction *but*.

   You can buy a ticket, but you can't get a good seat.

3. Write a compound sentence using the coordinating conjunction *or*.

   I can take my car, or we can go in your truck.

4. Write a compound sentence using the coordinating conjunction *nor*.

   My supervisor did not praise me, nor did she offer me a raise.

5. Write a compound sentence using the coordinating conjunction *for*.

   I will call you later, for I am busy right now.

6. Write a compound sentence using the coordinating conjunction *yet*.

   Jerry was angry, yet he did not raise his voice.

7. Write a compound sentence using the coordinating conjunction *so*.

   Brian's favorite team is playing, so he is going to the game.

OPTION 2: USING A SEMICOLON BETWEEN TWO SIMPLE SENTENCES

Sometimes you may want to combine two simple sentences (independent clauses) without using a coordinating conjunction. If you want to join two simple sentences that are related in their ideas and you do not want to use a coordinating conjunction, you can combine them with a semicolon.

two simple sentences:

S   V   S   V
I washed the floor. *He dusted* the furniture.

two simple sentences combined with a semicolon:

S   V   ; S   V
I washed the floor; *he dusted* the furniture.

Here are more examples of this option in use:

S   V   ;S V
He swam; I ran.

S   V   V ; S   V   V
*Jacy could*n't *sleep; she was thinking* about her job.

S   V   ; S   V
Skindiving is expensive; *you need* money for equipment.

Notice that when you join two simple sentences with a semicolon, the second sentence begins with a lowercase letter, not a capital letter.

Exercise 4

Practice

Recognizing Compound Sentences and Adding Semicolons

Add semicolons only where they are needed in the following sentences.

1. Howard took me into the hallway and asked me to apologize for

   my unkind remarks.

2. Denice will take the car to the tire store ; you can get a ride with
   Wayne.

3. Somebody took my umbrella ; I just left it here for a minute.

4. The location of the house makes it a perfect choice for a family

   with small children or a retired couple.

5. Dr. Fumiko is a demanding instructor ; he gives a test every week

   and assigns a paper once a month.

6. You can type your report on my computer ; I don't mind.

7. Elaine Karram loved children but thought taking child develop-

   ment classes would be too hard for her.

8. Matthew cried and begged his father for one last chance ; his

   father refused.

9. Last summer, Lisa and Patrick got jobs in Denver ; they loved the city.

10. Taking a speech class can give you confidence and boost your

    self-esteem.

TEACHING TIP:

Tell students not to place
a comma between the
complete subject and the
verb. See if any students
were tempted to place a
comma between "class"
and "can" in exercise item
10.

Exercise 5

Practice

More on Recognizing Compound Sentences and Adding Semicolons

Add semicolons only where they are needed in the following sentences.

1. My employer praised my work and offered me a chance to earn some extra money.

2. Your house is cold ; you should turn on the heat.

3. A scruffy terrier and a small brown Chihuahua leaped through the door and began barking with joy. ;

4. Working long hours can give you extra money ; it can also give you added stress.

5. Spike can't eat that cake ; he is allergic to the peanuts in it.

6. My credit card bill will be high ; I spent too much on clothes last month.

7. Nothing in the refrigerator looks appetizing to me I'll just go out for dinner.

8. Monica or her brother should sell the house or fix it up. ;

9. Gerard occasionally does the shopping ; Andy never does.

10. I received four phone calls last night they were all from Marta.

OPTION 3: USING A SEMICOLON AND A CONJUNCTIVE ADVERB

Sometimes you may want to join two simple sentences (independent clauses) with a connecting word called a **conjunctive adverb.** This word points out or clarifies a relationship between the sentences.

Info BOX

Some Common Conjunctive Adverbs

also	furthermore	likewise	otherwise
anyway	however	meanwhile	similarly
as a result	in addition	moreover	still
besides	incidentally	nevertheless	then
certainly	indeed	next	therefore
consequently	in fact	now	thus
finally	instead	on the other hand	undoubtedly

You can put a conjunctive adverb (CA) between simple sentences, but when you do, you still need a semicolon in front of the adverb.

two simple sentences:

S V   S   V
I got a tutor for College Algebra. *I improved* my grade.

two simple sentences joined by a conjunctive adverb and a semicolon:

S V   ; CA S   V
I got a tutor for College Algebra; *then I improved* my grade.

S V   ;   CA   S   V
I got a tutor for College Algebra; *consequently, I improved* my grade.

Punctuating After a Conjunctive Adverb

Notice the comma after the conjunctive adverb in the sentence, *I got a tutor for College Algebra; consequently, I improved my grade.* Here's the generally accepted rule:

> **Put a comma after the conjunctive adverb if the conjunctive adverb is more than one syllable long.**

For example, if the conjunctive adverb is a word like *consequently, furthermore,* or *moreover,* you use a comma. If the conjunctive adverb is one syllable, you do not have to add a comma after it. One-syllable conjunctive adverbs are words like *then* or *thus.*

punctuating with conjunctive adverbs:

Every month I paid my whole credit card debt; thus I avoided paying interest.

Every month I paid my whole credit card debt; consequently, I avoided paying interest.

Exercise 6

Practice

Recognizing and Punctuating Compound Sentences with Conjunctive Adverbs

Add semicolons and commas only where they are needed in the following sentences,

1. The football game was very close finally my team won.

2. Rick is an excellent skater in fact he won a speed skating award

   in high school.

3. Lennie loves to talk about his friends but never says very much

   about himself.

4. You can still stay at our house over the weekend.

5. I usually have a Diet Pepsi for breakfast however I've got to

   start the day in a healthier way.

6. Betty used to worry about graduating from high school now she is

   ordering her cap and gown for her college graduation.

7. My neighbors are celebrating the birth of a baby girl ; undoubtedly , they will put pink ribbons and a sign on their door.

8. The tea kettle on the stove began to whistle ; meanwhile , the cake in the oven began to burn.

9. Cheesecake is a delicious dessert but is full of calories.

10. Cheesecake is a delicious dessert ; on the other hand , it is full of calories.

 Exercise 7
Practice

More on Recognizing and Punctuating Compound Sentences with Conjunctive Adverbs

Add semicolons and commas only where they are needed in the following sentences.

1. You should think about joining our softball team ; incidentally , I am the captain.

2. Helen took two classes in summer school ; as a result , she can graduate next semester.

3. My car needs new brakes ; besides , the radiator is leaking.

4. I'll take Deanna to a fancy restaurant ; then I'll give her the ring.

5. I waved a toy bunny in front of the baby and danced around ; still he would not smile for the camera.

6. Tim always says he wants to get more exercise yet rarely goes outdoors.

7. I'll start the day with a walk on the beach ; next I'll drink a glass of fresh-squeezed orange juice.

8. You can take college classes at night and even register for one on the weekends.

9. Marcy's background in accounting will certainly help her in her new position at the Internal Revenue Service.

10. You have a good chance of getting a B in this course ; certainly , you should get a C.

👥 *Collaborate*

Exercise 8   Writing Sentences with Conjunctive Adverbs

Working with a partner or a group, write one sentence for each of the conjunctive adverbs below. When you have completed this exercise, share your answers with another group or with the class. The first one is done for you.

1. Write a compound sentence using *instead*.

She couldn't find her notes for her speech to the jury; instead, she

relied on her memory.

Answers Will Vary.

Possible answers shown
at right.

2. Write a compound sentence using *then*.

The doorbell rang; then someone pounded on the door.

3. Write a compound sentence using *furthermore*.

Gossip can be malicious; furthermore, it is often untrue.

4. Write a compound sentence using *on the other hand*.

I can make a high salary as an accountant; on the other hand, I would

be happier in a more creative field.

5. Write a compound sentence using *otherwise*.

I am writing myself a note; otherwise, I will forget to go to the post

office.

6. Write a compound sentence using *therefore*.

You helped me out last year; therefore, I'll help you out this year.

Practice

Exercise 9   Combining Simple Sentences Three Ways

Add (1) a comma, (2) a semicolon, or (3) a semicolon and a comma to the following sentences. Do not add, change, or delete any words; just add the correct punctuation.

1. Check the classified advertisements in the newspaper first ; then

you can start looking at apartments for rent.

2. Manuel has dozens of buddies , but he has no close friends.

3. My father loved to play chess ; moreover , he loved to watch others

play the game.

4. Bill took dozens of pictures' for he wanted to remember this meeting with his long-lost brother.

5. Mark answered the questions brilliantly; in fact' he was the smartest contestant on the quiz show.

6. My dog loves to catch a ball; however' he never returns it to me.

7. Nothing is wrong with the DVD player; it works perfectly.

8. This jacket is too small for me' so you can have it.

9. Keith has been sneezing all afternoon; he must be allergic to something in the house.

10. My boyfriend will never throw away his old football jersey' nor will he ever get rid of his Super Bowl ticket stubs.

11. Charlie's cat waited under the bed; then she jumped out and pounced at me.

12. I am working with a tutor in my math class; in addition' I joined a study group for my sociology class.

13. Dave and Alex volunteered for the crime watch committee' and James joined the residents' clean-up committee.

14. I forgot to bring a sweater' so I borrowed one from my cousin.

15. Once my brother cut his hair very short; now he wears it below his ears.

16. Broccoli is full of vitamins and healthy fiber' yet I hate the taste of it.

17. That reckless driver could have seriously hurt someone; in fact' he could have killed someone.

18. My mother always buys extra boxes of microwave popcorn; thus she always has snacks for unexpected visitors.

19. The police spent three hours at the crime scene; finally' they collected all the necessary evidence.

20. You could have asked me for a loan' or you could have gone to your sister for help with the rent.

Collaborate

Combining Simple Sentences

Following are pairs of simple sentences. Working with a partner or group, combine each pair into one sentence. Remember the three options for combining sentences: (1) a comma and a coordinating conjunction, (2) a semicolon, (3) a semicolon and a conjunctive adverb. When you have combined each pair into one sentence, exchange your exercise with another group. Write a new sentence below each sentence prepared by the other group. The first is done for you.

1. Takeout pizza for a family of six is expensive.
   My children and I make our own pizza at home.

   combination 1: Takeout pizza for a family of six is expensive, so my children and I make our own pizza at home.

   combination 2: Takeout pizza for a family of six is expensive; instead, my children and I make our own pizza at home.

Answers Will Vary.

Possible answers shown at right.

2. Mr. Garcia was demanding, impatient, and stingy with praise.
   He was the best music teacher in the school.

   combination 1: Mr. Garcia was demanding, impatient, and stingy with praise, but he was the best music teacher in the school.

   combination 2: Mr. Garcia was demanding, impatient, and stingy with praise; however, he was the best music teacher in the school.

3. Alonso's parents fought all the time.
   He has very little faith in marriage.

   combination 1: Alonso's parents fought all the time; as a result, he has very little faith in marriage.

   combination 2: Alonso's parents fought all the time; thus he has very little faith in marriage,

4. You spread rumors about me to everyone in school.
   You made fun of me in front of your friends.

   combination 1: You spread rumors about me to everyone in school, and you made fun of me in front of your friends.

   combination 2: You spread rumors about me to everyone in school; then you made fun of me in front of your friends.

5. Dana will not listen to my advice.
She will not accept a friendly warning from her sister.

combination 1: Dana will not listen to my advice, nor will she accept a friendly warning from her sister.

combination 2: Dana will not listen to my advice; moreover, she will not accept a friendly warning from her sister.

6. Kevin has been working at the health food store for two years.
He knows all about herbs and vitamin supplements.

combination 1: Kevin has been working at the health food store for two years, so he knows all about herbs and vitamin supplements.

combination 2: Kevin has been working at the health food store for two years; consequently, he knows all about herbs and vitamin supplements.

Exercise 11

 Connect

Punctuating Compound Sentences in a Paragraph

Add commas and semicolons only where they are needed in the paragraph below.

Our trip to Philadelphia was full of surprises. Some were pleasant surprises; others were not so pleasant. One surprise related to the weather. Kim and I are from Southern California, and we had never seen snow. We were visiting Philadelphia in January; consequently, we expected to see fluffy white flakes of falling snow. We did see some snow; however, it was slushy melted snow with a dirty gray tint. We also had a pleasant surprise in the city; our surprise was seeing history in a new way. I expected Independence Hall and the Liberty Bell to be boring, but they brought the past to life. Kim and I stood silently before them, for we were awed by these symbols of America's past. Our last surprise was more trivial yet also fine. We were introduced to the taste of a Philly cheese steak; now we can't stop dreaming of one. We will certainly go back to Philadelphia for more eye-opening and mouth-watering experiences.

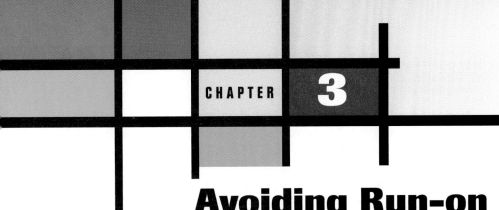

CHAPTER 3

Avoiding Run-on Sentences and Comma Splices

RUN-ON SENTENCES

If you run two independent clauses together without the necessary punctuation, you make an error called a **run-on sentence.** This error is also called a **fused sentence.**

run-on sentence error:
I worked hard in the class I earned a good grade.

run-on sentence error corrected:
I worked hard in the class, and I earned a good grade. (To correct this error, you need a comma before the coordinating conjunction *and.*)

run-on sentence error:
I worked hard in the class I earned a good grade.

run-on sentence error corrected:
I worked hard in the class; I earned a good grade. (To correct this error, you need a semicolon between the two independent clauses.)

Steps for Correcting Run-on Sentences

When you edit your writing, you can correct run-on sentences by following these steps:

Step 1: Check for two independent clauses.
Step 2: Check that the clauses are separated either by a coordinating conjunction (*and, but, or, nor, for, yet, so*) and a comma or by a semicolon.

Follow the steps in checking this sentence:

Spaghetti is cheap I buy it often.

Step 1: Check for two independent clauses. You can do this by check-ing for the subject-verb, subject-verb pattern that indicates two independent clauses:

S   V   S V
Spaghetti is cheap *I buy* it often.

The pattern indicates that you have two independent clauses.

Step 2: Check that the clauses are separated either by a coordinating conjunction (*and, but, or, nor, for, yet, so*) and a comma or by a semicolon.

There is no punctuation between the independent clauses, and there is no coordinating conjunction. You have a run-on sentence. You can correct it two ways:

run-on sentence corrected with a coordinating conjunction and a comma:
Spaghetti is cheap, *so* I buy it often.

run-on sentence corrected with a semicolon:
Spaghetti is cheap; I buy it often.

Follow the steps once more, checking this sentence:

I bought a new computer it is too complicated for me.

Step 1: Check for two independent clauses. Do this by checking the subject-verb, subject-verb pattern:

S   V   S V
I bought a new computer *it is* too complicated for me.

Step 2: Check that the clauses are separated either by a coordinating conjunction (*and, but, or, nor, for, yet, so*) and a comma or by a semicolon.

There is no punctuation between the independent clauses. There is no coor-dinating conjunction, either. Without the proper punctuation, this a run-on sentence. Correct it two ways:

run-on sentence corrected with a coordinating conjunction and a comma:
I bought a new computer, *but* it is too complicated for me.

run-on sentence error corrected with a semicolon:
I bought a new computer; it is too complicated for me.

Using the steps to check for run-on sentences can also help you to avoid unnecessary punctuation. Consider this sentence:

Alan stuffed the papers into the trash and carried the trash bag to the curb.

Step 1: Check for two independent clauses. Do this by checking the subject-verb, subject-verb pattern:

S   V   V
Alan stuffed the papers into the trash and *carried* the trash bag to the curb.

The pattern is *SVV*, not *SV, SV*. You have one independent clause, not two. The sentence is not a run-on sentence.

Following the steps in correcting run-on sentences can help you avoid a major grammar error.

Exercise 1

Practice

Correcting Run-on Sentences

Some of the sentences below are correctly punctuated. Some are run-on (fused) sentences—two simple sentences run together without any punctuation. If a sentence is correctly punctuated, write *OK* in the space provided. If it is a run-on sentence, put an *X* in the space provided and correct the sentence above the lines.

1. __X__   Norman gave his mother a birthday gift of a dozen roses[;] he wanted her to feel loved and special.

2. __X__   I sent you an e-mail _{, but} you never replied to it.

3. __X__   At the bottom of the suitcase was my cold medicine[;] it had leaked all over my clothes.

4. __OK__   Two of the oldest citizens in our town meet at the community center every morning and swim laps in the pool.

5. __X__   Eli is polite[;] he always opens the door for me.

6. __OK__   Young children on skateboards wobble and fall on the concrete pavement every afternoon.

7. __X__   Brett called his old girlfriend _{, for} he had just lost his new one.

8. __X__   Mr. Morris has been working at the bank for two years_{, yet} he has never received a promotion.

9. __OK__   I get a flu shot every year yet always get a bad case of the flu.

10. __OK__   The chili at Café Mexico looks weird but smells and tastes wonderful.

Exercise 2

Practice

More on Correcting Run-on Sentences

Some of the following sentences are correctly punctuated. Some are run-on (fused) sentences—two simple sentences run together without any punctuation. If the sentence is correctly punctuated, write *OK* in the space provided. If it is a run-on sentence, put an *X* in the space provided and correct the sentence above the lines.

1. __X__   My best friend comes from a wealthy family[;] thus he seems to have all the luck in the world.

2. __X__   You should develop a positive attitude[;] worrying and complaining only make your situation worse.

TEACHING TIP:

This may be a good time to advise students that computer "grammar/style checkers" may often designate a sentence as a run-on simply because of its length. Remind the class that such software may be beneficial at times, but it cannot guarantee accuracy.

3. _OK_   Newly baked bread from a bakery and two-day old bread from my refrigerator are completely different.

4. _X_   My little brother loves music videos *;* he watches them before and after school and long into the night.

5. _X_   It had been drizzling all day *;* then the rain began to pound the earth.

6. _X_   I needed some coffee *, so* I stopped at the supermarket.

7. _X_   Claudia will always remember Mr. Halaby *, for* he had faith in her acting ability.

8. _OK_   Mia stopped at a service plaza on the turnpike and asked for directions to the university.

9. _X_   Chocolate syrup was all over the kitchen counter *, and* it was dripping on the floor.

10. _OK_   Next month Brian will drive down from Charlotte and see me.

COMMA SPLICES

A **comma splice** is an error that occurs when you punctuate with a comma but should use a semicolon instead. If you are joining two independent clauses without a coordinating conjunction, you *must use* a semicolon. A comma isn't enough.

comma splice error:
The rain fell steadily, the valley filled with water.

comma splice error corrected:
The rain fell steadily; the valley filled with water.

comma splice error:
I lost my umbrella, now I have to buy a new one.

comma splice error corrected:
I lost my umbrella; now I have to buy a new one.

Correcting Comma Splices

When you edit your writing, you can correct comma splices by following these steps:

Step 1: Check for two independent clauses.
Step 2: Check that the clauses are separated by a coordinating conjunction (*and, but, or, nor, for, yet, so*). If they are, then a comma in front of the coordinating conjunction is sufficient. If they are not separated by a coordinating conjunction, you have a comma splice. Correct it by changing the comma to a semicolon.

Follow the steps to check for a comma splice in this sentence:

> The puppy jumped up, he licked my face.

Step 1: Check for two independent clauses. You can do this by check-ing for the subject-verb, subject-verb pattern that indicates two independent clauses.

> **S**   **V**   **S**   **V**
> The *puppy jumped* up, *he licked* my face.

Step 2: Check that the clauses are separated by a coordinating con-junction.

There is no coordinating conjunction. To correct the comma splice error, you must use a semicolon instead of a comma:

> **comma splice error corrected:**
> The puppy jumped up; he licked my face.

Be careful not to mistake a short word like *then* or *thus* for a coordi-nating conjunction. Only the seven coordinating conjunctions (*and, but, or, nor for, yet, so*), with a comma in front of them, can join independent clauses.

> **comma splice error:**
> Suzanne opened the letter, then she screamed with joy.

> **comma splice error corrected:**
> Suzanne opened the letter; then she screamed with joy.

Then is not a coordinating conjunction; it is a conjunctive adverb. When it joins two independent clauses, it needs a semicolon in front of it.

Also remember that conjunctive adverbs that are two or more syllables long (like *consequently, however, therefore*) need a comma after them *as well as* a semicolon in front of them when they join independent clauses:

> Anthony passed the placement test; consequently, he can take
> Advanced Mathematics.

(For a list of some common conjunctive adverbs, see Chapter 2).

Sometimes writers see commas before and after a conjunctive adverb and think the commas are sufficient. Check this sentence for a comma splice by following the steps:

> The van held all my tools, however, it used too much gas.

Step 1: Check for two independent clauses by checking for the subject-verb, subject-verb pattern.

> **S**   **V**   **S**   **V**
> The *van held* all my tools, however, *it used* too much gas.

Step 2: Check for a coordinating conjunction.

There is no coordinating conjunction. *However* is a conjunctive adverb, not a coordinating conjunction. Without a coordinating con-junction, a semicolon is needed between the two independent clauses.

> **comma splice corrected:**
> The van held all my tools; however, it used too much gas.

Following the steps in correcting comma splices can help you avoid a major grammar error.

TEACHING TIP:

When students are checking for comma splices, ask them to see if a period could be substituted for the comma. If so, the comma is probably incorrect, and a semicolon should be used instead.

Exercise **3**

Practice

Correcting Comma Splices

Some of the following sentences are correctly punctuated. Some contain comma splices. If the sentence is correctly punctuated, write *OK* in the space provided. If it contains a comma splice, put an *X* in the space provided and correct the sentence. To correct the sentence, you do not need to add words; just correct the punctuation.

1. __X__   The pale gray kitten was the most beautiful one at the shelter,⟨;⟩ they immediately decided to adopt it.

2. __X__   Elise ordered a big platter of ribs,⟨;⟩ she gave half of them to me.

3. __X__   Some movies begin with an exciting chase scene,⟨;⟩ then they turn into long and confusing stories of crime and betrayal.

4. __X__   I was rapidly searching my pockets for the tickets,⟨;⟩ meanwhile, my husband was getting impatient.

5. __X__   Nelson called the airport early this morning,⟨;⟩ thus he knew about the flight delays.

6. __OK__   Our house was surrounded by big trees, so it was shady and cool in the summer.

7. __X__   Two lanes on the highway were closed,⟨;⟩ nevertheless, we arrived at work on time.

8. __X__   You should always lock your car doors,⟨;⟩ otherwise, you risk a burglary or the theft of your car.

9. __X__   One reason for his fear of public speaking might be childhood experiences,⟨;⟩ another might be low self-esteem.

10. __OK__   Sammy and his parents can't forget the past, nor can they move beyond it.

Exercise **4**

Practice

More on Correcting Comma Splices

Some of the following sentences are correctly punctuated. Some contain comma splices. If the sentence is correctly punctuated, write *OK* in the space provided. If it contains a comma splice, put *X* in the space provided and correct the sentence. To correct the sentence, you do not need to add words; just correct the punctuation.

1. __OK__   My father has never seen an opera, yet he has always listened to them on the radio.

2. __X__   Carlos vowed to stop looking for the perfect woman,⟨;⟩ then he met her at his aunt's birthday party.

3. __X__   I was stopped for speeding on the interstate highway, however, I escaped with a warning.

4. __X__   Janice called the cable repair service and was put on hold for twenty minutes, as a result, she became frustrated and angry.

5. __X__   The Palace Grill is expensive, I eat there only on special occasions.

6. __OK__   My parents are away for the weekend, so I am having a party on Saturday night.

7. __X__   Baseball games can last for hours, moreover, they often have to go into extra innings.

8. __X__   My grandfather loves e-mail, he writes dozens of people every week.

9. __OK__   Your brother could drive you to the bus station, or you could ask Terry for a ride.

10. __OK__   My boss changed my schedule at the store, so I have to find a sitter for my little boy.

Exercise 5

👥 *Collaborate*

Completing Sentences

With a partner or a group, write the first part of each of the following incomplete sentences. Make your addition an independent clause. Be sure to punctuate your completed sentences correctly. The first one is done for you.

Answers Will Vary.

Possible answers shown at right.

1. My candle suddenly blew out;_____ then I saw the ghost.

2. The Sharks played well;_____ however, the team lost the game.

3. I kept shouting,_____ but no one came to my rescue.

4. We waited for an hour;_____ finally, the car started.

5. The teacher gave a surprise quiz;_____ now the students are upset.

6. Leo heard a noise outside;_____ therefore, he locked all the doors.

7. You must move the car now,_____ or the car will be towed away.

8. The passengers panicked;_____ meanwhile, the ship was sinking.

9. A crowd approached, and_____ somebody looked in the window.

10. I saw a fire; then_____ sirens began to scream through the neighborhood.

Connect

Exercise 6   Editing a Paragraph for Run-on Sentences and Comma Splices

Edit the following paragraph for run-on sentences and comma splices. There are five errors.

Being asked for advice puts me in a difficult position. A friend in trouble may ask for advice, but he or she may not really want my ideas. For example, I can tell a friend to apologize to his boss, however, my friend expected me to do something completely different. He expected me to be on his side of the dispute. I tried to help, as a result, I disappointed my friend. Sometimes, whatever I say can be dangerous for a friendship. For instance, a friend complains about her boyfriend and asks for my opinion. I tell her to end the relationship. She listens but decides to stay in the relationship, consequently, she sees me as a bad friend. On the other hand, she could listen to me and break up with her boyfriend. Soon she may regret her decision then she gets angry. Unfortunately, she is angry at me, not at herself. She blames me for my bad advice, soon she thinks the break-up is all my fault. Situations like these make me very careful about sharing my opinions.

CHAPTER 4

Beyond the Simple Sentence: Subordination

MORE ON COMBINING SIMPLE SENTENCES

You may remember these principles of grammar:

- A clause has a subject and a verb.
- An independent clause is a simple sentence; it is a group of words, with a subject and a verb, that makes sense by itself.

Chapter 2 described three options for combining simple sentences (independent clauses). There is another kind of clause called a **dependent clause.** It has a subject and a verb, but it does not make sense by itself. It cannot stand alone because it is not complete by itself. That is, it *depends* on the rest of the sentence to give it meaning. You can use a dependent clause as another option for combining simple sentences.

OPTION 4: USING A DEPENDENT CLAUSE TO BEGIN A SENTENCE

Often, you can combine simple sentences by changing an independent clause into a dependent clause and placing it at the beginning of the new sentence:

two simple sentences:

S V   S V
I missed my bus. *I slept* through my alarm.

changing one simple sentence into a beginning dependent clause:

                S V   S   V
Because *I slept* through my alarm, *I missed* my bus.

OPTION 5: USING A DEPENDENT CLAUSE TO END A SENTENCE

You can also combine simple sentences by changing an independent clause into a dependent clause and placing it at the end of the new sentence:

I missed my bus because I slept through my alarm.

Notice how one simple sentence can be changed into a dependent clause in two ways:

two simple sentences:

Nicholas played his guitar. Jared sang an old song.

changing one simple sentence into a dependent clause:

Nicholas played his guitar while Jared sang an old song.

or

While Jared sang an old song, Nicholas played his guitar.

Using Subordinating Words: Subordinating Conjunctions

Changing an independent clause to a dependent one is called **subordinating.** How do you do it? You add a subordinating word, called a **subordinating conjunction,** to an independent clause, which makes it dependent—less "important"—or subordinate, in the new sentence.

Keep in mind that the subordinate clause is still a clause; it has a subject and verb, but it doesn't make sense by itself. For example, here is an independent clause:

David cooks.

Somebody (David) does something (cooks). The statement makes sense by itself. But if you add a subordinating conjunction to the independent clause, the clause becomes dependent—incomplete, unfinished—like this:

When David cooks (When he cooks, what happens?)
Unless David cooks (Unless he cooks, what will happen?)
If David cooks (If he cooks, what will happen?)

Now, each dependent clause needs an independent clause to finish the idea:

dependent clause   independent clause
When David cooks, he makes wonderful meals.

dependent clause   independent clause
Unless David cooks, you will not get a decent dinner.

dependent clause independent clause
If David cooks, dinner will be delicious.

There are many subordinating conjunctions. When you put any of these words in front of an independent clause, you make that clause dependent. Following is a list of some subordinating conjunctions.

---

info BOX

Subordinating Conjunctions

after	before	so that	whenever
although	even though	though	where
as	if	unless	whereas
as if	in order that	until	whether
because	since	when	while

If you pick the right subordinating conjunction, you can effectively combine simple sentences (independent clauses) into a more sophisticated sentence pattern. Such combining helps you add sentence variety to your writing and helps to explain relationships between ideas.

simple sentences:

   S   V   V   S   V
Emily had never *studied* art. *She was* a gifted painter.

new combination:

          dependent clause   independent clause
Although Emily had never studied art, she was a gifted painter.

simple sentences:

S   V   S   V
I bought a new leash last night. My *puppy chewed* up his old one.

new combination:

         independent clause   dependent clause
I bought a new leash last night because my puppy chewed up his old one.

Punctuating Complex Sentences

A sentence that has one independent clause and one or more dependent clauses is called a **complex sentence.** Complex sentences are very easy to punctuate. See if you can figure out the rule for punctuating by yourself. Look at the following examples. All are punctuated correctly.

       dependent clause   independent clause
Whenever I visit my mother, I bring flowers.

  independent clause   dependent clause
I bring flowers whenever I visit my mother.

      dependent clause   independent clause
While he was talking, I was daydreaming.

  independent clause   dependent clause
I was daydreaming while he was talking.

In the examples above, look at the sentences that have a comma. Now look at the ones that don't have a comma. Both kinds of sentences are punctuated correctly. Do you see the rule?

When a dependent clause comes at the beginning of the sentence, the clause is followed by a comma. When a dependent clause comes at the end of a sentence, the clause does not need a comma.

TEACHING TIP:

Survey recent magazine and/or newspaper articles and make copies of short articles that incorporate a variety of sentence patterns. Ask students to spot prepositional phrases, coordinating conjunctions, and subordinating conjunctions. Some alert students may even spot comma errors or omissions.

Here are some correctly punctuated complex sentences:

Although he studied hard, he failed the test.
He failed the test although he studied hard.

Until I started running, I was out of shape.
I was out of shape until I started running.

Punctuating Complex Sentences

All of the following sentences are complex sentences—they have one independent clause and one or more dependent clauses. Add a comma to each sentence that needs one.

1. Unless I study tonight, I won't get a good grade on the test.

2. Ask Cristina for her biology notes when you see her in the library.

3. After Peter got a job in Memphis, he stopped driving to my house on weekends.

4. When the sky is a solid gray with no clouds, the atmosphere feels heavy and dull.

5. My little brother usually plays with the computer after he has dinner.

6. Whenever Amanda and Jack see an antique shop, they want to stop and look around.

7. Before he interviewed for the job at Data Dynamics, he got letters of recommendation from a teacher and a former employer.

8. My dog kept licking my face as I tried to cover my head with the blankets and go back to sleep.

9. As the sign says, there is no parking in this spot.

10. My father hasn't been back to Nigeria since he was twenty years old.

More on Punctuating Complex Sentences

All of the following sentences are complex sentences—they have one independent clause and one or more dependent clauses. Add a comma to each sentence that needs one.

1. Kevin is taking a few days of vacation before he starts his new job at the hotel.

2. Because you gave me such good directions to the arena, I was able to find it easily.

3. We should be able to pay the rent unless we have another big bill for car repairs.

4. Keshia is studying architecture because she is fascinated with the design and structure of buildings.

5. Even if you feel healthy, you should get regular physical examinations.

6. Since you don't like avocados, I will give the ones from our tree to Antonio.

7. The children went to bed after their father read them a story.

8. Sheila would love to have dinner where she and Marty went last Valentine's Day.

9. Danny will make the steaks while you make the salad.

10. Although much of police work is exhausting and tedious, many people see it as adventurous and glamorous.

 Combining Sentences

Practice

Combine each pair of sentences below into one smooth, clear sentence. The new combination should include one independent and one dependent clause and an appropriate subordinating word.

Answers Will Vary.

Possible answers shown at right.

1. The road was covered in broken glass. There had been a bad accident at the intersection.

   combined: The road was covered in broken glass because there had been a bad accident at the intersection.

2. Watching a game on television is enjoyable. It is never as exciting as watching it in the stadium.

   combined: Although watching a game on television is enjoyable, it is never as exciting as watching it in the stadium.

3. Courtney scrubbed the kitchen floor. Adam vacuumed the living room carpet.

   combined: Courtney scrubbed the kitchen floor while Adam vacuumed the living room carpet.

4. I open a can of tuna. My cat leaps onto the kitchen counter and reaches for a taste.

combined: Whenever I open a can of tuna, my cat leaps onto the kitchen counter and reaches for a taste.

5. You pack some warm clothing and a raincoat. You will be prepared for any kind of weather on your trip.

combined: If you pack some warm clothing and a raincoat, you will be prepared for any kind of weather on your trip.

6. Mr. Morita is willing to compromise on the lease. He will never be able to rent the building.

combined: Unless Mr. Morita is willing to compromise on the lease, he will never be able to rent the building.

7. Frank called to apologize to his mother. She remained angry at him.

combined: Frank called to apologize to his mother since she remained angry at him.

8. Most teens will buy the new shoes. They have seen them in the latest videos.

combined: Most teens will buy the new shoes after they have seen them in the latest videos.

9. Our school plans an outdoor activity. It begins to rain.

combined: Whenever our school plans an outdoor activity, it begins to rain.

10. I turn off the alarm clock. I stagger out of bed.

combined: I turn off the alarm clock before I stagger out of bed.

Exercise 4   **Creating Complex Sentences**

Collaborate

Do this exercise with a partner or a group. Each item below lists a dependent clause. Write two different sentences that include the dependent clause. One sentence should begin with the dependent clause; the other sentence should end with the dependent clause. The first one is done for you.

1. **dependent clause:** whenever I visit my grandmother

   sentence 1: Whenever I visit my grandmother, she tells me stories about life in Havana.

   sentence 2: I bring a box of chocolates whenever I visit my grandmother.

2. **dependent clause:** although he has never taken guitar lessons

   sentence 1: Although he has never taken guitar lessons, my brother is quite a good guitar player.

   sentence 2: Fred plays guitar in a rock 'n roll band although he has never taken guitar lessons.

3. **dependent clause:** unless you can find a way to earn $100.

   sentence 1: Unless you can find a way to earn $100, you can't buy the car battery.

   sentence 2: You will have to borrow money from your brother unless you can find a way to earn $100.

4. **dependent clause:** because we could never agree on anything

   sentence 1: Because we could never agree on anything, we made terrible roommates.

   sentence 2: Elizabeth and I divorced because we could never agree on anything.

5. **dependent clause:** while the sirens screamed

   sentence 1: While the sirens screamed, cars moved to the edge of the road.

   sentence 2: Everyone rushed for cover while the sirens screamed.

6. **dependent clause:** after she escaped from the burning building

   sentence 1: After she escaped from the burning building, Alicia was taken to the emergency room.

   sentence 2: Mrs. Brennan hugged her children after she escaped from the burning building.

7. dependent clause: since I have a long weekend coming up

sentence 1: Since I have a long weekend coming up, I am planning a camping trip.

sentence 2: I am in a good mood today since I have a long weekend coming up.

8. dependent clause: before we choose a new car

sentence 1: Before we choose a new car, we should think about our budget.

sentence 2: We can visit several car dealers before we choose a new car.

9. dependent clause: as an elderly lady struggled with two heavy bags

sentence 1: As an elderly lady struggled with two heavy bags, a kind man rushed to help her.

sentence 2: A young woman offered a shopping cart as an elderly lady struggled with two heavy bags.

10. dependent clause: even if you win the lottery

sentence 1: Even if you win the lottery, I won't marry you.

sentence 2: You will never be satisfied even if you win the lottery.

Exercise 5

∞ *Connect*

Editing a Paragraph for Complex Sentences

Edit this paragraph by adding commas where they are necessary. There are eight places that need commas.

The greatest luxury in my life is a totally free day. Even though I do not work on weekends I seem to have a series of jobs at home. Saturday is the time when I become a housekeeper. I toss out a week's worth of pizza boxes and soda cans as I vacuum and scrub. When I have gathered up all the dirty clothes on the chairs and floor my apartment is liveable again. Next I start on the laundry. While I sit at the coin laundry and watch my clothes toss in the dryer I try to read my biology assignment. After I have finished the laundry I barely have time to grab dinner at a fast-food restaurant. Sunday is devoted to more work. Since my refrigerator is empty my first chore is shopping. Even if I get the shopping done early I still have hours of work ahead of me. Now comes the homework. I read my psychology assignment, write my English paper, and review for my math test. Before I know it the day is over. As I end the weekend I can at least be proud of my neat apartment, clean clothes, well-stocked refrigerator, and well-tuned mind. I only hope that all my work will one day lead to more free time.

CHAPTER 5

Combining Sentences: A Review of Your Options

Combining sentences helps you to avoid a choppy writing style in which all your sentences are short. The pattern of one short sentence after another makes your writing repetitive and boring. When you mix the length of sentences, using some long ones and some short ones, you use a strategy called **sentence variety**.

You can develop a style that includes sentence variety by combining short, related sentences clearly and smoothly. There are several ways to combine sentences. The following chart helps you to see them all, at a glance. It also includes the punctuation necessary for each combination.

Info BOX

Options for Combining Sentences

	Coordination	
Option 1 Independent clause	, and , but , or , nor , for , yet , so	independent clause.
Option 2 Independent clause	;	independent clause.
Option 3 Independent clause	; also, ; anyway, ; as a result, ; besides, ; certainly, ; consequently,	independent clause.

Option 3 (continued) Independent clause	; finally, ; furthermore, ; however, ; in addition, ; incidentally, ; indeed, ; in fact, ; instead, ; likewise ; meanwhile, ; moreover, ; nevertheless, ; next ; now ; on the other hand, ; otherwise, ; similarly, ; still ; then ; therefore, ; thus ; undoubtedly,	independent clause.

Subordination

Option 4 Independent clause	after although as as if because before even though if in order that since so that though unless until when whenever where whereas whether while	dependent clause.

Option 5	After Although As As if Because Before Even though If In order that Since So that	Dependent clause, independent clause. (When you begin with a dependent clause, put a comma at the end of the dependent clause.)

(continued)

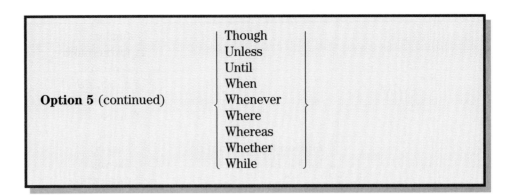

Option 5 (continued)	Though Unless Until When Whenever Where Whereas Whether While

Exercise **1**

Practice

TEACHING TIP:

Advise students not to rely too often on the word "and" when combining sentences. By avoiding "and," they can devise more effective ways to combine sentences.

Answers Will Vary.

Possible answers shown at right.

Combining Simple Sentences

Following are pairs of simple sentences. Combine each pair of sentences into one clear, smooth sentence. Create two new combinations for each pairing. The first one is done for you.

1. My car wouldn't start yesterday.

   The car battery was dead.

combination 1: My car wouldn't start yesterday because the battery was dead.

combination 2: The car battery was dead; as a result, my car wouldn't start yesterday.

2. Aunt Vivian doesn't like to exercise.
   She walks two miles every morning.

combination 1: Aunt Vivian doesn't like to exercise; nevertheless, she walks two miles every morning.

combination 2: Aunt Vivian doesn't like to exercise, but she walks two miles every morning.

3. I stretched to grab a jar of coffee on the top shelf.
   The jar fell and shattered all over the kitchen floor.

combination 1: When I stretched to grab a jar of coffee on the top shelf, the jar fell and shattered all over the kitchen floor.

combination 2: I stretched to grab a jar of coffee on the top shelf; then the jar fell and shattered all over the kitchen floor.

4. Roger never offers to pay for gas for my car.
   I am not giving him a ride to school anymore.

combination 1: Roger never offers to pay for gas for my car, so I am

not giving him a ride to school anymore.

combination 2: Because Roger never offers to pay for gas for my car,

I am not giving him a ride to school any more.

5. My parents always shop at Price Mart.
   The store has the best deals on fresh vegetables and bakery goods.

combination 1: My parents always shop at Price Mart since the

store has the best deals on fresh vegetables and bakery goods.

combination 2: My parents always shop at Price Mart, for the store

has the best deals on fresh vegetables and bakery goods.

6. The boy next door dresses up on Saturday nights.
   He is on his way to a club in town.

combination 1: The boy next door dresses up on Saturday nights

before he is on his way to a club in town.

combination 2: The boy next door dresses up on Saturday nights;

then he is on his way to a club in town.

7. My sisters meet for coffee on Sunday mornings.
   They gossip about the wild members of the family.

combination 1: Whenever my sisters meet for coffee on Sunday

mornings, they gossip about the wild members of the family.

combination 2: My sisters meet for coffee on Sunday mornings,

and they gossip about the wild members of the family.

8. Sergeant Morris is good-natured and patient.
   He will not tolerate any cruel or violent behavior.

combination 1: Sergeant Morris is good-natured and patient;

however, he will not tolerate any cruel or violent behavior.

combination 2: Although Sergeant Morris is good-natured and

patient, he will not tolerate any cruel or violent behavior.

9. Patrick washes and waxes his new car every weekend.
He is proud of it.

combination 1: Patrick washes and waxes his new car every weekend;

certainly, he is proud of it.

combination 2: As Patrick washes and waxes his new car every week-

end, he is proud of it.

10. Sharon couldn't get a better-paying job.
Sharon kept her old job at the restaurant.

combination 1: Because Sharon couldn't get a better-paying job, she

kept her old job at the restaurant.

combination 2: Sharon couldn't get a better-paying job, so she kept

her old job at the restaurant.

Collaborate

Create Your Own Text

Following is a list of rules for sentence combining through coordinating and subordinating sentences. Working with a group, create two examples of each rule and write those sentences on the lines provided. After your group has completed this exercise, share your examples with another group.

Option 1: You can join two simple sentences (two independent clauses) into a compound sentence with a coordinating conjunction and a comma in front of it. (The coordinating conjunctions are *and, but, or, nor, for, yet, so.*)

example 1: The sky was gray, so I took my umbrella.

_____

example 2: The offer sounded legitimate, yet Mr. Garcia was

suspicious.

Option 2: You can combine two simple sentences (two independent clauses) into a compound sentence with a semicolon between independent clauses.

example 1: Heather was angry; she refused to speak to

Sean.

example 2: My office is small; it has only two chairs and a desk.

_____

Option 3: You can combine two simple sentences (two independent clauses) into a compound sentence with a semicolon and a conjunctive adverb between independent clauses. (Some common conjunctive adverbs are *also, anyway, as a result, besides, certainly, consequently, finally, furthermore, however, incidentally, in addition, indeed, in fact, instead, likewise, meanwhile, moreover, nevertheless, next, now, on the other hand, otherwise, similarly, still, then, therefore, thus,* and *undoubtedly.*)

example 1: The singer from Brazil is the most talented; undoubtedly,

he will win the contest.

example 2: Kayla is a model; in fact, she has worked in fashion shows

in Paris.

Option 4: You can combine two simple sentences (two independent clauses) into a complex sentence by making one clause dependent. The dependent clause starts with a subordinating conjunction. If the dependent clause begins the sentence, the clause ends with a comma. (Some common subordinating conjunctions are *after, although, as, because, before, even though, if, in order that, since, though, unless, until, when, whenever, where, whereas, whether, while.*)

example 1: As I listened to the music, I began to fall asleep.

example 2: Unless you have a better idea, we can rent a movie

tonight.

Option 5: You can combine two simple sentences (two independent clauses) into a complex sentence by making one clause dependent. If the dependent clause comes after the independent clause, no comma is needed.

example 1: I won't go to the party unless you come with me.

example 2: Jason can't sleep if your music is too loud.

 Connect

Exercise 3 **Editing a Paragraph with Compound and Complex Sentences**

Edit the following paragraph, adding commas and semicolons where they are necessary and taking out unnecessary commas. There are ten errors.

(no comma)

Although, I love music, I do not like all the music I hear. If I am home in my

(no comma)

room I like to study with some music in the background. But, I do not want to hear

music blasting into my room from the house next door nor do I want to listen to my

(no comma)

brother playing his drums. I love to turn the music loud, when I drive my car down

;   ,

the highway however someone else's loud music blaring out of a car annoys me. My

,

cell phone plays a song whenever it rings. I love that ringing song yet listening to

;

other people's phones ringing a song irritates me. My CDs and tapes are my choice I

chose them to entertain, soothe, or amuse me. Those sounds are mine. Other peo-

ple's music may not be so pleasant. It can make me cover my ears, grit my teeth, or

clench my jaw. Who knows? Maybe my music is just as annoying to others.

 4

Practice

Combining Sentences in a Paragraph

In the following paragraph, combine each pair of underlined sentences into one clear, smooth sentence. Write your combination in the space above the old sentences.

Answers Will Vary.

Possible answers shown at right.

My job has both its hectic and its boring moments. I work behind the refresh-

When a movie is about to begin, the lines

ments counter at a movie theater. <u>A movie is about to begin. The lines at the</u>

at the counter are very long.

<u>counter are very long.</u> People crowd the counter and demand their popcorn,

They want their snacks fast because they do not want to

soda, and candy. <u>They want their snacks fast. They do not want to miss the begin-</u>

miss the beginning of the movie.

<u>ning of the movie.</u> During this period, I am very busy meeting impatient cus-

After the movie has started, a few people

tomers' demands for fast service. <u>The movie has started. A few people dribble out</u>

dribble out of the theater.

<u>of the theater.</u> It is easy to serve one or two people at a time. <u>My job becomes</u>

My job becomes

less stressful, but it is also very tedious.

<u>less stressful. It is also very tedious.</u> The time seems to pass more slowly. <u>I have</u>

I have

nothing to do; consequently, I have time to be bored.

<u>nothing to do. I have time to be bored.</u> My experience has led me to a conclusion

Crowds of customers may be pushy and rude; nevertheless,

about my work. <u>Crowds of customers may be pushy and rude. They make my</u>

they make my work day go by more quickly than one or two customers

<u>work day go by more quickly than one or two customers waiting politely at my</u>

waiting politely at my counter.

<u>counter.</u>

CHAPTER 6

Avoiding Sentence Fragments

A **sentence fragment** is a group of words that looks like a sentence, is punctuated like a sentence, but is not a sentence. Writing a sentence fragment is a major error in grammar because it reveals that the writer is not sure what a sentence is. The following groups of words are all fragments:

Fragments:
Because parents with small children want a car with room for a car seat, stroller, diaper bags, and toys.
Her father being an open-minded individual.
For example, the controversy over the safety of air bags.

There are two simple steps that can help you check your writing for sentence fragments.

Info BOX

Two Steps in Recognizing Sentence Fragments

Step 1: Check each group of words punctuated like a sentence; look for a subject and a verb.

Step 2: If you find a subject and a verb, check that the group of words makes a complete statement.

RECOGNIZING FRAGMENTS: STEP 1

Check for a subject and a verb. Some groups of words that look like sentences may actually have a subject but no verb, or they may have a verb but no subject, or they may have no subject *or* verb.

fragments:

The bowl with the bright gold rim. (*Bowl* could be the subject of the sentence, but there is no verb.)

Can't be a friend of mine from college. (There is a verb, *Can be*, but there is no subject.)

On the tip of my tongue. (There are two prepositional phrases, *On the tip* and *of my tongue*, but there is no subject or verb.)

Remember that an *-ing* verb by itself cannot be the main verb in a sentence. Therefore groups of words like the following ones may look like sentences but are missing a verb and are really fragments.

fragments:

The man cooking the Texas chili for the barbecue contest.

A few brave souls taking the plunge into the icy lake in mid-March.

My friend Cynthia being loyal to her selfish and manipulative sister.

An infinitive (*to* plus a verb) cannot be a main verb in a sentence, either. The following groups of words, which contain infinitives, are also fragments.

fragments:

Next week a representative of the airlines to meet with travel agents from across the country.

My hope to help the children of the war-torn nation.

Something nutritious to eat for supper.

Groups of words beginning with words like *also, especially, except, for example, for instance, in addition,* and *such as* need subjects and verbs. Without subjects and verbs, these groups can be fragments, like the ones below:

fragments:

Also a dangerous neighborhood in the late hours of the evening.

Especially a house with a large basement.

For example, a box of high-priced chocolates.

Checking for subjects and verbs is the first step in recognizing the major sentence errors called fragments.

TEACHING TIP:

Stress the concept of incomplete vs. complete thoughts when reviewing fragment rules. A fragment is an incomplete thought (it does not make sense by itself), but a sentence expresses a complete thought. For example, "The meeting last night" (incomplete thought) vs. "The meeting ran late last night." (complete thought).

Exercise 1   **Checking Groups of Words for Subjects and Verbs**

Practice   Some of the following groups of words have subjects and verbs; these are sentences. Some groups are missing subjects, verbs, or both; these are fragments. Put an *S* next to each sentence; put an *F* next to each fragment.

1. ___F___   Definitely hasn't seen Aretha with any of her friends from the office.

2. ___S___   For instance, people with allergies often get flu shots in the winter months.

3. ___F___   For example, a job interview at a radio station in Philadelphia.

4. ___F___   A frazzled student rushing up the stairs, trying to make it to class on time.

5. ___F___   Except for one man holding a flashlight and pointing to available parking spaces at the edge of the field.

6. __S__   Her purpose was to prevent another burglary at the store.

7. __F__   At a table in the back of the room with a few empty chairs.

8. __F__   The board's intention being to decide on a chairperson for the fundraising project.

9. __S__   In addition, the dinner was delicious.

10. __F__   Larry having a natural talent for getting along with all kinds of people.

Exercise 2   **More on Checking Groups of Words for Subjects and Verbs**

Practice   Some of the following groups of words have subjects and verbs; these are sentences. Some groups are missing subjects, verbs, or both; these are fragments. Put an *S* next to each sentence; put an *F* next to each fragment.

1. __F__   Someone from the service department to install my new refrigerator today.

2. __S__   Keith and Frank are taking their boat out on the river for some fishing.

3. __F__   The employee with the best record in customer relations and courtesy.

4. __F__   Could have been the sound of a prowler outside the window.

5. __S__   Nancy wants to finish her paper before noon.

6. __F__   Especially the last one in line at the airline check-in counter.

7. __F__   His reason for the delay being a flat tire on the way to work.

8. __F__   Has requested an early start for the golf tournament.

9. __S__   The sound of the wind filled the dark woods.

10. __S__   Checking the battery is a good idea.

RECOGNIZING FRAGMENTS: STEP 2

If you are checking a group of words to see if it is a sentence, the first step is to look for a subject and verb. If you find a subject and a verb, step 2 is to check that the group of words makes a complete statement. Many groups of words have both a subject and a verb but don't make sense by themselves. They are **dependent clauses.**

How can you tell if a clause is dependent? After you've checked each group of words for a subject and verb, check to see if it begins with one of the subordinating conjunctions that start dependent clauses.

> ## Info BOX
>
> ### Subordinating Conjunctions
>
> | | | | |
> |---|---|---|---|
> | after | before | so that | whenever |
> | although | even though | though | where |
> | as | if | unless | whereas |
> | as if | in order that | until | whether |
> | because | since | when | while |

A clause that begins with a subordinating conjunction is a dependent clause. When you punctuate a dependent clause as if it were a sentence, you have a kind of fragment called a **dependent-clause fragment.** These fragments do not make a complete statement.

> **dependent-clause fragments:**
> After she gave him a kiss. (What happened after she gave him a kiss?)
> Because lemonade tastes better than limeade. (What will happen because lemonade tastes better than limeade?)
> Unless you leave for the movie right now. (What will happen unless you leave for the movie right now?)

It is important to remember both steps in checking for fragments:

> **Step 1:** Check for a subject and a verb.
> **Step 2:** If you find a subject and verb, check that the group of words makes a complete statement.

 Checking for Dependent-Clause Fragments

Practice

Some of the following groups of words are sentences. Some are dependent clauses punctuated like sentences; these are sentence fragments. Put an *S* next to each sentence and an *F* by each fragment.

1. __F__ Whenever he calls me in the middle of the night and wants to talk.

2. __F__ As the painter carefully prepared the walls for a fresh coat of paint.

3. __S__ On the table near my bed is a box of tissues.

4. __F__ Even though James was studying criminal justice in his first year of college.

5. __S__ At parties my brother is shy and even withdrawn.

6. __F__ If Ron can find a babysitter for his daughter and get his work schedule changed.

7. __S__ Talking too much makes me hoarse.

8. __F__ Before my parents started saving for a new car.

9. __F__ Although my apartment is two miles from campus and I have no car.

10. __F__ Because Dean is not exactly sure about the status of his student loan.

Exercise 4
Practice

More on Checking for Dependent-Clause Fragments

Some of the following groups of words are sentences. Some are dependent clauses punctuated like sentences; these are sentence fragments. Put an *S* next to each sentence and an *F* by each fragment.

1. __S__ Without complaining, the little boy went off to bed.

2. __F__ When my best friend asks me for advice about his younger sister.

3. __F__ After my mother quit her job and started filling out applications for a new position.

4. __F__ Since I've started going to the gym twice a week.

5. __S__ Without Maureen there is no concert.

6. __F__ Because my son managed to climb out the window and not get hurt.

7. __F__ Even though the promotion at work pays more money.

8. __S__ From my son I received a ring with my birthstone in it.

9. __F__ Unless you can find a shortcut to the airport.

10. __S__ Then a light rain fell on the green fields.

Exercise 5
Practice

Using Two Steps to Recognize Sentence Fragments

Some of the following are complete sentences; some are sentence fragments. To recognize the fragments, check each group of words by using the two-step process:

Step 1: Check for a subject and a verb.
Step 2: If you find a subject and a verb, check that the group of words makes a complete statement.

Then put an *S* next to each sentence and an *F* next to each fragment.

INSTRUCTOR'S NOTE:

Some students will need much more practice than others when distinguishing sentences and fragments. They need to break their habit of automatically assuming a "long" entry is a sentence.

1. __F__ The real reason behind Simon's unhappiness being his dissatisfaction with his new and more demanding job.

2. __S__ The squeaking door in the bedroom needs to be repaired.

3. __F__ When you finally find a parking space near the downtown mall.

4. __S__ At the center of an enormous chocolate cake the baker placed a white chocolate heart.

5. __F__ Without a word of apology or a glance in the direction of the victim.

6. __F__ One bus company controlling all the bus routes in a large city.

7. __F__ For instance, someone willing to pay a large sum of money for a house with a view of the river.

8. __F__ As if my supervisor had already known about the reorganization of the company.

9. __F__ The results of the medical tests to be sent to me by the end of the week.

10. __S__ A few of the secretaries plan to take Lorraine to lunch tomorrow.

Exercise 6

Practice

More on Using Two Steps to Recognize Sentence Fragments

Some of the following are complete sentences; some are sentence fragments. To recognize the fragments, check each group of words by using the two-step process:

Step 1: Check for a subject and a verb.
Step 2: If you find a subject and a verb, check that the group of words makes a complete statement.

Then put an *S* next to each sentence and an *F* next to each fragment.

1. __F__ Becoming a long, boring conversation about my father's seven cousins in Puerto Rico.

2. __F__ Have always wanted a ride in a police helicopter.

3. __F__ Because Henry can't see a foot in front of him without his glasses.

4. __S__ Under the dining room table was a small dog.

5. __F__ Whenever my mother goes on a hunt for bargains at the open-air market.

6. __S__ Sometimes the kitchen is invaded by tiny ants.

7. __S__ Admitting a mistake can be difficult.

8. __F__ The diner being the only all-night restaurant in the area.

9. __S__ Down the hall came my best friend from high school and my old boyfriend.

10. __F__ One of the four finalists to compete in the international tournament next month.

CORRECTING FRAGMENTS

You can correct fragments easily if you follow the two steps for identifying them.

Step 1: Check for a subject and a verb. If a group of words is a fragment because it lacks a subject or a verb, or both, *add what is missing.*

fragment: Jonette giving ten percent of her salary. (This fragment lacks a main verb.)

corrected: Jonette gave ten percent of her salary. (The verb *gave* replaces *giving*, which is not a main verb.)

fragment: Can't study with the television on. (This fragment lacks a subject.)

corrected: Salvatore can't study with the television on. (A subject, *Salvatore*, is added.)

fragment: Especially at the end of the day. (This fragment has neither a subject nor a verb.)

corrected: I often feel stressed, especially at the end of the day. (A subject, *I*, and a verb, *feel*, are added.)

Step 2: If you find a subject and a verb, check that the group of words makes a complete statement. To correct the fragment, you can turn a dependent clause into an independent one by removing the subordinating conjunction, *or* you can add an independent clause to the dependent one, to create something that makes sense by itself.

fragment: When Mrs. Diaz offered him a job. (This statement does not make sense by itself. The subordinating conjunction *when* leads the reader to ask, "What happened when Mrs. Diaz offered him a job?" The subordinating conjunction makes this a dependent clause, not a sentence.)

corrected: Mrs. Diaz offered him a job. (Removing the subordinating conjunction makes this an independent clause— a sentence.)

corrected: When Mrs. Diaz offered him a job, he was very happy. (Adding an independent clause to the end of the sentence turns this into something that makes sense by itself.)

corrected: He was very happy when Mrs. Diaz offered him a job. (Adding an independent clause to the beginning of the sentence turns this into something that makes sense by itself.)

Note: Sometimes you can correct a fragment by adding it to the sentence before or after it.

fragment (in italics): *Even if he lowers the price.* I can't afford that car.
corrected: Even if he lowers the price, I can't afford that car.

fragment (in italics): Yvonne hates large parties. *Like the one at Matthew's house.*
corrected: Yvonne hates large parties like the one at Matthew's house.

You have several choices for correcting fragments: you can add words, phrases, or clauses; you can take words out or combine independent and dependent clauses. You can change fragments into simple sentences or create compound or complex sentences. If you create compound or complex sentences, be sure to use correct punctuation.

 Exercise 7

Practice

Answers Will Vary.

Possible answers shown at right.

Correcting Fragments

Correct each sentence fragment below in the most appropriate way.

1. Sometimes my little boy wants to sleep with a comforting object. Such as an old teddy bear or a soft blanket.

   corrected: Sometimes my little boy wants to sleep with a comforting object such as an old teddy bear or a soft blanket.

2. If you call me tomorrow. I will tell you all the latest news about Sandra and Emilio.

   corrected: If you call me tomorrow, I will tell you all the latest news about Sandra and Emilio.

3. Driving through the city on a wet, gray day. We saw a depressing mixture of decaying buildings and ragged streets.

   corrected: Driving through the city on a wet, gray day, we saw a depressing mixture of decaying buildings and ragged streets.

4. My grandfather used to spoil all his grandchildren. Especially Larry.

   corrected: My grandfather used to spoil all his grandchildren, especially Larry.

5. Because my CD player was stolen from my car. I have to drive around in silence.

   corrected: Because my CD player was stolen from my car, I have to drive around in silence.

6. Unless someone wants this old bookcase from my room.

   corrected: Unless someone wants this old bookcase from my room, I will throw it away.

7. The handsome young man in my math class sitting in the front row.

   corrected: The handsome young man in my math class was sitting in the front row.

8. Melissa is eager to start her new job. To begin to earn some money and learn more about the hotel business.

   corrected: Melissa is eager to start her new job, earn some money, and learn more about the hotel business.

9. My parents were discussing my bad behavior. As I climbed out of my bedroom window and sneaked into my friend's truck.

   corrected: My parents were discussing my bad behavior as I climbed out of my bedroom window and sneaked into my friend's truck.

10. Some of the regular customers at the restaurant asking for Alan as their server.

    corrected: Some of the regular customers at the restaurant were asking for Alan as their server.

Exercise 8   **Correcting Fragments Two Ways**

Collaborate   The following groups of words all contain fragments. With a partner or a group, construct two ways to eliminate the fragment. You can add words, phrases, or clauses, take out words, combine independent and dependent clauses, or attach a fragment to the sentence before or after it. When you have completed the exercise, be ready to share your answers with another group or with the class. The first one has been done for you.

1. When she calls me and starts complaining.

   corrected: When she calls me and starts complaining, I try to be sympathetic.

   corrected: She calls me and starts complaining.

Answers Will Vary.

Possible answers:

2. Even though my family had very little money.

   corrected: Even though my family had very little money, we were happy.

   corrected: I never felt deprived even though my family had very little money.

3. After I started my new job at the college bookstore. I had the money to pay for car repairs.

   corrected: After I started my new job at the college bookstore, I had the money to pay for car repairs.

   corrected: I had the money to pay for car repairs after I started my new job at the college bookstore.

4. If you see any bargains at the furniture store.

corrected: Let me know if you see any bargains at the furniture store.

corrected: If you see any bargains at the furniture store, give me a call.

5. Dennis making no effort to be polite to his grandmother.

corrected: Dennis made no effort to be polite to his grandmother.

corrected: Dennis was making no effort to be polite to his grandmother.

6. Whenever Carla throws a temper tantrum in the supermarket. Her mother quietly takes her out of the store.

corrected: Whenever Carla throws a temper tantrum in the supermarket, her mother quietly takes her out of the store.

corrected: Carla's mother quietly takes her out of the store whenever the child throws a temper tantrum in the supermarket.

7. Helen fell asleep in her seat. As the speaker lectured about the inner workings of the banking industry.

corrected: Helen fell asleep in her seat as the speaker lectured about the inner workings of the banking industry.

corrected: As the speaker lectured about the inner workings of the banking industry, Helen fell asleep in her seat.

8. At 6:00 a.m., when my alarm goes off.

corrected: At 6:00 a.m., when my alarm goes off, I am already awake.

corrected: I am in my deepest sleep when my alarm goes off at 6:00 a.m.

9. Unless you can pay me back by next Wednesday. I can't lend you the money for your rent.

corrected: Unless you can pay me back by next Wednesday, I can't lend you the money for your rent.

corrected: I can't lend you the money for your rent unless you can

pay me back by next Wednesday.

10. Even though José has been working for the company for ten years and deserves to be promoted to assistant manager.

corrected: Even though José has been working for the company for

ten years and deserves to be promoted to assistant manager, he is

always overlooked.

corrected: José has been working for the company for ten years and

deserves to be promoted to assistant manager.

Exercise 9

⊆⊂⊇ *Connect*

Editing Paragraphs for Fragments

Both of the paragraphs below contain sentence fragments. Edit the paragraphs, correcting the fragments by writing in the space above each fragment. There are seven fragments in the first paragraph and six fragments in the second.

1. I am usually very good-natured about lending my possessions to

I am usually very good-natured about lending my possessions to friends

friends and neighbors. Except when they don't return what they

and neighbors except when they don't return what they borrowed.

borrowed. Then I can be nasty and hot-tempered. For example,

For example, Bill,

after Bill, my friend in English class, asked to borrow my

my friend in English class, asked to borrow my English textbook.

English textbook. He said he had left his book at home and

wanted to borrow mine for an hour to do his assignment. Two

days later, he had not returned my book. I decided to give him a lit-

A week later, Bill had stopped coming to class and

tle more time. A week later, Bill had stopped coming to class and

had still not returned my book even though I had called and left a

had still not returned my book. Even though I had called and left

message on his voice mail several times.

a message on his voice mail several times. Becoming angrier and

I rang his doorbell

more frustrated, I decided to pay Bill a visit. I rang his doorbell

for about ten minutes before he decided to open the door. Finally,

for about ten minutes. Before he decided to open the door. Final-

I got the real story of the borrowed book. Bill had lost it and didn't

ly, I got the real story. Of the borrowed book. Bill had lost it and

want to face me because he knew I would be angry. Of course,

didn't want to face me. Because he knew I would be angry. Of

I was, especially after all of Bill's attempts to avoid me.

course, I was. Especially after all of Bill's attempts to avoid me.

As a result of this incident, I lost a friend but got Bill to pay for

my new book.

2. Last summer, my brother Oliver and I did a favor for my mother

My mother usually

that turned out to be a favor for ourselves. My mother usually

spends one day a week volunteering at a day care center for

spends one day a week. Volunteering at a day care center for

senior citizens. Unfortunately, she couldn't keep up her volunteer

senior citizens. Unfortunately, she couldn't keep up her volunteer

work last July because she was recovering from surgery.

work last July. Being that she was recovering from surgery. As a

result, she asked Oliver and me to fill in at the center for a month.

We thought it would be horrible and

We really didn't want to do it. Thought it would be horrible and

depressing with all the old people.

depressing with all the old people. However, we really couldn't say

no. Every Saturday, for a month, we visited the Lincoln Senior

Center and worked with three dozen seniors. At first, Oliver and I

were nervous. Some of the elderly people stared straight ahead

Some were shaking and mumbling.

and never smiled. Some shaking and mumbling. We didn't know

how to behave, but gradually we learned how to relate to the

seniors who could have been our grandparents. We smiled and

We played old music, and all

laughed and listened to their stories. We played old music, and all

of us sang along while some of us danced. If our friends had seen

of us sang along. While some of us danced. If our friends had seen

us, they would have thought we were crazy.

us. They would have thought we were crazy. Yet we had a good

time. We helped others feel happy, and we felt great. Now that my

mother is back to her own volunteering, Oliver and I often go with

her to visit our friends at the center.

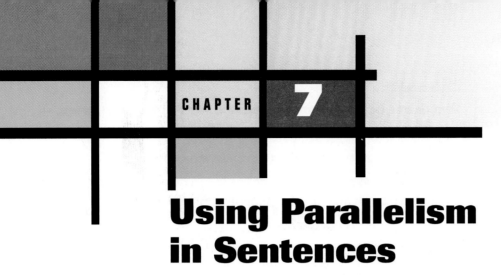

Using Parallelism in Sentences

Parallelism means balance in sentences. To create sentences with parallelism, remember this rule:

Similar points should get similar structures.

Often, you will include two or more points—related ideas, examples, or details—in one sentence. If you express these ideas in a parallel structure, they will be clearer, smoother, and more convincing.

Here are some pairs of sentences with and without parallelism:

not parallel: Of all the household chores, the ones I hate the most are cooking, to iron, and dusting.

parallel: Of all the household chores, the ones I hate the most are *cooking, ironing,* and *dusting.* (Three words are parallel.)

not parallel: When I need a pencil, I look in my purse, the table, and beside the telephone.

parallel: When I need a pencil, I look *in my purse, on the table,* and *beside the telephone.* (Three prepositional phrases are parallel.)

not parallel: Inez should get the promotion because she gets along with her co-workers, she works hard, and a knowledge of the business.

parallel: Inez should get the promotion because *she gets along with her co-workers, she works hard, and she knows the business.* (Three clauses are parallel.)

From these examples you can see that parallelism involves matching the structure of parts of your sentence. There are two steps that can help you check your writing for parallelism.

Info BOX

Two Steps in Checking a Sentence for Parallel Structure

Step 1: Look for the list in the sentence.

Step 2: Put the parts of the list into a similar structure.

You may have to change or add something to get a parallel structure.

ACHIEVING PARALLELISM

Let's correct the parallelism of the following sentence:

> **not parallel:** If you want to pass the course, you have to study hard, taking good notes, and attendance at every class.

To correct this sentence, we'll follow the steps.

> **Step 1:** Look for the list. If you want to pass the course, you have to do three things. Here's the list:
> 1. to study hard
> 2. taking good notes
> 3. attendance at every class

> **Step 2:** Put the parts of the list into a similar structure.
> 1. *to study* hard
> 2. *to take* good notes
> 3. *to attend* every class

Now revise to get a parallel sentence.

> **parallel:** If you want to pass the course, you have *to study* hard, *to take* good notes, and *to attend* every class.

If you follow steps 1 and 2, you can also write the sentence like this:

> **parallel:** If you want to pass the course, you have to *study* hard, *take* good notes, and *attend* every class.

But you can't write the sentence like this:

> **not parallel:** If you want to pass the course, you have to study hard, take good notes, and to attend every class.

Think of the list again. You can write

> If you want to pass the course, you have
> 1. to study
> 2. to take   } parallel
> 3. to attend

Or you can write

> If you want to pass the course, you have to
> 1. study
> 2. take   } parallel
> 3. attend

But you *cannot* write

> If you want to pass the course, you have to
> 1. study
> 2. take   } not parallel
> 3. to attend

In other words, either use *to* once (if it fits every part of the list), or use it with *every* part of the list.

Sometimes making ideas parallel means adding something to the sentence because all the parts of the list cannot match exactly.

> **not parallel:** After the toddler threw his bowl of cereal, oatmeal splattered down the walls, the floor, and the table.

> **Step 1:** Look for the list. After the toddler threw his bowl of cereal, oatmeal splattered
> 1. down the walls
> 2. the floor
> 3. the table

TEACHING TIP:

Ask students what they plan to do on their next school vacation or on a day off from work. List some responses on the board or on an overhead. Have students compose several sentences in parallel structure that incorporate information from the list.

As this sentence is written, *down* goes with *walls*, but it doesn't go with *floor* or *table*. Check the sense of this sentence by looking at each part of the list and how it is working in the sentence: "After the toddler threw his bowl of cereal, oatmeal splattered *down the walls*" is clear. But "oatmeal splattered *down the floor*"? Or "oatmeal splattered *down the table*"? These parts of the list are not right.

> **Step 2:** The sentence needs some words added to make the structure parallel.

> **parallel:** After the toddler threw his bowl of cereal, oatmeal splattered *down* the walls, *on* the floor, and *under* the table.

When you follow the two steps to check for parallelism, you can write clear sentences and improve your style.

Exercise 1

Practice

Answers Will Vary.

Possible answers shown at right.

Revising Sentences for Parallelism

Some of the following sentences need to be revised so they have parallel structures. Revise the ones that need parallelism.

1. The holiday parade begins on Seventh Street; Magnolia Avenue is where it ends.

revised: The holiday parade begins on Seventh Street and ends on

Magnolia Avenue.

2. My father is kind, calm, and has patience.

revised: My father is kind, calm, and patient.

3. On my day off, I spend all my time studying for my biology and English classes, clean my apartment, and doing huge piles of laundry.

revised: On my day off, I spend all my time studying for my biology and

English classes, cleaning my apartment, and doing huge piles of laundry.

4. While I am out of town, you can reach me by phone or e-mail.

revised: OK

5. Desmond is a leader with an attractive personality and who also has style.

   revised: Desmond is a leader with an attractive personality and style.

6. At the training session, the new sales representatives learned how to answer questions, handling complaints, and resolve requests for refunds.

   revised: At the training session, the new sales representatives learned how to answer questions, handle complaints, and resolve requests for refunds.

7. The car's price, its safety features, and what it looked like made it my first choice.

   revised: The car's price, safety features, and appearance made it my first choice.

8. My mother said she would never get into a small plane and trying skydiving, but she did both on her recent vacation.

   revised: My mother said she would never get into a small plane and try skydiving, but she did both on her recent vacation.

9. Having a baby is not as much work as when you take care of a baby.

   revised: Having a baby is not as much work as taking care of a baby.

10. When you first meet Jimmy, you may think he is outgoing and spontaneous, but he is really shy and cautious.

    revised: OK

Exercise 2

👥 *Collaborate*

Writing Sentences with Parallelism

With a partner or a group, complete each sentence. Begin by brainstorming a draft list; then revise the list for parallelism. Finally, complete the sentence in a parallel structure. You may want to assign one task (brainstorming a draft list, revising it, etc.) to each group member and then switch tasks on the next sentence. Following is a sample of how to work through each question, from list to sentence.

sample incomplete sentence: The three parts of college I like best are

Draft List	Revised List
1. new friends	1. making new friends
2. doing well in English	2. doing well in English
3. Fridays off	3. having Fridays off

sentence: The three parts of college I like best are making new friends, doing well in English, and having Fridays off.

1. Three ways to cut down on spending are

Draft List	Revised List
1. get rid of credit cards	1. get rid of credit cards
2. a budget	2. stick to a budget
3. record everything you spend	3. record everything you spend

sentence: Three ways to cut down on spending are to get rid of credit cards, stick to a budget, and record everything you spend.

2. Two suggestions for improving your grades are

Draft List	Revised List
1. more studying	1. study more
2. a study buddy	2. get a study buddy

sentence: Two suggestions for improving your grades are to study more and to get a study buddy.

3. Three good reasons to stay up late are

Draft List	Revised List
1. finish an assignment	1. finish an assignment
2. good movie	2. watch a good movie
3. talking with a friend	3. talk with a friend

sentence: Three good reasons to stay up late are to finish an assignment, watch a good movie, and talk with a friend.

4. Parents must pay close attention to teens because (give three reasons)

Draft List	Revised List
1. advice is important	1. need advice
2. would like support	2. appreciate support
3. approval	3. crave approval

sentence: Parents must pay close attention to teens because teens need advice, appreciate support, and crave approval.

5. Four ways you can help your elderly relatives are

Draft List	Revised List
1. call often	1. call them often
2. little gifts	2. bring them little gifts
3. chores	3. do their chores
4. listening skills	4. listen to their stories

sentence: Four ways you can help your elderly relatives are to call them often, bring them little gifts, do their chores, and listen to their stories.

Collaborate

Recognizing Parallelism in Famous Speeches

Some of the most famous speeches in history contain parallel structures. This parallelism adds emphasis and dignity to the points expressed. Working in a group, have one member read each segment of a speech aloud while the others listen carefully. Then underline all the words, phrases, clauses, or sentences that are in parallel form. When you have completed the exercise, share your answers with another group.

1. Inaugural Address
John F. Kennedy

President John F. Kennedy delivered this speech when he was inaugurated on January 20, 1961. His theme was the renewal of American values and the changes and challenges we must face.

Let the word go forth from this time and place, to friend and foe alike, that the torch has been passed to a new generation of Americans—born in this century, tempered* by war, disciplined by a hard and bitter peace, proud of our ancient heritage—and unwilling to witness or permit the slow undoing of those human rights to which this nation has always been committed, and to which we are committed today at home and around the world.

2. I Have a Dream
Martin Luther King, Jr.

Martin Luther King, Jr., a Southern minister, was a leading advocate of civil rights in the 1960s. He delivered this speech to 200,000 people in Washington, D.C., where they had gathered to demonstrate peacefully for the cause of equality.

---

*tempered means hardened, toughened

INSTRUCTOR'S NOTE:
You may need to tell students that the printed format for a speech differs considerably from a formal written paragraph or essay.

I have a dream that one day every valley shall be exalted, every hill and mountain shall be made low, the rough places shall be made plain, and the crooked places shall be made straight, and the glory of the Lord will be revealed, and all flesh shall see it together.

This is our hope. This is the faith that I go back to the South with.

With this faith we will be able to hew* out of the mountain of despair a stone of hope. With this faith, we will be able to transform the jangling discords of our nation into a beautiful symphony of brotherhood.

With this faith we will be able to work together, to pray together, to go to jail together, to stand up for freedom together, knowing that we will be free one day.

 Exercise 4

∞∞ *Connect*

Combining Sentences and Creating a Parallel Structure

In the paragraph below, some sentences should be combined in a parallel structure. Combine each cluster of underlined sentences into one sentence, with a parallel structure. Write your sentences in the lines above the old ones.

Parents who want to give their children a wonderful gift should read to their sons and daughters. The time spent reading with a child has many emotional

Reading creates a special bond between parent and child, brings
benefits. Reading creates a special bond between parent and child. Also, reading
comfort and warmth, and establishes a soothing and pleasant routine.
brings comfort and warmth. In addition, it establishes a soothing and pleasant

routine. All these results can come from a nightly bedtime story. Reading to chil-
Children who are read to
dren is also a wonderful way to develop their minds. Children who are read to
know how to handle books, to hold and open them, and to look at the
know how to handle books. They know how to hold and open them. They know
pages from front to back.
how to look at the pages from front to back. Most of all, they know that people
Parents with books can get
who can read have the power to enter new worlds. Parents with books can get
closer to their children and can open young minds.
closer to their children. Also, parents with books can be opening young minds.

_____

*__hew__ means to make or shape with cutting blows

☉☉☉ *Connect*

Revising a Paragraph for Parallelism

The following paragraph contains sentences with errors in parallelism. In the space above the lines, rewrite the sentences that contain errors in parallelism. There are five sentences with errors.

If you go to the fair, be prepared for three problems. The parking lots are

there are long lines for the rides

crowded, waiting in long lines for the rides, and the food is ridiculously over-

priced. As soon as you arrive at the fair, you'll see dozens of drivers circling the

are honking their horns

full parking lot, some impatient drivers are honking their horns, and frazzled

parking attendants directing cars to a distant dirt field. If you go straight to the

dirt field, you can save yourself some irritation. Next, you'll face some long lines

at the rides. Some of the lines stretch way past the ride itself, so be prepared to

come

wait or coming back another time. Whatever you do, be careful not to waste your

money on the fair food. A slimy hot dog costs $5.00, greasy popcorn is $4.00 for a

to buy

tiny box, and to buy a tiny soft drink is $4.00. Just bring your own snacks and

save your money. The fair is great fun for a Saturday afternoon, but it has its

having

drawbacks. Being prepared for its challenges means to have a better time.

CHAPTER **8**

Using Adjectives and Adverbs

WHAT ARE ADJECTIVES?

TEACHING TIP:

This chapter is a good place to remind students about sensory (sight, sound, smell, taste, and touch) details. Ask students to describe an extremely messy kitchen, a physician's examining room, a rude audience, etc. Some amusing descriptions should emerge, and students will see that adjectives often reflect one of the five senses.

Adjectives describe nouns (words that name persons, places, or things) or pronouns (words that substitute for a noun).

> **adjectives:**
> She stood in a *dark* corner. (*Dark* describes the noun *corner.*)
> I need a *little* help. (*Little* describes the noun *help.*)
> She looked *happy*. (*Happy* describes the pronoun *she.*)

An adjective usually comes before the word it describes:

> He gave me a *beautiful* ring. (*Beautiful* describes *ring.*)

Sometimes it comes after a *being* verb, a verb that tells what something is. Being verbs are words like *is, are, was, am, has been*. Words like *feels, looks, seems, smells, sounds,* and *tastes* are part of the group called being verbs.

> He seems *unhappy*. (*Unhappy* describes *he* and follows the being verb *seems.*)
> Alan was *confident*. (*Confident* describes *Alan* and follows the being verb *was.*)
> Your tires are *bald*. (*Bald* describes *tires* and follows the being verb *are.*)

 Recognizing Adjectives

Practice Circle the adjective in each of the following sentences.

1. Keith soaked in a warm bath.

2. The pie smells wonderful.

3. Robertine has been a (powerful) influence on my life.

4. The kitchen needs a (new) refrigerator.

5. We feel (sad).

6. An (ugly) stain covered the wall.

7. The (large) dog rushed at me.

8. The milk tastes (strange).

9. Jamie heard a (loud) noise in the basement.

10. They are (nervous) about the decision at the trial.

Exercise 2 **More on Recognizing Adjectives**

Practice Circle the adjective in each of the following sentences.

1. An (unlucky) player broke his ankle.

2. The door lead to a (narrow) hall.

3. Charlie's apology sounded (insincere).

4. My skin feels (dry).

5. Jesse has (long) legs.

6. Samantha is driving a (large) truck.

7. Marcus brought me an (exotic) plant.

8. (Greasy) dishes covered the table.

9. Nelson and Esther seem (upset) with their parents.

10. (Impatient) drivers can cause accidents.

ADJECTIVES: COMPARATIVE AND SUPERLATIVE FORMS

The **comparative** form of an adjective compares two persons or things. The **superlative** form compares three or more persons or things.

comparative: Your car is *cleaner* than mine.
superlative: Your car is the *cleanest* one in the parking lot.

comparative: Hamburger is *cheaper* than steak.
superlative: Hamburger is the *cheapest* meat on the menu.

comparative: Lisa is *friendlier* than her sister.
superlative: Lisa is the *friendliest* of the three sisters.

For most adjectives of one syllable, add *-er* to form the comparative, and add *-est* to form the superlative:

The weather is *colder* today than it was yesterday, but Friday was the *coldest* day of the year.

Orange juice is *sweeter* than grapefruit juice, but the *sweetest* juice is grape juice.

For longer adjectives, use *more* to form the comparative and *most* to form the superlative:

I thought College Algebra was *more difficult* than English; however, Beginning Physics was the *most difficult* course I ever took.

My brother is *more outgoing* than my sister, but my father is the *most outgoing* member of the family.

The three forms of adjectives usually look like this:

Adjective	Comparative (two)	Superlative (three or more)
sweet	sweeter	sweetest
fast	faster	fastest
short	shorter	shortest
quick	quicker	quickest
old	older	oldest

Or they may look like this:

Adjective	Comparative (two)	Superlative (three or more)
confused	more confused	most confused
specific	more specific	most specific
dangerous	more dangerous	most dangerous
confident	more confident	most confident
beautiful	more beautiful	most beautiful

However, there are some *irregular forms of adjectives:*

Adjective	Comparative (two)	Superlative (three or more)
good	better	best
bad	worse	worst
little	less	least
many, much	more	most

Exercise 3

Selecting the Correct Adjective Forms

Practice Write the correct form of the adjective in each of the following sentences.

1. I like both cars, but the little Toyota is the ____more practical____ (practical).

2. Of the three Reilly brothers, Dave is the ____youngest____ (young).

3. Anna believes skiing is _____more demanding_____ (demanding) than ice skating, but she calls ice hockey the _____most demanding_____ (demanding) of all winter sports.

4. That dinner was the _____best_____ (good) meal I have ever eaten.

5. Taking vitamins can be good for you, but even _____better_____ (good) is eating healthy foods filled with vitamins.

6. The thriller was the _____most confusing_____ (confusing) movie I've ever seen.

7. Harry is _____more conceited_____ (conceited) than his friend Patrick.

8. Working on Saturday night is _____worse_____ (bad) than working on Sunday.

9. Which of these three kittens is the _____smartest_____ (smart) one?

10. Three of my friends gave me the _____best_____ (good) birthday party I've ever had.

Exercise 4

Collaborate

Writing Sentences with Adjectives

Working with a partner or a group, write a sentence that correctly uses each of the following adjectives. Be prepared to share your answers with another group or with the class.

Answers Will Vary.

Possible answers shown at right.

1. more complicated Filing your income tax is more complicated than applying for a driver's license.

2. worst That was the worst movie I have ever seen.

3. cheaper A ticket to the Bahamas is cheaper than a ticket to Puerto Rico.

4. most disturbing Four children gave terrible accounts of the accident, but the youngest child's was the most disturbing.

5. weakest There are three bad players on the opposing team, and Wilson is the weakest of the three.

6. more enthusiastic My mother is more enthusiastic about moving than I am.

7. thinner That pizza crust is thinner than the crust at Romeo's Restaurant.

8. worse Yesterday's snowstorm was worse than last year's
   blizzard.

9. better I feel better than I did last night.

_____

10. more polite My nephew is more polite than his sister.

_____

WHAT ARE ADVERBS?

Adverbs describe verbs, adjectives, or other adverbs.

adverbs:

As she spoke, Steve listened *thoughtfully.* (*Thoughtfully* describes the verb *listened.*)

I said I was *really sorry* for my error. (*Really* describes the adjective *sorry.*)

The cook worked *very* quickly. (*Very* describes the adverb *quickly.*)

Adverbs answer questions like "How?" "How much?" "How often?" "When?" "Why?" and "Where?"

 Exercise 5

Practice

TEACHING TIP:

Group Work: Distribute copies of a recent local newspaper article about a prominent person or issue. Ask one group to find adjectives and the words they modify; ask the other group to find adverbs and the words they modify. Then ask each group to find the most descriptive sentences. Discuss why some sentences are more descriptive (effective) than others.

Recognizing Adverbs

Circle the adverbs in the following sentences.

1. After he identified the problem, the electrician examined the circuits (carefully).

2. The senator gave a (truly) memorable speech to the new citizens.

3. The angry customer spoke (rudely) to the cashier.

4. When the little boy asked questions, William answered (patiently).

5. Sam is not (really) interested in finishing college.

6. Nora listened (intently) as the teacher explained the test.

7. The sheriff spoke (calmly) to the crowd of anxious citizens.

8. Jill will call (tomorrow).

9. Fearful of slipping on the ice, Jill walked (very) cautiously.

10. Anthony took me to an (extremely) boring football game.

 Exercise 6

Practice

More on Recognizing Adverbs

Circle the adverbs in the following sentences.

1. Children (rarely) misbehave in the science museum.

2. Remember to visit (often).

3. Construction on the house is (nearly) finished.

4. I am not (completely) convinced of his innocence.

5. Dr. Jacobsen is a (highly) recommended heart specialist.

6. The line to the ticket booth is moving (slowly.)

7. The train from Philadelphia is (usually) on time.

8. When my father lost his job, the neighbors were (very) kind.

9. When the child began to whine, the exhausted mother answered (sharply).

10. Tom always spends his money (wisely).

Exercise 7

 *Collaborate*

Writing Sentences with Adverbs

Working with a partner or a group, write a sentence that correctly uses each of the following adverbs. Be prepared to share your answers with another group or with the class.

Answers Will Vary.

Possible answers shown at right.

1. sincerely The new mayor spoke sincerely.

2. really Her words were really convincing.

3. never Michael would never do anything to hurt me.

4. occasionally Jeremy occasionally stops by for a cup of coffee.

5. closely The detective looked closely at the evidence.

6. constantly I am constantly picking up your dirty dishes.

7. easily You can easily find a better apartment.

8. recently Steve has recently met a wonderful woman.

9. surely Michelle will surely get an A in Political Science.

10. angrily My partner angrily accused me of lying.

HINTS ABOUT ADJECTIVES AND ADVERBS

Do not use an adjective when you need an adverb. Some writers make the mistake of using an adjective when they need an adverb.

not this: Talk to me ~~honest~~.
but this: Talk to me honestly.

not this: You can say it ~~simple~~.
but this: You can say it simply.

not this: He was breathing ~~deep~~.
but this: He was breathing deeply.

Exercise 8

Practice

Changing Adjectives to Adverbs

In each pair of sentences, change the underlined adjective in the first sentence to an adverb in the second sentence. The first one is done for you.

1. a. That light is <u>bright</u>.

b. That light gleams _____ brightly _____.

2. a. Melissa is a <u>creative</u> decorator.

b. Melissa decorates _____ creatively _____.

3. a. My toddler does a <u>wild</u> dance.

b. My toddler dances _____ wildly _____.

4. a. The dog has a <u>ferocious</u> bark.

b. The dog barks _____ ferociously _____.

5. a. Carlos is a <u>safe</u> driver.

b. Carlos always drives _____ safely _____.

6. a. The detectives did <u>extensive</u> research into the crime.

b. The detectives researched the crime _____ extensively _____.

7. a. Mike made a <u>sarcastic</u> comment.

b. Mike commented _____ sarcastically _____.

8. a. My brother gave an <u>unkind</u> reply.

b. My brother replied _____ unkindly _____.

9. a. Naomi makes <u>frequent</u> trips to Jamaica.

b. Naomi _____ frequently _____ travels to Jamaica.

10. a. Norman has a <u>graceful</u> way of hitting the ball.

b. Norman hits the ball _____ gracefully _____.

Do Not Confuse *good* and *well,* or *bad* and *badly*

Remember that *good* is an adjective; it describes nouns. It also follows being verbs like *is, are, was, am,* and *has been*. Words like *looks, seems, smells, sounds,* and *tastes* are part of the group called being verbs. *Well* is an adverb; it describes verbs. (The only time *well* can be used as an adjective is when it means *healthy,* as in *I feel well today.*)

not this: You ran that race ~~good~~.
but this: You ran that race well.

not this: I cook eggs ~~good~~.
but this: I cook eggs well.

not this: How ~~good~~ do you understand grammar?
but this: How well do you understand grammar?

Bad is an adjective; it describes nouns. It also follows being verbs like *is, are, was, am, has been*. Words like *feels, looks, seems, smells, sounds,* and *tastes* are part of the group called being verbs. *Badly* is an adverb; it describes verbs.

not this: He feels ~~badly~~ about his mistake.
but this: He feels bad about his mistake. (*Feels* is a being verb; it is described by the adjective *bad.*)

not this: That soup smells ~~badly~~.
but this: That soup smells bad. (*Smells* is a being verb; it is described by the adjective *bad.*)

not this: He dances ~~bad~~.
but this: He dances badly.

Exercise 9

Practice

Using *good* and *well, bad* and *badly*

Write the appropriate word in the following sentences.

1. Bill rarely plays the piano, but when he does, he plays it
_____ well _____ (good, well).

2. I am saving my money to buy a _____ good _____ (good, well) pair of boots.

3. Don't go to the party if you don't feel _____ well _____ (good, well).

4. When David fell on the ice, he was hurt _____ badly _____ (bad, badly).

5. Peanut butter and chocolate go _____ well _____ (good, well) together.

6. After the child started crying, the mother felt _____ bad _____ (bad, badly) about scolding him.

7. In his first semester of college, Ivan is doing _____ well _____ (good, well).

8. I play softball _____ *badly* _____ (bad, badly), but I love the game.

9. Because he wanted the job _____ *badly* _____ (bad, badly), Jimmy wore his best clothes to the interview.

10. Amanda gave a _____ *good* _____ (good, well) speech in her Introduction to Communications class.

Do Not Use *more* + *-er* or *most* + *-est*

Be careful. Never write both an *-er* ending and *more*, or an *-est* ending and *most*.

> **not this:** I want to work with someone ~~more smarter~~.
> **but this:** I want to work with someone smarter.

> **not this:** Alan is the ~~most richest~~ man in town.
> **but this:** Alan is the richest man in town.

Use *than*, Not *then*, in Comparisons

When you compare things, use *than*. *Then* means *at a later time*.

> **not this:** You are taller ~~then~~ I am.
> **but this:** You are taller than I am.

> **not this:** I'd like a car that is faster ~~then~~ my old one.
> **but this:** I'd like a car that is faster than my old one.

When Do I Need a Comma Between Adjectives?

Sometimes you use more than one adjective to describe a noun:

> I visited a cold, dark cave.
> The cat had pale blue eyes.

If you look at the examples above, one uses a comma between the adjectives *cold* and *dark*, but the other doesn't have a comma between the adjectives *pale* and *blue*. Both sentences are correctly punctuated. To decide whether you need a comma, try one of these tests:

Test 1: Try to put *and* between the adjectives. If the sentence still makes sense, put a comma between the adjectives.

> **Check for comma:** I visited a cold, dark cave. (Do you need the comma? Add *and* between the adjectives.)

> **Add *and*:** I visited a cold and dark cave. (Does the sentence still make sense? Yes. You need the comma.)

> **Correct sentence:** I visited a cold, dark cave.

> **Check for comma:** The cat had pale blue eyes. (Do you need the comma? Add *and* between the adjectives.)

> **Add *and*:** The cat had pale and blue eyes. (Does the sentence still make sense? No. You do not need the comma.)

> **Correct sentence:** The cat had pale blue eyes.

Test 2: Try to reverse the order of the adjectives. If the sentence still makes sense, put a comma between the adjectives.

> **Check for comma:** I visited a cold, dark cave. (Do you need the comma? Reverse the order of the adjectives.)
>
> **Reverse the order of the adjectives:** I visited a dark, cold cave. (Does the sentence still make sense? Yes. You need the comma.)
>
> **Correct sentence:** I visited a cold, dark cave.
>
> **Check for comma:** The cat had pale blue eyes. (Do you need a comma? Reverse the order of the adjectives.)
>
> **Reverse the order of the adjectives:** The cat had blue pale eyes. (Does the sentence still make sense? No. You don't need a comma.)
>
> **Correct sentence:** The cat had pale blue eyes.

You can use Test 1 or Test 2 to determine whether you need a comma between adjectives.

Exercise 10

Practice

A Comprehensive Exercise on Using Adjectives and Adverbs

Correct any errors in using adjectives and adverbs (including punctuation errors) in the following sentences. Some sentences do not need correcting.

1. My sister is more athletic then I am. *than*

2. I am afraid the air pollution near the factory will get more worse. *more*

3. Ice cream tastes well on a summer day. *good*

4. Fatima is going to skip the movie because she is not feeling well.

5. I've worked at Tasty Doughnuts and Chicken Shack; Chicken Shack was the worst place for tips. *worse*

6. I bought a Hyundai because it is less expensive than a Ford.

7. Cherline is the most ambitious of the three sisters.

8. My little niece insisted on wearing a bright purple sweater and ragged wool slippers.

9. The eager salesperson spoke enthusiastic. *enthusiastically*

10. You should apologize because you were extreme rude to your old friend. *extremely*

Exercise 11

Practice

Another Comprehensive Exercise on Using Adjectives and Adverbs

Correct any errors in using adjectives and adverbs (including punctuation errors) in the following sentences. Some sentences do not need correcting.

1. Our plans for the trip became a total disaster.

2. A deserted decaying house stood before the weary travelers.

3. Your new fleece jacket looks good with those pants.

quickly

4. You will be late for work if you don't get dressed quick.

really

5. The woman in the television commercial tries to sound real sincere.

6. Mr. Ostrowsky is a highly respected business leader in the community.

~~most~~

7. Eliot told me the most saddest story about his grandparents.

8. Helen and I looked at three engagement rings; I think the one with three small diamonds is the most beautiful.

9. If you are looking for a way to spend an afternoon, there is
than
nothing better then a walk by the water.

well

10. Ted is not much of a talker, but he listens good.

Editing a Paragraph for Errors in Adjectives and Adverbs

Edit the following paragraph, correcting all the errors in the use of adjectives and adverbs. Write your corrections in the space above the errors. There are seven errors.

I am going to have to change my busy schedule, or I will be in trouble. Last
badly
week I did bad on my math test because I hadn't studied for it. Instead, I had

worked overtime at my job and managed to get only four hours of sleep. Yesterday,
(no comma)
when I thought I would have a little, private time to study, my sister was sick and

had to stay home from elementary school. So I was stuck at home, taking care of
than
her. That job is worst then going to work. Then last night my boss called and asked

me to fill in for one of the assistant managers. I wanted to say no, but my boss was
really
real desperate, so I went to work. Now, here I am, falling asleep in English class. I
good
know I could get a well grade in here, but it's hard for me to concentrate when I'm
~~more~~
so tired. Tonight I will think about how I can be more smarter about using my time. I
most
need to look at work, home, and school and decide which is more important.

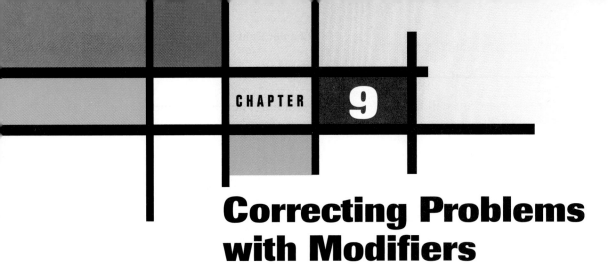

CHAPTER 9

Correcting Problems with Modifiers

Modifiers are words, phrases, or clauses that describe (modify) something in a sentence. All the following italicized words, phrases, and clauses are modifiers.

> **modifiers:**
> the *black* cat (word)
> the cat *in the corner* (phrase)
> the cat *that he adopted* (clause)

Sometimes modifiers limit another word. They make another word (or words) more specific:

> the basket *in the boy's bedroom* (tells which basket)
> *twenty* cookies (tells how many cookies)
> the card *that she gave me* (tells which card)
> They *seldom* visit. (tells how often)

Exercise 1

Practice

Recognizing Modifiers

In each of the following sentences, underline the modifiers (words, phrases, or clauses) that describe the italicized word.

1. Yesterday, Sarah gave me a *rose* <u>in a crystal vase</u>.

2. At the beginning of class, a *boy* <u>wearing a red baseball cap</u> left the room.

3. The *crowd* <u>waiting in line</u> began to push and shove against the fence.

4. My little brother Henry wanted a *brownie* <u>covered in chocolate frosting</u>.

5. Shantay studied for the test but wasn't ready for the <u>essay</u> *questions.*

6. The <u>heavy</u> *rain* drenched my clothes and soaked into my shoes.

7. <u>Captured in the woods,</u> the *fugitive* was taken to the county jail.

8. A <u>gray</u> *kitten* <u>with white paws</u> peeked out of the basket.

9. <u>Lying on the couch,</u> *Eric* fell into a deep sleep.

10. Dad's <u>old bedroom</u> *slippers,* <u>with their torn leather toes and ragged flannel lining,</u> made perfect toys for the dog.

 Finding Modifiers in Professional Writing

Practice

Following is an excerpt from an article by J. R. Miller in the *Miami Herald.* It is a description of the office of Luther Campbell, a controversial and popular rap artist of the 1980s. The writing makes effective use of specific details, particularly through using modifiers. After you read the description, underline the modifiers that describe each italicized word or phrase.

Luther Campbell's office could belong to any successful businessman: <u>Italian leather</u> *chairs* and a <u>sleekly modern</u> *slab of something* <u>dark and expensive</u> for a desk. But one entire wall is bristling with enough electronics to launch a Saturn V: speakers, turntable, tuner, amplifier, CD player, tape deck, and right smack in the middle of the wall a large television hooked directly into the <u>satellite</u> *dish* that is bolted onto the roof. Two large framed *posters* hang behind his desk. . . . Beside the row of <u>gold and platinum</u> *albums* <u>in chrome frames</u> are lithographs[*] of <u>Luther's</u> *heroes:* the martyred[*] Martin and Malcolm.[*]

* **lithographs** means prints
* **martyred** means killed for a cause or belief
* **Martin** and **Malcolm** are Martin Luther King, Jr., and Malcolm X

CORRECTING MODIFIER PROBLEMS

Modifiers can make your writing more specific and more vivid. Used effectively and correctly, modifiers give the reader a clear picture of what you want to say, and they help you to say it precisely. But modifiers have to be used correctly. You can check for errors with modifiers as you revise your sentences.

Info BOX

Three Steps in Checking for Sentence Errors with Modifiers

Step 1: Find the modifier.

Step 2: Ask, "Does the modifier have something to modify?"

Step 3: Ask, "Is the modifier in the right place, as close as possible to the word, phrase, or clause it modifies?"

If you answer *no* to either Step 2 or Step 3, you need to revise your sentence.

Review the three steps in the following example:

sample sentence: They were looking for a man walking a dog smoking a cigar.

Step 1: Find the modifier. The modifiers are *walking a dog* and *smoking a cigar.*

Step 2: Ask, "Does the modifier have something to modify?" The answer is yes. The man is walking a dog. The man is smoking a cigar. Both modifiers go with *a man.*

Step 3: Ask, "Is the modifier in the right place?" The answer is *yes* and *no.*

One modifier is in the right place:

a man *walking a dog*

The other modifier is not in the right place:

a dog *smoking a cigar*

The dog is not smoking a cigar. The sentence needs to be revised.

revised sentence: They were looking for a man *smoking a cigar and walking a dog.*

Here is another example of how to apply the three steps:

sample sentence: Slathered in whipped cream and nuts, she ate the hot fudge sundae.

Step 1: Find the modifiers. The modifiers are *Slathered in whipped cream and nuts* and *hot fudge.*

Step 2: Ask, "Does the modifier have something to modify?" The answer is yes. The sundae is *slathered in whipped cream and nuts,* and the sundae is *hot fudge.*

Step 3: Ask, "Is the modifier in the right place?" The answer is yes and no. The phrase *hot fudge* is in the right place:

hot fudge sundae

But *Slathered in whipped cream and nuts* is in the wrong place:

Slathered in whipped cream and nuts, she

She is not slathered in whipped cream and nuts. The sundae is. The sentence needs to be revised.

> **revised sentence:** She ate the *hot fudge* sundae *slathered in whipped cream and nuts.*

TEACHING TIP:

Tell students that misplaced modifiers are common errors. See if they can write misplaced modifiers intentionally, and then have them read their "incorrect" sentences to the class. Ask students to explain how the modifiers are in an illogical place. Some responses may be both amusing and instructive.

Caution: Be sure to put words like *almost, even, exactly, hardly, just, merely, nearly, only, scarcely,* and *simply* as close as possible to what they modify. If you put them in the wrong place, you may write a confusing sentence.

> **confusing sentence:** Brian only wants to buy toothpaste and shampoo. (The modifier that creates confusion here is *only*. Does Brian have only one goal in life—to be a toothpaste and shampoo buyer? Or are these the only items he wants to buy? To create a clearer sentence, move the modifier.)

> **revised sentence:** Brian wants to buy *only* toothpaste and shampoo.

The preceding examples show one common error in using modifiers. This error involves **misplaced modifiers**—words that describe something but are not where they should be in the sentence. Here is the rule to remember:

Put the modifier as close as possible to the word, phrase, or clause it modifies.

Exercise 3

Practice

Correcting Sentences with Misplaced Modifiers

Some of the following sentences contain misplaced modifiers. Revise any sentences that have a misplaced modifier by putting the modifier as close as possible to whatever it modifies.

1. With blood dripping from its wound, the man approached the lion.

   revised: The man approached the lion with blood dripping from its

   wound.

2. Terry was broke, but in the past few months, she had almost asked all of her friends for a loan and couldn't ask them again.

   revised: Terry was broke, but in the past several months, she had asked

   almost all of her friends for a loan and couldn't ask them again.

3. I'll be glad we were roommates years from now.

   revised: Years from now, I'll be glad we were roommates.

4. With a video camera, most of the crime was recorded by a woman.

   revised: Most of the crime was recorded by a woman with a video

   camera.

5. My brother heard that the volcano had erupted on the radio.

revised: My brother heard on the radio that the volcano had

erupted.

6. Waiting for a bus, I dropped my books and lost my chemistry homework.

revised: OK

_____

7. Jamal and Joey saw two rabbits on their way to work.

revised: On their way to work, Jamal and Joey saw two rabbits.

_____

8. Louise got into an argument with a man who took her parking space named Mr. Kelsoe.

revised: Louise got into an argument with a man named Mr. Kelsoe

who took her parking space.

9. After scoring the winning point, my coach asked me how I felt.

revised: My coach asked how I felt after scoring the winning

point.

10. My sister says I eat too many snacks, but I only eat fruit for snacks.

revised: My sister says I eat too many snacks, but I eat only fruit for

snacks.

Correcting Dangling Modifiers

The three steps for correcting modifier problems can help you recognize another kind of error. For example, let's use the steps to check the following sentence.

sample sentence: Cruising slowly through the Everglades, two alligators could be seen.

Step 1: Find the modifier. The modifiers are *Cruising slowly through the Everglades* and *two*.

Step 2: Ask, "Does the modifier have something to modify?" The answer is yes and no. The word *two* modifies *alligators*. But who or what is *cruising slowly through the Everglades?* There is no person mentioned in the sentence. The alligators are not cruising.

This kind of error is called a **dangling modifier.** It means that the modifier does not have anything to modify; it just dangles in the sentence. If you want to correct this kind of error, just moving the modifier will not work.

> **still incorrect:** Two alligators could be seen cruising slowly through the Everglades. (There is still no person cruising, and the alligators are not cruising.)

The way to correct this kind of error is to add something to the sentence. If you gave the modifier something to modify, you might come up with several correct sentences:

> **revised sentences:** *As we cruised slowly through the Everglades,* two alligators could be seen.
>
> Two alligators could be seen *when the visitors were cruising slowly through the Everglades.*
>
> *Cruising slowly through the Everglades, the people on the boat* saw two alligators.

Try the process for correcting dangling modifiers once more:

> **sample sentence:** Having struggled in the snow all day, a hot cup of coffee was welcome.

> **Step 1:** Find the modifier. The modifiers are *Having struggled in the snow all day, hot,* and *of coffee.*
> **Step 2:** Ask, "Does the modifier have anything to modify?" The answer is yes and no. The words *hot* and *of coffee* modify *cup,* but *Having struggled in the snow all day* doesn't modify anything. Who struggled? There is nobody mentioned in the sentence. To revise, put somebody in the sentence.

> **revised sentences:** Having struggled in the snow all day, Dan welcomed a hot cup of coffee.
>
> After we struggled in the snow all day, a hot cup of coffee was welcome.

Remember that you cannot correct a dangling modifier just by moving the modifiers. You have to give the modifier something to modify, so you must add something to the sentence.

Practice

Correcting Sentences with Dangling Modifiers

Some of the following sentences use modifiers correctly, but some have dangling modifiers. Revise the sentences that have dangling modifiers. To revise, you will have to add words and change words.

1. To move ahead in that company, the ability to accept change is necessary.

revised: To move ahead in that company, you must be able to accept

change.

2. With very little background in math, Adam struggled in his college math class.

   revised: OK
   _____

   _____

3. Driving in an ice storm, the car was run into a ditch.

   revised: Driving in an ice storm, I ran my car into a ditch.

   _____

4. Treated like a hero and followed by fans, life became exciting and wonderful.

   revised: Treated like a hero and followed by fans, Alan found life

   exciting and wonderful.

5. While cleaning out the garage, a spider bit his hand.

   revised: While Jim was cleaning out the garage, a spider bit his

   hand.

6. Deciding not to take on too many projects, my sister resigned from the club's hospitality committee.

   revised: OK
   _____

   _____

7. At the age of five, my family visited Arkansas.

   revised: When I was five, my family visited Arkansas.

   _____

8. Without comfortable shoes and light clothing, the walk through the hills will not be enjoyable.

   revised: Without comfortable shoes and light clothing, you will not

   enjoy the walk through the hills.

9. Ripped into pieces by my crazy dog, the newspaper was unreadable.

   revised: OK

   _____

10. When boarding the school bus, an argument between two first-graders started.

    revised: When they were boarding the school bus, two first-graders

    started an argument.

REVIEWING THE STEPS AND THE SOLUTIONS

It is important to recognize problems with modifiers and to correct these problems. Modifier problems can result in confusing or even silly sentences, and when you confuse or unintentionally amuse your reader, the reader misses your point.

Remember to check for modifier problems by using three steps and to correct each kind of problem appropriately.

Info BOX

A Summary of Modifier Problems

Checking for Modifier Problems

Step 1: Find the modifier.

Step 2: Ask, "Does the modifier have something to modify?"

Step 3: Ask, "Is the modifier in the right place?"

Correcting Modifier Problems

• If a modifier is in the wrong place (a misplaced modifier), put it as close as possible to the word, phrase, or clause it modifies.

• If a modifier has nothing to modify (a dangling modifier), add or change words so that it has something to modify.

Exercise 5

Practice

Revising Sentences with Misplaced or Dangling Modifiers

All of the sentences below have some kind of modifier problem. Write a new, correct sentence for each one. You can move, remove, add, or change words. The first one is done for you.

1. Shot in the chest, the ambulance took the robber to the emergency room.

   revised: The ambulance took the robber, shot in the chest, to the

   emergency room.

Answers Will Vary.

Possible answers shown at right.

2. After dusting the furniture and washing the floors, the apartment looked much better.

   revised: After we dusted the furniture and washed the floors, the

   apartment looked much better.

3. With a desire to help the victims of the storm, a fund was established at the local bank.

   revised: With a desire to help the victims of the storm, our

   community established a fund at the local bank.

4. He gave her a velvet box with a silver bracelet dressed in his best clothes.

   revised: _Dressed in his best clothes, he gave her a velvet box with a_

   silver bracelet.

5. Smearing finger paint on the other children, the teacher scolded the mischievous kindergartner.

   revised: _The teacher scolded the mischievous kindergartner smearing_

   finger paint on the other children.

6. An old photograph album was found in the attic that had been missing for years.

   revised: _An old photograph album that had been missing for years_

   was found in the attic.

7. At the graduation ceremony, Leon's mother nearly cried for an hour.

   revised: _At the graduation ceremony, Leon's mother cried for nearly_

   an hour.

8. Oozing oil under the hood, Marcy examined the old pickup truck.

   revised: _Marcy examined the old pickup truck oozing oil under the_

   hood.

9. To be a good parent, patience and a sense of humor are essential.

   revised: _To be a good parent, you have to have patience and a sense_

   of humor.

10. Scattered among the tall weeds, Billy saw small clusters of wild flowers.

    revised: _Billy saw small clusters of wild flowers scattered among the_

    tall weeds.

Exercise 6   Collaborate

Completing Sentences with Modifiers

Do this exercise with a partner or a group. Below are the beginnings of sentences. Complete each sentence by adding your own words. Be sure that each new sentence is free of modifier problems. When you have completed the exercise, share your sentences with another group or with the class. The first one is done for you.

1. Scorched and dry, <u>the toasted English muffin tasted like a chunk of</u>

<u>charcoal.</u>

2. Trapped in the haunted house, <u>the teenagers began to scream.</u>

_____

3. Complaining about the traffic jam, <u>Dan hit the car in front of him.</u>

_____

4. When asking for a favor, <u>you should try not to whine.</u>

_____

5. Caught in the act of robbing the store, <u>the woman surrendered with-</u>

<u>out a struggle.</u>

6. Upset by her supervisor's criticism, <u>Gilda couldn't sleep all night.</u>

_____

7. Swimming in shark-infested waters, <u>the divers struggled to get to</u>

<u>shore.</u>

8. Captured on videotape, <u>the incident seemed like a case of self-</u>

<u>defense.</u>

9. While talking on his cell phone, <u>Mr. Swenson heard a strange</u>

<u>noise.</u>

10. Held together with duct tape, <u>the doorknob was sure to fall off the</u>

<u>door.</u>

Exercise 7

⊖⊖⊖ _Connect_

Revising for Modifier Problems

The following paragraph has some modifier problems. Correct the errors by
writing above the lines. There are five errors.

      learn almost
You can almost learn anything you want to if you have the patience and

determination. My mother, for example, always wanted to learn to play the piano.

Because she came from a poor family,
Coming from a poor family, piano lessons were out of the question. When she left

home and began to earn her own money, my mother struggled to pay for her food

and rent. Once again, she put her dream aside. Then, married and raising a family,

she made other needs a priority.

other needs took priority. After her children were grown, my mother figured she

was too old to learn a new skill. Then my father surprised her with a gift certifi-

cate for ten piano lessons. At first she was terrified. With fingers stiff and

she found playing the simplest notes nearly impossible. Yet, with my

awkward, playing the simplest notes seemed impossible. Yet she kept practicing

father's support, she kept practicing.

with my father's support. Three years later, my mother plays the piano for her

club, her friends, and for family celebrations.

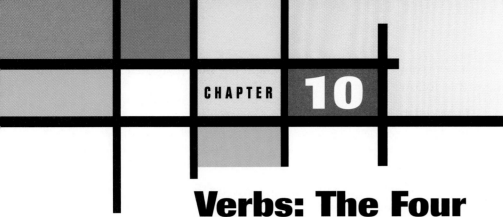

CHAPTER 10

Verbs: The Four Main Forms

Verbs are words that show some kind of action or being:

> verb
> My brother *washes* my car.

> verb
> The teddy bear *is* his oldest toy.

> verb
> Your cinnamon cake *smells* wonderful.

Verbs also tell about time:

> verb
> My brother *will wash* my car. (The time is future.)

> verb
> The teddy bear *was* his oldest toy. (The time is past.)

> verb
> Your cinnamon cake *smells* wonderful. (The time is present.)

The time of a verb is called its **tense.** You can say a verb is in the **present tense,** the **future tense,** the **past tense,** or many other tenses.

Using verbs correctly involves knowing which form of the verb to use and choosing the right verb tense.

USING STANDARD VERB FORMS

Many people use nonstandard verb forms in everyday conversation. But everyone who wants to write and speak effectively should know different levels of language, from the slang and dialect of everyday conversation to the **standard English** of college, business, and professional environments.

In everyday conversation, you might use **nonstandard forms** like the ones that follow:

Nonstandard Verb Forms

it seem	I faces	we was	you was
we goes	they don't	they talks	she work
you be	I be	he sell	it don't

But these are not correct forms in standard English. To become more familiar with standard verb forms, start with a review of the present tense.

THE PRESENT TENSE

Here are the standard verb forms of the verb *walk:*

Info BOX

Standard Verb Forms in the Present Tense

I walk	we walk
you walk	you walk
he, she, it walks	they walk

Take a closer look at the standard verb forms. Only one form is different:

he, she, it *walks*

This is the only form that ends in *-s* in the present tense.

In the present tense, use an *-s* or *-es* ending on the verb only when the subject is *he, she,* or *it,* or the equivalent of *he, she,* or *it.*

examples:
He *drives* to the store on Saturdays.
Larry *walks* his dog on Saturdays. (*Larry* is the equivalent of *he.*)
The cat *chases* the birds in my garden. (The *cat* is the equivalent of *it.*)
She *reminds* me of my sister.
It *looks* like a new car.
Your engine *sounds* funny. (The word *engine* is the equivalent of *it.*)
My daughter *watches* the news on television. (The word *daughter* is the equivalent of *she.*)

Take another look at the present tense. If the verb is a standard verb, like *work,* it will follow this form in the present tense:

I *work* on the weekends.	We *work* well together.
You *work* too hard.	You two boys *work* with Joe.
He *works* for his father.	They *work* near the mall.
She *works* in a bakery.	
It *works* on solar power.	

Exercise 1   Picking the Right Verb in the Present Tense

Practice

To familiarize yourself with standard verb forms in the present tense, underline the subject and circle the correct verb form in each of the following sentences.

1. Hoping for a good grade in Art Appreciation, <u>Jason</u> attend/attends every lecture.

2. A <u>meal</u> in a fancy restaurant cost/costs too much for me.

3. <u>Cynthia</u> and her <u>cousin</u> give/gives their old clothes to charity.

4. The <u>possibility</u> of a robbery frighten/frightens me.

5. That <u>waitress</u> serve/serves us every weekend.

6. <u>Sylvester</u> get/gets a new car once a year.

7. <u>He</u> wear/wears a different shirt every day.

8. In the evening, <u>I</u> sit/sits on my patio.

9. The <u>puppy</u> belong /belongs to my neighbor.

10. <u>He</u> clean /cleans offices for a living.

 Exercise 2   **More on Picking the Right Verb in the Present Tense**

Practice

To familiarize yourself with standard verb forms in the present tense, underline the subject and circle the correct verb form in each of the following sentences.

1. Your <u>plan</u> sound /sounds good to me.

2. <u>I</u> buy/ buys my clothes at sales.

3. <u>They</u> often travel/ travels in a camper.

4. <u>Melanie</u> hesitate /hesitates to act in a crisis.

5. <u>Margarine</u> taste /tastes like butter.

6. On the shore of the lake stand /stands a <u>pavilion</u>.

7. Tomorrow, <u>you</u> speak/speaks at the club breakfast.

8. His <u>behavior</u> raise /raises several questions.

9. A guilty <u>conscience</u> tear /tears you apart.

10. On my birthday, <u>Tommy</u> always send /sends me a card.

 **Exercise 3**   **Writing Sentences with Verbs in the Present Tense**

Collaborate

Below are pairs of verbs. Working with a partner or a group, write a sentence using each verb. Be sure your verbs are in the present tense, and make your sentences at least five words long. When you have completed the exercise, share your sentences with another group. The first one is done for you.

1. verbs: listen, listens

sentence 1. Every morning on their way to work, my parents listen to a boring radio station.

sentence 2. Sam always listens to my sad stories and silly complaints.

2. verbs: fear, fears

sentence 1. Lena and Miriam fear the loss of their jobs.

sentence 2. In a thunderstorm, Nick sometimes fears the lightning.

3. verbs: make, makes

sentence 1. You make the best pizza in town.

sentence 2. Listening to gossip makes me uncomfortable.

4. verbs: struggle, struggles

sentence 1. Each month, we struggle to pay the bills.

sentence 2. At night, the toddler struggles to get out of his crib.

5. verb: respect, respects

sentence 1. My neighbors respect the rights of others.

sentence 2. Don respects my right to disagree with him.

6. verbs: teach, teaches

sentence 1. My mother and father teach at the university.

sentence 2. Professor Klein teaches you how to think.

7. verbs: sell, sells

sentence 1. On Fridays, local farmers sell fruit at the market.

_____

sentence 2. My drug store sells milk and soft drinks.

_____

8. verbs: confuse, confuses

sentence 1. Children often confuse fun with danger.

_____

sentence 2. When he tries to explain further, he only confuses me.

_____

9. verbs: seem, seems

sentence 1. These bracelets seem too expensive for my budget.

_____

sentence 2. Barbados seems like a perfect vacation spot.

_____

10. verbs: appreciate, appreciates

sentence 1. I appreciate Richard's hard work.

_____

sentence 2. Marie appreciates the support of her friends.

_____

Exercise 4   **Revising a Paragraph for Errors in the Present Tense**

Connect

The following paragraph contains nine errors in the present tense verb forms. Correct the errors in the spaces above the lines.

       ask

My mother puts me through the same routine every time I asks to borrow

    looks

a few dollars. First, she look at me with a stern expression and questions me

about my spending habits. Then she delivers a long lecture about the state

of the economy. She ends her lecture by saying that money doesn't grow

       says

on trees and by bringing up my older brothers. She say Tom and Matthew

  borrow   _possess_

never borrows money from her because they possesses a strong

awareness of the value of a dollar. While my mother screams and yell, I *yells*
says nothing. Finally, she reaches in her purse and gives me the money I *say*
needs. Once again, I get the cash, and my mother get to feel righteous. *need* *gets*

THE PAST TENSE

The past tense of most verbs is formed by adding *-d* or *-ed* to the verb.

Info BOX

Standard Verb Forms in the Past Tense

I walked	we walked
you walked	you walked
he, she, it walked	they walked

Add *-ed* to *walk* to form the past tense. For some other verbs, you may add *-d*.

> The zookeeper *chased* the chimpanzee.
> I *trembled* with excitement.
> Paul *baked* a birthday cake for his daughter.

Exercise 5

Practice

Writing the Correct Form of the Past Tense

To familiarize yourself with the past tense, write the correct past tense form of each verb in the blank.

1. Last year, Amy and Chris _____*cooked*_____ (cook) a special dinner for our anniversary.

2. The counselor _____*excused*_____ (excuse) some of the students from class yesterday.

3. A recent letter from the bank _____*informed*_____ (inform) me about my ATM card.

4. Yesterday's paper _____*printed*_____ (print) a story about my old neighborhood.

5. Over the holidays, I _____*borrowed*_____ (borrow) a great book from Frank.

6. The chocolate bar she gave me _____*contained*_____ (contain) nuts and raisins.

7. After recognizing my error, I _____*erased*_____ (erase) it.

8. In high school, we seldom _____*managed*_____ (manage) to get to sleep before midnight.

9. Visitors to last week's carnival _____*enjoyed*_____ (enjoy) some wonderful rides and exhibits.

10. Many years ago, my grandfather _____*immigrated*_____ (immigrate) to this country.

Exercise 6

Practice

More on Writing the Correct Form of the Past Tense

To familiarize yourself with the past tense, write the correct past tense form of each verb in the blank space.

1. Last night, the two cooks _____*slaved*_____ (slave) over a hot stove.

2. All afternoon, the little boy _____*pasted*_____ (paste) brightly colored stickers in the book.

3. A long time ago, Mr. Chen _____*reported*_____ (report) the news on a local television station.

4. This morning, Omar _____*raced*_____ (race) through his breakfast.

5. Squirrels _____*nested*_____ (nest) in our attic for several months.

6. After drinking the milk, the kitten _____*purred*_____ (purr) loudly.

7. An old friend from my first job _____*visited*_____ (visit) me last winter.

8. Witnesses at the scene of last night's fire _____*described*_____ (describe) a loud explosion.

9. When I was a child, Cleavon _____*encouraged*_____ (encourage) me to study music.

10. At the end of the play, everyone _____*applauded*_____ (applaud) the cast.

Exercise 7

Collaborate

Writing Sentences with Verbs in the Present and Past Tense

Below are pairs of verbs. Working with a partner or a group, write a sentence using each verb. Each sentence should be five or more words long. When you have completed the exercise, share your sentences with another group. The first one is done for you.

1. **verbs:** recognizes, recognized

   sentence 1. Whenever I go to that coffee shop, the owner

   recognizes me.

   sentence 2. Yesterday my sister recognized a famous actor walking

   down our street.

2. **verbs:** place, placed

sentence 1. I always place those books on the desk.

sentence 2. My advisor placed me in the wrong math class.

3. **verbs:** mail, mailed

sentence 1. I mail my letters at the post office.

sentence 2. The company says it mailed the package last week.

4. **verbs:** attacks, attacked

sentence 1. A sore throat attacks you when you least expect it.

sentence 2. The storm attacked the coast yesterday.

5. **verbs:** sound, sounded

sentence 1. The rain and wind sound frightening.

sentence 2. The soft music sounded like a love song.

6. **verbs:** insults, insulted

sentence 1. Talking on a cell phone at the movies insults the other members of the audience.

sentence 2. Jackie was angry because someone insulted him.

7. **verbs:** demand, demanded

sentence 1. This product doesn't work; I demand a refund.

sentence 2. The furious customer demanded to see the manager.

8. verbs: dream, dreamed

sentence 1. _I often dream of a long hallway and dark stairs._

_____

sentence 2. _Last night I dreamed about a wedding._

_____

9. verbs: receives, received

sentence 1. _Every month, Eliot receives a check from the bank._

_____

sentence 2. _Last week, I received an e-mail from Josie._

_____

10. verbs: accept, accepted

sentence 1. _Simon and Leah accept responsibility for the error._

_____

sentence 2. _Dina accepted an invitation to a fancy party._

_____

Exercise 8

∞ *Connect*

Rewriting a Paragraph, Changing the Verb Tense

Rewrite the following paragraph, changing all the present tense verbs to the past tense. Write the changes in the space above the original words.

           worked   *hated*   *ignored*
    Jennifer works at a place she hates. Her coworkers ignore her, and her

criticized
boss criticizes her about the smallest details, including Jennifer's makeup and

      said   *looked*
hair style. She says Jennifer looks too sloppy to serve customers. Jennifer also

believed   *behaved*   *smiled*
believes that the customers behave very badly. Not one of them ever smiles

     said   *offered*   *considered*
or says "Thank you" when Jennifer offers assistance. Jennifer considers her

                    dreamed   *stayed*
job a punishment, and she dreams of quitting. She stays only because she

needed
needs the money.

THE FOUR MAIN FORMS OF A VERB

When you are deciding what form of a verb to use, you will probably rely on one of four verb forms: the present tense, the past tense, the present participle, or the past participle. You will use one of these forms or add a helping verb to it. As an example, look at the four main forms of the verb *walk:*

Info BOX

The Four Main Forms of a Verb

Present	Past	Present Participle	Past Participle
walk	walked	walking	walked

You use the four verb forms—present, past, present participle, past participle—alone or with helping verbs to express time (tense). Forms of regular verbs like *walk* are easy to remember.

Use the **present** form for the present tense:

They *walk* three miles every day.

The **past** form expresses past tense:

Steve *walked* to work yesterday.

The **present participle,** or *-ing* form, is used with helping verbs:

He *was walking* in a charity fund-raiser.
I *am walking* with a neighbor.
You *should have been walking* faster.

The **past participle** is the form used with the helping verbs *have, has,* or *had:*

I *have walked* down this road before.
She *has walked* to church for years.
The children *had walked* the dog before they went to school.

Of course, you can add many helping verbs to the present tense:

present tense:
We *walk* in a beautiful forest.

add helping verbs:
We *will* walk in a beautiful forest.
We *must* walk in a beautiful forest.
We *can* walk in a beautiful forest.

In **regular verbs,** the four verb forms are simple: the past form is created by adding *-d* or *-ed* to the present form; the present participle is formed by adding *-ing* to the present form; and the past participle is the same as the past form.

Exercise 9

 *Collaborate*

Writing Sentences Using the Four Main Forms of a Verb

Do this exercise with a partner or a group. Below are pairs of verbs. Write a sentence for each verb. Your sentences should be at least five words long. When you have completed this exercise, share your answers with another group or with the class. The first one is done for you.

1. **verbs:** hesitate, hesitating

   sentence 1. Since I had a car accident, I hesitate before getting into a car.

   sentence 2. The lawyers might have been hesitating about the deal.

Answers Will Vary.

Possible answers shown at right.

2. **verbs:** explained, explaining

   sentence 1. The chairperson explained the difficulties with the new agreement.

   sentence 2. Cory is explaining how to use the new printer.

3. **verbs:** complaining, complained (Put *have* in front of *complained.*)

   sentence 1. Our neighbors must have been complaining about the noise.

   sentence 2. My parents have complained to the city council.

4. **verbs:** climbed, climbing

   sentence 1. When I was younger, I climbed to the top of the tower.

   sentence 2. Omar has been climbing mountains for years.

5. **verbs:** accept, accepted (Put *had* in front of *accepted.*)

   sentence 1. We accept your generous offer.

   sentence 2. Amy had accepted Joe's invitation before she learned about the other party.

6. **verbs:** love, loved (Put *had* in front of *loved.*)

   sentence 1. Juliana and Dave love their new apartment.

   sentence 2. Mitch had loved Cindy since they were in college.

7. **verbs:** disappearing, disappeared (Put *has* in front of *disappeared.*)

   sentence 1. Jimmy has been disappearing on weekends.

   sentence 2. My best shirt has disappeared from my closet.

8. **verbs:** confront, confronted

   sentence 1. You should confront your uncle about the issue.

   sentence 2. I confronted the neighbor who always steals my newspaper.

9. **verbs:** wished, wishing

   sentence 1. The little boy wished for a baby brother.

   sentence 2. We were all wishing for warmer weather.

10. **verbs:** rebel, rebelled (Put *have* in front of *rebelled.*)

    sentence 1. Teenagers often rebel against their parents' rules.

    sentence 2. Infuriated by the new dress code, the students have rebelled.

IRREGULAR VERBS

The Present Tense of *be, have, do*

Irregular verbs do not follow the same rules for creating verb forms that regular verbs do. Three verbs that we use all the time—*be, have, do*—are irregular verbs. You need to study them closely. Look at the present tense forms for all three, and compare the standard present tense forms to the nonstandard ones. *Remember to use the standard forms for college or professional writing.*

present tense of *be*:

Nonstandard	Standard
~~I be~~ *or* ~~I is~~	I am
~~you be~~	you are
~~he, she, it be~~	he, she, it is
~~we be~~	we are
~~you be~~	you are
~~they be~~	they are

present tense of *have*:

Nonstandard	Standard
~~I has~~	I have
~~you has~~	you have
~~he, she, it have~~	he, she, it has
~~we has~~	we have
~~they has~~	they have

present tense of *do*:

Nonstandard	Standard
~~I does~~	I do
~~you does~~	you do
~~he, she, it do~~	he, she, it does
~~we does~~	we do
~~you does~~	you do
~~they does~~	they do

Caution: Be careful when you add *not* to *does*. If you're using the contraction of *does not*, be sure you write *doesn't*, instead of *don't*. Contractions should be avoided in most formal reports and business writing courses. Always check with your instructor about the use of contractions in your personal writing.

> **not this:** ~~He don't call me very often~~.
> **but this:** He doesn't call me very often.

Exercise 10

Practice

Choosing the Correct Form of *be*, *have*, or *do* in the Present Tense

Circle the correct form of the verb in each sentence.

1. I am sure the reporters on the scene has/(have) a deadline to meet.

2. On a day like today, I (am)/be happy to have such good friends.

3. The old washing machine still do/(does) a decent job of getting the clothes clean.

4. With a new car, we has/(have) higher car payments.

5. All my aunts and uncles be/(are) experts at telling ghost stories.

6. At the end of each month, I (am)/be confused about my lack of money.

7. I know that nobody do/(does) a better job than this cleaning service.

8. In his bedroom Peter (has)/have a big-screen television.

9. You know that David be/(is) thinking about his senior year.

10. The theater near our house (doesn't)/don't show movies after mid-night.

More on Choosing the Correct Form of *be, have,* or *do* in the Present Tense

Circle the correct form of the verb in each sentence.

1. Every Saturday morning I (do)/does the grocery shopping for my grandfather.

2. Cooking dinner for my family can be fun, but it do/(does) take time.

3. Other teams may brag, but I know that we (are)/be the fastest team on the court.

4. If you has/(have) any doubts about Diane's sincerity, you should talk to her.

5. I (do)/does the best I can for my family.

6. My cousin Tyra and I has/(have) a special bond.

7. When you smile that way, you (are)/be telling me a lie.

8. Deep down inside, you has/(have) a good heart.

9. When their parents have to work late, Daniella and Marc (do)/does their best to make dinner.

10. That old black dog be/(is) a gift from my brother-in-law.

Revising a Paragraph with Errors in the Present Tense of *be, have,* and *do*

The following paragraph contains five errors in the use of the present tense forms of *be, have,* and *do.* Correct the errors above the lines.

My brother's plan to sell our car is making me upset and indignant. Mike, my

            is

brother, says he be thinking about getting rid of our old Toyota. But my parents

gave that car to me and Mike so that we could use it to get to work and school.

       doesn't   *has*

Mike don't own the car by himself; therefore, he have no right to sell it alone.

Mike says he will split the sale money with me, but I am still angry with him. First

of all, he is not the sole owner of the car. Second, he can't make a decision about our property without informing me. The fact that he even considered selling the

car without telling me shows that he *has* have no respect for my wishes. He must

think I *am* is a brainless, passive person. His attitude toward me is what upsets me

the most.

The Past Tense of *be, have, do*

The past tense forms of these irregular verbs can be confusing. Again, compare the nonstandard forms to the standard forms. *Remember to use the standard forms for college or professional writing.*

past tense of *be*:

Nonstandard	Standard
~~I were~~	I was
~~you was~~	you were
~~he, she, it were~~	he, she, it was
~~we was~~	we were
~~you was~~	you were
~~they was~~	they were

past tense of *have*:

Nonstandard	Standard
~~I has~~	I had
~~you has~~	you had
~~he, she, it have~~	he, she, it had
~~we has~~	we had
~~you has~~	you had
~~they has~~	they had

past tense of *do*:

Nonstandard	Standard
~~I done~~	I did
~~you done~~	you did
~~he, she, it done~~	he, she, it did
~~we done~~	we did
~~you done~~	you did
~~they done~~	they did

Exercise 13

Practice

Choosing the Correct Form of *be*, *have*, or *do* in the Past Tense

Circle the correct verb form in each sentence.

1. The man across the street (did)/done the planting for the Community Center garden.

2. The Brazilian singers at the free concert exceeded my expectations; they was / (were), without a doubt, the best part of the entertainment.

3. Janet thought you relied on an interior decorator, but I told her you (did)/done all the decorating yourself.

4. This morning Luke couldn't find his key, but I know he have/(had) it yesterday.

5. When I lived at my grandmother's house, I (was)/were not allowed to stay up late.

6. A year ago, you was/(were) a total stranger; now you are my best friend.

7. A week ago, I (had)/has a bad case of the flu.

8. When you stood at the top of the Empire State Building, you has/(had) no fear of heights.

9. At last night's lecture on AIDS, the Student Council have/(had) an information booth.

10. When she couldn't get to her job, I (did)/done her a favor and drove her to work.

Practice

More on Choosing the Correct Form of *be*, *have*, and *do* in the Past Tense

Circle the correct verb form in each sentence.

1. Two hours after Melissa left, we was/(were) still unwrapping presents.

2. The sugar-free lemonade she served me (had)/have a peculiar taste.

3. My hair looks good because Lorraine (did)/done it for me last night.

4. People standing in line at the movies yesterday (had)/has to wait for at least an hour.

5. The girls in my kindergarten class was/(were) very bright and curious.

6. When he came over, he (had)/have a big bag of candy for his nephew.

7. All weekend they was/(were) waiting for the rain to stop.

8. For two months last summer I (was)/were a lifeguard for the city of Crystal Beach.

9. After she finished dinner, she (had)/have a cup of coffee with me.

10. Ted and Brian (did)/done the dishes while Ryan took out the garbage.

⊕⊕⊕ *Connect*

Revising a Paragraph with Errors in the Past Tense of *be*, *have*, and *do*

The following paragraph contains seven errors in the use of the past tense of *be*, *have*, and *do*. Correct the errors above the lines.

For no good reason, the local police gave me and my friends a hard time last

                                               were

night. Frank, Rickie, and I was just sitting on Rickie's truck and drinking Pepsi in front of the Quik Mart when a patrol car pulled up. The officer said he have a [*had*]

complaint about us, that we were causing a disturbance, and the store manager

wanted to get rid of us. I told the officer that it weren't against the law to sit in [*wasn't*]

front of a convenience store and drink soda. But he said it was private property

and the manager have a right to ask us to leave. The policeman done his best to [*had*] [*did*]

roust us, and eventually we has to leave. Because we were male and in our teens, [*had*]

we must have looked threatening to the store manager. Then, when a policeman

showed up, we got angry with him even though he was just doing his job. Most

likely he and the manager were upset, but my friends and I was, too. [*were*]

More Irregular Verb Forms

Be, *have*, and *do* are not the only verbs with irregular forms. There are many such verbs, and everybody who writes uses some form of an irregular verb. When you write and you are not certain you are using the correct form of a verb, check the following list of irregular verbs.

For each verb listed, the *present*, the *past*, and the *past participle* forms are given. The present participle isn't included because it is always formed by adding *ing* to the present form.

Irregular Verb Forms

TEACHING TIP:

Have students check the irregular verb forms that seem "strange" to them. For practice, discuss some of their choices and use them in sentences.

Present	Past	Past Participle
(Today I *arise*.)	(Yesterday I *arose*.)	(I have/had *arisen*.)
arise	arose	arisen
awake	awoke, awaked	awoken, awaked
bear	bore	born, borne
beat	beat	beaten
become	became	become
begin	began	begun
bend	bent	bent
bite	bit	bitten
bleed	bled	bled
blow	blew	blown
break	broke	broken
bring	brought	brought
build	built	built
burst	burst	burst
buy	bought	bought
catch	caught	caught
choose	chose	chosen
cling	clung	clung
come	came	come
cost	cost	cost
creep	crept	crept
cut	cut	cut

Present	Past	Past Participle
deal	dealt	dealt
draw	drew	drawn
dream	dreamed, dreamt	dreamed, dreamt
drink	drank	drunk
drive	drove	driven
eat	ate	eaten
fall	fell	fallen
feed	fed	fed
feel	felt	felt
fight	fought	fought
find	found	found
fling	flung	flung
fly	flew	flown
freeze	froze	frozen
get	got	got, gotten
give	gave	given
go	went	gone
grow	grew	grown
hear	heard	heard
hide	hid	hidden
hit	hit	hit
hold	held	held
hurt	hurt	hurt
keep	kept	kept
know	knew	known
lay (*to put*)	laid	laid
lead	led	led
leave	left	left
lend	lent	lent
let	let	let
lie (*to recline*)	lay	lain
light	lit, lighted	lit, lighted
lost	lost	lost
make	made	made
mean	meant	meant
meet	met	met
pay	paid	paid
ride	rode	ridden
ring	rang	rung
rise	rose	risen
run	ran	run
say	said	said
see	saw	seen
sell	sold	sold
send	sent	sent
sew	sewed	sewn, sewed
shake	shook	shaken
shine	shone, shined	shone, shined
shrink	shrank	shrunk
shut	shut	shut
sing	sang	sung
sit	sat	sat

Present	Past	Past Participle
sleep	slept	slept
slide	slid	slid
sling	slung	slung
speak	spoke	spoken
spend	spent	spent
stand	stood	stood
steal	stole	stolen
stick	stuck	stuck
sting	stung	stung
stink	stank, stunk	stunk
string	strung	strung
swear	swore	sworn
swim	swam	swum
teach	taught	taught
tear	tore	torn
tell	told	told
think	thought	thought
throw	threw	thrown
wake	woke, waked	woken, waked
wear	wore	worn
win	won	won
write	wrote	written

Exercise 16

Practice

Choosing the Correct Form of Irregular Verbs

Write the correct form of the verb in parentheses in the following sentences. Be sure to check the list of irregular verbs.

1. My year in the U.S. Marines has _____taught_____ (teach) me

more than you can imagine.

2. The witness told an incredible story, but he had

_____sworn_____ (swear) to tell the truth, under oath.

3. Last week, when the sun ___shone or shined___ (shine) so brightly, I

got a sunburn.

4. On several occasions, the aunts' nasty remarks have

_____hurt_____ (hurt) the child's feelings.

5. My parents were able to buy a house because a good friend

_____lent_____ (lend) them some money.

6. I was so tired last night I _____lay_____ (lie) down for a nap

before dinner.

7. Denise and Roy were munching on taco chips and watching the game; by the second half, they had _____eaten_____ (eat) all the chips.

8. The burglar heard a noise so he _____hid_____ (hide) in the closet.

9. Marisol had a painful knee injury last summer, but she _____bore_____ (bear) her burden with patience.

10. Julie used to be shy, but lately she has _____become_____ (become) more outgoing.

Exercise 17

Practice

More on Choosing the Correct Form of Irregular Verbs

Write the correct form of the verb in parentheses in the following sentences. Be sure to check the list of irregular verbs.

1. After the barbecue, he _____swam_____ (swim) in the ocean until sundown.

2. When they broke the curfew, Alan and Cody _____strung_____ (string) together a complicated story of a flat tire and a traffic jam.

3. Last year you _____led_____ (lead) me to believe I was eligible for a scholarship.

4. The travel agent has _____kept_____ (keep) his word about the discount air fares.

5. When you didn't call, I was sure you had _____gone_____ (go) to the library without me.

6. As the police officer returned the lost kitten, the little boy _____burst_____ (burst) into tears.

7. Mr. Dixon wouldn't let us ice skate on the pond; he said the pond had not _____frozen_____ (freeze) solid.

8. The soldier was injured in the attack, yet he _____bled_____ (bleed) very little.

9. The runner collapsed because he hadn't _____*drunk*_____

(drink) enough fluids.

10. After yesterday's class, we _____*chose*_____ (choose) to go to a

coffee shop for lunch.

Exercise 18   **Writing Sentences with Correct Verb Forms**

👥 *Collaborate*   Working with a partner or a group, write two sentences that correctly use each of the following verb forms. Each sentence should be five or more words long. In writing these sentences, you may add helping verbs to the verb forms, but you may *not* change the verb form itself. When your group has completed the exercise, share your answers with another group or with the class. The first one has been done for you.

1. verb: flown

sentence 1. To see me, my grandfather has flown nearly a thousand

miles.

sentence 2. We usually see ducks, but they have flown south for the

winter.

Answers Will Vary.

Possible answers shown at right.

2. verb: lain

sentence 1. My sick dog has lain on the sofa all week.

_____

sentence 2. When I have been really tired, I have lain on the floor of

the office and taken a nap.

3. verb: begun

sentence 1. That man has begun to irritate me.

_____

sentence 2. I wish we had begun the tennis lessons earlier.

_____

4. verb: lead

sentence 1. The school marching band will lead the parade.

_____

sentence 2. I can lead you to the right house.

_____

5. verb: rung

sentence 1. The phone has rung seven times this afternoon.

_____

sentence 2. You could have rung the doorbell.

_____

6. verb: torn

sentence 1. The wind has torn the banner to shreds.

_____

sentence 2. The note cards have been torn in half.

_____

7. verb: threw

sentence 1. I foolishly threw the check out with the garbage.

_____

sentence 2. My niece threw her chocolate pudding on the

floor.

_____

8. verb: wore

sentence 1. All the running wore me out.

_____

sentence 2. Yesterday Tom wore his new shoes to work.

_____

9. verb: waked

sentence 1. I have waked too late for the morning news.

_____

sentence 2. My poodle waked me with a big, sloppy kiss.

_____

10. verb: shook

sentence 1. Yesterday my father shook the governor's hand.

_____

sentence 2. During the earthquake, my apartment shook.

_____

Exercise 19   **Revising a Paragraph that Contains Errors in Irregular Verb Forms**

⊖⊖⊖ *Connect*   Nine of the irregular verb forms in the following paragraph are incorrect. Write the correct verb forms in the space above the lines.

I made a big mistake yesterday when I underestimated the power of the sun.

Yesterday, I decided to go to the beach and lie in the sun for a while. I hadn't

              begun

been outside for a while, and I had began to feel unhealthy. I packed up my car,

taking a blanket, some bottled water, and my portable CD player. I didn't take any

sunscreen because it was a cloudy day, and the sun shined only through the

   lay

clouds. I laid in the sun for at least an hour before I felt warm. Then I started to

                       slept

feel drowsy and chose to take a short nap. I must have sleeped for quite a while

        woke or waked   *become*

because when I woked up, my skin was hot. By last night, I had became feverish.

         flung

This morning, I flinged the sheets off my body because my skin felt so fiery. Then

  began   *frozen*

I begun to feel chills, as if my body had froze. I had a bad case of overexposure to

        known

the sun. If I had only knew what the sun could do to me, I would have been much

more careful.

CHAPTER 11

More on Verb Tenses

HELPING VERBS AND VERB TENSES

The main verb forms—present, past, present participle, and past participle—can be combined with *helping verbs* to create more verb tenses. Following is a list of some common helping verbs:

Info BOX			
Some Common Helping Verbs			
is	was	does	have
am	were	did	had
are	do	has	

These verbs change their form, depending on the subject:

> She *is* calling the ticket booth.
> I *am* calling the ticket booth.

Fixed-Form Helping Verbs

Some other helping verbs always keep the same form, no matter what the subject. These are the **fixed-form helping verbs.** Following are the fixed-form helping verbs.

Info BOX				
Fixed-Form Helping Verbs				
can	will	may	shall	must
could	would	might	should	

Notice how the helping verb *can* is in the same form even when the subject changes:

> She *can* call the ticket booth.
> I *can* call the ticket booth.

The Helping Verbs *can* and *could, will* and *would*

Can is used to show the present tense:

> Today, David *can* fix the washer.

Could is used to show the past tense:

> Yesterday, David *could* fix the washer.

Could is also used to show a possibility or a wish:

> David *could* fix the washer if he had the right tools.
> Harry wishes he *could* fix the washer.

Will points to the future from the present:

> Cecilia is sure she *will* win the case. (Today, in the present, Cecilia is sure she will win in the future.)

Would points to the future from the past:

> Cecilia was sure she *would* win the case. (In the past, Cecilia was sure she would win in the future.)

Would is also used to show a possibility or a wish:

> Cecilia *would* win the case if she prepared for it.
> Cecilia wishes she *would* win the case.

 Recognizing Helping Verbs

Practice

Underline the helping verbs in the following sentences.

1. I <u>do</u> think the referee is right.

2. When the supervisor speaks, you <u>should</u> pay more attention to her.

3. Tomorrow, the weather <u>may</u> turn warmer.

4. Last week, I <u>could</u> hardly speak because I had a bad cold.

5. Now I <u>can</u> speak normally.

6. <u>Does</u> that child ever sleep?

7. If we spend money on a computer, we <u>must</u> select a reliable one.

8. Even though the coach has a temper, she <u>does</u> keep it under control.

9. Desmond went to school in our neighborhood, so he <u>might</u> know my sister.

10. The King of France <u>shall</u> arrive in a golden carriage.

Exercise 2

Practice

Selecting *can* or *could*, *will* or *would*

In each of the following sentences, circle the correct helping verb.

1. Casey wished Juanita will/(would) call him more often.

2. Last year, I can/(could) use my husband's cell phone.

3. If the bedrooms were larger, I will/(would) buy the house.

4. When the baby smiles, you (can)/could see his resemblance to his mother.

5. When the phone rang, I can/(could) see Sherman run to answer it.

6. I am sure I (can)/could make the semifinals.

7. Last week, I felt I can/(could) solve the problem.

8. Mike knows that he (will)/would need a better job.

9. The detective believed the suspect will/(would) confess.

10. I wish you will/(would) stop worrying about the bills.

THE PRESENT PROGRESSIVE TENSE

The **progressive tense** uses the present participle (the *-ing* form of the verb) plus some form of *to be*. Following are examples of the **present progressive tense:**

Info BOX

The Present Progressive Tense

I am walking		we are walking	
you are walking	Singular	you are walking	Plural
he, she, it is walking		they are walking	

TEACHING TIP:

Since grammatical terms can be threatening to students, stress that memorizing the labels is not as important as knowing concepts and correct verb forms. (Many departmental tests and state "exit" exams ask students to recognize errors within a sentence, but they do not emphasize rote memorization of terminology.)

All these forms of the present progressive tense use an *-ing* form of the verb (*walking*) plus a present form of *to be* (*am, is, are*).

Be careful not to confuse the present progressive tense with the present tense:

present tense: Terry listens to music. (This sentence means that Terry *does* listen to music, but it does not say she is doing so at this moment.)

present progressive tense: Terry is listening to music. (This sentence means that Terry is listening to music at this moment.)

The present progressive tense shows us that the action is happening right now. The present progressive tense can also show future time:

Terry is listening to music later. (This sentence means that Terry will be listening to music in the future.)

 Exercise 3

Practice

Distinguishing Between the Present Tense and the Present Progressive Tense

Circle the correct verb tense in each of the following sentences. Be sure to look carefully at the meaning of each sentence.

1. On Saturdays, we are doing/(do) the laundry.

2. My boyfriend (is playing)/plays softball right now.

3. The doctor cannot see you now; she (is reading)/reads X-rays.

4. Sometimes I am feeling/(feel) happy about my decision.

5. Every time he tells a joke, he is making/(makes) a fool of himself.

6. Occasionally, the engine is making/(makes) a strange noise.

7. Tony is busy; he (is making)/makes tortillas for dinner.

8. Late at night, the dog is barking/(barks) at every little sound.

9. That cut on your hand looks serious; I (am calling)/call the doctor.

10. Whenever it rains, Cynthia and Mike are taking/(take) the bus to school.

THE PAST PROGRESSIVE TENSE

The **past progressive tense** uses the present participle (the *-ing* form of the verb) plus a past form of *to be* (*was, were*). Following are examples of the past progressive tense:

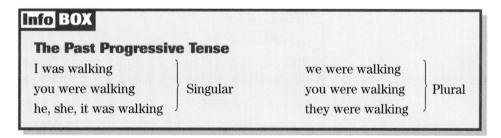

Info BOX

The Past Progressive Tense

I was walking		we were walking	
you were walking	Singular	you were walking	Plural
he, she, it was walking		they were walking	

Be careful not to confuse the past progressive tense with the past tense:

past tense: George walked carefully. (This sentence implies that George has stopped walking.)

past progressive tense: George was walking carefully when he slipped on the ice. (This sentence says that George was in the process of walking when something else happened: he slipped.)

Use the progressive tenses, both present and past, when you want to show that something was or is in progress.

Exercise 4

Practice

Distinguishing Between the Past Tense and the Past Progressive Tense

Circle the correct verb tense in each of the following sentences. Be sure to look carefully at the meaning of each sentence.

1. I (was changing)/changed my baby's diaper when she suddenly started to scream.

2. My sister was painting/(painted) her kitchen last night.

3. After I drank the cocoa, I was sleeping/(slept) soundly.

4. James was calling/(called) me before he called Marcia.

5. Sylvia and her mother (were driving)/drove back to Texas when they heard the news on the radio.

6. When I was seven, I was playing/(played) softball.

7. Two months ago, we were taking/(took) guitar lessons.

8. I (was staring)/stared out the window when the teacher called on me.

9. Before I could stop her, my mother was pushing/(pushed) money into my hand.

10. He was calling/(called) me all the time.

THE PRESENT PERFECT TENSE

The **present perfect tense** is made up of the past participle form of the verb plus *have* or *has* as a helping verb. Following are examples of the present perfect tense.

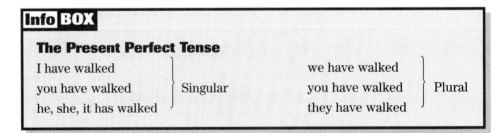

Info BOX

The Present Perfect Tense

I have walked	we have walked
you have walked Singular	you have walked Plural
he, she, it has walked	they have walked

Be careful not to confuse the present perfect tense with the past tense:

past tense: Jacqueline *studied* yoga for two years. (This sentence means that Jacqueline doesn't study yoga any more, but she did study it in the past.)

present perfect tense: Jacqueline *has studied* yoga for two years. (This sentence means that Jacqueline started studying yoga two years ago, and she is still studying it.)

The present perfect tense is used to show an action that started in the past but is still going on in the present.

Exercise 5   **Distinguishing Between the Past and Present Perfect Tenses**

Practice: Circle the correct verb tense in each of the following sentences. Be sure to look carefully at the meaning of each sentence.

1. Last week, Chief Ryman (captured)/has captured the convict

who escaped from the Pines Correctional Institution.

2. Our neighbors dumped/(have dumped) their garbage in an empty

lot for many years now.

3. My arthritis was/(has been) giving me trouble, yet I am reluctant to

go to the doctor.

4. He (served)/has served in the navy but left to become a police officer.

5. Nancy canceled her plane reservations and (notified)/has notified

the car rental agency.

6. Ice cream was/(has been) a popular dessert for years now.

7. We (worked)/have worked together at the Farmers' Market for six

months and are now opening our own restaurant.

8. Lenny (contacted)/has contacted four dry cleaning stores and

finally found one that cleans curtains.

9. I (waited)/have waited at the bus stop for an hour and then I gave

up and went home.

10. The cook and the cashier at the coffee shop worked/(have worked)

there since 1997.

THE PAST PERFECT TENSE

The **past perfect tense** is made up of the past participle form of the verb with *had* as a helping verb. You can use the past perfect tense to show more than one event in the past; that is, you can use it to show when two or more events happened in the past but at different times:

past tense: Alan *cut* the grass.
past perfect tense: Alan *had cut* the grass by the time David arrived. (Alan cut the grass *before* David arrived. Both events happened in the past, but one happened earlier than the other.)

past tense: The professor *lectured* for an hour.
past perfect tense: The professor *had lectured* for an hour when he pulled out a surprise quiz. (Lecturing came first; pulling out a surprise quiz came second. Both actions are in the past.)

The past perfect is especially useful because you write most of your essays in the past tense, and you often need to get further back into the past. Just remember to use *had* with the past participle of the verb, and you'll have the past perfect tense.

Practice

Distinguishing Between the Past and the Past Perfect Tenses

Circle the correct verb tense in the following sentences. Be sure to look carefully at the meaning of each sentence.

1. The bird flew/(had flown) out of the cage only seconds before I raced to close the cage door.

2. I needed crutches last week because I reinjured/(had reinjured) my knee playing football a month earlier.

3. Crystal won the art contest yesterday; she worked/(had worked) to win the award for years.

4. At the family dinner, I (kept)/had kept silent while my brother bragged about his new job.

5. Every Sunday, Leon (went)/had gone to lunch at his favorite Cuban restaurant.

6. Marian's mother wanted to know if we left/(had left) a package at her front door.

7. As Thomas (drove)/had driven the car with one hand, he used his other hand to point out famous landmarks.

8. My sister finished/(had finished) the coconut cake by the time I was ready for dessert.

9. He wondered if Sheila tossed/(had tossed) out the newspaper earlier in the day.

10. When the dog barked excitedly, the old man (ran)/had run to the window.

Small Reminders About Verbs

There are a few errors that people tend to make with verbs. If you are aware of these errors, you will be on the lookout for them as you edit your writing.

Used to: Be careful when you write that someone *used to* do, say, or feel something. It is incorrect to write *use to*.

   not this: Wendy ~~use to~~ make pancakes for breakfast.
   but this: Wendy *used to* make pancakes for breakfast.

not this: They ~~use to~~ live on my street.

but this: They *used to* live on my street.

Supposed to: Be careful when you write that someone is *supposed to* do, say, or feel something. It is incorrect to write *suppose to.*

not this: He was ~~suppose to~~ repair my watch yesterday.

but this: He was *supposed to* repair my watch yesterday.

not this: I am ~~suppose to~~ make dinner tomorrow.

but this: I am *supposed to* make dinner tomorrow.

Could have, should have, would have: Using *of* instead of *have* is another error with verbs.

not this: He ~~could of~~ sent me a card.

but this: He *could have* sent me a card.

not this: You ~~should of~~ been more careful.

but this: You *should have* been more careful.

not this: Norman ~~would of~~ enjoyed the music.

but this: Norman *would have* enjoyed the music.

Would have/had: If you are writing about that something that might have been possible but that did not happen, use *had* as the helping verb.

not this: If he ~~would have~~ been friendlier, he would not be alone now.

but this: If he *had* been friendlier, he would not be alone now.

not this: I wish the plane fare ~~would have~~ cost less.

but this: I wish the plane fare *had* cost less.

not this: If David ~~would have~~ controlled his temper, he would be a free man today.

but this: If David *had* controlled his temper, he would be a free man today.

Exercise 7   Connect

Editing a Paragraph for Small Errors in Verbs

Correct the eight errors in *used to, supposed to, could have, should have, would have,* and *would have/had* in the following paragraph. Write your corrections in the space above the lines.

Looking back on my high school years, I realize I should have acted different-

ly. First, I am sorry that I didn't take my senior year seriously. I ~~use~~ *used* to cut classes

all the time in my last year of high school. I believed that senior year was my last

chance to play and to live a wild life because I would soon be working a full-time

job or attending college. If I ~~would have~~ *had* taken senior year more seriously, I would

be having an easier time in my college classes, especially my math class. I should

~~of~~ *have* paid attention to my high school math teacher when he said I was ~~suppose~~ *supposed* to

study more. He warned me that I needed to know certain basic concepts if I

wanted to survive in college. I could ~~of~~ *have* learned a great deal from that man. Last, I

had
wish I ~~would of~~ taken a foreign language in high school. Then I could ~~of~~ entered
                                                                                            have

college with a foundation in French or Spanish and gone into an intermediate

level course. Instead, I am now required to take both Elementary and Intermedi-

had
ate French or Spanish in order to graduate. If I ~~would~~ have known in my senior

year what I know now, I would be having an easier time in college.

Exercise 8   **Collaborate**

Writing Sentences with the Correct Verb Forms

Do this exercise with a partner or a group. Write or complete each of the following sentences. When you have finished the exercise, be ready to share your answers with the group or with the class.

Answers Will Vary.

Possible answers shown at right.

1. Complete this sentence and add a verb in the correct tense:
He had spoken to my mother before he

   offered me a summer job in California.

2. Write a sentence that uses the words *done volunteer work* in the middle of the sentence.

   Bertine and Pierre have done volunteer work for Habitat for Humanity

   for four summers.

3. Complete this sentence and add a verb in the correct tense:
The painter was standing on the top rung of the ladder when he

   dropped the can of blue paint.

4. Write a sentence that includes the phrases *have been* and *for three years*.

   My parents have been planning this vacation for three years.

5. Complete this sentence: If Larry had taken better care of his car,

   he would not be spending so much on repairs now.

6. Write a sentence that contains the words *would have*.

   Shelley would have brought the baby pictures if she had known you

   were going to be here.

7. Write a sentence that includes both these helping verbs: *can* and *could.*

When Sam was ten, he could ride his bike to school; now, at sixteen,

he can ride in his friend's car.

8. Complete this sentence:

By the time the police arrived, the robbers

had escaped through the back door.

_____

9. Write a sentence that includes the words *for many years* and *has given.*

For many years, Mrs. Castellano has given us vegetables from her

garden.

10. Write a sentence that includes the words *Our family used to.*

Our family used to live at the end of a dirt road, but now the road is

a major highway.

Exercise 9

Connect

A Comprehensive Exercise: Editing a Paragraph for Errors in Verb Tense

Correct the eight errors in verb tense in the following paragraph. Write your corrections in the space above the lines.

An experience yesterday showed me just how resourceful I can be. Late in the

                                                          had

afternoon, I was alone in the office, working overtime. I just finished my work at my

                                  ran

workstation when I smelled smoke. I ~~have~~ ran to the outer office where I saw deep

                                            approached

gray smoke coming from a wastepaper basket. I ~~was approaching~~ the basket care-

fully; then I saw a large flame at the center of the smoke. The flame had already

spread from the basket to a nearby cardboard box. Immediately, I took action. I did

not stop to search frantically for a fire extinguisher. I did not run back to my desk to

                                     rushed   used

grab my briefcase or laptop. Instead, I ~~was~~ rushing outside to safety and ~~had~~ used

my cell phone to call the fire department. I calmed down when the firefighters

                        said   had

arrived. They ~~were saying~~ I ~~have~~ done the right thing by leaving a room full of paper

and flammable chemicals like toner for the copy machine. In the past, I often hoped

                                              can

I would behave well in a crisis. Now I know I ~~could~~.

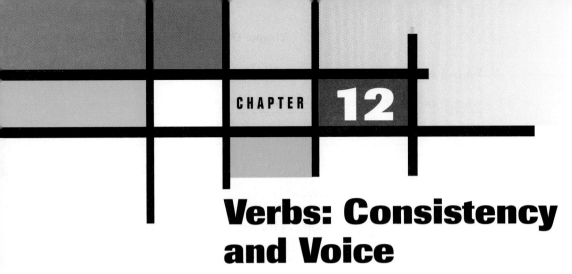

CHAPTER 12

Verbs: Consistency and Voice

Remember that your choice of verb form indicates the time (tense) of your statements. Be careful not to shift from one tense to another unless you have a reason to change the time.

CONSISTENT VERB TENSES

TEACHING TIP:

This is a good time to review parallel structure. See Chapter 7 for parallelism in sentences, pp. 71–78.

Staying in one tense (unless you have a reason to change tenses) is called **consistency of verb tense**.

> **incorrect shifts in tense:**
> He *raced* through the yellow light, *stepped* on the gas, and *cuts* off a
>   driver in the left lane.
> A woman in a black dress *holds* a handkerchief to her face and
>   *moaned* softly.

You can correct these errors by putting all the verbs in the same tense:

> **consistent present tense:**
> He *races* through the yellow light, *steps* on the gas, and *cuts* off a dri-
>   ver in the left lane.
> A woman in a black dress *holds* a handkerchief to her face and
>   *moans* softly.

> **consistent past tense:**
> He *raced* through the yellow light, *stepped* on the gas, and *cut* off a
>   driver in the left lane.
> A woman in a black dress *held* a handkerchief to her face and
>   *moaned* softly.

Whether you correct the errors by changing all the verbs to the present tense or by changing them all to the past tense, you are making the tense *consistent*. Consistency of verb tenses is important when you describe events because it helps the reader understand what happened and when it happened.

Exercise 1

Practice

Correcting Sentences That Are Inconsistent in Tense

In each sentence that follows, one verb is inconsistent in tense. Cross it out and write the correct tense above it. The first one is done for you.

1. The driver was extremely apologetic: she took full responsibility for
   looked
   the fender-bender, offered to pay all and ~~looks~~ very concerned.

2. When the leaves fall from the trees, my husband buys a stack of
   cleans
   firewood, ~~cleaned~~ the fireplace, and builds a warm, comforting fire.

3. Annoying sales calls come at dinner time and offer us magazine
   urge
   subscriptions, invite us to buy insurance, or ~~urged~~ us to get a
   burial plot.

4. Ronald and I belong to the same gym, and we ~~ran~~ into one
   run
   another in the pool or meet in the weight room.

5. My father took his car to City Automotive because he ~~likes~~ the
   liked
   service and trusted the mechanics.

6. For three days in a row we tried calling the station, but the line
   lost
   was always busy and we ~~lose~~ our patience.

7. He answers my questions sarcastically and seems irritated if I
   want
   ~~wanted~~ an explanation for his behavior.

8. Because the park closed at sundown, local teens ~~lose~~ a gathering
   lost
   place and looked for somewhere else to meet.

9. In our biology class, we went over the test grades and reviewed
   ran
   the test questions, but we ~~run~~ out of time for the new material.

10. Although Lucy claims she is on a budget, she ~~spent~~ more than I do
    spends
    when we go shopping.

Exercise 2

Connect

Editing Paragraphs for Consistency of Tense

Read the following paragraphs. Then cross out any verbs that are inconsistent in tense and write the corrections above them. Each paragraph has four errors.

1.   For my children, summer vacation means freedom from school,
but it is a difficult time for me. My two boys, Adam, age six, and Troy,

                        love
age seven, ~~loved~~ being out of school. They enjoy staying up late on

week nights and sleeping late in the morning. They are thrilled not to

have homework and expect the vacation period to be a long series of

                                am
fun and games. I, on the other hand, ~~was~~ confronted with several ques-

tions. I have to find someone or some place willing to care for my boys

        am
while I ~~was~~ at my job. Summer camp is expensive, and a five-day-a-

              costs
week sitter ~~cost~~ a fortune. I do not want to leave the boys with my

mother; they get bored, and she is too old to handle them. It takes some

thinking, but eventually I find ways to handle my vacation dilemma. I

usually find an activities program at the local YMCA and pay a neighbor

to watch the boys after the program. My sons are happy, and I am

relieved that the summer problems are solved.

2.   Raoul discovered a whole new side of himself when he took an art

class. At first Raoul did not want to take the class at all, but he needed a

humanities class in order to get his college degree. Since all the music

                                           had
and theater classes were closed, Raoul ~~has~~ no choice but to sign up for

a design class. He was sure the class would be full of talented artists,

                                would
and that he, a beginner, ~~will~~ make a fool of himself. However, the class

was
~~is~~ an introductory class, and everyone in it was on the same level as

Raoul. He soon discovered that he loved working with lines and colors

and creating such things as album covers and posters. Raoul's teacher

also praised Raoul for some outstanding work. Over the semester, Raoul

                                        learned
developed an appreciation for art and ~~learns~~ the importance of design in

everyday objects like billboards, magazines, and store windows.

Exercise 3   **Rewriting a Paragraph for Consistent Verb Tenses**

👥 *Collaborate*   The following paragraph has some inconsistencies in verb tenses: it shifts
between past and present tenses. Working with a group, correct the errors
in consistency by writing all the verbs in the past tense. You can write your
corrections in the space above the errors.

When you have completed the corrections, have one member of the group read the paragraph aloud, as a final check.

INSTRUCTOR'S NOTE:

Corrections in the past tense are above the lines.

was   couldn't   wanted had

My first car is a compromise car. I can't afford what I want, so I have to

It was

compromise. It's an old Ford with 100,000 miles on the speedometer. The car was

was

not too attractive on the outside: the paint job is dull from years of exposure to

had

the sun, a piece of chrome has fallen off, and two of the tires were missing hub-

was

caps. Mechanically, the car is a mix of good and bad. My Ford started right up on

were   guzzled

the coldest mornings, but the brake linings are shot, and the car guzzles gas. As

was

for the interior, the upholstery is torn, so I disguised the tear with cheap seat cov-

had

ers. The dash has a small crack; on the other hand, the speakers were in good

wanted   had was

shape. What I want was a shiny, fast, new sport utility vehicle. What I have is an

was   ran

ancient Taurus. But it is mine, and it runs .

PASSIVE AND ACTIVE VOICE

TEACHING TIP:

The word "voice" may confuse students. Spend a few minutes discussing how this term applies to grammar.

Verbs not only have tenses; they have voices. When the subject in the sentence is doing something, the verb is in the ***active voice***. When something is done to the subject, the verb is in the ***passive voice***.

active voice:

I designed the album cover. (*I*, the subject, did it.)
My friends from college raised money for the homeless shelter.
   (*Friends*, the subject, did it.)

passive voice:

The album cover was designed by me. (The *cover*, the subject, didn't do anything. It received the action—it was designed.)
Money for the homeless shelter was raised by my friends from college. (*Money*, the subject, didn't do anything. It received the action—it was raised.)

Notice what happens when you use the passive voice instead of the active voice:

active voice: I designed the album cover.
passive voice: The album cover was designed by me.

TEACHING TIP:

Stress that the passive voice is easily overused. Remind students that using the active voice whenever possible leads to stronger and more precise writing.

The sentence in the passive voice is two words longer than the one in the active voice. However, the sentence that used the passive voice doesn't add any information, nor does it state the facts any more clearly than the one in the active voice.

Using the passive voice can make your sentences wordy, it can slow them down, and it can make them boring. The passive voice can also confuse readers. When the subject isn't doing anything, readers may have to look carefully to see who or what *is doing* something. Look at this sentence, for example:

A famous city landmark is being torn down.

Who is tearing down the landmark? In this sentence, it's impossible to find the answer to that question.

Of course, there will be times when you have to use the passive voice. For example, you may have to use it when you don't know who did something, as in these sentences:

Lana's car was stolen last week.
A bag of garbage was scattered all over my neighbor's lawn.

But in general, you should avoid using the passive voice; instead, rewrite sentences so they are in the active voice.

 Exercise 4
Practice

Rewriting Sentences, Changing the Passive Voice to the Active Voice

In the following sentences, change the passive voice to the active voice. If the original sentence doesn't tell you who or what performed the action, add words that tell you who or what did it. The first one is done for you.

1. One of Shakespeare's plays was performed at Green River High School last night.

    rewritten: Students at Green River High School performed one of Shakespeare's plays last night.

Answers Will Vary.

Possible answers shown at right.

2. Cecilia was promoted to assistant manager of Quality Food Mart by her boss.

    rewritten: Cecilia's boss promoted her to assistant manager of Quality Food Mart.

3. An offer to buy the house was made.

    rewritten: Mr. and Mrs. Reilly offered to buy the house.

4. On some weekends, the beach is closed by the lifeguards.

    rewritten: On some weekends, the lifeguards close the beach.

5. José's father was rescued from a burning house.

    rewritten: A stranger rescued José's father from a burning house.

6. An agreement has been signed by the buyer and the seller.

    rewritten: The buyer and seller have signed an agreement.

7. A delicious breakfast was made and eaten.

rewritten: Ingrid made and ate a delicious breakfast.

8. Apologies for the cruel joke have been offered.

rewritten: I offered my apologies for the cruel joke.

9. Great care was put into the preparations for the party.

rewritten: The family put great care into the preparations for the party.

10. A number of alternatives were considered by the disciplinary committee.

rewritten: The disciplinary committee considered a number of alternatives.

Exercise 5

Collaborate

Answers Will Vary.

Possible answers shown at right.

Rewriting a Paragraph, Changing It to the Active Voice

Do this exercise with a partner or a group. Rewrite the paragraph below, changing all the verbs that are in the passive voice to the active voice. To make these changes, you may have to add words, omit words, or change the structure of sentences. Write your changes in the space above the lines. Be ready to read your new version of the paragraph to another group or to the class.

the city council reached an important decision.   It decided
Last night an important decision was reached by the city council. A decision
to add bike paths along all main roads.   Cyclists were overjoyed by the
to add bike paths along all main roads was made. Cyclists have been made over-
news because they have been campaigning for bike paths for years.
joyed by the news because the paths have been campaigned for, by cyclists, for
Bike riders have suffered from dangerous conditions.
years. Dangerous conditions have been suffered by the bike riders. In addition,
impatient motorists have frequently harassed cyclists.
harassment by impatient motorists has been frequently endured by cyclists.
The lack of bike paths created an ugly conflict between drivers and cyclists.
An ugly conflict between drivers and cyclists was created by the lack of bike
But the city council has removed all the danger and bad feeling.
paths. But all the bad feeling and danger has been changed by the city council.
Bike paths will make bicycle riding safer and more pleasant.
Bicycle riding will be made safer and more pleasant by bike paths.

Avoiding Unnecessary Shifts in Voice

Just as you should be consistent in the tense of verbs, you should be consistent in the voice of verbs. Do not shift from active to passive, or vice versa, without a good reason to do so.

active   passive
shift: *Carl wrote* the song, but the *credit was taken* by Tom.

active   active
rewritten: *Carl wrote* the song, but *Tom took* the credit.

passive
shift: Several *suggestions were made* by the vice president,

active
yet the *president rejected* all of them.

active
rewritten: The *vice president made* several suggestions, yet

active
the *president rejected* all of them.

Being consistent can help you to write clearly and smoothly.

Exercise 6	**Rewriting Sentences to Correct Shifts in Voice**
Practice	Rewrite the following sentences so that all the verbs are in the active voice. You may change the wording to make the sentences clear, smooth, and consistent in voice.

Answers Will Vary.

Possible answers shown at right.

1. My feelings were hurt by Andrea when she called me selfish.

   rewritten: Andrea hurt my feelings when she called me selfish.

2. A set of keys was found in the purse; the detective also discovered an old photograph in the purse.

   rewritten: The detective found a set of keys and an old photograph in the purse.

3. Lamar's attitude can be changed by you because you are honest with him.

   rewritten: You can change Lamar's attitude because you are honest with him.

4. It was agreed by a group of neighbors that the grass needs regular cutting.

   rewritten: A group of neighbors agreed that the grass needs regular cutting.

5. The crowd cheered the Olympic swimmer as a record for the backstroke was broken by her.

   rewritten: The crowd cheered the Olympic swimmer as she broke a record for the backstroke.

6. I was healthy all year until I was given the measles.

rewritten: <u>I was healthy all year until I got the measles.</u>

_____

7. If a secret meeting was set up by the players, they didn't tell me.

rewritten: <u>If the players set up a secret meeting, they didn't tell me.</u>

_____

8. The teacher expected excellence and a serious attitude was demanded from her students.

rewritten: <u>The teacher expected excellence and demanded a serious</u>

<u>attitude from her students.</u>

9. Some of my classmates are money-hungry; new cars, jewelry, and fine clothes are worshiped.

rewritten: <u>Some of my classmates are money-hungry; they worship</u>

<u>new cars, jewelry, and fine clothes.</u>

10. Minneapolis was chosen by the committee as the site of the conference; it is an accessible and friendly city.

rewritten: <u>The committee chose Minneapolis as the site of the</u>

<u>conference; it is an accessible and friendly city.</u>

Exercise 7

⊝⊝⊝ _Connect_

Editing a Paragraph for Consistency in Voice

The following paragraph contains five unnecessary shifts to the passive voice. Correct these shifts. Write your corrections in the space above the errors. You can add words, omit words, or change words.

When we invited friends to dinner, Dale and I worked together and cleaned

We felt

the apartment in no time. It was felt that we should fix up the apartment for our

guests. We did not want them to think we lived like pigs, so we put our heads

we devised a plan for a quick clean-up.   _Dale would make the_

together. Soon, a plan for a quick clean-up was devised. Beds were to be made

beds,   _I cleaned the kitchen_

by Dale, and I would pick up all the clothes on the floor. Then the kitchen was to

be cleaned while Dale vacuumed the living room. We worked fast since our

we had created a

friends were arriving in an hour. Just before they arrived, a reasonably clean

reasonably clean apartment.

apartment had been created by us. We were proud to show our friends the results

of our hard work.

A Comprehensive Exercise: Editing a Paragraph for Errors in Consistent Verb Tense and Voice

The following paragraph has four errors related to verb tense and voice. Correct the errors in the space above the lines.

she would have made a better choice.

If Danielle had taken my advice, then a better choice would have been made

by her. Instead, she rushed into the purchase of a car and bought a lemon. She

didn't listen to my warnings about getting a mechanic to test the car before she

was

bought it, or about shopping around for the best car deal. Danielle is too eager to

has been

have her own car, so she took the first car that caught her eye. She was impetu-

ous and impatient for years. In all the time I have known her, Danielle has never

stopped to think, and she did not think clearly yesterday. Rushing into a bad deal,

signed

she purchased a car with a cracked engine block and bad brakes. She just signs

the papers on the dotted line and wasted a great deal of her money.

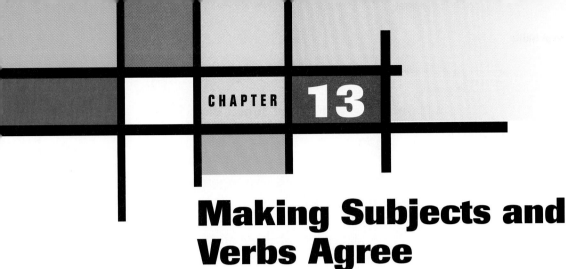

CHAPTER 13

Making Subjects and Verbs Agree

Subjects and verbs have to agree in number. That means a singular subject must be matched with a singular verb form and a plural subject must be matched with a plural verb form.

singular subject, singular verb
> *Nicole races* out of the house in the morning.

> **plural subject,**   **plural verb**
> *Christine, Michael, and Marie take* the train to work.

> **singular subject, singular verb**
> The old *song reminds* me of Mexico.

> **plural subject, plural verb**
> Greasy *hamburgers upset* my stomach.

Caution: Remember that a regular verb has an *-s* ending in one singular form in the present tense—the form that goes with *he, she, it,* or their equivalents:

-s endings in the present tense:

He *takes* good care of his dog.
She *concentrates* on her assignments.
It *looks* like a nice day.
Eddie *buys* high-octane gasoline.
Nancy *seems* pleased.
The apartment *comes* with cable television.

PRONOUNS USED AS SUBJECTS

Pronouns can be used as subjects. **Pronouns** are words that take the place of nouns. When pronouns are used as subjects, they must agree in number with verbs.

Following is a list of the subject pronouns and the regular verb forms that agree with them, in the present tense: **143**

Info BOX

Subject Pronouns and Present Tense Verb Forms

Pronoun	Verb	
I	walk	
you	walk	} all singular forms
he, she, it	walks	
we	walk	
you	walk	} all plural forms
they	walk	

In all the following sentences, the pronoun used as the subject of the sentence agrees in number with the verb:

singular pronoun, singular verb
I take good care of my daughter.

singular pronoun, singular verb
You sing like a professional entertainer.

singular pronoun, singular verb
She argues with conviction and courage.

plural pronoun, plural verb
We want a better deal on the apartment.

plural pronoun, plural verb
They accept my decision about moving.

Exercise 1   **Editing a Paragraph for Simple Errors in Subject-Verb Agreement**

⊖⊖⊖ *Connect*   There are six errors in subject-verb agreement in the following paragraph. If the verb does not agree with its subject, cross out the incorrect verb form and write the correct one above it.

My brother has a Saturday ritual that never varies. He always ~~wake~~ *wakes* up at the same time, 7:00 a.m. The first thing he ~~do~~ *does* is jog around the neighborhood to get his energy level up. Then he goes to the coffee shop on our street and brings home cups of freshly brewed coffee and a bag of jelly doughnuts. As he eats this breakfast, he watches cartoons on television. They are stupid, he admits, but they ~~makes~~ *make* him laugh. After the cartoons are over, he gets in his car and drives to his friend Joe's house. He and Joe ~~watches~~ *watch* any game— football, basketball, hockey—they can find on television. Drinking Pepsi and eating potato chips, they watch the games all afternoon. When it is time for dinner, they head for a sports bar that ~~show~~ *shows* games on a big-screen television. My brother ~~love~~ *loves* his Saturdays of sports and junk food.

SPECIAL PROBLEMS WITH AGREEMENT

Agreement seems fairly simple, doesn't it? If a subject is singular, use a singular verb form; if a subject is plural, use a plural verb form. However, there are certain problems with agreement that will come up in your writing. Sometimes it is difficult to find the subject of a sentence; at other times, it can be difficult to determine whether a subject is singular or plural.

Finding the Subject

When you are checking for subject-verb agreement, you can find the real subject of the sentence by first eliminating the prepositional phrases. To find the real subject, put parentheses around the prepositional phrases. Then it will be easy to find the subject because nothing in a prepositional phrase can be the subject of a sentence.

prepositional phrases in parentheses:

S   V
A person (with good math skills) *is* a good candidate (for the job).

S   V
One (of the children) (from the village) (in the hills) *is* my cousin.

S   V
The *restaurant* (down the road) (from Cindy's house) *is* open all night.

S   V
Roy, (with his charm and style), *is* popular (with the ladies).

Exercise 2

Practice

Finding the Subject and Verb by Recognizing Prepositional Phrases

Put parentheses around all the prepositional phrases in the following sentences, and identify the subject and verb by writing an *S* or a *V* above them.

               S (   )V   (   )
1. A person with your talents is an asset to any company.

           S (   )(   )V
2. The cookies in the dairy case at the supermarket are slice-and-
               (   )
bake cookies for busy families.

  (   ) S   V
3. With no sense of responsibility, Jeff missed the most important
   (   )
day of his son's life.

         S (   )V   (   )
4. The beautiful cat on my bed is a former stray from the animal shelter.

        S (   )(   )V   (   )(
5. The people at the end of the line are some friends of mine from
)
Davenport.

        S   (   ) V   (
6. A salesperson from an insurance company offered us a deal on life
)
insurance.

        S (   )(   )(   )V
7. One of the funniest movies on my list of all-time favorites is
            (   )
<u>Scream,</u> a horror film with many laughs.

8. In the autumn, she carves a pumpkin into a smiling face.

9. In a panic, I searched between the pages of the newspaper for my lost credit card.

10. On his day off, Nelson drives from Parkview to Kingsbury in three hours.

Exercise 3

Practice

Selecting the Correct Verb Form by Identifying Prepositional Phrases

In the following sentences, put parentheses around all the prepositional phrases; then circle the verb that agrees with the subject.

1. The girl with the dark eyes (is/are) giving me a signal from the other side of the room.

2. Several of the items in her closet (is/are) worth a great deal of money.

3. A realistic assessment of the city's problems (is/are) coming from the director of the budget committee.

4. The commuters on the stalled train (has/have) no idea of the length of the delay.

5. A quick meal between classes (isn't/aren't) good for your digestion.

6. The last bell of the school day (was/were) a signal for whooping and shouting among the students.

7. One of the letters on the table (is/are) a note from your mother with a check in it.

8. The oil stain under my car (makes/make) me afraid of big car repair bills.

9. One of the easiest forms of exercise (is/are) walking with a dog.

10. A representative of the airlines (has/have) announced a delay in the departure of the flight.

Changed Word Order

You are probably used to looking for the subject of a sentence in front of the verb, but not all sentences follow this pattern. Questions, sentences beginning with words like *here* or *there*, and other sentences change the word order. Therefore, you have to check carefully for subject-verb agreement:

sentences with changed word order:

Where *are* the *packages*?
(V) (S)

When *is Mr. Hernandez giving* the exam?
(V) (S) (V)

Behind the trees *is* a picnic *table*.
(V) (S)

There *are crumbs* on the floor.
(V) (S)

There *is* an *answer* to your question.
(V) (S)

Exercise 4

Practice

Making Subjects and Verbs Agree in Sentences with Changed Word Order

In each of the following sentences, underline the subject; then circle the correct verb form.

1. There is/are some unhappy people on that plane.

2. Among the travelers was/were a tourist from a small city in China.

3. Beneath the cherry trees sits/sit a bird with bright yellow feathers.

4. When is/are your grandparents moving to California?

5. By the edge of the road was/were a vegetable stand with bright orange pumpkins.

6. Here is/are your copies of the lease.

7. At the back of my mind was/were a plan for the term paper.

8. Where has/have the football players gone?

9. From the top of the stadium comes/come a piercing scream.

10. Beyond the city limits is/are a popular night club and a sports club.

Exercise 5

Collaborate

TEACHING TIP:

Before students begin this exercise, remind them that a verb must always agree with its subject and that subjects are not always found at the beginning of sentences.

Writing Sentences with Subject-Verb Agreement in Changed Word Order

Do this exercise with a partner or a group. Complete the following, making each into a sentence. Be sure the subject and verb agree. The first one is done for you.

1. From the back of the room came three loud cheers.

2. At the back of the dark closet hides a little mouse.

3. There are an old suitcase and a trunk in the attic.

4. Among the objects in the treasure chest was *a map.*

5. Beyond the mountains is *a log cabin.*

6. Below the old castle stand *ancient oak trees.*

7. With every good action comes *a feeling of achievement.*

8. On the edge of the bridge is *a seagull.*

9. Around the concert stage sit *some eager fans.*

10. Here is *a dish of strawberries.*

COMPOUND SUBJECTS

A **compound subject** is two or more subjects joined by *and, or,* or *nor.* When subjects are joined by *and,* they are usually plural:

compound subjects joined by *and*:

   S   S   V
Bill and *Chris are* good tennis players.

       S   S   V
The *garage* and the *basement are* full of water.

     S   S   V
A *restaurant* and a *motel are* across the road.

Caution: Be sure to check for a compound subject when the word order changes.

compound subjects in changed word order:

     V   S   S
There *are* a *restaurant* and a *motel* across the road. (Two things, a restaurant and a motel, are across the road.)

   V   S   S
Here *are* your *notebook* and *pencil.* (Your notebook and pencil, two things, are here.)

When subjects are joined by *or, either . . . or, neither . . . nor, not only. . . but also,* the verb form agrees with the subject closest to the verb.

compound subjects with *or, either . . . or, neither . . . nor, not only . . . but also*:

singular S   plural S, plural V
Christine or the *neighbors are* making dinner.

   plural S   singular S, singular V
The *neighbors* or *Christine is* making dinner.

       singular S   plural S plural V
Not only my *mother* but also my *brothers were* delighted with the gift.

       plural S   singular S, singular V
Not only my *brothers* but also my *mother was* delighted with the gift.

       plural S   singular S, singular V
Either the *tenants* or the *landlord has* to back down.

singular S   plural S, plural V
Either the *landlord* or the *tenants have* to back down.

plural S   singular s, singular V
Neither the rose *bushes* nor the lemon *tree fits* in that corner of
the yard.

singular S   plural S, plural V
Neither the lemon *tree* nor the rose *bushes fit* in that corner of
the yard.

Exercise 6

Practice

Making Subjects and Verbs Agree: Compound Subjects

Circle the correct form of the verb in each of the following sentences:

1. Heavy blankets or a thick quilt (is/are) essential in this cold weather.

2. After that enormous dinner, Stephen and Michelle (was/were) ready to fall asleep.

3. There (is/are) a new movie theater and a pizza place near the mall.

4. Either Ms. Lin or her uncles (subscribes/subscribe) to <u>Newsweek</u>.

5. At the bottom of the page (is/are) a photograph of the Vietnam Wall and a poem.

6. The boys or the babysitter (is/are) at home.

7. Here (is/are) a box of toys from your kindergarten days and an old scrapbook.

8. Not only the bus driver but also the passengers (is/are) enjoying the new bus.

9. Professor Wykowski or Professor Stein (is/are) lecturing on acid rain today.

10. Washing my car and listening to my CDs (was/were) typical weekend activities for me.

Exercise 7

Practice

Recognizing Subjects and Verbs: a Review

Being sure that subjects and verbs agree often depends on recognizing subject and verbs in sentences with changed word order, prepositional phrases, and compound subjects. To review the subject-verb patterns of sentences, underline all the subjects and verbs in the following selection. Put an **S** above the subjects and a **V** above the verbs.

This excerpt is from an essay by Edna Buchanan, a former prize-winning journalist for the *Miami Herald* and now a famous crime novelist.

Miami's Most Dangerous Profession

Miami's most dangerous profession is not police work or fire fighting; it is driving a cab. For taxi drivers, many of them poor immigrants, murder is an occupational hazard. All-night gas station attendants and convenience store clerks used to be at high risk, but steps were taken to protect them. Gas pumps now switch to self-serve after dark, with exact change only, and the attendants are locked in bullet-proof booths. Convenience stores were redesigned and drop safes were installed, leaving little cash available.

But the life of a taxi driver is just as risky as it was twenty years ago when I covered my first killing of a cabbie. Bullet-proof glass could be placed between the driver and passengers, but most owners say it is too expensive, and besides, there is no foolproof way to protect oneself totally from somebody riding in the same car.

Indefinite Pronouns

Certain pronouns, called **indefinite pronouns**, always take a singular verb.

Info BOX

Indefinite Pronouns

one	nobody	nothing	each
anyone	anybody	anything	either
someone	somebody	something	neither
everyone	everybody	everything	

If you want to write clearly and correctly, you must memorize these words and remember that they always use singular verbs. Using your common sense isn't enough because some of these words seem plural: for example, *everybody* seems to mean more than one person, but in grammatically correct English, it takes a singular verb. Here are some examples of the pronouns used with singular verbs:

indefinite pronouns and singular verbs:

singular S   singular V
Each of my friends *is* athletic.

singular S   singular V
Everyone in the supermarket *is looking* for a bargain.

singular S   singular V
Anybody from our Spanish class *is* capable of translating the letter.

TEACHING TIP:

Emphasize that indefinite words often end in the words "one," "body," or "thing," and since these words are singular, students can then remember to use the singular verb form.

singular S   singular V

Someone from the maintenance department *is* working on the heater.

singular S   singular V

One of Roberta's nieces *is* in my sister's ballet class.

singular S   singular V

Neither of the cakes *is* expensive.

You can memorize the indefinite pronouns as the *-one*, *-thing*, and *-body* words—every*one*, every*thing*, every*body*, and so on—plus *each*, *either*, and *neither*.

Exercise 8

Practice

Making Subjects and Verbs Agree: Using Indefinite Pronouns

Circle the correct verb in the following sentences.

1. Anybody from the Southern states (knows/know) about hot summers.

2. Each of the boys (sends/send) money to Aunt Lucille.

3. (Is/Are) something the matter with the television?

4. Nothing in the refrigerator (looks/look) appetizing.

5. Neither of the dogs (barks/bark) when the doorbell rings.

6. Someone in our neighborhood (is/are) playing a radio.

7. Everything in the attic and in the basement (needs/need) to be sorted and boxed.

8. I don't think anybody in our family (wants/want) a big celebration for New Year's Eve.

9. Something in the soup or in the vegetables (smells/smell) strange.

10. One of Matthew's worst habits (is/are) worrying about insignificant details.

Exercise 9

Practice

Making Subjects and Verbs Agree: Using Indefinite Pronouns

Circle the correct verb in the following sentences.

1. Here (is/are) everybody from school.

2. Nobody with good math skills (is/are) afraid of that test.

3. Everybody in my exercise class (wears/wear) black tee shirts.

4. (Has/Have) anyone from White Plains called?

5. Somebody at the movies ((was)/were) annoying me.

6. If you look closely, nothing in those books ((talks)/talk) about the subject.

7. I know that neither of the brothers ((has)/have) an athletic scholarship.

8. Each of the muffins ((is)/are) wrapped in tissue paper.

9. Anyone from the suburbs ((has)/have) to take the train to the city.

10. You can have rice pudding or lemon cake; either ((is)/are) included in the price of the dinner.

Editing for Subject-Verb Agreement in a Paragraph with Indefinite Pronouns

The following paragraph has five errors in the agreement of indefinite pronouns and verbs. Correct the errors in the spaces above the lines.

It is unfortunate that many people refuse to get involved in their community. Of course, everyone in town have *has* some excuse for not doing volunteer work, joining a club, or participating in a community program. One of the biggest excuses is, "I'm too busy." But everyone knows, deep down, that people can always find time to do what they truly want to do. Everybody in our hectic society cope *copes* with responsibilities at home, or at work, or at school, yet sometimes the busiest people are the ones who find time to get involved in their communities. Another common excuse is, "I don't have any talents to offer a club or a volunteer group." Talent, however, isn't an issue. It doesn't take talent to clean up a neglected park. Anybody are *is* capable of serving food in a soup kitchen. Somebody with no singing voice or musical skills are *is* still welcome at a community playhouse, to build scenery or sell tickets. There are *is* something for everybody to contribute to a community, and contributing can be fun.

Collective Nouns

Collective nouns refer to more than one person or thing.

Info BOX

Some Common Collective Nouns

team	company	council
class	corporation	government
committee	family	group
audience	jury	crowd

Collective nouns usually take a singular verb.

collective nouns and singular verbs:

singular S, singular V
The *class is meeting* in the library today.

singular S, singular V
The *audience was* bored.

singular S, singular V
The *jury is examining* the evidence.

A singular verb is used because the group is meeting, or feeling bored, or examining, *as one unit.*

Collective nouns take a plural verb *only* when the members of the group are acting individually, not as a unit.

collective noun with a plural verb:

plural S,   plural V
The football *team are arguing* among themselves. (The phrase *among themselves* shows that the team is not acting as one unit.)

Exercise 11

Practice

Making Subjects and Verbs Agree: Using Collective Nouns

Circle the correct verb in each of the following sentences:

1. His family (is/are) celebrating the Fourth of July with a big

barbecue at home.

2. The Classic Automobile Club (was/were) founded in 1965.

3. The board of directors (is/are) considering the cost of advertising

for a new treasurer.

4. The company with the most awards for quality (is/are) Food

Service America.

5. My team of bowlers (is/are) friendly and funny.

6. The jury (has/have) reached a verdict.

7. A group of visitors to the museum (was/were) quarreling among

themselves.

8. After the concert, the audience ((was)/were) screaming for an encore.

9. While the coach lectures and shouts, the team ((looks)/look) serious.

10. Our Student Council never ((sponsors)/sponsor) dances on weeknights.

MAKING SUBJECTS AND VERBS AGREE: A REVIEW

As you have probably realized, making subjects and verbs agree is not as simple as it first appears. But if you can remember the basic ideas in this section, you will be able to apply them automatically as you edit your own writing. Following is a quick summary of subject-verb agreement:

Info BOX

Making Subjects and Verbs Agree: A Summary

1. Subjects and verbs should agree in number: singular subjects get singular verbs; plural subjects get plural verbs.

2. When pronouns are used as subjects, they must agree in number with verbs.

3. Nothing in a prepositional phrase can be the subject of a sentence.

4. Questions, sentences beginning with *here* or *there*, and other sentences can change word order.

5. Compound subjects joined by *and* are usually plural.

6. When subjects are joined by *or*, *either . . . or*, *neither . . . nor*, or *not only . . . but also*, the verb form agrees with the subject closest to the verb.

7. Indefinite pronouns always take singular verbs.

8. Collective nouns usually take singular verbs.

 A Comprehensive Exercise on Subject-Verb Agreement

Practice   This exercise covers all the rules on subject-verb agreement. Circle the correct verb form in the following sentences.

1. The softball team (is/(are)) debating the manager's decision among

   themselves.

2. A company in the suburbs ((provides)/provide) transportation to

   and from the city.

3. How (was/(were)) the cookies from the new bakery?

4. Each year, faith and optimism (grows/(grow)) in the renovated

   neighborhoods of my city.

5. Anybody with a golden retriever ((knows)/know) that breed needs

   regular exercise.

6. Beneath the layers of tissue paper (was/were) two lace scarves.

7. Each of Isaac's friends (is/are) connected to the music business.

8. Neither Maria nor her children (like/likes) living on a farm.

9. A job applicant with experience in retailing and good computer skills (has/have) an advantage over less qualified applicants.

10. If the weather doesn't get warmer, someone (is/are) going to have an accident on the ice.

Exercise 13

Practice

Another Comprehensive Exercise on Subject-Verb Agreement

This exercise covers all the rules on subject-verb agreement. Circle the correct verb form in the following sentences.

1. There (is/are) a turkey sandwich and some macaroni salad in the refrigerator.

2. Everything in Senator Davis' speeches (seems/seem) logical to me.

3. When the days get longer, the family (has/have) summer picnics in the park.

4. In times of war, the government of the United States (has/have) called on citizens to enlist in the armed forces.

5. Nothing in his chest of toys (delights/delight) my son more than his teddy bear.

6. Yesterday there (was/were) a violent incident at the Pinetree Apartments.

7. Where in the world (is/are) your books?

8. Either of the girls (is/are) a good choice for class president.

9. Two weeks ago, everyone in our class (was/were) wearing heavy sweaters.

10. Sometimes the most expensive cars needs/need the most maintenance.

Exercise 14

 *Collaborate*

Writing Sentences with Subject-Verb Agreement: A Comprehensive Exercise

Working with a partner or a group, write two sentences for each of the following phrases. Use a verb that fits and put it in the present tense. Be sure that the verb agrees with the subject. The first one is done for you.

1. A group of Ecuadoran students visits my high school once a year, in the fall.

   A group of Ecuadoran students corresponds with a group of high school seniors from Milwaukee.

2. A box of firecrackers is not a toy.

   A box of firecrackers leads to tragedy almost every year.

3. Neither Dracula nor Frankenstein has many friends.

   Neither Dracula nor Frankenstein is a modern monster.

4. The crowd at the prize fight wants a dramatic conflict.

   The crowd at the prize fight is smaller than I expected.

5. Everyone at the movies is a fan of action films.

   Everyone at the movies is waiting in line for tickets.

6. Not only the pilot but also the passengers are shaken by the turbulence.

   Not only the pilot but also the passengers are glad the flight is over.

7. Each of his brothers works at the family restaurant.

   Each of his brothers plays soccer on the weekends.

8. Someone with psychic powers is investigating the case of the

missing suitcase.

Someone with psychic powers is the main character in the movie.

_____

9. The freshman class has to register today.

_____

The freshman class is having a picnic on the lawn.

_____

10. Everything in my computer files is related to my business.

_____

Everything in my computer files needs to be backed up.

_____

Exercise 15

👥 *Collaborate*

Create Your Own Text on Subject-Verb Agreement

Work with a partner or a group to create your own grammar handbook. Following is a list of rules on subject-verb agreement. Write two sentences that are examples of each rule. Write an *S* above the subject of each sentence and a *V* above the verb. After you've completed this exercise, trade it for another group's exercise. Check that group's examples while it checks yours. The first one is done for you.

Rule 1: Subjects and verbs should agree in number: singular subjects get singular verb forms; plural subjects get plural verb forms.

example 1:
      S V
    An apple is a healthy snack.

_____

example 2:
      S   V
    Runners need large quantities of water.

_____

Answers Will Vary.

Possible answers shown at right.

Rule 2: When pronouns are used as subjects, they must agree in number with verbs.

example 1:
      S V
    He is a conscientious worker.

_____

example 2:
      S V
    They are my closest relatives.

_____

Rule 3: Nothing in a prepositional phrase can be the subject of a sentence.

example 1:
$$\overset{S}{\text{Everybody}} \text{ in the apartments } \overset{V}{\text{wants}} \text{ a better lease.}$$

example 2:
$$\overset{S}{\text{One}} \text{ of the swimmers in the semifinals } \overset{V}{\text{is}} \text{ my boyfriend.}$$

Rule 4: Questions, sentences beginning with *here* or *there*, and other sentences can change word order.

example 1:
$$\overset{V}{\text{Here}} \text{ are your algebra } \overset{S}{\text{workbook}} \text{ and Spanish } \overset{S}{\text{dictionary.}}$$

example 2:
$$\overset{V}{\text{Where}} \text{ are my } \overset{S}{\text{hat}} \text{ and } \overset{S}{\text{coat?}}$$

Rule 5: Compound subjects joined by *and* are usually plural.

example 1:
$$\overset{S}{\text{Nicholas}} \text{ and } \overset{S}{\text{Mack}} \overset{V}{\text{ are}} \text{ your nearest neighbors.}$$

example 2:
$$\overset{S}{\text{Dusting}} \text{ and } \overset{S}{\text{sweeping}} \overset{V}{\text{ are}} \text{ time-consuming.}$$

Rule 6: When subjects are joined by *or, either . . . or, neither . . . nor,* or *not only . . . but also,* the verb form agrees with the subject closest to the verb.

example 1:
$$\text{Neither } \overset{S}{\text{Gary}} \text{ nor his } \overset{S}{\text{sisters}} \overset{V}{\text{ have}} \text{ the address.}$$

example 2:
$$\text{The } \overset{S}{\text{dogs}} \text{ or the } \overset{S}{\text{cat}} \overset{V}{\text{ has}} \text{ been digging in the yard.}$$

Rule 7: Indefinite pronouns always take singular verbs.

example 1:
$$\overset{S}{\text{Everybody}} \text{ in the office } \overset{V}{\text{knows}} \text{ Sal.}$$

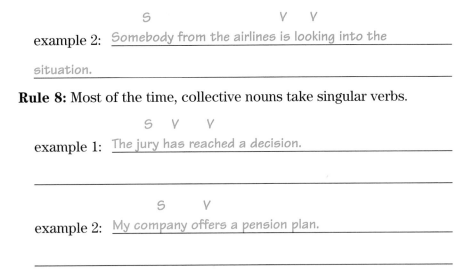

example 2: Somebody from the airlines is looking into the

situation.

Rule 8: Most of the time, collective nouns take singular verbs.

example 1: The jury has reached a decision.

example 2: My company offers a pension plan.

Exercise 16

⊖⊖⊖ *Connect*

A Comprehensive Exercise: Editing a Paragraph for Subject-Verb Agreement

The following paragraph has seven errors in subject-verb agreement. Correct the errors in the spaces above the lines.

         is
  The Lymon Company are making a change that will be very welcome to

many employees. My husband, who works for the Lymon Company, came

home yesterday and told me the news. The company is building a day care

center for the workers' children on the grounds of the factory. My husband

       are   *have*
and I am delighted by the news. We has two children under the age of five,

               have
and neither a babysitter nor local day care centers has worked out for us.

The construction of a center at my husband's workplace is a dream come

          is
true. Among his deepest desires are the wish to be near his children during

the day so he can check on them. This wish will soon come true. My hus-

band is not the only employee at Lymon who is thrilled by the day care plan.

           is
Everyone with small children are talking about the new child-care facilities.

The facilities will make the Lymon factory a more attractive place to work.

In fact, any parent with two job offers is now more likely to choose working

                has
at Lymon because child care is available. The company have made a wise

decision.

CHAPTER 14

Using Pronouns Correctly: Agreement and Reference

Pronouns are words that substitute for nouns. A pronoun's **antecedent** is the word or words it replaces.

pronouns and antecedents:

antecedent   pronoun
George is a wonderful father; *he* is loving and kind.

                    antecedent   pronoun
Suzanne wound the *clock* because *it* had stopped ticking.

             antecedent   pronoun
Talking on the phone is fun, but *it* takes up too much of my time.

           antecedent   pronoun
Joanne and David know what *they* want.

 antecedent   pronoun
Christopher lost *his* favorite baseball cap.

   antecedent   pronoun
The *horse* stamped *its* feet and neighed loudly.

Exercise 1

Practice

Identifying the Antecedents of Pronouns

In each of the following sentences, a pronoun is underlined. Circle the word or words that are the antecedent of the underlined pronoun.

1. (My best friend and her sister) are looking for an apartment they can afford.

2. Sylvia loves (fattening desserts), but I never eat them.

3. (Taking the stairs) is good for you; it gives you some much-needed exercise.

4. (Michael,) will <u>you</u> please answer me?

5. (The little girl) would not let go of <u>her</u> Barbie doll.

6. Last week (Trina and I) were exhausted; <u>we</u> had to work overtime every night.

7. (The bird on my lawn) seems to have hurt <u>its</u> wing.

8. (The detectives) are certain <u>they</u> have solved the mystery.

9. The sailors asked (the captain) for another day off, but <u>he</u> wouldn't give it to them.

10. (The fans at last night's game) lost <u>their</u> patience with the umpire.

AGREEMENT OF A PRONOUN AND ITS ANTECEDENT

A pronoun must agree in number with its antecedent. If the antecedent is singular, the pronoun must be singular. If the antecedent is plural, the pronoun must be plural.

singular antecedents, singular pronouns:

singular antecedent   singular pronoun
The *dog* began to bark wildly; *it* hated being locked up in the cellar.

singular antecedent   singular pronoun
Maria spends most of *her* salary on rent.

plural antecedents, plural pronouns:

plural antecedent   plural pronoun
Carlos and Ronnie went to Atlanta for a long weekend; *they* had a good time.

plural antecedent   plural pronoun
Cigarettes are expensive, and *they* can kill you.

SPECIAL PROBLEMS WITH AGREEMENT

Agreement of pronoun and antecedent seems fairly simple: If an antecedent is singular, use a singular pronoun. If an antecedent is plural, use a plural pronoun. There are, however, some special problems with agreement of pronouns, and these problems will come up in your writing. If you become familiar with the explanations, examples, and exercises that follow, you'll be ready to handle special problems.

Indefinite Pronouns

Certain words, called **indefinite pronouns,** are always singular. Therefore, if an indefinite pronoun is the antecedent, the pronoun that replaces it must be singular. Here are the indefinite pronouns:

Info BOX

Indefinite Pronouns

one	nobody	nothing	each
anyone	anybody	anything	either
someone	somebody	something	neither
everyone	everybody	everything	

You may think that *everybody* is plural, but in grammatically correct English, it is a singular word. Therefore, if you want to write clearly and correctly, memorize these words as the *-one*, *-thing*, and *-body* words: every*one*, every*thing*, every*body*, any*one*, any*thing*, and so on, plus *each*, *either*, and *neither*. If any of these words is an antecedent, the pronoun that refers to it is singular.

TEACHING TIP:

Most students will want to use "their" with "everyone." Tell students to look at the ending. The word "one" is singular, and it is thus a reminder to use the singular "his or her."

indefinite pronouns as antecedents:

indefinite pronoun antecedent,   singular pronoun

Each of the women skaters did *her* best in the Olympic competition.

indefinite pronoun antecedent   singular pronoun

Everyone nominated for Father of the Year earned *his* nomination.

Avoiding Sexism

Consider this sentence:

Everybody in the cooking contest prepared _____ best dish.

How do you choose the correct pronoun to fill this blank? You can write

Everybody in the cooking contest prepared *his* best dish.

if everybody in the contest is male. Or you can write

Everybody in the cooking contest prepared *her* best dish.

if everybody in the contest is female. Or you can write

Everybody in the cooking contest prepared *his* or *her* best dish.

if the contest has male and female entrants.

In the past, most writers used *his* to refer to both men and women when the antecedent was an indefinite pronoun. Today, many writers try to use *his or her* to avoid sexual bias. If you find using *his or her* is getting awkward and repetitive, you can rewrite the sentence and make the antecedent plural.

Correct: *The entrants* in the cooking contest prepared *their* best dishes.

But you can not shift from singular to plural:

Incorrect: ~~Everybody in the cooking contest prepared their best dish.~~

 Making Pronouns and Their Antecedents Agree: Simple Agreement and Indefinite Pronouns

Practice

In each of the following sentences, write the appropriate pronoun in the blank space. Look carefully for the antecedent before you choose the pronoun.

1. After Ellen finished the assignment, _____*she*_____ felt relieved and satisfied.

2. A few of the regular customers in my store want _____*their*_____ groceries packed in boxes, not bags.

3. Someone from the men's athletic club must have lost _____*his*_____ wallet.

4. Has anyone from the Girl Scouts offered _____*her*_____ help to the elderly couple next door?

5. I just realized that the kitchen cabinets are greasy; I'm going to clean _____*them*_____ right away.

6. Either of the little girls could have left _____*her*_____ crayons on the couch.

7. One of my uncles was kind enough to offer me the use of _____*his*_____ truck.

8. A single father with a large family may become overwhelmed by the stress of trying to take care of _____*his*_____ children.

9. Each of the sisters believes that a degree in business administration will lead _____*her*_____ to a good job.

10. Watching television can be relaxing; _____*it*_____ can also be boring.

Exercise 3

Connect:

Editing a Paragraph for Errors in Agreement: Indefinite Pronouns

The following paragraph contains six errors in agreement where the antecedents are indefinite pronouns. Correct the errors in the space above the lines.

My cousin Tina is glad she dropped out of her college sorority; she found joining the sorority was a disappointment. Tina had expected all the girls in the sorority to be friendly and outgoing. Instead, most of them were superior and snobbish. Everyone made a point of showing off ~~their~~ *her* expensive clothes and elegant jewelry. Tina felt that she could not keep up with such rich females. In addition, each of the members flaunted ~~their~~ *her* family background. One of the

                                    her

girls bragged about their millionaire father; another said she came from a family of famous brain surgeons. Tina, whose father is a baker, was made to feel inferior. Finally, Tina left the sorority because the club was devoted to superficial activities. Tina said that every conversation focused on the next party, and

                          her

if anyone brought up their need to study, the others laughed. Everyone was

                   her   *her*

obsessed with their hair and their outfit for the next social event. Tina decided that she would look for a sorority with more mature, secure members.

Collective Nouns

Collective nouns refer to more than one person or thing.

Info BOX

Some Common Collective Nouns

team	company	council
class	corporation	government
committee	family	group
audience	jury	crowd

Most of the time, collective nouns take a singular pronoun:

collective nouns and singular pronouns:

collective noun   singular pronoun
The *jury* in the murder trial announced *its* verdict.

collective noun   singular pronoun
The *company* I work for has been in business a long time; *it* started in Atlanta, Georgia.

Collective nouns are usually singular because the group that is announcing a verdict or starting a business is acting as one—as a unit. Collective nouns take a plural *only* when the members of the group are acting individually, not as a unit:

collective noun and a plural pronoun:

collective noun,   plural pronoun
The *team* signed *their* contracts yesterday. (The members of the team sign contracts individually.)

Exercise 4

Practice

Making Pronouns and Antecedents Agree: Collective Nouns

Circle the correct pronoun in each of the following sentences.

1. The sophomore class had (its/their) individual yearbook photos taken yesterday.

2. That pharmaceutical corporation had a reputation for being good to (its/their) employees.

3. The audience for the concert was enormous; (it/they) filled the stadium.

4. Impact Motors designed a new entrance to (its/their) service department.

5. A scholarship committee will examine your application and then notify you of (its/their) decision.

6. The family lived in different parts of the country; (it/they) rarely saw each other.

7. Several of the groups met to plan (its/their) annual children's fair.

8. Denise is furious with the telephone company; (it/they) over-charged her for some long-distance calls.

9. Our team had lost (its/their) final game of the season.

10. The rebel army began to disintegrate when the soldiers began to fight among (itself/themselves).

Exercise 5   **Editing a Paragraph for Errors in Agreement: Collective Nouns**

The following paragraph contains six errors in agreement where the antecedent is a collective noun. Correct the errors in the spaces above the lines.

    Yesterday, Albert was very upset with our city government. Albert and his neighbors wanted the city government to close off one end of Maple Street. The residents of Maple Street, including Albert, felt that many motorists were using Maple Street as a shortcut and speeding through the formerly quiet street. The residents petitioned the government, but the government refused the residents' request, reasoning that closing the road would be expensive. Albert felt very frustrated. He shouted about the government and said ~~they~~ it had grown out of touch with ~~their~~ its citizens. Furthermore, Albert said, ~~they~~ it had created a dangerous situation by allowing Maple Street to remain open. When the city government was faced with a major

it

accident on Maple Street, they would be responsible for deaths or injuries.

Its

Their decision would have disastrous consequences, Albert said. Albert

ranted on until he decided to take the neighborhood petition to the County

it

Commission; he thought they might be more sympathetic.

Exercise 6

👥 *Collaborate:*

Writing Sentences with Pronoun-Antecedent Agreement

Working with a partner or a group, write a sentence for each of the following pairs of words, using each pair as a pronoun and its antecedent(s). The first pair is done for you.

1. men . . . their

sentence: **The men at the dance were wearing their best clothes.**

_____

2. The U.S. Navy . . . its

sentence: The U.S. Navy changed its policy on earning college credits.

_____

3. someone . . . his or her

sentence: Someone left his or her wallet under this desk.

_____

4. millionaires . . . they

sentence: The millionaires on the quiz show certainly earned their

money; they knew all kinds of information.

5. worrying . . . it

sentence: Leonard should stop worrying; it doesn't do any good.

_____

6. either . . . his

sentence: Either of the brothers might bring his camera.

_____

7. everything . . . its

sentence: Everything in the drawer was in its proper place.

_____

8. Sal and Ryan . . . their

sentence: _Sal and Ryan are working on their sailboat._

_____

9. anyone . . . his or her

sentence: _Did anyone in the class complete his or her test?_

_____

10. cat . . . its

sentence: _The cat rubbed its head against my legs._

_____

PRONOUNS AND THEIR ANTECEDENTS: BEING CLEAR

Remember that pronouns are words that replace or refer to other words, and those other words are called *antecedents*.

Make sure that a pronoun has one clear antecedent. Your writing will be vague and confusing if a pronoun appears to refer to more than one antecedent or if a pronoun doesn't have any specific antecedent to refer to. Such confusing language is called a problem with *reference of pronouns*.

When a pronoun refers to more than one thing, the sentence can become confusing or silly:

pronouns refer to more than one thing:

Carla told Elaine that her car had a flat tire. (Whose car had a flat tire? Carla's? Elaine's?)

Josh woke to the shrieking alarm clock, buried his head in his pillow, and threw it across the room. (What did Josh throw? The pillow? The clock? His head?)

If there is no one, clear antecedent, you must rewrite the sentence to make the reference clear. Sometimes the rewritten sentence may seem repetitive, but a little repetition is better than a lot of confusion.

unclear: Carla told Elaine that her car had a flat tire.
clear: Carla told Elaine that Carla's car had a flat tire.
clear: Carla told Elaine that Elaine's car had a flat tire.
clear: Carla told Elaine, "Your car has a flat tire."
clear: Carla told Elaine, "My car has a flat tire."

unclear: Josh woke to the shrieking alarm clock, buried his head in his pillow, and threw it across the room.
clear: Josh woke to the shrieking alarm clock, buried his head in his pillow, and threw the clock across the room.

Sometimes the problem is a little more confusing. Can you spot what's wrong with this sentence?

Linda was able to negotiate for a raise which pleased her. (What pleased Linda? The raise? Or the fact that she was able to negotiate for it?)

TEACHING TIP:

This is a good place to discuss the vague use of "they" and how often it is used incorrectly in conversation and in writing. Stress that vague references can be confusing and misleading. Write this sentence on the board: "The management doesn't know what they are doing." Who, exactly, are "they"? "Management" is a collective noun, so "they" should be changed to "it." The incorrect "they" could be construed as either employees or employers.

Be very careful with the pronoun *which*. If there is any chance that using *which* will confuse the reader, rewrite the sentence and get rid of *which*:

clear: Linda was pleased that she was able to negotiate for a raise.
clear: Linda was pleased by the raise she negotiated.

Sometimes a pronoun has nothing to refer to; it has no antecedent.

pronouns with no antecedent:

When Mary took the television to the repair shop, they said the television couldn't be repaired. (Who are "they"? Who said the television couldn't be repaired? The television service personnel? The customers? The repairmen?)

I have always been interested in designing clothes and have decided that's what I want to be. (What does *that* refer to? The only word it could refer to is *clothes.* You certainly don't want to be clothes. You don't want to be a dress or a suit.)

If a pronoun lacks an antecedent, add an antecedent or eliminate the pronoun.

add an antecedent: When Mary took the television to the repair shop and asked *the service personnel* for an estimate, they said the television couldn't be repaired.

eliminate the pronoun: I have always been interested in designing clothes and have decided I want to be a fashion designer.

To check for clear reference of pronouns, underline any pronouns that may not be clear. Then try to draw a line from that pronoun to its antecedent. Are there two or more possible antecedents? Is there no antecedent? In either case, you need to rewrite.

Exercise 7

Practice

Rewriting Sentences for Clear Reference of Pronouns

Rewrite the following sentences so that the pronouns have clear references. You can add, take out, or change words.

1. Oscar told Victor that he had a bad temper.

   rewritten: *Oscar told Victor that Victor had a bad temper.*

Answers Will Vary.

Possible answers shown at right.

2. I will never go to the Golden Palace again; they charge too much for dinner.

   rewritten: *I will never go to Golden Palace again; the restaurant charges too much for dinner.*

3. Bill decided not to apply for a part-time job which worried his parents.

   rewritten: *Bill's parents were worried because he decided not to apply for a part-time job.*

4. My mother is a computer systems analyst, but I am not interested in it.

rewritten: My mother is a computer systems analyst, but I am not interested in computers.

5. My father lost his temper with Harry because he was being rude and thoughtless.

rewritten: My father lost his temper with Harry because Harry was being rude and thoughtless.

6. Corinna asked her roommate if she could go to the party.

rewritten: Corrinna asked her roommate, "Can you go to the party?"

7. A van skidded on the ice and hit a pickup truck, but it was not badly damaged.

rewritten: A van skidded on the ice and hit a pickup truck, but the truck was not badly damaged.

8. They never gave me a chance to explain when they arested me for drunk driving.

rewritten: The police never gave me a chance to explain when they arrested me for drunken driving.

9. The manager told the assistant manager that his job was in danger of being eliminated.

rewritten: The manager told the assistant manager, "Your job is in danger of being eliminated."

10. Don finally made a sale which encouraged him.

rewritten: Don was encouraged that he finally made a sale.

Exercise 8 *Collaborate*

Revising Sentences with Problems in Pronoun Reference: Two Ways

Do this exercise with a partner or a group. Each of the following sentences contains a pronoun with an unclear antecedent. Because the antecedent is unclear, the sentence can have more than one meaning. Rewrite each sentence twice, to show the different meanings. The first one is done for you.

1. Mrs. Klein told Mrs. Yamaguchi her dog was digging up the flower beds.

   sentence 1: Mrs. Klein told Mrs. Yamaguchi, "Your dog is digging up the flower beds."

   sentence 2: Mrs. Klein told Mrs. Yamaguchi that Mrs. Klein's dog was digging up the flower beds.

2. Wayne's father let him bring his new motorcycle to the race.

   sentence 1: Wayne's father let him bring Wayne's new motorcycle to the race.

   sentence 2: Wayne's father said, "You may bring my new motorcycle to the race."

3. The antique vase hit the glass tabletop, but it did not break.

   sentence 1: The antique vase hit the glass tabletop, but the vase did not break.

   sentence 2: The antique vase hit the glass tabletop, but the tabletop did not break.

4. She put the sandwich next to the salad and began to eat it.

   sentence 1: She put the sandwich next to the salad and began to eat the sandwich.

   sentence 2: She put the sandwich next to the salad and began to eat the salad.

5. Julia asked Stacy if she was invited to the wedding.

   sentence 1: Julia asked Stacy, "Are you invited to the wedding?"

   sentence 2: Julia asked Stacy, "Am I invited to the wedding?"

6. Teresa easily found a new house which made her happy.

   sentence 1: Teresa was happy that it was easy to find a new house.

   sentence 2: Teresa's new house, which she found easily, made her happy.

7. After the children splashed water on the adults, they ran away.

sentence 1: After the children splashed water on the adults, the

adults ran away.

sentence 2: After the children splashed water on the adults, the

children ran away.

8. Ron took the cake out of the box and gave it to me.

sentence 1: Ron took the cake out of the box and gave the cake

to me.

sentence 2: Ron took the cake out of the box and gave the box to

me.

9. Arnold saw his father at his graduation.

sentence 1: Arnold saw his father at Arnold's graduation.

_____

sentence 2: Arnold saw his father at his father's graduation.

_____

10. Joe told Mike he needed a vacation.

sentence 1: Joe told Mike that Joe needed a vacation.

_____

sentence 2: Joe told Mike that Mike needed a vacation.

_____

Editing a Paragraph for Errors in Pronoun Reference

Connect

The following paragraph contains five errors in pronoun reference. Correct the errors in the spaces above the lines.

After much confusion and indecision, I have finally made a career

choice. For years, I have been trying to pick a career that would be practical

the counselors
and financially rewarding. In high school, they told me to look into such

fields as business, accounting, or computers. I tried to commit to one of

these areas, but I never felt satisfied. After much soul searching, I realized I

that I want to be a ballet dancer.
have always loved ballet, and I decided that's what I want to be. Of course, I

, and that career displeased my parents.

took years to choose a career which displeased my parents. My mother told

my mother's

me that her sister Edna had said her dreams of being an actress were fool-

ish. My mother said my dreams were equally foolish. My father warned me

a career in ballet

that in ten years I would see that it was a waste of my time. But in spite of

my parents' disapproval, I know I have to follow my heart.

CHAPTER 15

Using Pronouns Correctly: Consistency and Case

When you write, you write from a point of view, and each point of view gets its own form. If you write from the first person point of view, your pronouns are in the *I* (singular) or *we* (plural) forms. If you write from the second person point of view, your pronouns are in the *you* form, whether they are singular or plural. If you write from the third person point of view, your pronouns are in the *he*, *she*, or *it* (singular) or *they* (plural) forms.

Different kinds of writing may require different points of view. When you are writing a set of directions, for example, you might use the second person (you) point of view. For an essay about your childhood, you might use the first person (I) point of view.

Whatever point of view you use, be consistent in using pronouns. That is, do not shift the form of your pronouns without some good reason.

> **not consistent:** The last time *I* went to that movie theater, the only seat *you* could get was in the front row.
> **consistent:** The last time *I* went to that movie theater, the only seat *I* could get was in the front row.

> **not consistent:** By the time the shoppers got into the store, *they* were so jammed into the aisles that *you* couldn't get to the sales tables.
> **consistent:** By the time the shoppers got into the store, *they* were so jammed into the aisles that *they* couldn't get to the sales tables.

 Exercise 1

Practice

Consistency in Pronouns

Correct any inconsistency in point of view in the following sentences. Cross out the incorrect pronoun and write the correct one above it.

    1. Breakfast is a meal I eat on the run because I am always late for

    work and ~~you~~ never have time to cook a big breakfast.

2. After the students are seated at their desks, the professor circu-
  them
  lates an attendance sheet for you to sign.

3. Motorists must use caution when they enter the toll plaza; if they
  they
  rush through the gates, you can be hit by another driver.

4. In the college snack bar, students sit at long tables, socialize with
  their
  their friends, or do your homework.
                                                                          I
5. I am very tactful when I ask my mother for money because you

  don't want to put her in a bad mood.

6. Although the weather was sunny, we took an umbrella in case
  we
  you got caught in a shower.
                                         they
7. They avoided Paul because you couldn't put up with his constant

  complaining.

8. When we drove into central Florida, the rain was coming down
        we
  so hard you could barely see the road.
                                              I
9. Every time I run into Dean, you know he has a story to tell me.

10. The first time I ate barbecued chicken, I thought it was so deli-
        I'd
  cious you'd never want to eat anything else.

 **Exercise 2**

Collaborate

Rewriting Sentences with Consistency Problems

Do this exercise with a partner or group. Rewrite the following sentences, correcting any errors in the consistency of pronouns. To make the corrections, you may have to change, add, or take out words.

Answers Will Vary.
Possible answers shown
at right.

1. You could tell the atmosphere was tense when we walked in and
  saw our friends sitting in silence.

  rewritten: *We could tell the atmosphere was tense when we walked in*

  and saw our friends sitting in silence.

2. For me, Sunday is the best day of the week; I particularly like waking up as late as I want, watching my favorite morning news
  shows, and lounging around in your pajamas.

  rewritten: *For me, Sunday is the best day of the week; I particularly*

  like waking up as late as I want, watching my favorite morning news

  shows, and lounging around in my pajamas.

3. Children who are given too much freedom too early can become insecure and confused; you need limits to make you feel safe and cared for.

   rewritten: Children who are given too much freedom too early can become insecure and confused; they need limits to make them feel safe and cared for.

4. If you truly want to succeed in college, students must put college at the top of their schedules and devote most of your time to studying.

   rewritten: If they truly want to succeed in college, students must put college at the top of their schedules and devote most of their time to studying.

5. I won't offer to drive Brian to class because you'll lose patience waiting for Brian to show up, and I'll be in a bad mood the rest of the day.

   rewritten: I won't offer to drive Brian to class because I'll lose patience waiting for Brian to show up, and I'll be in a bad mood the rest of the day.

6. Sophomores who want to register for next semester have to make an appointment with your advisor before they can sign up for classes.

   rewritten: Sophomores who want to register for next semester have to make an appointment with their advisor before they can sign up for classes.

7. The best part of my speech class is that you can relax when someone else is giving a speech.

   rewritten: The best part of my speech class is that I can relax when someone else is giving a speech.

8. When I entered the studio, the place was so quiet that you could have heard a pin drop.

   rewritten: When I entered the studio, the place was so quiet that I could have heard a pin drop.

9. Before the painter paints new wood, he has to be sure you have covered the wood with primer.

rewritten: *Before the painter paints new wood, he has to be sure*

that he has covered the wood with primer.

10. There's no reason for me to apologize to Jack; he'll just carry a grudge against you anyway.

rewritten: *There's no reason for me to apologize to Jack; he'll just*

carry a grudge against me anyway.

~~Connect~~

Exercise 3   Editing a Paragraph for Consistency of Pronouns

The following paragraph has four errors in consistency of pronouns. Correct the errors above the lines.

I have a perfect system for completing my holiday shopping early. First, I begin way ahead of time. As early as July, I visit the best sales and begin stock-piling gifts for members of my family. By September, I have made a list of all the people ~~you~~ [I] want to buy for and what ~~you've~~ [I've] already bought. I circle the names of those who still need gifts. Then I visit the malls, looking specifically for gifts for the people on my list. By October, I have completed nearly all my shopping. From November on, I avoid the malls and do the remainder of my shopping by catalog. Catalog shopping is quick and easy, and it keeps ~~you~~ [me] out of the stores when they are jammed with desperate shoppers trying to beat ~~me~~ [I] to the bargains. When the holidays finally roll around, you can enjoy them because there is no last-minute shopping to make me crazy.

CHOOSING THE CASE OF PRONOUNS

Pronouns have forms that show number and person, and they also have forms that show **case.** Following is a list of three cases of pronouns:

Info BOX

Pronouns and Their Case
Singular Pronouns

	Subjective Case	Objective Case	Possessive Case
1st person	I	me	my, mine
2nd person	you	you	your, yours
3rd person	he, she, it	him, her, it	his, her, hers, its

Plural Pronouns			
	Subjective Case	**Objective Case**	**Possessive Case**
1st person	we	us	our (ours)
2nd person	you	you	your (yours)
3rd person	they	them	their (theirs)

Rules for Choosing the Case of Pronouns

The rules for choosing the case of pronouns are simple:

1. When a pronoun is used as a subject, use the subjective case.
2. When a pronoun is used as the object of a verb or the object of a preposition, use the objective case.
3. When a pronoun is used to show possession, use the possessive case.

Here are some examples of the correct use of pronouns:

pronouns used as subjects:
She calls the office once a week.
Sylvia wrote the letter, and *we* revised it.
When Guy called, *I* was thrilled.

pronouns used as objects:
The loud noise frightened *me.*
The card was addressed to *him.*
Sadie's dog always traveled with *her.*

pronouns used to show possession:
The criticism hurt *her* feelings.
Our car is nearly new.
The restaurant changed *its* menu.

Exercise 4   **Choosing the Right Case of Pronouns: Simple Situations**

Practice   Circle the correct pronoun in each of the following sentences.

1. (He/Him/His) visited the city museum yesterday.

2. A week ago, Jennifer borrowed (I/me/my) best dress.

3. Dave and Brenda drove straight to Cleveland; then (they/them/their) stopped for the night.

4. (I/Me/My) need a good job for the summer.

5. Frank invited (we/us/our) to a party at the beach.

6. Cynthia asked Mark to go to the dance with (she/her).

7. Paulette and Enrique are celebrating (they/them/their) fifth anniversary.

8. Uncle Tim should give the money to (we/us/our).

9. (He/Him/His) research paper was excellent.

10. Christopher scored the winning point, but (I/me/my) contributed to the victory.

PROBLEMS CHOOSING PRONOUN CASE

Choosing the Right Pronoun Case in a Related Group of Words

You need to be careful in choosing pronoun case when the pronoun is part of a related group of words. If the pronoun is part of a related group of words, isolate the pronoun. Next, try out the pronoun choices. Then decide which pronoun is correct and write the correct sentence. For example, which of these sentences is correct?

Diane had a big surprise for Jack and *I*.

or

Diane had a big surprise for Jack and *me*.

To chose the correct sentence, follow these steps:

Step 1: Isolate the pronoun. Eliminate the related words *Jack and.*
Step 2: Try each case.

Diane had a big surprise for *I*.

or

Diane had a big surprise for *me*.

Step 3: Decide which pronoun is correct and write the correct sentence.

correct sentence: Diane had a big surprise for Jack and *me*.

The pronoun acts as an object, so it takes the objective case.

To be sure that you understand the principle, try working through the steps once more. Which of the following sentences is correct?

Next week, my sister and *me* will start classes at Bryant Community College.

or

Next week, my sister and *I* will start classes at Bryant Community College.

Step 1: Isolate the pronoun. Eliminate the related words *my sister and.*
Step 2: Try each case.

Next week, *me* will start classes at Bryant Community College.

Next week, *I* will start classes at Bryant Community College.

Step 3: Decide which pronoun is correct and write the correct sentence.

correct sentence: Next week, my sister and *I* will start classes at Bryant Community College.

Common Errors with Case of Pronouns

In choosing the case of pronouns, be careful to avoid these common errors:

1. *Between* is a preposition. The pronouns that follow it are objects of the preposition: between *us,* between *them,* between *you and me.* It is never correct to write between *you and I.*

   examples:
   not this: What I'm telling you must be kept strictly between you and ~~I~~.
   but this: What I'm telling you must be kept strictly between you and me.

2. Never use *myself* as a replacement for *I* or *me.*

   examples:
   not this: My family and ~~myself~~ are grateful for your expressions of sympathy.
   but this: My family and I are grateful for your expressions of sympathy.
   not this: The scholarship committee selected Nadine and ~~myself.~~
   but this: The scholarship committee selected Nadine and me.

3. The possessive pronoun *its* has no apostrophe.

   examples:
   not this: The stale coffee lost ~~it's~~ flavor.
   but this: The stale coffee lost its flavor.

Exercise 5

Practice

Choosing the Right Case of Pronoun: Problems with Pronoun Case

Circle the correct pronoun in each of the following sentences.

1. Cristina was able to open her new store after she received a great deal of help from her cousins and (me/myself).

2. Basic training can be very difficult, but the program has (it's/its) benefits.

3. I told Sylvia she could come to the wedding with Freddie and (I/me).

4. When David won the lottery, he gave half of his winnings to (they/them) and Carlos.

5. Stuck in traffic, Dr. Chen and (he/him) used the cell phone to call the office.

6. My mother thinks the judges will have a hard time choosing between the student from Texas and (me/myself).

7. The people in the nursing home always welcome Sandra and (I/me) when we visit.

8. The neighbors and (we/us) spent the weekend cleaning up the streets.

9. My wife and I moved to San Diego to find more job opportunities

for her and (I/me).

10. Ed and (I/me) watched an old movie last night.

Practice

More on Choosing the Right Case of Pronoun: Problems with Pronoun Case

Circle the correct pronoun in each of the following sentences.

1. Just try to keep it a secret between you and (I/me).

2. My friends and (I/myself) want to thank you for this honor.

3. Once I started working, staying out late lost (its/it's) appeal for me.

4. We were able to settle the argument between David and (me/myself).

5. My father said he couldn't have painted the house without the help

of my sister and (I/me).

6. Last week, Danny and (he/him) borrowed a van from Jesse.

7. The leadership award was a great honor for Lisa and (I/me).

8. At the dinner, Debbie and (she/her) wouldn't talk to Jim.

9. My sister arranged a wonderful treat for my girlfriend and (I/me).

10. I think the tree is diseased; it is losing too many of (its/it's) leaves.

Collaborate

Write Your Own Text on Pronoun Case

Working with a partner or a group, write two sentences that could be used as examples for each of the following rules. The first one is done for you.

Rule 1: When a pronoun is used as a subject, use the subjective case.

example 1: They study for tests in the math lab.

example 2: Caught in the rain, she ran for cover.

Answers Will Vary.

Possible answers shown at right.

Rule 2: When a pronoun is used as the object of a verb or the object of a preposition, use the objective case. (For examples, write one sentence in which the pronoun is the object of a verb and one in which the pronoun is the object of a preposition.)

example 1: My boss praised me.

example 2: The photographer took a picture of me.

Rule 3: When a pronoun is used to show ownership, use the possessive case.

example 1: _Manny took his car to the repair center._

example 2: _Mr. and Mrs. Cohen love their dog._

Rule 4: When a pronoun is part of a related group of words, isolate the pronoun to choose the case. (For examples, write two sentences in which the pronoun is part of a related group of words.)

example 1: _Uncle Carl and I have the same birthday._

example 2: _The speech was a tribute to Mrs. Jansen and her._

 Exercise 8

Connect

Editing a Paragraph for Case of Pronouns

The following letter has five errors in pronoun case. Correct the errors in the space above the lines.

Dear Professor Walker,

If you could give us an extension on the writing assignment, you would
                                                                me.
really help Steve Lopez and I. We both work at Home Warehouse, and we
                                                  I
have had to work overtime all week. Me and Steve have been getting home

after midnight, and it's been impossible for us to get our homework done.
                                                             its
We have asked our boss for time off, but Home Warehouse has it's policy
                              I
about working overtime, and Steve and myself have to follow that policy.

Since we have been so busy working, we haven't started the writing assign-

ment. If you could extend the deadline, we could do a good job on our

papers, and we wouldn't tell the rest of the class about our extension. It
                                               me.
would be a secret between Steve and I.

Sincerely,

Richard Lesniak

CHAPTER 16

Punctuation

You probably know much about punctuation already. In fact, you probably know many of the rules so well that you punctuate your writing automatically. However, there are times when every writer wonders, "Do I need a comma here?" or "Should I capitalize this word?" The following review of the basic rules of punctuation can help you answer such questions.

THE PERIOD

INSTRUCTOR'S NOTE:

Grammar handbooks routinely stipulate that a comma should be placed before "Jr." and "Sr." However, most newspapers and magazines now omit this comma use. A publication's style sheet may occasionally conflict with traditional grammatical rules for student essays.

Periods are used two ways:

1. Use a period to mark the end of a sentence that makes a statement.

   examples:
   My father gave me an exciting new book.
   After the dance, we went to a coffeehouse for a snack.

2. Use a period after abbreviations.

   examples:
   Mr. Vinh
   Carlos Montoya, Sr.
   11:00 a.m.
   Dr. J. T. Mitchell

THE QUESTION MARK

Use a question mark after a direct question.

   examples:
   Do you have any spare change?
   Wasn't that song beautiful?

If a question is not a direct question, do not use a question mark.

   examples:
   I wonder if it will rain tonight.
   Nadine asked whether I had cleaned the kitchen.

Exercise 1

Practice

Punctuating with Periods and Question Marks

Add the necessary periods and question marks to the following sentences.

1. Brian questioned whether I really believed Suzanne's story .

   Ms.
2. Do you think Ms Ross will ever miss a day of class ?

3. If you are going to the store, can you pick up some milk ?

   Mr.   *B.S.*
4. Mr Wing wants to earn a B S in chemistry .

5. I was wondering if you would like to car pool with me .

   a.m.
6. Norman cannot get to sleep before 3:00 a m, so he has a hard time

   waking up in the morning .

7. Has anyone seen my umbrella ?

8. We asked the teacher if she was going to give us a quiz .

   Jr.
9. Charles Pulaski, Jr inherited the factory from his father .

10. Why not call a plumber to fix the sink ?

Exercise 2

Collaborate

Punctuating with Periods and Question Marks

Do this exercise with a partner. First, by yourself, write a paragraph that needs periods and question marks, but leave out those punctuation marks. Then exchange paragraphs with your partner, and add the necessary periods and question marks to your partner's paragraph. Finally, you and your partner should check each other's punctuation.

Write a paragraph of at least six sentences, using the topic sentence below.

New students have many questions about college, but their questions are soon answered. _____

_____

_____

_____

_____

_____

_____

_____

THE SEMICOLON

There are two ways to use semicolons:

1. Use a semicolon to join two independent clauses.

> **examples:**
> Aunt Celine can be very generous; she gave me fifty dollars for my birthday.
> The ice storm was horrible; our town endured five days without electricity.

If the independent clauses are joined by a conjunctive adverb, you still need a semicolon. You will also need a comma after the conjunctive adverb if the conjunctive adverb is more than one syllable long.

> **examples:**
> I called the towing service; then I waited impatiently for the tow truck to arrive.
> Stephen forgot about the exam; therefore, he was not prepared for it.

2. If a list contains commas and the items on it need to be clarified, use a semicolon to separate the items. Note how confusing the following lists would be without the semicolons.

> **examples:**
> The student government presidents at the conference represented Mill Valley High School, Springfield; Longfellow High School, Riverdale; Kennedy High School, Deer Creek; and Martin Luther King High School, Rocky Hills.
> The members of the musical group were Janet Reese, guitar; Richelle Dennison, drums; Sandy Simon, bass; and Lee Vickers, vocalist.

 Exercise 3

Practice

Punctuating with Semicolons

Some of the following sentences need semicolons; some do not. Add the necessary semicolons. (You may need to change some commas to semicolons.)

1. Contestants in the talent contest came from Miami, Florida, Dallas, Texas, Chicago, Illinois, Los Angeles, California, and Boston, Massachusetts.

2. A large dog bounced out of the van the animal began to jump all over me.

3. The weather was exceptionally warm for this time of year consequently, we decided to walk to the store instead of drive.

4. Sylvia called a number of stores but couldn't find the right kind of light bulb.

5. At the club meeting last night, these people were elected: Samantha Monceau, president, Mark Chang, first vice president, Alan Deschamps, second vice president, and Tom Robinson, treasurer.

6. For three years, my father worked at two jobs ; thus he was able to make a down payment on a house.

7. A good haircut can make your hair look better and can enhance your best features.

8. Take the car ; I don't need it tonight.

9. When you go hiking, you need to buy good shoes, warm socks, sturdy clothing, a comfortable hat, and a roomy backpack.

10. My brother loves late-night television ; he can watch it all night.

Exercise 4   **Punctuating with Semicolons**

Connect

Add semicolons where they are needed in the following paragraph.

David's first day at work was stressful ; nevertheless, he came out of the experience with a sense of accomplishment. The showroom floor where he began work was more crowded and busy than he had expected. Moreover, the customers all seemed to be in a hurry ; they wanted to be helped immediately. David tried to take care of everyone but was overwhelmed by the demands of so many people. The manager of the store was encouraging ; she told David things would slow down in the afternoon. By 3:00 p.m., David had learned to cope ; moreover, the showroom had really emptied out. David's boss had been right ; the pace was much slower in the afternoon. By the time David left, he felt less stressed and more confident. He had survived his first day at American Furniture Galleries without making any major mistakes. The worst was over ; better days were ahead.

THE COMMA

There are four main ways to use a comma, and there are other, less important ways. Memorize the four main ways. If you can learn and understand these four rules, you will be more confident and correct in your punctuation. That is, you will use a comma only when you have a reason to do so; you will not be scattering commas in your sentences simply because you think a comma might fit, as many writers do. The four main ways to use a comma are as a *lister*, a *linker*, an *introducer*, or an *inserter* (two commas).

1. Comma as a lister

Commas separate items in a series. These items can be words, phrases, or clauses.

commas between words in a list:

Charles was fascinated by Doreen because she was smart, sassy, and funny.

commas between phrases in a list:

I wanted a house on a quiet street, in a friendly neighborhood, and with a school nearby.

commas between clauses in a list:

In a single year my brother joined the army, he fought in the Gulf War, and he was decorated for valor.

Note: In a list, the comma before *and* is optional, but most writers use it.

 Exercise 5

Practice

Using the Comma as a Lister

Add commas only where they are needed in the following sentences.

1. Skiing snowboarding and surfing all demand tremendous agility and fitness.

2. The letter you lost could be in your bureau drawer on the night stand or behind the bookcase.

3. I needed eggs milk bread and orange juice from the supermarket.

4. When my mother was in college, she had part-time jobs as a waitress stock clerk bank teller gas station attendant and lifeguard.

5. The whole apartment is filled with green white and yellow wallpaper.

6. I hated my roommate I missed my friends and I was very homesick at summer camp.

7. Joining a club taking a class and doing volunteer work are three good ways to meet people.

8. San Diego Philadelphia Boston and Chicago are cities I've visited explored and loved.

9. Charlie was rude Cindy was thoughtless and Bill was obnoxious when they stayed at my house last month.

10. Romance can be fun exciting and fulfilling, but it can also be scary painful and disappointing.

2. Comma as a linker

A comma and a coordinating conjunction link two independent clauses. The coordinating conjunctions are *and, but, or, nor, for, yet, so.* The comma goes before the coordinating conjunction.

comma before coordinating conjunctions:

You can pick up the pizza, and I'll set the table.

The movie was long, but it was action-packed.

Diane will fly home for summer vacation, or her parents will visit her.

Our house had no basement, nor did it have much of an attic.

Norbert was thrilled by the A in Organic Chemistry, for he had studied really hard all semester.

Mr. Weinstein has lived in the neighborhood for a year, yet no one knows him very well.

The front door was open, so I went right in.

Note: Before you use a comma, be careful that the coordinating conjunction is linking two independent clauses:

> **no comma:** Veronica wrote poetry and painted beautiful portraits.
> **use a comma:** Veronica wrote poetry, and she painted beautiful portraits.

 Exercise 6

Practice

Using the Comma as a Linker

Add commas only where they are needed in the following sentences.

1. Christopher called me twice last night but wouldn't give a straight answer to my question.

2. The car has very low mileage and it runs like a new car.

3. Steve is cutting back on his spending for he wants to pay off his credit cards.

4. Anyone can check books out of the city library or use the computers in the reference section.

5. The sun was in my eyes so I couldn't see the road very well.

6. Professor Rotonda never assigns papers nor does he give essay tests.

7. A few of the players on the local softball team meet at Sloppy Joe's and grab a meal after the game.

8. Carly gave my son a baby blanket and she embroidered his name on it.

9. I always plan to clean up my bedroom yet I never seem to get around to it.

10. Sam makes a cheesecake loaded with calories but it's too good to pass up.

3. Comma as an introducer
Put a comma after introductory words, phrases, or clauses in a sentence.

comma after an introductory word:

No, I can't afford that car.

comma after an introductory phrase:

In my opinion, that car is a lemon.

comma after an introductory clause:

When the baby smiles, I am the happiest father on earth.

Exercise 7

Practice

Using the Comma as an Introducer

Add commas only where they are needed in the following sentences.

1. Sure, I'll be happy to collect your mail while you're away.

2. After you called me, I felt better about our little disagreement.

3. No one in my family has cable television, but my cousin has a satellite dish.

4. Whenever Tyrone visits, he brings a cake or cookies for my grandfather and me.

5. On my only day off, I try to sleep a little later than usual.

6. Crying loudly, the toddler held up his bruised finger.

7. On a bright sunny day in July, Amanda became a lawyer.

8. Unfortunately, you can't get tickets for that boxing match; it's sold out.

9. Before you lose your temper, count to ten.

10. With a wicked grin, my brother grabbed the last chocolate chip cookie and ran.

4. Comma as an inserter
When words in phrases that are not necessary are inserted into a sentence, put a comma on *both* sides of the inserted material.

commas around inserted material:
Her science project, a masterpiece of research, won first prize.
Selena's problem, I believe, is her fear of failure.
Julio, stuck by the side of the road, waited for the tow truck.
Artichokes, a delicious vegetable, are not always available at the local market.

Using commas as inserters requires that you decide what is essential to the meaning of the sentence and what is nonessential.

TEACHING TIP:

To emphasize the difference between essential and nonessential information, write the following sentence on the board: "My grandmother who rides a motorcycle is eighty." Inserting commas implies the writer has one grandmother; omitting commas implies the writer has two grandmothers.

> **If you do not need material in a sentence, put commas around the material.**
>
> **If you need material in a sentence, do not put commas around the material.**

For example, consider this sentence:

The woman who was promoted to captain was Jack's wife.

Do you need the words *who was promoted to captain* to understand the meaning of the sentence? To answer this question, write the sentence without the words:

The woman was Jack's wife.

Reading the shorter sentence, you might ask, "What woman?" The words *who was promoted to captain* are essential to the sentence. Therefore, you do not put commas around them.

correct: The woman who was promoted to captain was Jack's wife.

Remember that the proper name of a person, place, or thing is always sufficient to identify it. Therefore, any information that follows a proper name is inserted material; it is not essential and gets commas on both sides.

proper names and inserted material:
Gloria Chen, who lives in my apartment building, won the raffle at Dominion High School.
Suarez Electronics, which just opened in the mall, has great deals on color televisions.

Note: Inserted material often begins with one of these *relative pronouns: who, which, that.* If you have to choose between *which* and *that, which* usually begins inserted material that is not essential:

The movie, which was much too long, was a comedy.

That usually begins inserted material that is essential.

The puppy that I want is a miniature poodle.

Note: Sometimes the material that is needed in a sentence is called *essential* (or *restrictive*), and the material that is not needed is called *non-essential* (or *non-restrictive*).

 Using Commas as Inserters (Two Commas)

Practice Add commas only where necessary in the following sentences.

1. The silver and turquoise ring that I wanted cost two hundred dollars.

2. Tony Russell, from my old neighborhood, is a high-powered attorney now.

3. My favorite movie, unfortunately, is not available on video.

4. Her boyfriend, thinking he could please her with flowers, brought her a dozen yellow roses.

5. The salesman's best offer, which he called a rock-bottom price, was still too high for my budget.

6. Captain Crunch, which my mother fed us every morning, is still my choice for breakfast.

7. Someone who loves tennis is still a good choice for the camp counselor's job.

8. Nicole wanted to rent <u>The Bodyguard</u>, her favorite movie, over the weekend.

9. A bad habit that really bothers me is constant complaining.

10. The teacher who helped me the most was my history teacher.

 Exercise 9   **Punctuating with Commas: The Four Main Ways**

Practice   Add commas only where they are needed in the following sentences.

1. Whether it rains or shines, we'll have the Arts Fair on Saturday.

2. Even Jason, with all his good intentions, couldn't help the confused teen.

3. She blasted the radio throughout the apartment but couldn't find comfort in the music.

4. Coffee Corner, which serves great espresso, is open until midnight.

5. Aaron picked up an armchair, a coffee table, and a bookcase at his neighbor's garage sale.

6. Louis took me out to dinner last night, so I want to do something nice for him.

7. Children love to play with puppies, but small children must learn how to treat the animals.

8. Tulips look wonderful in flower beds, in bright colored pots, and in window boxes.

9. When I get a chance, I'll have to write a letter to Aunt Cecilia and thank her for the birthday present.

10. While you were sleeping, a burglar cleaned out your closet.

Exercise 10

Practice

More on Punctuating with Commas: The Four Main Ways

Add commas only where they are needed in the following sentences.

1. On the best summer weekends, we take our dog for long walks, or we jog near the lake.

2. My mother used to warn us against the dangers of driving too fast, drinking too much, and speaking too freely.

3. The dress that I longed for was hanging in the window of Mason's Department Store.

4. I know, of course, that you weren't invited to the party.

5. The man who won the championship title will speak tonight.

6. Richard Mannheim, who won the championship title, will speak tonight.

7. The little boy begged and pleaded, yet he couldn't get his mother to give him the toy.

8. Dad, do you have any spare change?

9. The chicken was not very well cooked, nor was it attractively presented.

10. Until you taught me how to swim, I was afraid of the water.

 **Exercise 11**

Collaborate

The Four Main Ways to Use Commas: Create Your Own Examples

Do this exercise with a partner or a group. Below are the rules for the four main ways to use commas. For each rule, write two sentences that are examples. The first one is done for you.

Rule 1: Use a comma as a lister.

example 1: I have old photos stashed in my attic, in my closet, and in the garage.

example 2: The movie was long, dull, and pointless.

Rule 2: Use a comma as a linker.

example 1: Jennifer can drive to Tucson, or she can fly.

example 2: The ceiling was cracked, and the pipes were rusty.

Rule 3: Use a comma as an introducer.

example 1: Sure, I can give you a ride to the bank.

example 2: On her bad days, my grandmother has difficulty walking.

Rule 4: Use a comma as an inserter (two commas).

example 1: Milk, which is high in calcium, is good for your bones.

example 2: You could, with very little trouble, fill out an application.

 Exercise 12   Connect

The Four Main Ways to Use Commas

Add commas where they are needed in the following paragraph. Do not add or change any other punctuation; just add commas.

Believe it or not, I actually enjoy cleaning my apartment. I can't say that I look forward to cleaning, but I do find some satisfaction in the chore. First of all, I find the physical exercise of washing the floors, scrubbing the sinks, and dusting the furniture to be a good way to relieve stress. Even when I am tired, the activity of cleaning seems to energize me. I also like the sense of accomplishment that comes when I have defeated the mildew and conquered the dust bunnies again. A clean living space is, I think, an achievement. After all, it take some self-discipline to make myself grab the mop, pail, and Comet when I could be lounging around. Getting my chores done has its rewards. The part that I like best of all is being able to enjoy my sparkling new apartment—until it gets dirty again!

Other Ways to Use a Comma

Besides the four main ways, there are other ways to use a comma. Reviewing these uses will help you feel more confident as a writer.

1. **Use commas with quotations.** Use a comma to set off a direct quotation from the rest of the sentence.

examples:
Sylvia warned me, "Don't swim there."
"I can give you a ride," Alan said.

Note that the comma that introduces the quotation goes before the quotation marks. But once the quotation has begun, commas (or periods) go inside the quotation marks.

2. Use commas with dates and addresses. Put commas between the items in dates and addresses.

examples:
August 29, 1981, is the day we were married.
I had an apartment at 2323 Clover Avenue, Houston, Texas, until I was
  transferred to California.

Notice the comma after the year in the date, and the comma after the date in the address. These commas are needed when you write a date or an address within a sentence.

3. Use commas in numbers. Use commas in numbers of one thousand or larger.

examples:
He owed me $1,307.
That wall contains 235,991 bricks.

4. Use commas for clarity. Add a comma when you need to make something clear.

examples:
She waltzed in, in a stunning silk gown.
Whatever you did, did the trick.
I don't have to apologize, but I want to, to make things right between us.
Not long after, the party ended.

Exercise 13   Other Ways to Use a Comma

Practice   Add commas where they are needed in the following sentences.

1. Professor Milovich advised me "Whatever you choose choose

   carefully."

2. March 23 1998 was the day we attended Uncle Simon's funeral.

3. "No one has a right to say that to me" the angry customer shouted.

4. He wanted $1250 for the motorcycle, but I offered him $975 in cash.

5. Soon after the jury adjourned for the day.

6. Rebekah is moving to Chicago Illinois when she finishes college.

7. A fortune teller once told me "You have a dark stranger in your

   future."

8. Send the package to me at 257 Sanford Drive Davenport Iowa as

   soon as you can.

9. "I'd rather be happy than rich" my father always said.

10. At my job in Okemos Michigan I made $15000 a year.

Practice

Punctuating with Commas: A Comprehensive Exercise

Add commas where they are needed in the following sentences.

1. He never apologized to my sister, nor did he pay her the money that he owed.

2. If you win, win graciously.

3. David Wong, who comes from Georgia, has never seen the Empire State Building.

4. I mailed that birthday card on April 5, 1997, but it didn't arrive until April 23, 1998.

5. Children who are afraid of the dark should not visit the Halloween Fun House.

6. Sarah offered Sam money, she gave him advice, she listened to his complaints, yet Sam never felt close to her.

7. Dad, do you know someone who lives at 101 Ranch Road, Billings, Montana?

8. After all, you've done enough for the family that lives down the street.

9. Anton called the house yesterday and asked to speak to my sister.

10. "Let's have a party for Halloween," my little sister said, but my mother ignored her.

Practice

Punctuating with Commas: Another Comprehensive Exercise

Add commas where they are needed in the following sentences.

1. One of the greatest things about you, Josh, is your sense of humor.

2. The sunset at the beach was a mix of pink, violet, and golden streaks.

3. Sal's Pizza, which is doing a great business, is starting a take-out service.

4. Neil quit his job because he was sick of answering the phone, taking orders from customers, listening to complaints, and working until nearly midnight.

5. The woman who gave me the necklace is my godmother.

6. Whenever Luis borrows my car he fills the tank with gas.

7. In the years to come I'll be glad I went to college so I don't mind working hard at college assignments now.

8. Amy and Vito spent $2200 on living room furniture for they wanted their new house to look elegant.

9. After Tanika heard her brother's apology she declared "I never knew you could be so foolish but I have to forgive you."

10. Since you've been gone I've started a mail-order business and hired your father-in-law.

Collaborate

Punctuating with Commas

Working alone, write a paragraph that is at least six sentences long. The paragraph should require at least five commas, but leave the commas out. Then give your paragraph to a partner; let your partner add the necessary commas. Meanwhile, you punctuate your partner's paragraph. When you are both finished, check each other's answers.

Write your paragraph in the lines below, using the sentence given to you as the topic sentence.

Of all the places I remember from my childhood, one place stands out.

_____

_____

_____

_____

_____

_____

_____

THE APOSTROPHE

Use the apostrophe in the following ways:

1. Use an apostrophe in contractions to show that letters have been omitted.

examples:

do not	=	don't
she will	=	she'll
he would	=	he'd
is not	=	isn't
will not	=	won't

Use an apostrophe to show that numbers have been omitted, too.

example:
the winter of 1999 = the winter of '99

Note: Your instructor may want you to avoid contractions in formal assignments. Be sure to follow his or her instructions.

2. Use an apostrophe to show possession. If a word does not end in -*s*, show ownership by adding an apostrophe and -*s*.

examples:
the car belongs to Maria	=	Maria's car
the toy is owned by my cousin	=	my cousin's toy
the hat belongs to somebody	=	somebody's hat

If two people own something, put the '*s* on the last person's name.

Jack and Joe own a dog   =   Jack and Joe's dog

If a word already ends in '*s* and you want to show ownership, just add an apostrophe.

examples:
The doll belongs to Dolores	=	Dolores' doll
two girls own a cat	=	the girls' cat
Mr. Ross owns a house	=	Mr. Ross' house

3. Use an apostrophe and -*s* for special uses of time, and to create a plural of numbers mentioned as numbers, letters mentioned as letters, and words that normally do not have plurals.

special use of time: It took a *month's* work.
numbers mentioned as numbers: Add the *7's*.
letters mentioned as letters: Dot your *i's*.
words that normally do not have plurals: Give me some more *thank you's*.

Caution: Be careful with apostrophes. Possessive pronouns like *his*, *hers*, *theirs*, *ours*, *yours*, and *its* do not take apostrophes.

not this: I was sure the dress was ~~her's~~.
but this: I was sure the dress was hers.

not this: The movie has ~~it's~~ flaws.
but this: The movie has its flaws.

Do not add an apostrophe to a simple plural.

not this: The pudding comes in three ~~flavor's~~.
but this: The pudding comes in three flavors.

TEACHING TIP:

Remind students that some plural nouns do not end in "s," so this rule applies (for example, "He looked for the men's restroom").

INSTRUCTOR'S NOTE:

Some students have learned that the "proper" way to indicate possession for proper names ending in "s" is to add '*s*. You can assure students that either *James'* or *James's*, for example, is acceptable. However, you can also note that newspapers and magazines have their own style sheets and preferences for their writers to follow.

TEACHING TIP:

Write *customer's* (singular possessive), *customers'* (plural possessive), and *customers* (simple plural) on the board. Have students write a sentence for each version of the word. At random, ask a few students to put their versions on the board. Some students may still have difficulty breaking the habit of automatically using an apostrophe on simple plural nouns.

Exercise 17

Practice

Punctuating with Apostrophes

Add apostrophes where they are needed in the following sentences.

1. I was on my way to the mens locker room when I saw Dr. Thomas grandson at one of the weight-training machines.

2. Teresa found a house key that looked like it belonged to her neighbors, but they said it wasn't theirs.

3. Skateboarding lost its appeal for me when I broke three ribs in a fall at the courthouse steps.

4. You can't be blamed for trying to get what's yours.

5. Maxine was sure she'd be invited to Richard and Lee's birthday party.

6. Iris' sister pronounces her *r*'s strangely.

7. In the summer of '99, I bought two jars of expensive moisturizing cream.

8. It's not how the company sells its products that I dislike; it's the high prices.

9. He'd rather be filling out orders than listening to people's complaints.

10. The woman's generous donation was given to a women's health center.

 Exercise 18   **More on Punctuating with Apostrophes**

Practice   Add apostrophes where they are needed in the following sentences.

1. My aunt kept complaining about Los Angeles' lack of public transportation and its traffic jams.

2. The old farm had acres of apple trees and lush green meadows.

3. I won't go to the concert if it's raining too hard.

4. Roberta insisted that the books under the seat were hers.

5. I'm not interested in anybody's opinion except yours.

6. She's tired of hearing *maybes* instead of *certainlys*.

7. Sally is driving to her sister and brother-in-law's house for the weekend.

8. They're not sure whether the books are yours.

9. Arthur's going to the races at the fairgrounds tomorrow.

10. When she writes, she has a fancy way of writing her *q*'s.

Exercise 19 **Punctuating with Apostrophes**

Connect Edit the following paragraph, correcting the eleven errors related to apostrophes. You need to add some apostrophes and eliminate the unnecessary apostrophes.

> Its a shame how a good restaurant can lose its high standards over the years. When I was a child, my parents used to take me to Fran's Pancake House as a special treat. Frans had the best pancakes in town, but it also served a wonderful array of breakfast food, from scrambled egg's with sausage's to homemade muffins and doughnuts. My family would go to Fran's on Saturdays and wed eat so much brunch that we wouldnt eat again until dinner. The food was good and plentiful, the price's were reasonable, and the waitresses were always friendly and kind. I remember one waitress who always gave me extra butter for my pancake's. Unfortunately, time hasn't been good to the restaurant. Last week I went back there after ten years, and I found a crowded, noisy restaurant. I was hoping that the crowd signaled good food and low prices, but the food wasnt a bit like it used to be. Its about the quality of a fast-food place, but the prices are high. I wonder if Fran still owns Frans Pancake House. If so, I wonder how Fran feels about losing the quality that used to be hers.

THE COLON

A colon is used at the end of a complete statement. It introduces a list or explanation.

> **colon introducing a list:**
> When my father went to the Bahamas, he brought me back some lovely gifts: a straw bag, a shell necklace, and some Bahamian perfume.

> **colon introducing an explanation:**
> The salesperson was very helpful: he told us about special discounted items and the free gift wrap service.

Remember that the colon comes after a complete statement. What comes after the colon explains or describes what came before the colon. Look once more at the two examples, and you'll see the point.

> When my father went to the Bahamas, he brought me back some lovely gifts: a straw bag, a shell necklace, and some Bahamian perfume. (The words after the colon, *a straw bag, a shell necklace, and some Bahamian perfume,* describe the lovely gifts.)
> The salesperson was very helpful: he told us about special discounted items and the free gift wrap service. (The words after the colon,

he told us about special discounted items and the free gift wrap service, explain what the salesperson did to be helpful.)

Some people use a colon every time they put a list in a sentence, but this is not a good rule to follow. Instead, remember that a colon, even one that introduces a list, must come after a complete statement.

not this: ~~If you are going to the drug store, remember to pick up: toothpaste, dental floss, and mouthwash.~~

but this: If you are going to the drug store, remember to pick up these items: toothpaste, dental floss, and mouthwash.

A colon may also introduce a long quotation.

colon introducing a long quotation:
In a speech to the alumni at Columbia University, Will Rogers joked about what a big university it was and said: "There are 3,200 courses. You spend your first two years in deciding what course to take, the next two years in finding the building that these courses are given in, and the rest of your life in wishing you had taken another course."

Practice

Punctuating with Colons

Add colons where they are needed in the following sentences.

1. If you need more desserts for the party, you can call Tina Woo and ask her to bring cookies, ice cream, and cupcakes.

2. Last night Marco looked anxious he kept fidgeting and couldn't concentrate on the conversation.

3. When we camp out, we always bring some first-aid supplies bandages, antiseptic cream, aspirin, and antacid.

4. The food at the reunion banquet was disgusting greasy roast beef, watery boiled potatoes, limp green beans, and stale rolls.

5. After a long pause, the police officer said she would let me off with a warning.

6. When I realized my wallet was missing, I looked everywhere in my car, under the bed, in the garage, and even in the flower beds.

7. To find his lost key, the boy searched between the sofa cushions, behind the curtains, and under the rug.

8. Gina has a valuable collection of early American toys a hand-carved rocking horse, a rag doll, and three small wooden animals.

9. Yesterday, when I went back to my old school, I noticed several changes the students seemed young, the hallways seemed narrow, and the classrooms looked tiny.

10. Yesterday, when I went back to my old school, I noticed the students seemed young, the hallways seemed narrow, and the classrooms looked tiny.

THE EXCLAMATION MARK

The exclamation mark is used at the end of sentences that express strong emotion.

appropriate: Mr. Zimmerman, you've just become the father of triplets!

inappropriate: The dance was fabulous! (*Fabulous* already implies excitement and enthusiasm, so you don't need the exclamation mark.)

Be careful not to overuse the exclamation mark. If your choice of words is descriptive, you should not have to rely on the exclamation mark for emphasis. Use it sparingly, for it is easy to rely on exclamation marks instead of using better vocabulary.

THE DASH

Use a dash to interrupt a sentence; use two dashes to set off words in a sentence. The dash is somewhat dramatic, so be careful not to overuse it.

examples:
Helena's frustration at her job made her an angry woman—a mean, angry woman.
My cousins Celia and Rick—the silly fools—fell off the dock when they were clowning around.

PARENTHESES

Use parentheses to set off words in a sentence.

examples:
The movies he rented (<u>Anger Management</u>, <u>Spiderman</u>, <u>Agent Cody Banks</u>) were all too silly for me.
Note: In student essays, movies are underlined. In publications, movies are in italics.
Simon nominated Justin Lewis (his best friend) as club treasurer.

Note: Commas in pairs, dashes in pairs, and parentheses are all used as inserters. They set off inserted material that interrupts the flow of the sentence. The least dramatic and smoothest way to insert material is to use commas.

THE HYPHEN

A hyphen joins two or more descriptive words that act as a single word.

examples:
Mr. Handlesman was wearing a custom-made suit.
My great aunt's hair is a salt-and-pepper color.

 Exercise 21

Practice

Punctuating with Exclamation Marks, Dashes, Parentheses, and Hyphens

In the following sentences, add exclamation marks, dashes, parentheses, and hyphens where they are needed. Answers may vary because some writers may use dashes instead of parentheses.

1. I decided to wear a coat my second best one to the children's carnival.

2. You've just won a million dollars in the sweepstakes

3. Dolores Chang who used to go to high school with me is now a famous heart surgeon.

4. Dr. Menelli thinks Steve is a self centered young man.

5. There's a tarantula in my bed

6. The restaurant an old fashioned diner does a good business on Saturday nights.

7. My father's toy soldiers to my amazement turned out to be valuable antiques.

8. Jasmine spent all afternoon looking for a one of a kind birthday gift for me.

9. City Lights formerly called City Electric is a good place to look for lamps.

10. He's a smooth talker no doubt about it.

QUOTATION MARKS

Use quotation marks for direct quotations, for the titles of short works, and for other, special uses.

1. Put quotation marks around direct quotations, (a speaker or writer's exact words).

quotation marks around direct quotations:
Ernest always told me, "It is better to give than to receive."
"Nobody goes to that club," said Ramon.
"We could go to the movies," Christina offered, "but we'd better hurry."
My mother warned me, "Save your money. You'll need it for a rainy day."

Look carefully at the preceding examples. Note that a comma is used to introduce a direct quotation, and that, at the end of the quotation, a comma or a period goes inside the quotation marks.

Ernest always taught me, "It is better to give than to receive."

Notice how direct quotations of more than one sentence are punctuated. If the quotation is written as one unit, quotation marks go before the first quoted word and after the last quoted word:

My mother warned me, "Save your money. You'll need it for a rainy day."

But if the quotation is not written as one unit, the punctuation changes:

"Save your money," my mother warned me. "You'll need it for a rainy day."

Caution: Do *not* put punctuation marks around indirect quotations.

indirect quotation: Tyree asked if the water was cold.
direct quotation: Tyree asked, "Is the water cold?"

indirect quotation: She said that she needed a break from work.
direct quotation: She said, "I need a break from work."

2. Put quotation marks around the titles of short works. If you are writing the title of a short work like a short story, an essay, a newspaper or magazine article, a poem, or a song, put quotation marks around the title.

quotation marks around the titles of short works:
My father's favorite poem is "The Raven" by Edgar Allan Poe.
When I was little, I used to sing "Twinkle, Twinkle, Little Star."
I couldn't think of a good title, so I just called my essay "How I Spent My Summer Vacation."

If you are writing the title of a longer work like a book, movie, magazine, play, television show, or record album, underline the title.

underlining the titles of longer works:
My favorite childhood movie was <u>Star Wars</u>.
For homework, I have to read an article called "Children and Reading Skills" in <u>Time</u> magazine.

In printed publications such as books or magazines, titles of long works are put in italics. But when you are writing by hand, typing, or using a word processor, underline the titles of long works.

3. There are other, special uses of quotation marks. You use quotation marks around special words in a sentence.

quotation marks around special words:
When you say "sometimes," how often do you mean?
People from Boston say "frappe" when they mean "milkshake."

If you are using a quotation within a quotation, use single quotation marks.

a quotation within a quotation:
Janey said angrily, "You took my car without permission, and all you can say is, 'It's no big deal.' "
Aunt Mary said, "You need to teach that child to say 'please' and 'thank you' more often."

Punctuating with Quotation Marks

Practice   Add quotation marks where they are needed in the following sentences.

    1. Last night around nine, Samantha called to ask whether I had seen her brother.

    2. "You'll never be happy," my grandmother used to say, "until you find someone to love."

    3. That radio station has been playing "Jingle Bells" every hour.

    4. Mark seemed really sincere when he said that he wanted to come to the dance but couldn't get a ride.

    5. "Have you seen my brother?" Samantha asked when she called around nine last night.

    6. "It's been one thing after another. I've spent the whole day handling minor emergencies," said my father.

    7. "It's been one thing after another," my father said. "I've spent the whole day handling minor emergencies."

    8. The toddler calls his sister "Baba" because he can't pronounce "Barbara."

    9. Alexander declared, "When you refused to say 'I'm sorry,' our friendship ended."

    10. I think the word "gone" is the saddest word in the language.

 More on Punctuating with Quotation Marks

Practice   Add quotation marks where they are needed in the following sentences.

    1. In high school, I had to read a story called "The Black Cat."

    2. Instead of criticizing me, my sister said, "give me some encouragement."

    3. Jill wondered whether she could borrow some money until payday so she could pay her overdue electric bill.

    4. "I wonder if I can trouble you for a moment," my neighbor said. "I seem to have lost my keys."

    5. "Absolutely not," my mother said, when I asked her if I could borrow her car.

6. Our building superintendent always says he'll get to it when we ask him to do a repair, but he never follows through.

7. "Style" is a hard word to define because it has many meanings.

8. Dave said, "I apologize. I should have said 'please' before I grabbed the last piece of cake."

9. "The computer is too slow," he complained. "It is old and outdated," he added.

10. Without a map, you won't be able to find that house.

CAPITAL LETTERS

There are ten main situations when you capitalize.

1. Capitalize the first word of every sentence.

examples:
Sometimes we take a walk on the beach.
An apple is a healthy snack.

2. Capitalize the first word in a direct quotation if the word begins a sentence.

examples:
Jensina said, "Here is the money I owe you and a little something extra."
"Here is the money I owe you," Jensina said, "and a little something extra." (Notice that the second section of this quotation does not begin with a capital letter because it does not begin a sentence.)

3. Capitalize the names of persons.

examples:
Ingrid Alvorsen and Sean Miller invited me to their wedding.
I asked Father to visit me.

Do not capitalize words like *mother*, *father*, or *aunt* if you put a possessive in front of them.

names with possessives:
I asked my father to visit me.
She disliked her aunt.

4. Capitalize the titles of persons.

examples:
I worked for Dr. Mabala.
She is interviewing Dean Richards.

Do not capitalize when the title is not connected to a name.

a title not connected to a name:
I worked for that doctor.
She is interviewing the dean.

5. Always capitalize nationalities, religions, races, months, days of the week, documents, organizations, holidays, and historical events or periods.

examples:
In eighth grade, I did a project on the American Revolution.
At my son's nursery school, the students presented a program to celebrate Thanksgiving.
Every Tuesday night, he goes to meetings at the African-American Club.

Use small letters for the seasons.

a season with a small letter:
I always look forward to the coming of winter.

6. Capitalize the names of particular places.

examples:
I used to attend Hawthorne Middle School.
My friends like to stroll through City Center Mall.

Use small letters if a particular place is not given.

small letter for no particular place:
My friends like to stroll through the mall.

7. Use capital letters for geographic locations.

examples:
Lisa wanted to attend a college in the South.
I love autumn in the Midwest.

But use small letters for geographic directions.

small letter for a geographic direction:
The easiest way to find the airport is to drive south on the freeway.

8. Capitalize the names of specific products.

examples:
I need some Tylenol for my headache.
Melanie eats a Snickers bar every day.

But use small letters for a general type of product.

small letter for a general product:
Melanie eats a candy bar every day.

9. Capitalize the names of specific school courses.

examples:
My favorite class is Ancient and Medieval History.
Alicia is taking Introduction to Computers this fall.

But use small letters for a general academic subject.

small letter for a general subject:
Before I graduate, I have to take a computer course.

10. Capitalize the first and last words in the titles of long or short works, and capitalize all other significant words in the title.

examples:
I loved the movie <u>A Man Apart</u>.
There is a beautiful song called "I Will Always Love You."

(Remember that the titles of long works, like movies, are underlined; the titles of short works, like songs, are placed within quotation marks.)

Punctuating with Capital Letters

Add capital letters where they are needed in the following sentences.

1. My teachers in high school never made me take a psychology course.

2. The house I want to buy is just north of riverside drive near the
   Riverside Drive
   Springfield County Garden Club
   springfield county garden club.

3. Felipe gave his mother a beautiful tablecloth made of irish linen.
   Irish

4. "let's go see my brother," Tina said, "and borrow his truck."
   Let's

5. I want to explore the west over the summer and stay away until
   West
   Labor Day
   labor day.

6. My former teacher, who is now dean Roth, told me he is looking
   Dean
   Spanish Club
   for a new president of the spanish club.

7. Last sunday I spent the whole afternoon in front of the television,
   Sunday
   Pepsi   Doritos
   drinking pepsi and eating doritos.

8. I saw a copy of the declaration of independence at an exhibit at
   Declaration of Independence
   Hillsborough Art Center
   the hillsborough art center.

9. I once asked aunt louise if she liked being my aunt.
   Aunt Louise

10. I am writing to the president of the company about the

    deteriorating condition of the concert hall.

Punctuating with Capital Letters: Creating Your Own Examples

Do this exercise with a partner or a group. Below is a list giving situations when you should—or should not—use capital letters. Write a sentence at least five words long as an example for each item on the list.

1. Capitalize the names of particular places.

   example: Alicia is taking a trip to St. Louis, Missouri.

2. Use capital letters for geographic locations.

   example: Mimi and Steve were born in the South.

3. Use small letters for geographic directions.

   example: Greg lives north of the post office.

4. Capitalize historic events.

   example: My class is studying the Vietnam War.

5. Capitalize nationalities.

example: <u>The speaker is a Venezuelan journalist.</u>

6. Capitalize the names of persons.

example: <u>I saw a movie starring Denzel Washington.</u>

7. Do not capitalize words like *mother*, *father*, or *uncle* if you put a possessive in front of them.

example: <u>Rosa got the book from her uncle.</u>

8. Capitalize the titles of persons.

example: <u>Senator Jones is visiting our school today.</u>

9. Don't capitalize when the title is not connected to a name.

example: <u>I have seen the senator speak at two ceremonies.</u>

10. Capitalize the names of specific products.

example: <u>Harry grabbed the box of Kleenex.</u>

Exercise 26

 Connect

Punctuating with Quotation Marks, Underlining, and Capital Letters

Following is a paragraph with some blank spaces. Fill in the blanks, remembering the rules for using quotation marks, underlining, and capital letters. When you have completed the exercise, be ready to share your responses with members of the class.

When I think about last year, I remember some very specific details. I

remember that the song I was always listening to was called

<u>Capitalize and put the title in quotation marks.</u>, and the singer I admired

most was <u>Capitalize a proper name.</u>. The one movie I remember best is,

<u>Capitalize and underline the title.</u> and the television program I recall

watching is <u>Capitalize and underline the title.</u>. There are several places I

associate with last year, also. Among them are a store called

<u>Capitalize the store name.</u>, the school nearest to my home, called

<u>Capitalize the school name.</u>, and a place I always wanted to go to, but never

visited, called <u>Capitalize the place name.</u>. When I think of last year, I real-

ize that I spent many hours eating at a fast-food restaurant named

<u>Capitalize the place name.</u>   My favorite cold drink was

<u>Capitalize a brand name.</u>. Today, I realize that some of my habits and tastes

have changed, yet I am still very much connected to the specific places and

things of the past.

NUMBERS

Spell out numbers that take one or two words to spell out.

examples:
The coat cost seventy dollars.
Bridget sent two hundred invitations.

Use hyphens to spell out numbers from twenty-one to ninety-nine.

examples:
Clarissa, twenty-three, is the oldest daughter.
I mailed sixty-two invitations.

Use numerals if it takes more than two words to spell a number.

examples:
The company sold 367 toy trains.
The price of the car was $15,629.

Also use numerals to write dates, times, and addresses.

examples:
You can visit him at 223 Sailboat Lane.
I receivd my diploma on June 17, 1998.
We woke up at 6:00 a.m., bright and early.

Use numerals with *a.m.* and *p.m.*, but use words with *o'clock*.

example:
We woke up at six o'clock, bright and early.

ABBREVIATIONS

Although you should spell out most words rather than abbreviate them, you may use common abbreviations like *Mr.*, *Mrs.*, *Ms.*, *Jr.*, *Sr.*, and *Dr.* when they are used with a proper name. Abbreviations may also be used for references to time and for organizations widely known by initials.

examples:
I gave Dr. Lambert my medical records.
The phone rang at 3:00 a.m. and scared me out of a sound sleep.
Nancy got a job with the FBI.

Spell out the names of places, months, days of the week, courses of study, and words referring to parts of a book.

not this: I visited a friend in Philadelphia, ~~Penn.~~
but this: I visited a friend in Philadelphia, Pennsylvania.

not this: My brother skipped his ~~phys. ed.~~ class yesterday.
but this: My brother skipped his physical education class yesterday.

not this: Last week, our garbage was not picked up on ~~Weds.~~ or ~~Sat.~~,
   so I called the ~~Dept.~~ of Sanitation.

but this: Last week, our garbage was not picked up on Wednesday
   or Saturday, so I called the Department of Sanitation.

 Exercise 27

Practice

Punctuating with Numbers and Abbreviations

Correct any errors in punctuating with numbers and abbreviations in the
following sentences.

1. Mr. Zemeki's IBM computer cost over two thousand dollars.

2. My favorite vacation was in my jr. [junior] year when I took a school trip
   to Boston, Mass., [Massachusetts,] to see the historical sites.

3. Can I borrow your trig. [trigonometry] notes for the chapt. [chapter] I missed?

4. Norris will be twenty one [twenty-one] tomorrow.

5. I signed the lease for a place at Hamilton Apts. [Apartments] on Feb. [February] 1, 1997.

6. Lucinda gave fifty seven [fifty-seven] dollars to the disaster relief fund; she
   made the money working for the dr. [doctor] in our neighborhood clinic.

7. I asked her to give me 3 [three] or 4 [four] good reasons to drop my psych. [psychology]
   class.

8. Raina is hoping to attend Cal. [California] State U. [University] next year, so she is taking a
   trip to California to explore the university.

9. Last night I watched MTV until ten thirty-five [10:35] p.m.

10. I was looking for a prof. [professor] who would do more than lecture about
   history.

Exercise 28

Practice

Punctuation: A Comprehensive Exercise

In the following sentences, add punctuation where it is needed and correct
any punctuation errors.

1. My sister gave me a great book called The house on mango street [The House on Mango Street;]
   Ill [I'll] give it to you when Im [I'm] finished with it.

2. Pet Haven, the oldest pet supply store in town, works with the local
   animal shelter.

3. Leo studied cooking in France; thus he has been exposed to many
   new recipes and techniques.

4. After Lonny finished medical school he worked at Jackson

Memorial Hospital
memorial hospital.

5. Mr Rivera asked if there was a pharmacy nearby

6. Mr Rivera asked Is there a pharmacy nearby

7. I enjoyed my three cats antics but sometimes those cats drove me

crazy.

8. You could borrow the money from your father on the other hand

you could take out a bank loan.

9. Chocolate cake which is my favorite dessert is a disaster for my

diet because its full of fat.

10. "If you can give me five minutes Lisa said I'll be ready to leave.

Punctuation: Another Comprehensive Exercise

Practice   In the following sentences, add punctuation where it is needed and correct
any punctuation errors.

1. Customers can be pushy and salespeople can be rude but both

groups need to learn patience if the marketplace is to become

friendly again.

2. My car had a problem with its electrical system so I spent

$247
two hundred and forty-seven dollars in repairs.

3. My mother always used to sing a song by James Taylor called

"You've Got a Friend."
You've got a friend.

January 23, 2000,   ,Florida,
4. Jeff and I were married on Jan. 23 2000 in Tallahassee Fla. but

moved farther south a year later.

Schindler's List.
5. One movie that I will never forget is Schindlers List.

, Mom,
6. Sure you can borrow my hairdryer mom but remember to bring it

back.

Agnes'   :
7. Last night, I washed and ironed all of Agnes summer dresses her

ruffled yellow one her blue pinafore and her pink sundress.

8. When you call Rafael remind him to buy soda potato chips dip and salsa for the mens softball game tomorrow.

9. I woke up at *6:00 a.m.,* 6 a.m. so I had time to eat breakfast before I went to Miami-Dade *College* college.

10. Unless he does some work on that *beat-up* beat up house he wont be able to sell it.

Exercise 30   **Adding Punctuation to Paragraphs**

The following paragraphs come from an article in *People* magazine. They tell the true story of two people on the *Titanic*, the famous ship that sank when it hit an iceberg in 1912.

As you read the paragraphs, you will notice that they are missing some punctuation (twenty-three punctuation marks). Add the necessary punctuation.

Isidor and Ida Strauss: Inseparable in Life, Then in Death

Ida Strauss refused at least two opportunities to escape the sinking *Titanic*, choosing instead to die with her husband of fifty-one years, a well known philanthropist* who owned Macy's department store News that the couple had shared their fate came as no surprise to their six children and many friends. When they were apart they wrote to each other every day says Joan Adler, director of the Strauss *Historical Society.* historical society "She called him my darling papa. He called her my darling momma. " For years, they even celebrated their different birthdays on the same day.

As the *Titanic* went down, Ida sixty-three refused the pleas of officers to climb into a lifeboat, insisting instead that her maid take her place and handing the young woman her fur coat (I wont need this anymore, she said). She was finally cajoled* into boarding the second to last lifeboat, only to clamber* out again as Isidor sixty-seven stepped away. Last seen clasped in an embrace Ida and Isidor are memorialized in a Bronx cemetery with a monument inscribed, "Many waters cannot quench love, neither can the floods drown it "

*philanthropist: a person who donates money to charity
*cajoled: persuaded
*clamber: climb

CHAPTER 17

Spelling

No one is a perfect speller, but there are ways to become a better speller. If you can learn a few spelling rules, you can answer many of your spelling questions.

VOWELS AND CONSONANTS

To understand the spelling rules, you need to know the difference between vowels and consonants. **Vowels** are the letters *a, e, i, o, u,* and sometimes *y.* **Consonants** are all the other letters.

The letter *y* is a vowel when it has a vowel sound.

examples:
silly (The *y* sounds like *ee*, a vowel sound.)
cry (The *y* sounds like *i*, a vowel sound.)

The letter *y* is a consonant when it has a consonant sound.

examples:
yellow (The *y* has a consonant sound.)
yesterday (The *y* has a consonant sound.)

SPELLING RULE 1: DOUBLING A FINAL CONSONANT

Double the final consonant of a word if all three of the following are true:

1. the word is one syllable, or the accent is on the last syllable,
2. the word ends in a single consonant preceded by a single vowel, and
3. the ending you are adding starts with a vowel.

examples:

begin	+	ing	=	beginning
shop	+	er	=	shopper
stir	+	ed	=	stirred
occur	+	ed	=	occurred
fat	+	est	=	fattest
pin	+	ing	=	pinning

Exercise 1   **Doubling a Final Consonant**

Practice   Add *-ed* to the following words by applying the rules for double consonants.

1. refer   referred   6. expel   expelled

2. scatter   scattered   7. abandon   abandoned

3. plan   planned   8. wonder   wondered

4. trick   tricked   9. suffer   suffered

5. offer   offered   10. prefer   preferred

SPELLING RULE 2: DROPPING THE FINAL *e*

Drop the final *e* before you add an ending that starts with a vowel.

examples:

observe	+	ing	=	observing
excite	+	able	=	excitable
fame	+	ous	=	famous
create	+	ive	=	creative

Keep the final *e* before an ending that starts with a consonant.

examples:

love	+	ly	=	lovely
hope	+	ful	=	hopeful
excite	+	ment	=	excitement
life	+	less	=	lifeless

Exercise 2   **Dropping the Final *e***

Practice   Combine the following words and endings by following the rule for dropping the final *e*.

1. cure   +   able   curable

2. time   +   less   timeless

3. shape   +   ly   shapely

4. come   +   ing   coming

5. shape   +   ing   shaping

6. advertise   +   ment   advertisement

7. terminate   +   ion   termination

8. defense   +   ive   defensive

9. tame   +   ness   tameness

10. debate   +   able   debatable

SPELLING RULE 3: CHANGING THE FINAL *y* TO *i*

When a word ends in a consonant plus *y*, change the *y* to *i* when you add an ending.

examples:

try	+	es	=	tries
silly	+	er	=	sillier
rely	+	ance	=	reliance
tardy	+	ness	=	tardiness

Note: When you add *-ing* to words ending in *y*, always keep the *y*.

examples:

cry	+	ing	=	crying
rely	+	ing	=	relying

Exercise 3

Practice

Changing the Final *y* to *i*

Combine the following words and endings by applying the rule for changing the final *y* to *i*.

1. copy + er   *copier*

2. pretty + ness   *prettiness*

3. buy + er   *buyer*

4. mercy + less   *merciless*

5. copy + ing   *copying*

6. carry + ed   *carried*

7. annoy + ance   *annoyance*

8. pity + ful   *pitiful*

9. cry + es   *cries*

10. dismay + ed   *dismayed*

SPELLING RULE 4: ADDING *-s* OR *-es*

Add *-es* instead of *-s* to a word if the word ends in *ch*, *sh*, *ss*, *x*, or *z*. The *-es* adds an extra syllable to the word.

examples:

box	+	es	=	boxes
witch	+	es	=	witches
class	+	es	=	classes
clash	+	es	=	clashes

Exercise 4

Practice

Adding -s or -es

Add -s or -es to the following words by applying the rule for adding -s or -es.

1. vanish   vanishes   6. stretch   stretches

2. church   churches   7. wander   wanders

3. trespass   trespasses   8. clock   clocks

4. bunch   bunches   9. fizz   fizzes

5. fox   foxes   10. retreat   retreats

SPELLING RULE 5: USING *ie* OR *ei*

Use *i* before *e* except after *c*, or when the sound is like *a*, as in *neighbor* and *weigh*.

examples of *i* before *e*:

relief   niece   friend   piece

examples of *e* before *i*:

conceive   sleigh   weight   receive

Exercise 5

Practice

Using *ie* or *ei*

Add *ie* or *ei* to the following words by applying the rules for using *ie* or *ei*.

1. dec _e_ _i_ ve   6. th _i_ _e_ f

2. rec _e_ _i_ pt   7. v _e_ _i_ n

3. tr _i_ _e_ d   8. ch _i_ _e_ f

4. bel _i_ _e_ f   9. perc _e_ _i_ ve

5. fr _e_ _i_ ght   10. ach _i_ _e_ ve

INSTRUCTOR'S NOTE:

One common exception is the word "science."

Exercise 6

Practice

Spelling Rules: A Comprehensive Exercise

Combine the following words and endings by applying the spelling rules.

1. tax   +   s *or* es   taxes

2. guy   +   s *or* es   guys

3. fly   +   s *or* es   flies

4. beauty +   ful   beautiful

5. deserve +   ing   deserving

6. home   +   less   homeless

7. care   +   ful   careful

8. care	+	ing	caring
9. defer	+	ed	deferred
10. scan	+	er	scanner

Exercise 7

Practice

Spelling Rules: Another Comprehensive Exercise

Combine the following words and endings by applying the spelling rules.

1. steady	+	ness	steadiness
2. ship	+	ment	shipment
3. ship	+	ed	shipped
4. regret	+	ing	regretting
5. catch	+	s *or* es	catches
6. pass	+	s *or* es	passes
7. handy	+	er	handier
8. weigh	+	es	weighes
9. marry	+	ed	married
10. murmur	+	ed	murmured

Exercise 8

👥 *Collaborate*

Creating Examples for the Spelling Rules

Working with a partner or a group, write examples for the following rules.

Spelling Rule 1: Doubling the Final Consonant
Double the final consonant of a word if all three of the following are true:

1. the word is one syllable or the accent is on the last syllable,

2. the word ends in a single consonant preceded by a single vowel, and

3. the ending you added starts with a vowel.

example:

Answers Will Vary.

Possible answers shown at right.

1. Write a word that is one syllable (or the accent is on the last syllable), and that ends in a consonant preceded by a single vowel: _____infer_____

2. Write an ending that starts with a vowel: _____ed_____

3. Combine the word and the ending : _____inferred_____

Spelling Rule 2: Dropping the Final *e*
Drop the final *e* before you add an ending that starts with a vowel.

example:

1. Write a word that ends with an *e:* _____hate_____

2. Write an ending that starts with a vowel: _____ *ing* _____

3. Combine the word and the ending: _____ *hating* _____

Spelling Rule 3: Changing the Final *y* to *i*
When a word ends in a consonant plus *y*, change the *y* to *i* when you add an ending.

example:

1. Write a word that ends in a consonant plus *y:* _____ *sky* _____

2. Write an ending: _____ *es* _____

3. Combine the word and the ending: _____ *skies* _____

Spelling Rule 4: Adding *-s* or *-es*
Add *-es* instead of *-s* to a word if the word ends in *ch, sh, ss, x,* or *z*. The *-es* adds an extra syllable to the word.

example:

1. Write a word that ends in *ch, sh, ss, x,* or *z:* _____ *fax* _____

2. Add *-es* to the word: _____ *faxes* _____

Spelling Rule 5: Using *ie* or *ei*
Use *i* before *e*, except after *c*, or when the sound is like *a*, as in *neighbor* and *weigh*.

examples:

1. Write three words that use *i* before *e:* _____ *believe, relief, chief* _____

2. Write one word that uses *ei:* _____ *deceive.* _____

Exercise 9

☞ *Connect*

Editing a Paragraph for Spelling

Correct the twelve spelling errors in the following paragraph. Write your corrections above each error.

                                                 believe
        I have never been able to spell. I beleive my spelling problems come
                       difficulties
from several difficultys. First of all, I don't know how to use a dictionary.
                                               referred
Whenever I had a spelling problem in grade school, my teachers refered me

to a dictionary. But if I didn't know how to spell that word, how did I know
                               tries
where to look it up? After several trys, I always gave up. Second, I am a per-

son who doesn't have much patience, especially when I write. I am someone
               writing   *rushes*
who dislikes writing and who rushs through my assignments. I don't take
                                             looking
the time to correct errors, and I don't spend much time lookking for spelling
     mistakes   *relieved*
mistaks. I am so releived to have finished the paper, I don't want to spend

any more time on it. Third, I don't believe that spelling is very important. I

putting   *making*

figure that the purpose of puting words on paper is making a point. There-

Unfortunately

fore, if you get my point, the spelling shouldn't matter. Unfortunatly, most

people believe that spelling does matter, and so I guess I have to spend

some time learning this skill.

HOW DO YOU SPELL IT? ONE WORD OR TWO?

Sometimes you can be confused about certain words. You are not sure whether to combine them to make one word or to spell them as two words. The lists below show some commonly confused words.

Words That Should Not Be Combined

a lot	each other	high school
all right	even though	good night
a while	every time	living room
dining room	in front	no one

Words That Should Be Combined

another	nevertheless
bathroom	newspapers
bedroom	playroom
bookkeeper	roommate
cannot	schoolteacher
downstairs	southeast, northwest, etc.
good-bye, goodbye, or good-by	throughout
grandmother	worthwhile
nearby	yourself, myself, himself, etc.

Words Whose Spelling Depends on Their Meaning

one word: *Already* means "before."
He offered to do the dishes, but I had *already* done them.

two words: *All ready* means "ready."
My dog was *all ready* to play Frisbee.

one word: *Altogether* means "entirely."
That movie was *altogether* too confusing.

two words: *All together* means "in a group."
My sisters were *all together* in the kitchen.

one word: *Always* means "every time."
My grandfather is *always* right about baseball statistics.

two words: *All ways* means "every path" or "every aspect."
We tried *all ways* to get to the beach house.
He is a gentleman in *all ways*.

one word: *Anymore* means "any longer."
I do not want to exercise *anymore*.

two words: *Any more* means "additional."
Are there *any more* pickles?

one word: *Anyone* means "any person at all."
Is *anyone* home?

two words: *Any one* means "one person or thing in a special group."
I'll take *any one* of the chairs on sale.
He offered to give *any one* of the students a ride home.

one word: *Apart* means "separate."
Liam stood *apart* from his friends.

two words: *A part* is "a piece or section."
I read *a part* of the chapter.

one word: *Everyday* means "ordinary."
Tim was wearing his *everyday* clothes.

two words: *Every day* means "each day."
Sam jogs *every day*.

one word: *Everyone* means "all the people."
Everyone has bad days.

two words: *Every one* means "all the people or things in a specific group."
My father asked *every one* of the neighbors for a donation to the Red Cross.

one word: *Thank-you* is an adjective that describes a certain kind of note or letter.
Heather wrote her grandfather a *thank-you* note.

two words: We state our gratitude by saying, *"Thank you."*
"Thank you for lending me your car," Kyle said.

 Exercise 10

Practice

How Do You Spell It? One Word or Two?

Circle the correct word in the following sentences.

1. It was an (altogether/all together) beautiful ceremony; I was happy

to see my family (altogether/all together) at the wedding.

2. Celeste went to (highschool/high school) with (everyone/

every one) of the contestants in the cooking contest.

3. The decorator painted the (diningroom/dining room) a pale green, but

he painted (apart/a part) of the (bedroom/bed room) a bright orange.

4. If Mr. Han (cannot/can not) write the letter, you should write it

(yourself/your self).

5. Sue and Anna live (nearby/near by), and they see (eachother/

each other) often.

6. I told my (roommate/room mate) I had (already/all ready) called

the (highschool/high school).

7. When my brother left, he said (goodnight/good night) but not

(good-bye/good bye).

8. When I woke up, I did my (everyday/every day) chores, just the

way I (always/all ways) do.

9. (Throughout/Through out) the night, Paul listened for the sound of

a door opening (downstairs/down stairs).

10. An article in the (newspaper/news paper) said the accident victim

was going to be (alright/all right).

Exercise 11   **How Do You Spell It? One Word or Two?**

 Connect   The following paragraph contains ten errors in word combinations. Correct
the errors in the space above each line.

high school
My highschool education helped me to grow emotionally and intellectu-

ally. Even though I was not the best student, I know that I learned some-
every one
thing from everyone of my classes. My history class taught me that the past
altogether
is an all together fascinating subject, and my history teacher showed me
schoolteacher
what being a school teacher is all about. In my art class, I saw that people in
all ways
every culture want to add beauty to their lives in always and at all times. My

consumer math class helped me to be a better bookkeeper. My biology class
Nevertheless
was my toughest class, and at first I hated it. Never the less, I learned
cannot
from it. My instructor showed me that I can not treat a laboratory like a
playroom Another
play room. An other thing she did was give me a new respect for the
no one
environment. She taught me that noone has a right to abuse our natural

resources. I will always be grateful to her and to all my high school teachers

for introducing me to new skills and ideas.

A LIST OF COMMONLY MISSPELLED WORDS

Below is a list of words you use often in your writing. Study this list and use
it as a reference.

TEACHING TIP:

Ask students to circle any word that does not seem "right" to them. Such words can go on their personal spelling list. Also remind students to use a dictionary whenever possible; too many students prefer to jot down several versions of a word to see which one "looks correct," but such habits only reinforce poor spelling.

1. absence
2. absent
3. accept
4. accommodate
5. achieve
6. ache
7. acquire
8. across
9. actually
10. advertise
11. again
12. all right
13. a lot
14. almost
15. always
16. amateur
17. American
18. answer
19. anxious
20. apology
21. apparent
22. appetite
23. appreciate
24. argue
25. argument
26. asked
27. athlete
28. attempt
29. August
30. aunt
31. author
32. automobile
33. autumn
34. avenue
35. awful
36. awkward
37. balance
38. basically
39. because
40. becoming
41. beginning
42. behavior
43. belief
44. believe
45. benefit
46. bicycle
47. bought
48. breakfast
49. breathe
50. brilliant
51. brother
52. brought
53. bruise
54. build
55. bulletin
56. bureau
57. buried
58. business
59. busy
60. calendar
61. cannot
62. career
63. careful
64. catch
65. category
66. caught
67. cemetery
68. cereal
69. certain
70. chair
71. cheat
72. chicken
73. chief
74. children
75. cigarette
76. citizen
77. city
78. college
79. color
80. comfortable
81. committee
82. competition
83. conscience
84. convenient
85. conversation
86. copy
87. cough
88. cousin
89. criticism
90. criticize
91. crowded
92. daily
93. daughter
94. deceive
95. decide
96. definite
97. dentist
98. dependent
99. deposit
100. describe
101. desperate
102. development
103. different
104. dilemma
105. dining
106. direction
107. disappearance
108. disappoint
109. discipline
110. disease
111. divide
112. doctor
113. doesn't
114. don't
115. doubt
116. during
117. dying
118. early
119. earth
120. eighth
121. eligible
122. embarrass
123. encouragement
124. enough
125. environment
126. especially
127. etc.
128. every
129. exact
130. exaggeration
131. excellent
132. except
133. exercise
134. excite
135. existence
136. expect
137. experience
138. explanation
139. factory
140. familiar
141. family
142. fascinating
143. February
144. finally
145. forehead
146. foreign
147. forty
148. fourteen
149. friend
150. fundamental
151. general
152. generally
153. goes
154. going
155. government
156. grammar
157. grateful
158. grocery
159. guarantee

160. guard
161. guess
162. guidance
163. guide
164. half
165. handkerchief
166. happiness
167. heavy
168. height
169. heroes
170. holiday
171. hospital
172. humorous
173. identity
174. illegal
175. imaginary
176. immediately
177. important
178. independent
179. integration
180. intelligent
181. interest
182. interfere
183. interpretation
184. interrupt
185. iron
186. irrelevant
187. irritable
188. island
189. January
190. jewelry
191. judgment
192. kindergarten
193. kitchen
194. knowledge
195. laboratory
196. language
197. laugh
198. leisure
199. length
200. library
201. listen
202. loneliness
203. lying
204. maintain
205. maintenance
206. marriage
207. mathematics
208. meant
209. measure
210. medicine
211. million
212. miniature
213. minute
214. muscle
215. mysterious
216. naturally
217. necessary
218. neighbor
219. nervous
220. nickel
221. niece
222. ninety
223. ninth
224. occasion
225. o'clock
226. often
227. omission
228. once
229. operate
230. opinion
231. optimist
232. original
233. parallel
234. particular
235. peculiar
236. perform
237. perhaps
238. permanent
239. persevere
240. personnel
241. persuade
242. physically
243. pleasant
244. possess
245. possible
246. potato
247. practical
248. prefer
249. prejudice
250. prescription
251. presence
252. president
253. privilege
254. probably
255. professor
256. psychology
257. punctuation
258. pursue
259. quart
260. really
261. receipt
262. receive
263. recognize
264. recommend
265. reference
266. religious
267. reluctantly
268. remember
269. resource
270. restaurant
271. rhythm
272. ridiculous
273. right
274. sandwich
275. Saturday
276. scene
277. schedule
278. scissors
279. secretary
280. seize
281. several
282. severely
283. significant
284. similar
285. since
286. sincerely
287. soldier
288. sophomore
289. strength
290. studying
291. success
292. surely
293. surprise
294. taught
295. temperature
296. theater
297. thorough
298. thousand
299. tied
300. tomorrow
301. tongue
302. tragedy
303. trouble
304. truly
305. twelfth
306. unfortunately
307. unknown
308. until
309. unusual
310. using
311. variety
312. vegetable
313. Wednesday
314. weird
315. which
316. writing
317. written
318. yesterday

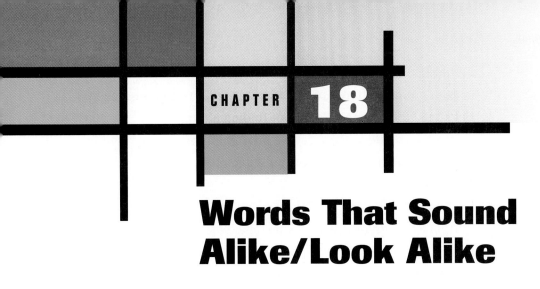

CHAPTER 18

Words That Sound Alike/Look Alike

WORDS THAT SOUND ALIKE/LOOK ALIKE

Words that sound alike or look alike can be confusing. Here is a list of some of these confusing words. Study this list, and make a note of any words that give you trouble.

a, an, and

A is used before a word beginning with a consonant or consonant sound.

> Jason bought *a* car.

An is used before a word beginning with a vowel or vowel sound.

> Nancy took *an* apple to work.

And joins words or ideas.

> Pudding *and* cake are my favorite desserts.
> Fresh vegetables taste delicious, *and* they are nutritious.

accept, except

Accept means "to receive."

> I *accept* your apology.

Except means "excluding."

> I'll give you all my books *except* my dictionary.

addition, edition

An *addition* is something that is added.

> My father built an *addition* to our house in the form of a porch.

An *edition* is an issue of a newspaper or one of a series of printings of a book.

> I checked the latest *edition* of the <u>Daily News</u> to see if my advertisement is in it.

advice, advise

Advice is an opinion offered as a guide; it is what you give someone.

> Betty asked for my *advice* about finding a job.

Advise is what you do when you give an opinion offered as a guide.

> I couldn't *advise* Betty about finding a job.

affect, effect

Affect means "to influence something."

> Getting a bad grade will *affect* my chances for a scholarship.

Effect means "a result" or "to cause something to happen."

> Your kindness had a great *effect* on me.
> The committee struggled to *effect* a compromise.

allowed, aloud

Allowed means "permitted."

> I'm not *allowed* to skateboard on those steps.

Aloud means "out loud."

> The teacher read the story *aloud*.

all ready, already

All ready means "ready."

> The dog was *all ready* to go for a walk.

Already means "before."

> David had *already* made the salad.

altar, alter

An *altar* is a table or place in a church.

> They were married in front of the *altar*.

Alter means "to change."

> My plane was delayed, so I had to *alter* my plans for the evening.

angel, angle

An *angel* is a heavenly being.

> That night, I felt an *angel* guiding me.

An *angle* is the space within two lines.

> The road turned at a sharp *angle*.

are, our

Are is a verb, the plural of *is*.

> We *are* friends of the mayor.

Our means "belonging to us."

> We have *our* family quarrels.

beside, besides

Beside means "next to."

> He sat *beside* me at the concert.

Besides means "in addition."

> I would never lie to you; *besides*, I have no reason to lie.

brake, break

Brake means "to stop" or "a device for stopping."

> That truck *brakes* at railroad crossings.
> When he saw the animal on the road, he hit the *brakes*.

Break means "to come apart" or "to make something come apart."

> The eggs are likely to *break*.
> I can *break* the seal on that package.

breath, breathe

Breath is the air you take in, and it rhymes with "death."

> I was running so fast that I lost my *breath*.

Breathe means "to take in air."

> He found it hard to *breathe* in high altitudes.

buy, by

Buy means "to purchase something."

> Sylvia wants to *buy* a shovel.

By means "near," "by means of," or "before."

> He sat *by* his sister.
> I learn *by* taking good notes in class.
> *By* ten o'clock, Nick was tired.

capital, capitol

Capital means "a city" or "wealth."

> Albany is the *capital* of New York.
> Jack invested his *capital* in real estate.

A *capitol* is a building.

> The city has a famous *capitol* building.

cereal, serial

Cereal is a breakfast food or a type of grain.

> My favorite *cereal* is Cheerios.

Serial means "in a series."

> Look for the *serial* number on the appliance.

choose, chose

Choose means "to select." It rhymes with "snooze."

> Today I am going to *choose* a new sofa.

Chose is the past tense of *choose*.

> Yesterday I *chose* a new rug.

close, clothes, cloths

Close means "near" or "intimate." It can also mean "to end or shut something."

> We live *close* to the train station.
> James and Margie are *close* friends.
> Noreen wants to *close* her eyes for ten minutes.

Clothes are wearing apparel.

> Eduardo has new *clothes*.

Cloths are pieces of fabric.

> I clean the silver with damp *cloths* and a special polish.

coarse, course
Coarse means "rough" or "crude."

> The top of the table had a *coarse* texture.
> His language was *coarse*.

A *course* is a direction or path. It is also a subject in school.

> The hurricane took a northern *course*.
> In my freshman year, I took a *course* in drama.

complement, compliment
Complement means "complete" or "make better."

> The colors in that room *complement* the style of the furniture.

A *compliment* is praise.

> Trevor gave me a *compliment* about my cooking.

conscience, conscious
Your *conscience* is your inner, moral guide.

> His *conscience* bothered him when he told a lie.

Conscious means "aware" or "awake."

> The accident victim was not fully *conscious*.

council, counsel
A *council* is a group of people.

> The city *council* meets tonight.

Counsel means "advice" or "to give advice."

> I need your *counsel* about my investments.
> My father always *counsels* me about my career.

decent, descent
Decent means "suitable" or "proper."

> I hope Mike gets a *decent* job.

Descent means "the process of going down, falling, or sinking."

> The plane began its *descent* to the airport.

desert, dessert
A *desert* is dry land. To *desert* means "to abandon."

> To survive a trip across the *desert*, people need water.
> He will never *desert* a friend.

Dessert is the sweet food we eat at the end of a meal.

> I want ice cream for *dessert*.

do, due

Do means "perform."

    I have to stop complaining; I *do* it constantly.

Due means "owing" or "because of."

    The rent is *due* tomorrow.
    The game was canceled *due* to rain.

does, dose

Does is a form of *do*.

    My father *does* the laundry.

A *dose* is a quantity of medicine.

    Whenever I had a cold, my mother gave me a *dose* of cough syrup.

fair, fare

Fair means "unbiased." It can also mean "promising" or "good."

    The judge's decision was *fair*.
    José has a *fair* chance of winning the title.

A *fare* is a fee for transportation.

    My subway *fare* is going up.

farther, further

Farther means "at a greater physical distance."

    His house is a few blocks *farther* down the street.

Further means "greater" or "additional." Use it when you are not describing a physical distance.

    My second French class gave me *further* training in French conversation.

flour, flower

Flour is ground-up grain, an ingredient used in cooking.

    I use whole wheat *flour* in my muffins.

A *flower* is a blossom.

    She wore a *flower* in her hair.

forth, fourth

Forth means "forward."

    The pendulum on the clock swung back and *forth*.

Fourth means "number four in a sequence."

    I was *fourth* in line for the tickets.

hear, here

Hear means "to receive sounds in the ear."

    I can *hear* the music.

Here is a place.

    We can have the meeting *here*.

heard, herd
Heard is the past tense of *hear.*

> I *heard* you talk in your sleep last night.

A *herd* is a group of animals.

> The farmer has a fine *herd* of cows.

hole, whole
A *hole* is an empty place or opening.

> I see a *hole* in the wall.

Whole means "complete" or "entire."

> Silvio gave me the *whole* steak.

isle, aisle
An *isle* is an island.

> We visited the *isle* of Capri.

An *aisle* is a passageway between sections of seats.

> The flight attendant came down the *aisle* and offered us coffee.

its, it's
Its means "belonging to it."

> The car lost *its* rear bumper.

It's is a shortened form of *it is* or *it has.*

> *It's* a beautiful day.
> *It's* been a pleasure to meet you.

knew, new
Knew is the past tense of *know.*

> I *knew* Teresa in high school.

New means "fresh, recent, not old."

> I want some *new* shoes.

know, no
Know means "to understand."

> They *know* how to play soccer.

No is a negative.

> Carla has *no* fear of heights.

Exercise 1   **Words That Sound Alike/Look Alike**

Practice   Circle the correct word in the following sentences.

1. David has traveled ((farther)/further) than I have, and he is so clever

   at finding bargains that he rarely pays full (fair/(fare)).

2. The jury was (conscience/(conscious)) of the prosecutor's hints that

   the (cereal/(serial)) killer had no ((conscience)/conscious).

3. I'm nearly deaf; you must come over (hear/(here)) so I can
   ((hear)/here) you.

4. The Oakwood Student ((Council)/Counsel) meets on the
   (forth/(fourth)) floor of the library building.

5. When I ((heard)/herd) the trucks outside my window, they sounded
   like a (heard/(herd)) of cattle running down the street.

6. ((Does)/Dose) Olivia ever (complement/(compliment)) you on your
   appearance or even say you have a ((decent)/descent) hairstyle?

7. Cristina and Amy are such ((close)/clothes/cloths) friends they wear
   each other's (close/(clothes)/cloths).

8. My little nephew insisted on helping me cook; he spilled
   ((flour)/flower) all over the kitchen floor and poured a (hole/(whole))
   gallon of milk down the sink.

9. Some people believe that a guardian ((angel)/angle) is right
   ((beside)/besides) them when they are in trouble.

10. I had an elaborate dinner ((all ready)/already) for her arrival, but
    she said she had (all ready/(already)) eaten.

Exercise 2

Collaborate

Words That Sound Alike/Look Alike

Working with a partner or a group, write one sentence for each of the words below. When you have completed this exercise, exchange it with another group's exercise for evaluation.

Answers Will Vary.

Possible answers shown at right.

1. a. its   The fish has lost its flavor.

   b. it's   I think it's warm enough to swim.

2. a. are   Nelson and Karen are guitar players.

   b. our   My husband and I bake our own bread.

3. a. accept   Brad is ready to accept your apology.

   b. except   Everyone except Peter liked the movie.

4. a. brake   I have never used my emergency brake.

   b. break   We must not break our promise to Dad.

5. a. buy   You can buy a birthday card at the supermarket.

   b. by   The package should arrive by Saturday.

6. a. choose   Today I can choose my engagement ring.

   b. chose   Last year, Julian chose to enter the military.

7. a. desert   They saw a film about the Sahara Desert.

   b. dessert   My favorite part of dinner is dessert.

8. a. conscience George must have a guilty conscience.

   b. conscious The speaker was not conscious of his error.

9. a. cereal   Sugary cereal is not good for children.

   b. serial   The dishwasher has a serial number on its door.

10. a. forth   From the depths of the crowd, a man came forth.

    b. fourth   Mr. Carson got his fourth parking ticket.

 Connect

Exercise 3   **Correcting Errors in Words That Sound Alike/Look Alike**

The following paragraph has eight errors in words that sound alike or look alike. Correct the errors in the space above each error.

                    choose
I am not sure how to chose a career. I want a job that pays well, so that

                                           capital
I can live a comfortable life and retire with enough capitol to maintain my

               course   *allowed*
lifestyle. Of coarse, I also want to work in a place where I am aloud to

express myself. It would be awful just to sit and stare at a computer screen

                                                breathe
all day. If I were trapped in a tiny office all day, I don't think I could breath.

On the other hand, it may be foolish to expect too much of a job. A good job

is hard to find, and maybe I should settle for financial security even if the

                               advice
work is boring. I think I should get some advise about my career because

                                                counsel
my choice will affect my entire future. Besides, some wise council can help

                       whole
me stop worrying about the hole issue.

MORE WORDS THAT SOUND ALIKE/LOOK ALIKE

lead, led
When *lead* rhymes with *need*, it means "to give direction, to take charge."
When *lead* rhymes with *bed*, it is a metal.

> The marching band will *lead* the parade.
> Your bookbag is as heavy as *lead*.

Led is the past form of *lead* when it means "to take charge."

> The cheerleaders *led* the parade last year.

loan, lone

A *loan* is something you give on the condition that it be returned.

> When I was broke, I got a *loan* of fifty dollars from my aunt.

Lone means "solitary, alone."

> A *lone* shopper stood in the checkout line.

loose, lose

Loose means "not tight."

> In the summer, *loose* clothing keeps me cool.

To *lose* something means "to be unable to keep it."

> I'm afraid I will *lose* my car keys.

moral, morale

Moral means "upright, honorable, connected to ethical standards."

> I have a *moral* obligation to care for my children.

Morale is confidence or spirit.

> After the game, the team's *morale* was low.

pain, pane

Pain means "suffering."

> I had very little *pain* after the surgery.

A *pane* is a piece of glass.

> The girl's wild throw broke a window *pane*.

pair, pear

A *pair* is a set of two.

> Mark has a *pair* of antique swords.

A *pear* is a fruit.

> In the autumn, I like a *pear* for a snack.

passed, past

Passed means "went by." It can also mean "handed to."

> The happy days *passed* too quickly.
> Janice *passed* me the mustard.

Past means "a time before the present." It can also mean "beyond" or "by."

> The family reunion was like a trip to the *past*.
> Rick ran *past* the tennis courts.

patience, patients

Patience is calm endurance.

> When I am caught in a traffic jam, I should have more *patience*.

Patients are people under medical care.

> There are too many *patients* in the doctor's waiting room.

peace, piece

Peace is calmness.

> Looking at the ocean brings me a sense of *peace*.

A *piece* is a part of something.

> Norman took a *piece* of coconut cake.

personal, personnel

Personal means "connected to a person." It can also mean "intimate."

> Whether to lease or own a car is a *personal* choice.
> That information is too *personal* to share.

Personnel are the staff in an office.

> The Digby Electronics Company is developing a new health plan for its *personnel.*

plain, plane

Plain means "simple," "clear," or "ordinary." It can also mean "flat land."

> The restaurant serves *plain* but tasty food.
> Her house was in the center of a windy *plain.*

A *plane* is an aircraft.

> We took a small *plane* to the island.

presence, presents

Your *presence* is your attendance, your being somewhere.

> We request your *presence* at our wedding.

Presents are gifts.

> My daughter got too many birthday *presents.*

principal, principle

Principal means "most important." It also means "the head of a school."

> My *principal* reason for quitting is the low salary.
> The *principal* of Crestview Elementary School is popular with students.

A *principle* is a guiding rule.

> Betraying a friend is against my *principles.*

quiet, quit, quite

Quiet means "without noise."

> The library has many *quiet* corners.

Quit means "stop."

> Will you *quit* complaining?

Quite means "truly" or "exactly."

> Victor's speech was *quite* convincing.

rain, reign, rein

Rain is wet weather.

> We have had a week of *rain.*

To *reign* is to rule; *reign* is royal rule.

> King Arthur's *reign* in Camelot is the subject of many poems.

A *rein* is a leather strap in an animal's harness.

> When Charlie got on the horse, he held the *reins* very tight.

right, rite, write

Right means "a direction (the opposite of left)." It can also mean "correct."

> To get to the gas station, turn *right* at the corner.
> On my sociology test, I got nineteen out of twenty questions *right*.

A *rite* is a ceremony.

> I am interested in the funeral *rites* of other cultures.

To *write* is to set down words.

> Brian has to *write* a book report.

sight, site, cite

A *sight* is something you can see.

> The truck stop was a welcome *sight*.

A *site* is a location.

> The city is building a courthouse on the *site* of my old school.

Cite means "to quote an authority." It can also mean "to give an example."

> In her term paper, Christina wanted to *cite* several computer experts.
> When my father lectured me on speeding, he *cited* the story of my best
>   friend's car accident.

sole, soul

A *sole* is the bottom of a foot or shoe.

> My left boot needs a new *sole*.

A *soul* is the spiritual part of a person.

> Some people say meditation is good for the *soul*.

stair, stare

A *stair* is a step.

> The toddler carefully climbed each *stair*.

To *stare* is to give a long, fixed look.

> I wish that woman wouldn't *stare* at me.

stake, steak

A *stake* is a stick driven into the ground. It can also mean "at risk" or "in question."

> The gardener put *stakes* around the tomato plants.
> Keith was nervous because his career was at *stake*.

A *steak* is a piece of meat or fish.

> I like my *steak* cooked medium rare.

stationary, stationery

Stationary means "standing still."

> As the speaker presented his speech, he remained *stationary*.

Stationery is writing paper.

> For my birthday, my uncle gave me some *stationery* with my name
>   printed on it.

than, then

Than is used to compare things.

My dog is more intelligent *than* many people.

Then means "at that time."

I lived in Buffalo for two years; *then* I moved to Albany.

their, there, they're

Their means "belonging to them."

My grandparents donated *their* old television to a women's shelter.

There means "at that place." It can also be used as an introductory word.

Sit *there,* next to Simone.
There is a reason for his happiness.

They're is a short form of *they are.*

Jaime and Sandra are visiting; *they're* my cousins.

thorough, through, threw

Thorough means "complete."

I did a *thorough* cleaning of my closet.

Through means "from one side to the other." It can also mean "finished."

We drove *through* Greenview on our way to Lake Western.
I'm *through* with my studies.

Threw is the past form of *throw.*

I *threw* the moldy bread into the garbage.

to, too, two

To means "in a direction toward." It is also a word that can go in front of a verb.

I am driving *to* Miami.
Selena loves *to* write poems.

Too means "also." It also means "very" or "excessively."

Anita played great golf, Adam did well, *too.*
It is *too* kind of you to visit.

Two is the number.

Mr. Almeida owns *two* clothing stores.

vain, vane, vein

Vain means "conceited." It also means "unsuccessful."

Victor is *vain* about his dark, curly hair.
The doctor made a *vain* attempt to revive the patient.

A *vane* is a device that moves to indicate the direction of the wind.

There was an old weather *vane* on the barn roof.

A *vein* is a blood vessel.

I could see the *veins* in his hands.

waist, waste

The *waist* is the middle part of the body.

He had a leather belt around his *waist.*

Waste means "to use carelessly." It also means "thrown away because it is useless."

I can't *waste* my time watching trashy television shows.
That manufacturing plant has many *waste* products.

wait, weight

Wait means "to hold oneself ready for something."

I can't *wait* until my check arrives.

Weight means "heaviness."

He tested the *weight* of the bat.

weather, whether

Weather refers to the conditions outside.

If the *weather* is warm, I'll go swimming.

Whether means "if."

Whether you help me or not, I'll paint the hallway.

were, we're, where

Were is the past form of *are.*

Only last year, we *were* scared freshmen.

We're is the short form of *we are.*

Today *we're* confident sophomores.

Where refers to a place.

Show me *where* you used to play basketball.

whined, wind, wined

Whined means "complained."

Polly *whined* about the weather because the rain kept her indoors.

Wind (when it rhymes with *find*) means "to coil or wrap something" or "to turn a key."

Wind that extension cord or you'll trip on it.

Wind (when it rhymes with *sinned*) is air in motion.

The *wind* blew my cap off.

If someone *wined* you, he treated you to some wine.

My brother *wined* and dined his boss.

who's, whose

Who's is a short form of *who is* or *who has.*

Who's driving?
Who's been stealing my quarters?

Whose means "belonging to whom."

I wonder *whose* dog this is.

woman/women

Woman means "one female person."

A *woman* in the supermarket gave me her extra coupons.

Women means "more than one female person."

Three *women* from Missouri joined the management team.

wood, would

Wood is the hard substance in the trunks and branches of trees.

I have a table made of a polished *wood*.

Would is the past form of *will*.

Albert said he *would* think about the offer.

your, you're

Your means "belonging to you."

I think you dropped *your* wallet.

You're is the short form of *you are*.

You're not telling the truth.

Exercise 4

Practice

Words That Sound Alike/Look Alike

Circle the correct word in the following sentences.

1. I told the salesman I (wood/(would)) rather have a ((wood)/would) fence ((than)/then) a metal one.

2. (Were/We're/(Where)) is the cake you ((were)/we're/where) supposed to bring to the birthday party?

3. Carl is ((waiting)/weighting) for me to decide (weather/(whether)) I want to go to the movies.

4. During the (rain/(reign)/rein) of Queen Elizabeth I, England suffered (thorough/(through)/threw) many political and religious conflicts.

5. The photographer insisted that the model remain ((stationary)/stationery) while he took some extra photographs.

6. I'm bringing my son, and (to/too/(two)) of my sisters are bringing ((their)/there) children, (to/(too)/two).

7. The (principal/(principle)) I live by is, "Don't (waist/(waste)) time worrying."

8. My grandson had (quiet/quit/(quite)) a temper tantrum when I told him to be ((quiet)/quit/quite) and (quiet/(quit)/quite) interrupting me.

9. It's better to tell the (plain/plane) truth (than/then) to lie.

10. I work on a construction (sight/site/cite) near (to/too/two) of the city's most famous landmarks.

   **Words That Look Alike/Sound Alike**

Collaborate

Working with a partner or a group, write one sentence for each of the words below. When you have completed this exercise, exchange it with another group's completed exercise for evaluation.

Answers Will Vary.

Possible answers shown at right.

1. a. stair   The top stair creaks a little.

    b. stare   I wish the woman wouldn't stare at me.

2. a. vain   Phyllis is a bit vain about her cooking skills.

    b. vane   The farmer studied the weather vane on the roof.

    c. vein   A nurse drew blood from a vein in my arm.

3. a. were   My sons were at a soccer game yesterday.

    b. we're   Ricky and I drove all night; we're exhausted.

    c. where   Diane knows where the old quilt is.

4. a. whose   Sarah wondered whose car had been stolen.

    b. who's   Brian knows who's taking dance lessons.

5. a. your   You should not lose your temper.

    b. you're   You're my best friend.

6. a. stake   The surveyor put a stake to mark the boundary.

    b. steak   He's thinking about a grilled steak and potatoes.

7. a. personal   I have personal reasons for my decision.

    b. personnel   The personnel at the law firm seem friendly.

8. a. peace   Our feuding cousins are finally at peace.

    b. piece   I need a piece of duct tape to fix this pipe.

9. a. moral   Dr. Castellano is a kind and moral counselor.

    b. morale   The layoffs at the factory created low morale.

10. a. loose   The child pulled at a loose thread on her jacket.

    b. lose   Our team cannot lose that game.

Exercise 6

Connect

Correcting Errors in Words That Sound Alike/Look Alike

The following paragraph has eight errors in words that sound alike or look alike. Correct the errors in the space above each error.

Every April, my college has a celebration called The Rites of Spring. Stu-

                        too   *to*

dents, faculty, and administrators, to, enjoy this time too welcome a new

and hopeful season. The art department sponsors a giant outdoor exhibit of

                          wood

photography, pottery, and would carving. Students in the horticulture pro-

                                           waiting

gram display the spring blossoms we've all been weighting for, for so long.

Creative students read poetry on a stage backed with flowers. Everyone enjoys

the music provided by the music department. The combination of art, music,

poetry, and flowers makes this celebration a special time. It is the first campus

                                  weather   *rains*

activity to be held outdoors after months of bad whether. And even if it reins,

                                                                morale

the festival goes on—indoors. A time to celebrate spring is good for the moral

                                          personnel

of everyone: teachers, students, and administrative personal.

Exercise 7

Practice

Words That Sound Alike/Look Alike: A Comprehensive Exercise

Circle the correct word in the following sentences.

1. I think Antonia needs to be more (*conscious*/conscience) of the (hole/*whole*) situation.

2. (Its/*It's*) too bad you forgot to bring (a/*an*) pencil with (a/*an*) eraser.

3. I'm not sure what (affect/*effect*) the (*weather*/whether) will have on his plans.

4. David asked Maria to (advice/*advise*) him about what (close/*clothes*/cloths) to wear.

5. My brother never thought I would get (thorough/*through*/threw) Algebra I; (beside/*besides*), he never believed I would get an A.

6. Bill (*knew*/new) I would never (*desert*/dessert) him in bad times.

7. The dog jumped on (*its*/it's) hind legs when it (*heard*/herd) me unwrap the (stake/*steak*).

8. The weather (vain/(vane)/vein) was tilted at a strange (angel/(angle)).

9. Children are not (aloud/(allowed)) in that movie unless (their/there/(they're)) accompanied by an adult.

10. My grandmother started (wait/(weight)) training at a gym; she is an exceptional ((woman)/women).

 Exercise 8

Practice

Words That Sound Alike/Look Alike: Another Comprehensive Exercise

Circle the correct word in the following sentences.

1. She was ((all ready)/already) to wax the car, but Damian had (all ready/(already)) done it.

2. Tom wrecked his (forth/(fourth)) ((pair)/pear) of shoes by walking in puddles; in ((addition)/edition), he got mud on his slacks.

3. On my way to work, I ((passed)/past) a big dog that did nothing but (stair/(stare)) at me.

4. Can you tell me ((whose)/who's) ((cereal)/serial) is spilled all over the floor?

5. The (patience/(patients)) at the children's clinic were thrilled with the gaily wrapped (presence/(presents)).

6. My sister needs a (brake/(break)) from her job; she does nothing (accept/(except)) work.

7. Vanessa gave me a ((loan)/lone) so I could ((buy)/by) gas for my car.

8. My coat was made of a ((coarse)/course) fabric that felt like a (peace/(piece)) of a blanket.

9. I'm paying you a (complement/(compliment)) when I say (your/(you're)) a (fare/(fair)) boss.

10. We ((know)/no) he will never (quiet/(quit)/quite) the team as long as he is healthy.

Exercise 9

Connect

Correcting Words That Sound Alike/Look Alike: A Comprehensive Exercise

The following paragraph has eleven errors in words that sound alike or look alike. Correct the errors in the space above each line.

                                                                  breathe

        Horror movies scare me so much that I can hardly breath. I remember

one night when I was home alone, watching an old Dracula movie on televi-

sion. By the middle of the movie I was so terrified that I couldn't leave my

                                       break

chair, even during a commercial brake. Once the movie was over and I went

                     hear

to bed, I began to here strange noises outside. Soon the noises seemed to be

                                         lone

moving closer, and I was certain that a loan vampire was walking up the

stairs   _would_

stares and wood soon arrive at my bedroom door. There was nothing I

                         stake

could do. I couldn't drive a steak through his heart, which was the way the

                                      wait

hero killed the vampire in the movie. All I could do was weight for my

doom. After what seemed like hours, I fell asleep. The next morning, I told

                     are   _lose_

myself that horror movies our silly and fake and that I should never loose

any sleep over another movie. Unfortunately, every time I see a scary movie,

             advice

I forget my own advise.

CHAPTER 19

Using Prepositions Correctly

INSTRUCTOR'S NOTE:

Students often misuse prepositions in their writing because interchanging them is common in conversation. Reviewing the lists in this chapter periodically will help reinforce standard use of prepositional expressions.

Prepositions are usually short words that often signal a kind of position, possession, or other relationship. The words that come after the preposition are part of a **prepositional phrase.** You use prepositions often because there are many expressions that contain prepositions.

Sometimes it is difficult to decide on the correct preposition. The following pages explain kinds of prepositions and their uses, and list some common prepositions.

PREPOSITIONS THAT SHOW TIME

At a specific time means "then."

> I will meet you *at* three o'clock.
> *At* 7:00 p.m., he closes the store.

By a specific time means "no later than" that time.

> You have to finish your paper *by* noon.
> I'll be home *by* 9:30.

Until a specific time means "continuing up to" that time.

> I talked on the phone *until* midnight.
> I will wait for you *until* 7:00 p.m.

In a specific time period is used with hours, minutes, days, weeks, months, or years.

> *In* a week, I'll have my diploma.
> My family hopes to visit me *in* August.
> **Note:** Write *in* the morning, *in* the afternoon, *in* the evening, but *at* night.

For a period of time means "during" that time period.

> James took music lessons *for* five years.
> I studied *for* an hour.

241

Since means "from then until now."

> I haven't heard from you *since* December.
> Juanita has been my friend *since* our high school days.

On a specific date means "at that time."

> I'll see you *on* March 23.
> The restaurant will open *on* Saturday.

During means "within" or "throughout" a time period.

> The baby woke up *during* the night.
> Robert worked part-time *during* the winter semester.

PREPOSITIONS TO INDICATE PLACE

On usually means "on the surface of," "on top of."

> Put the dishes *on* the table.
> They have a house *on* Second Avenue.

In usually means "within" or "inside of."

> Put the dishes *in* the cupboard.
> They have a house *in* Bolivia.

At usually means "in," "on," or "near to."

> I'll meet you *at* the market.
> The coffee shop is *at* the corner of Second Avenue and Hawthorne Road.
> Jill was standing *at* the door.

EXPRESSIONS WITH PREPOSITIONS

TEACHING TIP:

Point out that one can "agree with" someone's view and "approve of" someone's actions. Incorrectly using "agree with" (as in "I agree with his closing the plant") instead of "approve of" is a common error in writing and conversation.

angry about: You are *angry about* a thing.

> Suzanne was *angry about* the dent in her car.

angry at: You are *angry at* a thing.

> Carl was *angry at* the cruel treatment of the refugees.

angry with: You are *angry with* a person.

> Richard became *angry with* his mother when she criticized him.

approve of, disapprove of: You *approve* or *disapprove of* a thing, or of a person or group's actions.

> I *approve of* the new gun law.
> I *disapprove of* smoking in public places.

argue about: You *argue about* some subject.

> We used to *argue about* money.

argue for: You *argue for* something you want.

> The Student Council *argued for* more student parking.

argue with: You *argue with* a person.

> When I was a child, I spent hours *arguing with* my little sister.

arrive at: You *arrive at* a place.

> We will *arrive at* your house tomorrow.

between, among: You use *between* with two. You use *among* with three or more.

> It will be a secret *between* you and me.
> We shared the secret *among* the three of us.

bored by, bored with: You are *bored by* or *bored with* something. Do *not* write *bored of.*

> The audience was *bored by* the long movie.
> The child became *bored with* her toys.
> **not this:** ~~I am bored of school.~~

call on: You *call on* someone socially or to request something of a person.

> My aunt *called on* her new neighbors.
> Our club will *call on* you to collect tickets at the door.

call to: You *call to* someone from a distance.

> I heard him *call to* me from the top of the hill.

call up: You *call up* someone on the telephone.

> When she heard the news, Susan *called up* all her friends.

differ from: You *differ from* someone, or something *differs from* something.

> Roberta *differs from* Cheri in hair color and height.
> A van *differs from* a light truck.

differ with: You *differ with* (disagree with) someone about something.

> Theresa *differs with* Mike on the subject of food stamps.

different from: You are *different from* someone; something is *different from* something else. Do *not* write *different than.*

> Carl is *different from* his older brother.
> The movie was *different from* the book.
> **not this:** ~~The movie was different than the book.~~

grateful for: You are *grateful for* something.

> I am *grateful for* my scholarship.

grateful to: You are *grateful to* someone.

> My brother was *grateful to* my aunt for her advice.

interested in: You are *interested in* something.

> The children were *interested in* playing computer games.

look at: You *look at* someone or something.

> My sister *looked at* my haircut and laughed.

look for: You *look for* someone or something.

> David needs to *look for* his lost key.

look up: You *look up* information.

> I can *look up* his address in the phone book.

made of: Something or someone is *made of* something.

> Do you think I'm *made of* money?
> The chair was *made of* plastic.

need for: You have a *need for* something.

> The committee expressed a *need for* better leadership.

object to: You *object to* something.

> Lisa *objected to* her husband's weekend plans.

obligation to: You have an *obligation to* someone.

> I feel an *obligation to* my parents, who supported me while I was in college.

opportunity for: You have an *opportunity for* something; an *opportunity* exists *for* someone.

> The new job gives her an *opportunity for* a career change.
> A trip to China is a wonderful *opportunity for* Mimi.

pay for: You *pay* someone *for* something.

> I have to *pay* the plumber *for* the repairs to my sink.

pay to: You *pay* something *to* someone.

> Brian *paid* fifty dollars *to* the woman who found his lost dog.

popular with: Something or someone is *popular with* someone.

> Jazz is not *popular with* my friends.

prefer . . . to: You *prefer* something *to* something.

> I *prefer* jazz *to* classical music.

prejudice against: You have a *prejudice against* someone or something.

> My father finally conquered his *prejudice against* women drivers.

> **Note:** Remember to add *-ed* when the word becomes an adjective.

> He is *prejudiced* against scientists.

protect against: Something or someone *protects against* something or someone.

> A good raincoat can *protect* you *against* heavy rain.

protect from: Something or someone *protects from* something or someone.

> A good lock on your door can *protect* you *from* break-ins.

qualification for: You have a *qualification for* a position.

> Andre is missing an important *qualification for* the job.

qualified to: You are *qualified to* do something.

> Tim isn't *qualified to* judge the paintings.

quote from: You *quote* something *from* someone else.

> The graduation speaker *quoted* some lines *from* Shakespeare.

reason for: You give a *reason for* something.

> He offered no *reason for* his rude behavior.

reason with: You *reason with* someone.

> Sonny tried to *reason with* the angry motorist.

responsible for: You are *responsible for* something.

> Luther is *responsible for* the mess in the kitchen.

responsible to: You are *responsible to* someone.

> At the restaurant, the waiters are *responsible to* the assistant manager.

rob of: You *rob* someone *of* something.

> His insult *robbed* me *of* my dignity.

similar to: Someone or something is *similar to* someone or something.

> Your dress is *similar to* a dress I had in high school.

succeed in: You *succeed in* something.

> I hope I can *succeed in* getting a job.

superior to: Someone or something is *superior to* someone or something.

> My final paper was *superior to* my first paper.

take advantage of: You *take advantage of* someone or something.

> Maria is going to *take advantage of* the fine weather and go to the beach.

take care of: You *take care of* someone or something.

> Rick will *take care of* my cat while I'm away.

talk about: You *talk about* something.

> We can *talk about* the trip tomorrow.

talk over: You *talk over* something.

> The cousins met to *talk over* the plans for the anniversary party.

talk to: You *talk to* someone.

> I'll *talk to* my father.

talk with: You *talk with* someone.

> Esther needs to *talk with* her boyfriend.

tired of: You are *tired of* something.

> Sylvia is *tired of* driving to work.

wait for: You *wait for* someone or something.

> Jessica must *wait for* Alan to arrive.

wait on: You use *wait on* only if you wait on customers.

> At the diner, I have to *wait on* too many people.

Exercise 1

Practice

Choosing the Correct Preposition

Circle the correct preposition in each of the following sentences.

1. Susan told me that she would have the room ready (by/**in**) an hour.

2. We drove around Manchester (**for**/since) two hours.

3. We could find a good used car (**at**/in) Olsen Auto Market.

4. Dennis has a studio apartment (in/**on**) Orchard Street.

5. I couldn't find the cold pills (**in**/on) the bathroom drawer.

6. Magda and Pierre stayed up (by/**until**) midnight, talking about old times.

7. When Eddie gets upset, it is impossible to reason (for/**with**) him.

8. My boss said I was responsible (**for**/to) the mess in the kitchen.

9. The shipment of oranges will arrive (at/to) the warehouse next week.

10. The ceremony was so long that I became bored (of/with) it.

Exercise 2   **Choosing the Correct Preposition**

Practice   Circle the correct preposition in each of the following sentences.

1. Every time my sister sees a spider, she thinks she has to call (to/up) an exterminator.

2. Nora differs (from/with) Andy on the issue of capital punishment.

3. Nancy hasn't had a cigarette (in/on) a month.

4. I saw him riding (in/on) a car yesterday; he waved at me from the back seat.

5. If I finish college, I will be more likely to succeed (at/in) the business world.

6. Leon is waiting (on/for) Miguel and Tina; they are twenty minutes late.

7. The management told me I needed additional qualifications (for/to) the position of assistant manager.

8. We can divide the cooking (among/between) the four of us.

9. Yvette is a good swimmer, but she prefers tennis (over/to) swimming.

10. My little brother was sitting in a tree and calling (on/to/up) his friends below.

Exercise 3   **Writing Sentences Using Expressions with Prepositions**

 *Collaborate*   Do this exercise with a partner or a group. Below are pairs of expressions with prepositions. Write a sentence that contains each pair. The first one is done for you.

1. a. argue with   b. object to

    sentence: In college, I used to argue with my roommate whenever he

    would object to my loud music.

Answers Will Vary.
Possible answers shown at right.

2. a. angry about   b. complain to

    sentence: They were so angry about the leak in the apartment that

    they decided to complain to the landlord.

3. a. grateful for   b. succeed in

sentence: Susanna is grateful for the good education that enabled
her to succeed in politics.

4. a. succeed in   b. capable of

sentence: To succeed in business, you must be capable of planning
and developing your strategies.

5. a. interested in   b. bored by

sentence: Natasha is interested in fashion but bored by lectures on
the history of fashion.

6. a. call on   b. qualified to

sentence: Crystal will call on her former swimming coach to see if he
knows anyone qualified to work as a lifeguard.

7. a. prejudice against   b. superior to

sentence: Some ignorant people have a prejudice against foreigners
and feel superior to anyone who cannot speak English.

8. a. grateful to   b. opportunity for

sentence: My brother was grateful to the scholarship committee; it
gave him an opportunity for advanced study in Africa.

9. a. pay for   b. pay to

sentence: You have to pay for the use of Cameron Park; you pay a
small fee to the attendant at the entrance.

10. a. responsible to   b. different from

sentence: Larry is the owner's son but is still responsible to the night
manager; Larry is not different from the other workers.

 *Collaborate*

Writing Sentences Using Expressions with Prepositions

Do this exercise with a partner. Review the list of expressions with prepositions in this chapter. Select five expressions that you think are troublesome for writers. Write the expressions below. Then exchange lists with your partner. Your partner will write a sentence for each expression on your list; you will write sentences for his or her list. When you have completed the exercises, check each other's sentences.

1. expression: _____

    sentence: _____

2. expression: _____

    sentence: _____

3. expression: _____

    sentence: _____

4. expression: _____

    sentence: _____

5. expression: _____

    sentence: _____

Exercise 5

∞ *Connect*

Using Prepositions Correctly

The following paragraph has seven errors in prepositions. Correct the errors in the space above each error.

I usually don't go to horror movies because I hate scenes filled with blood.

However, I recently saw a horror movie that changed my opinion of frighten-

ing films. I went because my best friend persuaded me to take a chance on a

                                          with
movie that is very popular for all age groups and all kinds of audiences. My

                                                              to
friend said the movie was excellent and swore I would not object at any of the

                                                                  against
violent scenes. Even though I entered the theater with a real prejudice on this

                                                in
kind of film, I was pleasantly surprised. I found myself interested on the plot

and characters, and I was happy to note that the horror in the film didn't come

                                            in
from blood and gore. It came from the suspense and mystery on the movie.

The use of darkness, shadows, and eerie music created most of the thrills. I am

    to
grateful for my friend for taking me to this movie, and I have learned that

                        from
some horror movies are different than others.

Exercise 6

👥 *Collaborate*

Recognizing Prepositional Phrases in a Famous Speech

Do this exercise with a group. Following is part of a famous speech by Winston Churchill, a prime minister of Great Britain during World War II. When Churchill gave this speech in 1940, the Nazis had just defeated the British troops at Dunkirk, France. In this speech, Churchill explained the events at Dunkirk and then rallied the nation to keep fighting.

To do this exercise, have one member of your group read the speech aloud while the other members listen. Then underline all the prepositional phrases in it. Be ready to share your answers with another group.

We shall not flag* nor fail. We shall go on <u>to the end</u>. We shall fight

<u>in France</u> and <u>on the seas and oceans</u>; we shall fight <u>with growing confi-

dence and growing strength</u> in the air.

We shall defend our island whatever the cost may be; we shall fight

<u>on beaches</u>, <u>on landing grounds</u>, <u>in fields</u>, <u>in streets</u> and <u>on the hills</u>. We

shall never surrender and even if, which I do not <u>for a moment</u> believe, this

island or a large part <u>of it</u> were subjugated* and starving, then our empire

<u>beyond the seas</u>, armed and guarded <u>by the British Fleet</u>,* would carry on

the struggle until <u>in God's good time</u> the New World, <u>with all its power and

might</u>, sets forth <u>to the liberation and rescue of the Old</u>.

_____

***flag:** to lose energy
***subjugated:** conquered by the enemy
***the fleet:** a group of warships

Writing in Steps

The Process Approach

Introduction

Learning by Doing

Writing is a skill, and like any other skill, writing improves with practice. Through a menu of activities, this part of the book gives you the opportunity to improve your writing. Some activities can be done alone; some ask that you work with a partner or with a group. You can do some in the classroom; some can be done at home. The important thing to remember is that *good writing takes practice;* you can learn to write well by writing.

Steps Make Writing Easier

Writing is easier if you *don't try to do everything at once.* Producing a piece of effective writing demands that you think, plan, focus, and draft; then rethink, revise, edit, and proofread. You can become frustrated if you try to do all these things at the same time.

To make the task of writing easier, this section breaks the process into four major parts:

Thought Lines

In this step, you *think* about your topic, and you gather ideas. You *react* to your own ideas and add more ideas to your first thoughts. Or you react to other people's ideas as a way of generating your own writing material.

Outlines

In this step, you learn to *plan* your writing. You examine your own ideas and begun to *focus* them around one main idea. Planning involves combining, dividing, and even discarding the ideas you started with. It involves more thinking about the point you want to make and devising the best way to express it.

Rough Lines

In this step, your thinking and planning begin to shape themselves into a piece of writing. You complete a *draft* of your work, a rough version of the finished product. And then you think again as you examine the draft and check it. Checking it begins the process of *revision,* "fixing" the draft so that it takes the shape you want and expresses your ideas clearly.

Final Lines

In this step, you give the final draft of your writing one last, careful *review*. When you prepare the final copy of your work, you *proofread* and concentrate on identifying and correcting any mistakes in word choice, spelling, mechanics, or punctuation you may have overlooked. This step is the *final check* of your work to make sure your writing is the best that it can be.

These four steps in the writing process—*thought lines, outlines, rough lines,* and *final lines*—always overlap. You may be changing your plan (the *outlines* stage) even as you work on the *rough lines* of your paper, and there is no rule that says you cannot move back to an earlier step when you need to. Thinking of writing as a series of steps helps you see the process as a *manageable task*. You can avoid doing everything at once and becoming overwhelmed by the challenge.

Once you learn these four steps, you can put them to use. As you work through the writing chapters of this book, you will work with examples of each of the four steps and practice them.

CONTENTS

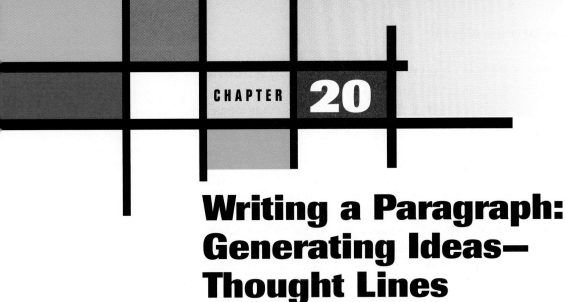

CHAPTER 20

Writing a Paragraph: Generating Ideas— Thought Lines

The paragraph is the basic building block of most writing. It is a group of sentences focusing on one idea or one point. Keep this concept in mind: *one idea for each paragraph.* Focusing on one idea or one point gives a paragraph *unity.* If you have a new point, start a new paragraph.

You may ask, "Doesn't this mean a paragraph will be short? How long should a paragraph be, anyway?" To convince a reader of one main point, you need to make it, support it, develop it, explain it, and describe it. There will be shorter and longer paragraphs, but for now, you can assume your paragraph will be between seven and twelve sentences long.

This chapter will guide you through the first step of the writing process, the thought lines, where you generate ideas for your paragraph.

BEGINNING THE THOUGHT LINES

Suppose your instructor asks you to write a paragraph about family. To write effectively, you need to know your *purpose* and your *audience.* In this case, you already know your purpose: to write a paragraph that makes some point about family. You also know your audience since you are writing this paragraph for your instructor and classmates. Often, your purpose is to write a specific type of paper for a class. However, you may have to write with a different purpose for a particular audience. Writing instructions for a new employee at your workplace, or writing a letter of complaint to a manufacturer, or composing a short autobiographical essay for a scholarship application are examples of different purposes and audiences.

Freewriting, Brainstorming, Keeping a Journal

Once you have identified your purpose and audience, you can begin by finding some way to *think* on paper. To gather ideas, you can use the techniques of freewriting, brainstorming, or keeping a journal.

Freewriting Give yourself ten minutes to write whatever comes into your mind on the subject. If you can't think of anything to write, just write "I can't think of anything to write" over and over until you think of something else. The main goal of **freewriting** is to *write without stopping*. Don't stop to tell yourself, "This is stupid," or "I can't use any of this in a paper." Just write. Let your ideas flow. Write freely. Here's an example:

Freewriting about Family

> Family. Family. Whose family? What is a family? What does she want me to write about? I'm not married. I don't have a family. Sure, my mother. I guess I have a big <u>other</u> family, too. Cousins, aunts, uncles. But my basic family is my mother and brother Tito. Is that a family? She's a good mom. Always takes care of me. Family ties. Family matters. How a family treats children.

Brainstorming **Brainstorming** is like freewriting because you write whatever comes into your head, but it is a little different because you can *pause to ask yourself questions* that will lead to new ideas. When you brainstorm alone, you "interview" yourself about a subject. Or you can brainstorm within a group.

If you are brainstorming about family, alone or with a partner or group, you might begin by listing ideas and then add to the ideas by asking and answering questions. Here's an example:

Brainstorming about Family

> Family.
>
> Family members.
>
> **Who is your favorite family member?**
> I don't know. Uncle Ray, I guess.
>
> **Why is he your favorite?**
> He's funny. Especially at those family celebrations.
>
> **What celebrations?**
> Birthdays, anniversaries, dinners. I hated those dinners when I was little.
>
> **Why did you hate them?**
> I had to get all dressed up.
>
> **What else did you hate about them?**
> I had to sit still through the longest, most boring meals.
>
> **Why were they boring?**
> All these grown-ups talking. My mother made me sit there, politely.
>
> **Were you angry at your mother?**
> Yes. Well, no, not really. She's strict, but I love her.

If you feel as if you are running out of ideas in brainstorming, try to form a question out of what you've just written. For example, if you write, "Families are changing," you could form these questions:

What families? How are they changing? Are the changes good? Why? Why not?

Forming questions helps you keep your thoughts flowing, and you will eventually arrive at a suitable focus for your paragraph.

Keeping a Journal A **journal** is a notebook of your personal writing, a notebook in which you write regularly and often. *It is not a diary, but it is a place to record your experiences, reactions, and observations.* In it, you can write about what you've done, heard, seen, read, or remembered. You can include sayings that you'd like to remember, news clippings, snapshots—anything that you'd like to recall or consider. Journals are a great way to practice your writing and a great source of ideas for writing.

If you were asked to write about family, for example, you might look through entries in your journal in search of ideas, and you might see something like this:

Journal Entry about Family

I was at Mike's house last night. We were just sitting around, talking and listening to CDs. Then we were bored, so we decided to go to the movies. When we left, we walked right past Mike's mother in the kitchen. Mike didn't even say goodbye or tell her where we were going. Mike is so rude to his mother. He can't stand her. Lots of my friends hate their parents. I'm lucky. I'm close to my mother.

Finding Specific Ideas

Whether you freewrite, brainstorm, or consult your journal, you end up with something on paper. Follow these first ideas; see where they can take you. You are looking for specific ideas, each of which can focus the general one you started with. At this point, you do not have to decide which specific idea you want to write about. You just want to narrow your range of ideas.

You might ask, "Why should I narrow my ideas? Won't I have more to say if I keep my topic big?" But remember that a paragraph has one idea. You want to say one thing clearly, and you want to use convincing details that support your main idea. If you write one paragraph on the broad topic of family, for example, you will probably make only general statements that say very little and bore your reader.

General ideas are big, broad ones. Specific ideas are narrow. If you scanned the freewriting example on family, you might underline many specific ideas that could be topics.

Family. Family. Whose family? What is a family? What does she want me to write about? I'm not married. I don't have a family. Sure, <u>my mother</u>. I guess I have a <u>big other family</u>, too. Cousins, aunts, uncles. But <u>my basic family</u> is my mother and brother Tito. Is that a family? <u>She's a good mom</u>. <u>Always takes care of me</u>. Family ties. Family matters. How a family treats children.

Consider the underlined parts. Many of them are specific ideas about family. You could write a paragraph about one underlined item or about several related items.

Another way to find specific ideas is to make a list after brainstorming, underlining specific ideas. Here is an underlined list about family:

> Family.
> Family members.
> Uncle Ray.
> He's funny. Especially at those family celebrations.
> Birthdays, anniversaries, dinners. I hated those dinners when I was little.
> I had to get all dressed up.
> I had to sit still through the longest, most boring meals.
> All these grownups, talking. My mother made me sit there, politely.
> She's strict, but I love her.

These specific ideas could lead you to specific topics.

If you reviewed the **journal entry** on family, you would be able to underline many specific ideas:

> I was at Mike's house last night. We were just sitting around, talking and listening to CDs. Then we were bored, so we decided to go to the movies. When we left, we walked right past Mike's mother in the kitchen. Mike didn't even say goodbye or tell her where we were going. Mike is so rude to his mother. He can't stand her. Lots of my friends hate their parents. I'm lucky. I'm close to my mother.

Remember, following the steps can lead you to specific ideas. Once you have some specific ideas, you can pick one idea and develop it.

<table>
<tr><td>

Exercise 1

Practice

TEACHING TIP:

Group Work: You can assign several students (or rows) to a particular topic or ask them to work collaboratively on it. Once students have completed the task, you can select a spokesperson for each group to share its best questions with the rest of the class.

Answers Will Vary.

Possible answers shown at right.

</td><td>

Brainstorming Questions and Answers

Following are several general topics. For each one, brainstorm by writing three questions and answers related to the topic that could lead you to specific ideas. The first topic is done for you.

1. **general topic:** home computers

   Question 1. Do I need my home computer?

   Answer 1.   Sure. I use it all the time.

   Question 2. But what do I use it for?

   Answer 2.   Games. Surfing the Internet.

   Question 3. So I don't use it for anything serious, do I?

   Answer 3.   It helps me do research and type my papers.

2. **general topic:** sports injuries

   Question 1. Have you ever hurt yourself playing a sport?

   Answer 1.   Once I chipped my tooth falling off a skateboard.

   Question 2. Is skateboarding dangerous?

   Answer 2.   Sure, but not as dangerous as some sports.

   Question 3. What other sports?

   Answer 3.   Hockey. Think of all the broken noses. Football.

</td></tr>
</table>

3. general topic: childhood fears

Question 1. What are most children afraid of?

Answer 1. The bogeyman. Something coming at them in the dark.

Question 2. Where do these fears come from?

Answer 2. Maybe from children's imagination or from movies.

Question 3. Do you remember a movie that scared you?

Answer 3. An old movie about a werewolf. And one with zombies.

4. general topic: violent movies

Question 1. Are movies too violent?

Answer 1. Yes, certainly. But people go to see the violence.

Question 2. Do you mean people like the violence?

Answer 2. Sure, it's exciting. It creates suspense.

Question 3. Can't movies be exciting without so much violence?

Answer 3. Probably. But they would not be as popular.

5. general topic: employment

Question 1. What's your dream job?

Answer 1. I'd like to be a music promoter.

Question 2. Why would this be a good job?

Answer 2. I would travel all the time, meet celebrities.

Question 3. How do you get a job like that?

Answer 3. I have to learn about business and public relations.

Exercise 2 **Finding Specific Ideas in a List**

Practice

Following are general topics; each general topic is followed by a list of words or phrases about the general topic. It is the kind of list you could make after brainstorming. Underline the words or phrases that are specific and could lead you to a specific topic. The first list is done for you.

1. general topic: sleeping habits

how people sleep

snoring all night

everyone sleeps

why people toss and turn

ways of sleeping

2. **general topic:** pets

<u>litter box training</u>

all kinds of pets

<u>obedience school</u>

<u>adopting a shelter dog</u>

animals and people

3. **general topic:** exercise

<u>finding good running shoes</u>

physical activity

<u>benefits of a health club</u>

<u>exercising with a friend</u>

getting exercise

4. **general topic:** shoppers

people in stores

<u>bargain hunters</u>

buyers of merchandise

<u>last-minute shoppers</u>

<u>shopaholics</u>

5. **general topic:** health

anatomy and physiology

<u>getting enough vitamins</u>

<u>cold remedies</u>

staying well

doctors

 Finding Specific Ideas in Freewriting

Practice

Following are two samples of freewriting. Each is a written response to a different topic. Read each sample, and then underline any words or phrases that could become the focus of a paragraph.

Freewriting on the Topic of Cooking

What do I know about cooking? I'm a guy. I never cook. <u>My mom cooks really well</u>. My girlfriend cooks, too. <u>She can't cook like my mother</u>. <u>I did cook, once</u>. It was a <u>disaster</u>. <u>Nearly set my apartment on fire when I tried to cook a turkey</u>. I love turkey. My mother makes <u>a great turkey dinner</u>. <u>Home cooking</u>. Nothing like it. It's great. That's cooking. <u>Home cooking is better than a restaurant</u> any day.

Freewriting on the Topic of Jobs

My first job. My boss was Mr. Silvero. Now I have a woman boss. Male vs. female bosses, pro and con. My first job was a summer job when I was still in high school. High school jobs. They don't pay much. Good experience, though. Mr. Silvero taught me a lot.

 **Collaborate**

Finding Topics through Freewriting

Begin this exercise alone; then complete it with a partner or group. First, pick one of the topics and freewrite on it for ten minutes. Then read your freewriting to your partner or group. Ask your listener(s) to jot down any words or phrases that lead to a specific subject for a paragraph.

Your listener(s) should read the jotted-down words or phrases to you. You will be hearing a collection of specific ideas that came from *your* writing. As you listen, underline the words in your freewriting.

Freewriting Topics (pick one):

    a. sports

    b. money

    c. crime

Freewriting on _____ (name of topic chosen)

_____

_____

_____

_____

_____

_____

_____

_____

Selecting an Idea

After you have a list of specific ideas, you must pick one and try to develop it by adding details. To pick an idea about family, you could survey the ideas you gathered through freewriting. Review the following freewriting in which the specific ideas are underlined:

Family. Family. Whose family? What is a family? What does she want me to write about? I'm not married. I don't have a family. Sure, my mother. I guess I have a big other family, too. Cousins, aunts, uncles. But my basic family is my mother and brother Tito. Is that a family? She's a good mom. Always takes care of me. Family ties. Family matters. How a family treats children.

Here are the specific ideas (the underlined ones) in a list:

my mother   She's a good mom
a big other family   Always takes care of me
my basic family

Looking at these ideas, you decide to write your paragraph on this topic: My Mother.

Now you can begin to add details.

Adding Details to an Idea

You can develop the one idea you picked a number of ways:

1. *Check your list* for other ideas that seem to fit the one you've picked.
2. *Brainstorm*—ask yourself more questions about your topic and use the answers as details.
3. *List any new ideas* you have that may be connected to your first idea.

One way to add details is to go back and check your list for other ideas that seem to fit with the topic of My Mother. You find these entries:

She's a good mom. Always takes care of me.

Another way to add details is to brainstorm some questions that will lead you to more details. These questions do not have to be connected to each other; they are just questions that could lead you to ideas and details.

Question: What makes your mom a good mom?
Answer: She works hard.

Question: What work does she do?
Answer: She cooks, cleans.

Question: What else?
Answer: She has a job.

Question: What job?
Answer: She's a nurse.

Question: How is your mother special?
Answer: She had a rough life.

Another way to add details is to list any ideas that may be connected to your first idea of writing about your mother. The list might give you more specific details:

makes great chicken casserole
good-looking for her age
lost her husband
went to school at night

If you tried all three ways of adding details, you would end up with this list of details connected to the topic of My Mother:

she's a good mom.   she had a rough life.
always takes care of me.   makes great chicken casserole
she works hard.   good-looking for her age
she cooks, cleans.   lost her husband
she has a job.   went to school at night
she's a nurse.

You now have details that you can work with as you move into the next stage of writing a paragraph.

This process may seem long, but once you have worked through it several times, it will become nearly automatic. When you think about ideas before you try to shape them, you are off to a good start.

Info BOX

Beginning the Thought Lines: A Summary

The thought lines stage of writing a paragraph enables you to gather ideas. This process begins with four steps:

1. *Think on paper and write down any ideas that you have about a general topic.* You can do this by freewriting, brainstorming, or keeping a journal.

2. *Scan your writing for specific ideas that have come from your first efforts.* List these ideas.

3. *Pick one specific idea.* This idea will be the topic of your paragraph.

4. *Add details to your topic.* You can add details by reviewing your early writing, by questioning, and by thinking further.

FOCUSING THE THOUGHT LINES

Once you have a topic and some ideas about the topic, your next step is to *focus* your topic and ideas around some point. Two techniques that you can use are to

- mark a list of related ideas, or
- map related ideas

Marking Related Ideas

To develop a marked list, take another look at the list developed under the topic, My Mother. In this list, you'll notice some of the items have been marked with letters that represent categories for related items.

H   marks ideas about your mother at home.
J   marks ideas about your mother's job.
B   marks ideas about your mother's background.

Following is a marked list of ideas related to the topic My Mother.

H	She's a good mom.	**B**	She had a rough life.
H	Always takes care of me.	**H**	makes great chicken casserole
H & J	She works hard.		good-looking for her age
H	She cooks and cleans.	**B**	lost her husband
J	She has a job	**B**	went to school at night
J	She's a nurse.		

You have probably noticed that one item, *She works hard*, is marked with two letters, H and J, because your mother works hard both at home and on the job. One item on the list, *good-looking for her age*, isn't marked. Perhaps you can come back to this item later, or perhaps you will decide you don't need it in your paragraph.

To make it easier to see what ideas you have and how they are related, try *grouping related ideas*, giving each list a title, like this:

my mother at home
She's a good mom.   Always takes care of me
She works hard.   She cooks, cleans.
makes great chicken casserole

my mother at her job
She has a job.   She's a nurse.
She works hard.

my mother's background
She had a rough life.   lost her husband
went to school at night

Mapping

Another way to focus your ideas is to mark your first list of ideas and then cluster the related ideas into separate lists. You can *map* your ideas like this:

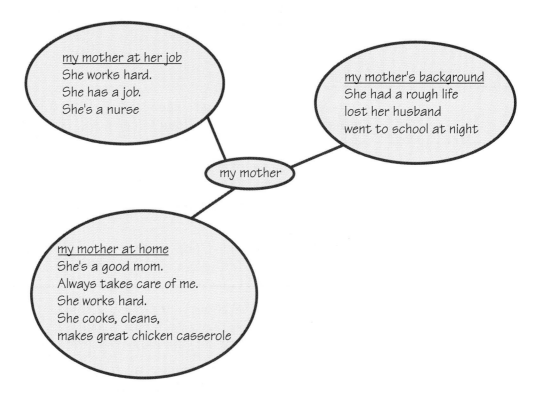

Whatever way you choose to examine and group your details, you are working toward a focus, a point. You are asking and beginning to answer the question, "Where do the details lead?" The answer will be the main idea of your paragraph, which will be stated in the topic sentence.

Exercise 5

Practice

Grouping Related Items in Lists of Details

Following are lists of details. In each list, circle the items that seem to fit in one group; then underline the items that seem to belong to a second group. Some items may not belong in either group. The first list is done for you.

1. **topic:** my favorite aunt

   always cheerful   unusual appearance

   tells jokes   orange hair

   gives me compliments   an accountant

   laughs at her troubles   outrageous hats

   dresses in wild colors   drives a jeep

2. **topic:** a snowstorm

   traffic jam   heating bills

   little driving visibility   slick roads

   icicles gleaming on trees   dazzling white hills

   children home from school   exquisite snowflakes

   beautiful snowdrifts   roads closed

3. **topic:** reasons to quit smoking

   nicotine patch   stained teeth

   tobacco smell on clothes   emphysema

   lung cancer   nicotine gum

   heart disease   teenage smokers

   bad breath   no-smoking areas

4. **topic:** my first job

   long hours   on my feet too long

   had my own spending money   restaurant waitress

   rude customers   ugly uniform

   boss was nice   friendly coworkers

   too many job responsibilities   forced to work weekends

5. **topic:** my mother's house

   brick patio   wooden floors

   apple tree in the yard   my favorite house

   border of roses   cozy kitchen

   attic bedroom   nasty landlord

   old-fashioned bathroom   near my school

Forming a Topic Sentence

To form a topic sentence, do the following:

1. Review your details and see if you can form some general idea that will summarize the details.
2. Write that general idea in one sentence.

The sentence that summarizes the details is the *topic sentence*. It makes a general point, and the more specific details you have gathered will support this point.

To form a topic sentence about your mother, you can ask yourself questions about the details. First, there are many details about your mother. You can ask yourself, "What kinds of details do I have?" You have details about your mother's background, about her job, and about her role as a mother. You might ask, "Can I summarize those details?" You might then summarize those details to get the topic sentence:

INSTRUCTOR'S NOTE:

You may want to point out such style changes as "mother" instead of "mom" and "difficult" instead of "rough" in the topic sentence.

My mother survived difficult times to become a good parent and worker.

Check the sentence against your details. Does it cover your mother's background? Yes, it mentions that she survived *rough times*. Does it cover her job? Yes, it says she is a *good worker*. Does it cover her role as a mother? Yes, it says she is a *good parent*. The topic sentence is acceptable; it is a general idea that summarizes the details.

Hints about Topic Sentences

1. Be careful. *Topics are not the same as topic sentences. A topic is the subject you will write about. A topic sentence states the main idea you have developed on a topic.* Consider the differences between the following topics and topic sentences:

topic: my mother
topic sentence: My mother survived rough times to become a good parent and worker.

topic: effects of drunk driving
topic sentence: Drunk driving hurts the victims, their families, and friends.

Exercise 6

👥 *Collaborate*

Turning Topics into Topic Sentences

Do this exercise with a partner or group. The following list contains some topics and some topic sentences. Have someone read the list aloud. As the list is read, decide which items are topics. Put an *X* by those items. On the lines following the list, rewrite the topics into topic sentences.

1. __X__ One way to lose weight

2. __X__ Why fish make good pets

3. _____ Poor planning wrecked my wedding

4. __X__ How to change a tire easily and safely

5. _____ My father is my best friend

6. _____   I learned compassion at my job

7. _X_   A great city to visit

8. _____   Speeding is foolish and selfish

9. _X_   A bad cold

10. _____   Voice mail can be irritating

Rewrite the topics. Make each one into a topic sentence.

1. Exercise is one way to lose weight.

2. Fish make good pets because they are easy to care for.

4. There are five steps to changing a tire easily and safely.

7. New York is a great city to visit because it is huge, diverse, and exciting.

9. A bad cold can put a person into a bad mood.

2. *Topic sentences do not announce;* they make a point. Look at the following sentences and notice the differences between the sentences that announce and the topic sentences.

announcement: The subject of this paper will be my definition of a bargain.
topic sentence: A bargain is a necessary item that I bought at less than half the regular price.

announcement: I will discuss the causes of depression in teenagers.
topic sentence: Depression in teenagers can be caused by stress at home, work, or school.

Exercise 7

👥 *Collaborate*

Turning Announcements into Topic Sentences

Do this exercise with a partner or group. The following list contains some topic sentences and some announcements. Have someone read this list aloud. As the list is read, decide whether items are announcements. Put an *X* by those items. On the lines following the list, rewrite the announcements, making them topic sentences.

1. _____   I learned to be a good tennis player by practicing regularly.

2. _X_   How to become a good dancer is the subject of this paper.

3. _X_   The pressures on teenagers will be explained.

4. _____   Working mothers feel stressed at home, at work, and in social gatherings.

5. _X_   I will explain the reasons for attending a college near your home.

6. _____ Buying at thrift shops can save you money and give you quality merchandise.

7. _X_ Why our school needs a bigger parking lot is the issue to be discussed.

8. _X_ The three characteristics of a good friend are the topic of this essay.

9. _____ A real leader is responsible, confident, and generous.

10. _X_ This essay will tell you why people watch soap operas.

Rewrite the announcements. Make each one a topic sentence.

Answers Will Vary.

Possible answers shown at right.

2. People become good dancers through dedication and practice.

3. Teenagers feel pressured by parents, teachers, and peers.

5. Attending a college near home can save you time and money.

7. Our school needs a bigger parking lot for reasons of convenience and safety.

8. A good friend is loyal, understanding, and generous.

10. Some people watch soap operas just to follow the lives of evil characters.

3. *Topic sentences should not be too broad* to develop in one paragraph. A topic sentence that is too broad may take many pages of writing to develop. Look at the following broad sentences and then notice how they can be narrowed.

too broad: Television violence is bad for children. (This sentence is too broad because "television violence" could include anything from bloody movies to the nightly news, and "children" could mean anyone under 18. Also, "is bad for children" could mean anything from "causes nightmares" to "provokes children to commit murder.")

a narrower topic sentence: Violent cartoons teach preschoolers that hitting and hurting is fun.

too broad: Education changed my life. (This sentence is so broad, you would have to talk about your whole education, and your whole life, to support it.)

a narrower topic sentence: Studying for my high school equivalency diploma gave me the confidence to try college.

Exercise 8

👥 *Collaborate*

Revising Topic Sentences That Are Too Broad

Do this exercise with a partner or group. Following is a list of topic sentences. Some are too broad to support in one paragraph. Have someone read this list aloud. As the list is read, decide which sentences are too broad. Put an *X* by those sentences. On the lines following the list, rewrite those sentences, focusing on a limited idea—a topic sentence—that could be supported in one paragraph.

1. __X__   Working can be very frustrating.

2. _____   Getting children to go to bed is the hardest part of babysitting.

3. __X__   College was a big change for me.

4. __X__   Television has too much influence on people.

5. __X__   Divorce can be very hard on children.

6. _____   Beer advertising on television makes drinking seem like a way to be popular.

7. _____   My brother grew up when he started working.

8. _____   A college math class forced me to learn how to study.

9. _____   Christopher developed self-confidence when he joined a boxing club.

10. _____   When parents argue, teenagers can feel torn and confused.

Rewrite the broad sentences. Make each one more limited.

Answers Will Vary.

Possible answers shown at right.

1. Working as a phone salesperson can be very frustrating.

3. A college instructor inspired me to study for a new career.

4. Late-night television keeps me from getting enough sleep.

5. Children of divorced parents can be used as prizes in a power struggle.

_____

_____

4. *Topic sentences should not be too narrow* to develop in one paragraph. A topic sentence that is too narrow can't be supported by details. It may be a fact which can't be developed. A topic sentence that is too narrow leaves you with nothing more to say.

too narrow:	We had fog yesterday.
a better, expanded topic sentence:	Yesterday's fog made driving difficult.
too narrow:	I moved to Nashville when I was twenty.
a better, expanded topic sentence:	When I moved to Nashville at age twenty, I learned to live on my own.

Exercise 9

👥 *Collaborate*

Revising Topic Sentences That Are Too Narrow

Do this exercise with a partner or group. Following is a list of topic sentences. Some of them are too narrow to be developed in a paragraph. Have someone read the list aloud. As the list is read, decide which sentences are too narrow. Put an *X* by those sentences. On the lines following the list, rewrite those sentences as broader topic sentences that could be developed in a paragraph.

1. __X__ Jack's truck is a new Ford.

2. _____ A station wagon is a more practical car than a sport utility vehicle.

3. __X__ Our house is in a valley near some farms.

4. _____ Living in the center of town has three advantages.

5. __X__ The sun on the beach was hot.

6. __X__ Christine gave me a tie.

7. _____ Mr. Rodriguez's offer of a ride was generous and thoughtful.

8. _____ When Dana made me a cake, she showed me her love.

9. __X__ Levar's haircut cost fifty dollars.

10. _____ Betty asked to borrow $100, but I had reasons for refusing her request.

Rewrite the narrow sentences. Make each one broader.

Answers Will Vary.

Possible answers shown at right.

1. Jack's new truck is a big improvement over his old one.

3. Having a house in the country has several advantages.

5. We should not have stayed at the beach for three hours.

6. Christine's gift to me showed little imagination or care.

9. Levar's new haircut was, in several ways, a disaster.

Once you have a topic sentence, you have completed the thought lines stage of writing. This stage begins with free, unstructured thinking and writing. As you work through the thought lines process, your thinking and writing will become more focused.

Info BOX

Focusing the Thought Lines: A Summary

The thought lines stage of writing a paragraph enables you to develop an idea into a topic sentence and related details. You can *focus* your thinking by working in steps.

1. Try marking a list of related details or mapping to group your ideas.

2. Write a topic sentence that summarizes your details.

3. Check your topic sentence. Be sure that it makes a point and focuses the details you have developed. Be sure that it is a sentence (not a topic), is not too broad or too narrow, and is not an announcement.

Exercise 10

Practice

Recognizing and Writing Good Topic Sentences

Some of the following are good topic sentences. Others are not; they are topics (not topic sentences), or announcements, or they are too broad, or too narrow. Put an *X* next to the ones that are not good topic sentences and rewrite them in the lines following the list.

1. __X__   How you can get the best deal on textbooks.

2. _____   Hitchhiking is a dangerous form of transportation.

3. __X__   Education has always been difficult for me.

4. __X__   On Fridays, my bank stays open late.

5. __X__   Sources of protein in a healthy diet.

6. __X__   Too many people are committing violent crimes.

7. __X__   Several risks associated with skydiving will be the subject of this paper.

8. _____   Vitamin C can be found in many popular foods.

9. __X__   A new way to meet people.

10. _____   A twenty-four-hour pharmacy is a neighborhood asset.

Rewrite the faulty topic sentences:

Answers Will Vary.

Possible answers shown at right.

1. You can get the best deal on textbooks by doing some investigating.

3. Taking notes has always been difficult for me.

4. My bank's later hours on Fridays appeal to many customers.

5. A healthy diet contains protein from a variety of sources.

6. Carjacking is the latest violent crime to hit my street.

7. Skydiving can be a risky sport.

9. A new way to meet people is to visit a chat room online.

Exercise 11

Practice

Writing Topic Sentences for Lists of Details

Following are lists of details that have no topic sentences. Write an appropriate topic sentence for each one.

Answers Will Vary.

Possible answers shown at right.

1. **topic sentence:** It is better to walk than to drive.

_____

Walking is good exercise.
Walking saves money spent on gas for a car.
Walkers don't get stuck in traffic.

Walkers get to enjoy their surroundings.
Cars pollute the air, but walkers don't.
Walking is less stressful than driving.

2. topic sentence: Professor Spinetti is a supportive but demanding

teacher.

Professor Spinetti is a patient teacher.
He is willing to answer questions.
He gives extra help after class.
He has many office hours for student conferences.
He demands students' best work.
Professor Spinetti is very strict about deadlines.
He gives many assignments.

3. topic sentence: Mugs are made of many materials, they hold many

liquids, and they are decorated in many ways.

coffee mugs
soup mugs
mugs with sayings on them
plastic mugs
mugs with cartoon characters
beer mugs
china mugs
mugs with college names
glass mugs

4. topic sentence: Don is an imperfect friend.

Don says he is my friend.
Calls me at midnight to talk
Talks behind my back
Likes to tell me his problems
Always wants to do things on weekends
Borrows my money and car
Gives me advice
Never offers to pay for anything

5. topic sentence: Sean is a wonderful father, husband, and

employee.

Spends time with his children every weekend
Tries to be home to tuck them in at night
Works overtime to support his family
Shares household chores with his wife
Arrives at work early
Volunteers for work projects so he may be promoted
Gives his wife love and respect

CHAPTER 21

Writing a Paragraph: Devising a Plan—Outlines

Once you have a topic sentence, you can begin working on an *outline* for your paragraph. The outline is a *plan* that helps you stay focused in your writing. The outline begins to form when you write your topic sentence and the details beneath it.

CHECKING YOUR DETAILS

You can now look at your list and ask yourself an important question: "Do I have enough details to support my topic sentence?" Remember, your goal is to write a paragraph of seven to twelve sentences.

Consider this topic sentence and list of details:

topic sentence: Fresh fruit is a good dessert.
details: tastes good
healthy
easy

Does the list contain enough details for a paragraph of seven to twelve sentences? Probably not.

Adding Details When There Are Not Enough

To add details, try brainstorming. Ask yourself some questions:

What fruit tastes good?
What makes fruit a healthy dessert?
Why is it easy? How can you serve it?

By brainstorming, you may come up with these details:

topic sentence: Fresh fruit is a good dessert.
details: tastes good
a ripe peach or a juicy pineapple tastes delicious

crunchy apples always available and satisfying
plump strawberries are great in summer
healthy
low in calories
rich in vitamins and fiber
easy
served as it is
in a fruit salad
mixed with ice cream or sherbet
no cooking necessary

Keep brainstorming until you feel you have enough details for a seven-to-twelve-sentence paragraph. Remember, it is better to have too many details than to have too little, for you can always edit the extra details later.

TEACHING TIP:

Stress that the order of details in this list may not necessarily be the order of details in a final version of the outline and final version of a paragraph. (See pp. 277-278 on coherence.)

Answers Will Vary.

Possible answers shown at right.

Exercise 1

Collaborate

Adding Details to Support a Topic Sentence

Do this exercise with a partner or group. The following topic sentences have some—but not enough—details. Write sentences to add details to each list.

1. **topic sentence:** Renting a movie on video has many advantages over seeing a movie in a theater.

   details:
   1. You don't have to get dressed up to see a video at home.
   2. You can stop the video to get a snack or answer the phone.
   3. Renting a video is cheaper than buying a movie ticket.
   4. Two or more people can view a video for one rental fee.
   5. You can view the video more than once during the rental period.
   6. At home, you don't have to put up with the loud, rude audiences of the movies.

2. **topic sentence:** My car is full of items that need to be cleaned or thrown out.

   details:
   1. The floor mats are covered in dust and leaves.
   2. There is an empty Kleenex box on the back seat.
   3. Also on the back seat is a filthy blanket.

   4. Three rusty wire hangers hang from a door handle.

5. A large, sticky paper cup is on the floor.

_____

6. Next to it are some paper packets of salt

and pepper.

7. Also on the floor is a broken umbrella.

_____

3. topic sentence: People go to the mall for a number of reasons.

details:

    1. Some people go to buy one specific piece of clothing and then leave.

    2. Others are there to enjoy the air conditioning on a hot day.

    3. Some go to eat in the food court.

_____

    4. Others are window shopping.

_____

    5. Parents often go to walk their babies in

strollers.

    6. Bargain hunters go to check the latest

sales.

4. topic sentence: I listen to some kind of music nearly all day.

details:

    1. I hear soft background music at the supermarket.

    2. I jog with a personal stereo that plays a CD of world music.

    3. When I wake up, my son is singing a song from _Sesame Street_.

    4. I listen to music on the radio while I drive.

    5. When I am put on hold on the telephone, I

wait while music plays.

    6. Even the nightly news on television has a

theme song.

7. I play my CDs when I study. _____

_____

5. **topic sentence:** Not all fast-food restaurants offer the same kinds of food.

details: 1. Some offer pizza.

2. Others sell deli subs.

3. Many sell burgers and fries. _____

_____

4. Some sell fried chicken. _____

_____

5. Others sell tacos and tortillas. _____

_____

6. Others specialize in Chinese food. _____

_____

Eliminating Details That Do Not Relate to the Topic Sentence

Sometimes, what you thought were good details don't relate to the topic sentence because they don't fit or support your point. Eliminate details that don't relate to the topic sentence. For example, the following list contains details that don't relate to the topic sentence. Those details are crossed out.

topic sentence: My neighbors are making my home life unbearable.
details: play their albums loud at 3 a.m.
I can't sleep
leave garbage all over the sidewalk
~~come from Philadelphia~~
sidewalk is a mess
insects crawl all over their garbage
~~I carefully bag my garbage~~
they argue loudly and bang on the walls
my privacy is invaded
park their van in my parking space

 Exercise 2 **Eliminating Details That Do Not Fit**

Practice

Following are topic sentences and lists of details. Cross out the details that do not fit the topic sentence.

1. **topic sentence:** Some professional athletes set a bad example for the children who admire them.
details: One basketball player choked a coach.
~~I think basketball has become more of a business than a sport.~~

A baseball player spit at an umpire.

Several football players have been charged with abusing their wives or girlfriends.

~~I used to collect autographs of famous players.~~

Some hockey players are notorious for fighting on the ice.

Children see this behavior and think it is acceptable.

2. topic sentence: Caps are worn by all kinds of people in all kinds of places.

details: Truckers wear caps when they drive.

Men on tractors wear caps with the name of the tractor company.

~~Caps are inexpensive.~~

Children in Little League wear baseball caps.

There are caps to protect fishermen from the sun.

Servers in some restaurants have to wear caps.

Some ladies wear baseball caps covered in sequins to match their fancy clothes.

College bookstores sell students caps printed with the name of the college.

~~Years ago, businessmen used to wear hats to work.~~

Teens wear caps when they're having a bad hair day.

3. topic sentence: Daniella is known for bringing something for every occasion.

details: If she visits someone in the hospital, she always brings flowers.

~~Fresh flowers are really expensive.~~

Daniella brings dessert when you invite her for dinner.

She brings me candy when she stops by.

When Celeste had a baby, Daniella brought the baby a knitted blanket.

I invited her to a picnic, and she came with an extra bag of ice.

Daniella always takes an extra pencil to class for the person who forgot one.

4. topic sentence: When I was ten, my six-year-old brother made a hobby out of teasing me.

details: Jimmy liked to pull my hair and run away.

He called me "chicken."

Sometimes he would sing, "Little chicken, little chicken" to me.

~~Jimmy was my mother's favorite.~~

In my father's car, Jimmy would kick me.

When I fought back, Jimmy blamed me for the fight.

~~My father drove an old Toyota.~~

~~Jimmy borrowed my books and games without telling me.~~

~~He never gave them back.~~

5. topic sentence: The new movie theater was very glamorous.

details: The exterior was made to look like a rock-and-roll drive-in restaurant.

Neon lights were shaped like guitars and musical notes.
Rock music blasted outside the ticket booths.
~~The ticket prices were reasonable.~~
~~The movies showing were the same as the ones at the theater down the block.~~
The concessions area sold gourmet pizza as well as popcorn and candy.
It also had a coffee bar with cappuccino.

From List to Outline

Take another look at the topic sentence and list of details on the topic of My Mother:

topic sentence:	My mother survived difficult times to become a good parent and worker.
details:	She's a good mom.
	Always takes care of me
	She works hard.
	She cooks, cleans.
	makes a great chicken casserole
	She has a job.
	She's a nurse.
	She had a rough life.
	lost her husband
	went to school at night

After you scan the list, you will be ready to develop the outline of a paragraph.

The outline is a plan for writing, and it can be a kind of draft in list form. It sketches what you want to write and the order in which you want to present it. An organized, logical list will make your writing unified because each item on the list will relate to your topic sentence.

When you plan, keep your topic sentence in mind:

My mother <u>survived difficult times</u> to become <u>a good parent</u> and <u>worker</u>.

Notice that the key words are underlined and lead to key phrases:

survived difficult times
a good parent
a good worker

Can you put the details together so that they connect to one of these key phrases?

survived difficult times
She had a rough life, lost her husband, went to school at night

a good parent
She's a good mom, Always takes care of me, She cooks, cleans, makes a great chicken casserole

a good worker
She works hard, She has a job, She's a nurse

With this kind of grouping, you have a clearer idea of how to organize a paragraph. You may have noticed that the details grouped under each phrase explain or give examples that are connected to the topic sentence. You may also have noticed that the detail "She works hard" is placed under the phrase "a good worker." It could also be placed under "a good parent," so it would be your decision where to place it.

Now that you have grouped your ideas with key phrases and examples, you can write an outline:

An Outline for a Paragraph on My Mother

topic sentence:	My mother survived difficult times to become a good parent and worker.
details: **difficult times**	She had a rough life. She lost her husband. She went to school at night.
a good parent	She's a good mom and always takes care of me. She cooks and cleans. She makes a great chicken casserole.
a good worker	She works hard at her job. She's a nurse.

As you can see, the outline combines some details from the list. Even with these combinations, the details are very rough in style. As you reread the list of details, you may notice places that need more combining, places where ideas need more explaining, and places that are repetitive. Keep in mind that an outline is merely a rough organization of your paragraph.

As you work through the steps of designing an outline, you can check for the following:

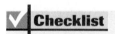 **Checklist**

A Checklist for an Outline

✔ **Unity:** Do all the details relate to the topic sentence? If they do, the paragraph will be unified.

✔ **Support:** Do I have enough supporting ideas? Can I add to those ideas with more specific details?

✔ **Coherence:** Are the ideas listed in the right order? If the order of the points is logical, the paragraph will be coherent.

Coherence

Check the sample outline again, and you'll notice that the details are grouped in the same order as in the topic sentence: First, details about your mother's difficult life; then, details about your mother as a parent; finally, details about your mother as a worker. Putting details in an order that matches the topic sentence is a logical order for this paragraph. It makes the paragraph *coherent*.

Determining the Order of Details

Putting the details in logical order makes the ideas in the paragraph easier to follow. The most logical order for a paragraph depends on the subject of the paragraph. If you are writing about an event, you might use **time order** (such as telling what happened first, second, and so forth); if you are arguing some point, you might use **emphatic order** (such as saving your most convincing idea for last); if you are describing a room, you might use **space order** (such as describing from left to right or from top to bottom).

| Exercise 3 | **Coherence: Putting Details in the Right Order** |

Practice

These outlines have details that are in the wrong order. In the space provided, number the sentences so that they are in the proper order: *1* would be the number for the first sentence, and so on.

1. topic sentence: My last day at my job was sadder than I had expected. (Put the sentences in time order, from first to last.)

___2___ Everyone went through the morning routine as usual.

___4___ I spent my afternoon feeling hurt and insulted.

___3___ At lunchtime, no one even asked me out for a farewell lunch.

___1___ When I first came in, no one acted as if he or she remembered it was my last day.

___5___ Just as we were closing the store, my boss and co-workers surprised me with a big cake and other treats.

___6___ I left feeling grateful for their thoughtfulness.

___7___ I was also sad to leave these kind people.

2. topic sentence: My son looked as if he had fallen into a mud pit. (Put the sentences in space order: from head to foot.)

___6___ Jackie's white sneakers were covered in a gray-green muck.

___4___ His shorts were wet with slime.

___2___ His eyelashes were covered with mud.

___1___ Jackie's hair was flat and matted with dirt.

___5___ Mud and twigs clung to his socks.

___3___ His yellow tee shirt had thick blotches of dirt.

3. topic sentence: Driving without a seat belt is foolish and dangerous.
(Put the sentences in emphatic order, from the least important reason to the most important.)

___4___ You can be killed.

___1___ If the police see you without your belt, you can get a ticket.

___2___ You can be bumped and bruised in a minor fender bender.

___3___ You can be severely hurt in a more serious accident.

4. topic sentence: The speech was long, boring, and confusing. (Put the sentences in the same order as in the topic sentence.)

<u>5</u>   The speaker jumped from topic to topic.

<u>6</u>   One minute he was talking about pollution; then he was telling a joke.

<u>3</u>   He spoke in a monotone.

<u>4</u>   He was putting me to sleep.

<u>1</u>   I checked my watch after thirty minutes.

<u>2</u>   He went on for another forty minutes.

Where the Topic Sentence Goes

INSTRUCTOR'S NOTE:

Students may be uncomfortable hearing that topic sentences are not necessarily at the beginning of a paragraph. Depending on your teaching preference or your department's curriculum/exit test for this course, you may need to stress that topic sentences in formal academic essays are often found at or near the beginning of a paragraph and that students should always follow instructions given in class.

The outline format helps you organize your ideas. The topic sentence is written above the list of details. This position helps you remember that the topic sentence is the main idea and that the details that support it are written under it. You can easily check each detail on your list against your main idea. You can also check the unity (relevance) and coherence (logical order) of your details.

When you actually write a paragraph, the topic sentence does not necessarily have to be the first sentence in the paragraph. Read the following paragraphs, and notice where each topic sentence is placed.

Topic Sentence at the Beginning of the Paragraph

<u>Dr. Chen is the best doctor I have ever had</u>. Whenever I have to visit him, he gives me plenty of time. He does not rush me through a physical examination and quickly hand me a prescription. Instead, he takes time to chat with me and encourages me to describe my symptoms. He examines me carefully and allows me to ask as many questions as I want. After I am dressed, he discusses his diagnosis, explains what medicine he is prescribing, and tells me exactly how and when to take the medication. He tells me what results to expect from the medication and how long it should take for me to get well. Dr. Chen acts as if he cares about me. I believe that is the most important quality in a doctor.

Topic Sentence in the Middle of the Paragraph

The meal was delicious, from the appetizer of shrimp cocktail to the dessert of strawberry tarts. Marcel had even taken the time to make home-baked bread and fresh pasta. <u>Marcel had worked hard on this dinner, and his hard work showed</u>. Everything was served on gleaming china placed on an immaculate tablecloth. There were fresh flowers in a cut glass bowl at the center of the table, and there was a polished goblet at every place setting. The pale green napkins had been carefully ironed and folded into precise triangles.

Topic Sentence at the End of the Paragraph

I woke up at 5:00 a.m. when I heard the phone ringing. I rushed to the phone, thinking the call was some terrible emergency. Of course, it was just a wrong number. Then I couldn't get back to sleep because I was shaken by being so suddenly awakened and irritated by the wrong number. The day got worse as it went along. My car stalled on the freeway, and I had to get towed to a repair shop. The repair cost me $250. I was three hours late for work and missed an important training session with my boss. On my way out of work, I stepped into an enormous puddle and ruined a new pair of shoes. <u>Yesterday was one of those days when I should have stayed in bed</u>.

Be sure to follow your own instructor's directions about placement of the topic sentence.

 Identifying the Topic Sentence

Practice Underline the topic sentence in each of the following paragraphs.

1. Last week I had just gotten out of bed when I had an unpleasant surprise. I was in the kitchen, making myself some instant coffee, when I ran my hand through my tangled hair. I suddenly realized that one of my earrings, a small gold ball, was gone. Since I knew I had been wearing it when I went to bed, I figured it was somewhere in the apartment. I crawled on the floor, checked the corners and crannies, and shook out the bed sheets and pillows. I looked everywhere. I couldn't find it. The next day, I looked again but once more found nothing except dust and crumbs. Finally, I was forced to give up. Then, yesterday, I was again making coffee. As I spooned the last of the coffee granules out of the jar, a small gold ball appeared at the bottom. It was my earring. <u>I have now realized that sometimes objects get lost in the strangest places</u>.

2. <u>Larry is addicted to cookies</u>. He keeps a bag of chocolate chip cookies in his car, and he has been known to drive with one hand on the wheel and one in the cookie bag. At the food court in the mall, he will skip the tacos and burgers and head straight for the freshly baked cookies. Everyone at the local bakery knows Larry. For his birthday, the staff makes Larry a giant cookie, the size of a flat cake, and writes "Happy Birthday" on it, in icing. The local Girl Scouts also know Larry well, for he is their biggest buyer of Girl Scout cookies.

3. I was going to give my father a tie for Father's Day, but then I realized he has very little use for ties. He used to wear ties to work, but now his office doesn't require them. When he dresses up, he wears a sports coat but no tie. <u>Most men don't wear ties anymore.</u> My boyfriend, for example, works in the construction business, so he doesn't wear a tie to work. Also, he refuses to go to any restaurant or club that requires ties. My brother rarely wears ties, either. He is a college student and never dresses up. In fact, I'm not sure he owns a tie. He probably borrows one of my father's old ties if he needs one.

CHAPTER **22**

Writing a Paragraph: Writing, Revising, and Editing the Drafts— Rough Lines

An outline is a draft of a paragraph in list form. Once you have an outline, you are ready to write the list in paragraph form, to "rough out" a draft of your assignment.

Rough Lines The *rough lines* stage of writing is the time to draft, revise, edit, and draft again. You may write several **drafts** or versions of the paragraph in this stage. Writing several drafts is not an unnecessary chore or a punishment. It is a way of taking pressure off yourself. By revising in steps, you are telling yourself, "The first try doesn't have to be perfect."

Review the outline on the topic of My Mother. You can create a first draft of this outline in the form of a paragraph. (*Remember that the first line of each paragraph is indented.*) In the draft of the following paragraph, the first sentence of the paragraph is the topic sentence.

A First Draft of a Paragraph on My Mother

My mother survived difficult times to become a good parent and worker. She had a rough life. She lost her husband. She went to school at night. She's a good mom and always takes care of me. She cooks and cleans. She makes a great chicken casserole. She works hard at her job. She's a nurse.

282

Revising and Editing the Draft

TEACHING TIP:

Remind students that revising a first draft can take considerably more time than they think. Rearranging the sequence of points in a logical order, as well as adding more specific details, may require going back to the initial outline. Students should periodically review the checklist as they revise their drafts.

Once you have a first draft, you can begin to think about revising and editing it. **Revising** means rewriting the draft to change the structure, the order of the sentences, and the content. **Editing** includes making changes in the choice of words, in the selection of the details, in the punctuation, and in the patterns and kinds of sentences. It may also include adding **transitions,** words, phrases, or sentences that link ideas.

One easy way to begin the revising and editing process is to read your work aloud to yourself. As you do so, listen carefully to your words and concentrate on their meaning. Each question in the following checklist will help you focus on a specific part of revising and editing. The name (or key term) for each part is in parentheses.

✔ Checklist

A Checklist for Revising the Draft of a Paragraph (with key terms)

✔ Am I staying on my point? (unity)

✔ Should I eliminate any ideas that do not fit? (unity)

✔ Do I have enough to say about my point? (support)

✔ Should I add any details? (support)

✔ Should I change the order of my sentences? (coherence)

✔ Is my choice of words appropriate? (style)

✔ Is my choice of words repetitive? (style)

✔ Are my sentences too long? Too short? (style)

✔ Should I combine any sentences? (style)

✔ Am I running sentences together? (grammar)

✔ Am I using complete sentences? (grammar)

✔ Can I link my ideas more smoothly? (transitions)

If you apply the checklist to the draft of the paper on My Mother, you will probably find these rough spots:

- The sentences are very short and choppy.
- Some sentences could be combined.
- Some words are repeated often.
- Some ideas need more details for support.
- The paragraph needs transitions: words, phrases, or sentences that link ideas.

Consider the following revised draft of the paragraph, and notice the changes, underlined, that have been made in the draft:

A Revised Draft of a Paragraph on My Mother

topic sentence: **sentences combined** **transition**	My mother survived difficult times to become a good parent and worker. <u>Her hard times began when she lost her</u>

(continued)

details added	husband. At his death, she was only nineteen
details added, transition	and had a baby, me, to raise. She sur-
	vived by going to school at night to
details added, transition	train for a career. Even though she lives
	a stressful life, she is a good mom. She
details added	always takes care of me. She listens to
	my problems, encourages me to do my best,
details added	and praises all my efforts. She cleans
	our apartment until it shines, and she
	makes dinner every night. She makes a
transition	great chicken casserole. In addition,
details added	she works hard at her job. She is a nurse
	at a home for elderly people, where she
	is on her feet all day and is still kind
	and cheerful.

When you are revising your own paragraph, you can use the checklist to help you. Read the checklist several times; then reread your draft, looking for answers to the questions on the list. If your instructor agrees, you can work with your classmates. You can read your draft to a partner or group. Your listener(s) can react to your draft by applying the questions on the checklist and by making notes about your draft as you read. When you have finished reading aloud, your partner(s) can discuss their notes about your work.

Practice

Revising a Draft for Unity

Some of the sentences in the following paragraph do not fit the topic sentence. (The topic sentence is the first sentence in the paragraph.) Cross out the sentences that do not fit.

When a toy becomes a fad, some parents teach their children the wrong lessons. Every year, it seems that one particular toy is the rage, and every child just has to have it immediately. ~~When I was little I had a Tickle-Me-Elmo doll.~~ Some parents camp out all night in front of a toy store so they can be sure to get the latest toy for their son or daughter. Such behavior teaches children that it is really important to have the newest toy, and that their parents are supposed to give them everything the children want. ~~Toys cost too much these days.~~ Some parents take their children to the toy store, and the children see their mother or father pushing, shouting, and shoving to get the newest toy. The children learn that it is acceptable to hurt others to get what you want. ~~The children see the same thing when their parents cut off other drivers on the highways.~~ Trying to please their children, parents can end up teaching them to be greedy, selfish, and overly aggressive.

Collaborate

Answers Will Vary.

Possible answers shown at right.

Adding Support to a Draft

Do this exercise with a partner or group. The following paragraph needs more details to support its point. Add the details in the blank spaces provided.

Our trip to Florida was a disappointment. First of all, the weather was terrible. (Add two sentences of details.) It rained most of the time, and the rain was hard and driving, like a constant storm. When it wasn't raining, it was hot and steamy.

In addition, the amusement park we visited was too crowded for us to enjoy. For example, the parking lots were so full, we had to wait thirty minutes for a parking space. (Add one sentence of details about the crowding.) Inside the park, we waited at least an hour for each ride.

Worst of all, I got sick on our trip. (Add two sentences of detail.) I think I caught some kind of flu; anyway, I spent the entire time coughing and sneezing. One day I felt so miserable that I stayed in bed all day.

I'm glad I got to see Florida, but I wish my visit had been more enjoyable.

Practice

Revising a Draft for Coherence

In the following paragraph, one sentence is in the wrong place. Move it to the right place in the paragraph by drawing an arrow from the sentence to its proper place.

Damien's gift to his mother was dazzling. He handed her an elegantly wrapped box. Inside the tissue paper was a beautiful silver and turquoise necklace. On top of the box was a blue silk rose tied with shiny blue ribbon. The ribbon covered blue wrapping paper dotted with silver stars. When she tore off the wrapping paper and opened the lid of the box, Damien's mother saw a nest of silver and blue tissue paper. She plunged her hands into the soft tissue paper to discover her gift. (The underlined sentence belongs here.)

Exercise **4**

👥 *Collaborate*

Revising a Draft for Style

Do this exercise with a partner or a group. The following paragraph is repetitive in its word choice. Replace each underlined word with a word that is less repetitive. Write the new word above the underlined one.

Answers Will Vary.

Possible answers shown at right.

There are some drinks that go with certain seasons. On a cold winter

chilly
day, for example, I don't want a <u>cold</u> glass of lemonade or iced tea. I want

something hot to drink, like cocoa or cappuccino. In contrast, when the

sweltering
weather is <u>hot</u>, I can't imagine drinking hot coffee. Summer is the time I

crave orange juice straight from the refrigerator or Pepsi in a glass full of

frosty
crushed ice. The <u>cold</u> touch of an ice-filled glass against my forehead is

steamy
one of the joys of a hot day. Similarly, warming my hands on the <u>hot</u> sur-

face of a mug of coffee makes winter feel comfortable. So whether the

sizzling freezing
weather is <u>hot</u> or <u>cold</u>, there are beverages that make the temperature

feel better!

Exercise **5**

Practice

Revising a Draft by Combining Sentences

The following paragraph has many short, choppy sentences that are under-lined. Wherever you see two or more underlined sentences clustered next to each other, combine them into one clear, smooth sentence. Write your revised version of the paragraph in the spaces above the lines. To review ways to combine sentences, see Chapter 5.

Answers Will Vary.

Possible answers shown at right.

He visits every used bookstore in our town,
Jose loves mysteries. <u>He visits every used bookstore in our town. He</u>
looking for mysteries he hasn't read yet.
<u>looks for mysteries he hasn't read yet.</u> He is a member of the Mystery Book

On weekends, he works with a drama group that stages mystery
Club. <u>On weekends, he works with a drama group. The group stages mystery</u>
plays at local restaurants.
<u>plays. The plays are staged at local restaurants.</u> The plays are part of a din-

ner theater show that involves the audience in solving the mystery.
In addition to reading mysteries and acting in them, Jose enjoys
<u>In addition to reading mysteries and acting in them, Jose enjoys</u>
watching mysteries on television, at the movies, and on video.
<u>watching mysteries on television. He sees them at the movies. He</u>

<u>enjoys them on video.</u> Some day, Jose will write a mystery of his own. I

am sure it will be excellent because Jose already knows everything there

is to know about dark crimes, dangerous secrets, and suspenseful endings.

Revising a Draft by Correcting Run-Together Sentences

Practice

The following paragraph has some run-together (run-on) sentences. Correct the run-ons by writing in the spaces above the lines. To review ways to correct run-on sentences, see Chapter 3.

I love to watch the dogs in my neighborhood when they are being taken

for a walk. One large boxer I know walks calmly and slowly, his head held

proudly. Other dogs are so emotional they can hardly suppress their excite-

                                     ; (or . He)

ment. One terrier pulls at his leash he has to sniff every tree and inspect

every inch of sidewalk. A big black Labrador jumps up to greet every

                               .Every (or ;)

passerby. Then there are the happy dogs every day I see a big golden retriev-

er smiling, with her tennis ball in her mouth. She knows she is on her way

to the park to play "fetch." A tiny Yorkshire terrier trots proudly as she dis-

                                   ; (or . However,)

plays a tiny pink satin bow in her topknot. I love dogs however, I do not

have a pet of my own. Therefore, I rely on the dogs in my neighborhood to

bring me amusement, entertainment, and joy.

Editing a Paragraph for Complete Sentences

Practice

The following paragraph has some incomplete sentences (sentence fragments). Correct the fragments by writing in the spaces above the lines. To
review ways to correct sentence fragments, see Chapter 6.

Answers Will Vary.

Possible answer shown
at right.

Food can be a source of disagreement in my family. My mother insists

on serving large, elaborate meals even when nobody is very hungry. She

                                     My father

becomes angry and hurt by our indifference to all her hard work. My father

also likes to cook such food as barbecued ribs and grilled fish.

also likes to cook. Such food as barbecued ribs and grilled fish. My sister,

who is a vegetarian, refuses to eat either my mother's or my father's cook-

Instead, she buys her own food, preferring to eat yogurt and organic

ing. Instead she buys her own food. Preferring to eat yogurt and organic

vegetables.

vegetables. When I come to visit with a bag full of gourmet meats, salads,

                             My mother is upset because I didn't let

and cakes, I cause an argument. My mother is upset. Because I didn't let her

her do the cooking, while my sister won't eat the meat, the nonorganic

do the cooking. While my sister won't eat the meat, the nonorganic salads

salads full of pesticides, or the cakes full of refined sugar.

full of pesticides, or the cakes full of refined sugar. Meanwhile, my father

wants to know why we couldn't have a barbecue.

CHAPTER 23

Writing a Paragraph: Polishing, Proofreading, and Preparing the Final Copy—Final Lines

The final lines of your paragraph are the result of careful thinking, planning, and revising. After many drafts, and when you are satisfied with the result, read the final draft to polish and proofread. You can avoid too many last-minute corrections if you check your last draft carefully for the following:

- spelling errors
- punctuation errors
- mechanical errors
- word choice
- a final statement

CORRECTING THE FINAL DRAFT OF A PARAGRAPH

Take a look at the following final draft of the paragraph on My Mother. The draft has been corrected directly above the crossed-out material. You will notice corrections in spelling, punctuation, mechanics, and word choice. You'll notice that the slang term, "mom," has been changed to "mother." At the end, you'll notice that a final statement has been added to unify the paragraph.

A Corrected Draft of a Paragraph on My Mother

My mother survived difficult ~~time's~~ **times** to become a good ~~parrent~~ **parent**

and worker. Her hard times began when she lost her husband.

At his death, ~~She~~ **she** was only nineteen and had a baby, me, to

She   **night**
raise. ~~she~~ survived by going to school at ~~nite~~ to train for a
                        still   **today**
career. Even though she lives a stressful life, she is a good
mother   **always takes**   **problems**
~~mom~~. She ~~allways take~~ care of me. She listens to my ~~prolems~~,
encourages
~~encourage~~ me to do my best, and praises all my efforts. She
                                    shines
cleans our apartment until it ~~shine~~, and she makes dinner every
                        delicious
night. She makes a ~~great~~ chicken casserole. In addition, she

works hard at her job. She is a nurse at a home for elderly peo-
                                all day
ple, where she is on her feet ~~allday~~ and is still kind and cheer-

ful. At work or at home, my mother is an inspiration to me.

Exercise 1

Practice

Correcting the Errors in the Final Lines of a Paragraph

Proofread the following paragraph, looking for errors in word choice, spelling, punctuation, and mechanics. Correct the fourteen errors by crossing out each mistake and writing the correction above it.

My sister is so involved in her nighttime soap opera that she is missing out
            real   Wednesday   If
on ~~reel~~ life. She has to watch her show every ~~Wensday~~ night. ~~if~~ she is not going
                                    sets   won't
to be home that night, she ~~set's~~ her VCR to tape the show. But lately she ~~wont~~
                        doesn't
even go out on Wednesdays because she ~~dont~~ want to miss the latest episode
                                    wear   one
of the soap opera. She has started to ~~ware~~ her hair like ~~on~~ of the characters on
                                                        too
the show, and I think she is starting to sound like that character, ~~to.~~ When

some of the actors from that show made an appearance at a local mall, my sis-
                    one there
ter was the first ~~on their~~ to see them. She is the president of the local fan club.
                stupid   watches
I think the show is ~~stuppid~~ and silly, but I don't care if she ~~watchs~~ it. I am just
worried
~~worry~~ that it is taking over her life.

Exercise 2

Practice

More on Correcting the Errors in the Final Lines of a Paragraph

Proofread the following paragraph, looking for errors in word choice, spelling, punctuation, and mechanics. Correct the fifteen errors by crossing out each mistake and writing the correction above it.

                            terrify   Halloween
An old ghost story used to ~~terriffy~~ me. I first heard it one ~~halloween~~ when
            boys
some older ~~boy's~~ were swapping tales on a dark playground. The story was
                                        Supposedly
about an old building in the neighborhood. ~~Supposably~~ a man was murdered in

the basement, many year ago. The story said that you could still here the man

groaning on dark nights. In addition, the story claimed that no one had ever

lived in the house since the murder. that story haunted me for year's. I was

afraid to passed that building, expesially at night. Then the building was

demolished. A disco was built in it's place. I was happy because I figured that

nobody could hears the groans of the Ghost over the noise of the disco, so the

spirit had probally moved on. Finely, I stopped being afraid.

(Handwritten corrections above the text: years, hear, That, years, pass, especially, its, hear, ghost, probably, Finally)

GIVE YOUR PARAGRAPH A TITLE

When you prepare the final copy of your paragraph, you may be asked to give it a title. The title should be short and should fit the subject of the paragraph. For example, an appropriate title for the paragraph on your mother could be "My Wonderful Mother" or "An Inspiring Mother." Check with your instructor to see if your paragraph needs a title. (In this book, the paragraphs do not have titles.)

Exercise 3

👥 *Collaborate*

Creating a Title

With a partner or group, create a title for the following paragraph.

Title: _Missing the Seasons_____

My family left New Jersey when I was seven years old, and I am very happy living in Florida. However, sometimes I feel homesick for the North. At Christmas, especially, I wish I could see the snow fall and then run outdoors to make a snowman. In December, it feels strange to string outdoor lights on palm trees. I also miss the autumn, when the leaves on the trees turn fiery red and gold. Sometimes my aunt in New Jersey sends me an envelope of autumn leaves, and I remember the crackle of leaves beneath my feet and the smell of the burning leaves in the fall bonfires. Life is different in Florida where we enjoy sunshine all year. We are spared the icy gray days of a Northern winter, the slush of melting snow, and the gloomy rain of early spring. I now live in a place that is always warm and bright, but sometimes I miss the changing seasons of my first home.

REVIEWING THE WRITING PROCESS

In four chapters, you have worked through *four important steps* in writing. As you become more familiar with the steps and working through them, you will be able to work more quickly. For now, try to remember the four steps:

> **Info BOX**
>
> ### The Steps of the Writing Process
>
> *Thought Lines:* gathering ideas, thinking on paper through freewriting, brainstorming, or keeping a journal.
>
> *Outlines:* planning the paragraph by grouping details, focusing the details with a topic sentence, listing the support, and devising an outline.
>
> *Rough Lines:* drafting the paragraph, then revising and editing it.
>
> *Final Lines:* preparing the final version of the paragraph, with one last proofreading check for errors in preparation, spelling, punctuation, and mechanics.

Following are the outlines, rough lines, and final lines versions of the paragraph on My Mother. Notice how the assignment evolved through the steps of the writing process.

An Outline for a Paragraph on My Mother

topic sentence: My mother survived difficult times to become a good parent and worker.

details:
She had a rough life.
She lost her husband.
She went to school at night.
She's a good mom and always takes care of me.
She cooks and cleans.
She makes a great chicken casserole.
She works hard at her job.
She's a nurse.

A Revised Draft of a Paragraph on My Mother

My mother survived difficult times to become a good parent and worker. Her hard times began when she lost her husband. At his death, she was only nineteen and had a baby, me, to raise. She survived by going to school at night to train for a career. Even though she lives a stressful life, she is a good mom. She always takes care of me. She listens to my problems, encourages me to do my best, and praises all my efforts. She cleans our apartment until it shines, and she makes dinner every night. She makes a great chicken casserole. In addition, she works hard at her job. She is a nurse at a home for elderly people, where she is on her feet all day and is still kind and cheerful.

A Final Version of a Paragraph on My Mother
(Changes from the draft are underlined.)

My mother survived difficult times to become a good parent and worker. Her hard times began when she lost her husband. At his death, she was only nineteen and had a baby, me, to raise. She survived by going to school at night to train for a career. Even though she <u>still</u> lives a stressful life <u>today</u>, she is a good <u>mother</u>. She always takes care of me. She listens to my problems, encourages me to do my best, and praises all my efforts. She cleans our apartment until it shines, and she makes dinner every night. She makes a <u>delicious</u> chicken casserole. In addition, she works hard at her job. She is a nurse at a home for elderly people, where she is on her feet all day and is still kind and cheerful. <u>At work or at home, my mother is an inspiration to me.</u>

Lines of Detail: A Walk-Through Assignment

Write a paragraph about a friend. To write this paragraph, follow these steps:

Step 1: For fifteen minutes, freewrite or brainstorm about a friend.

Step 2: Survey your freewriting or brainstorming and underline any specific ideas you can find. Put these ideas in a list.

Step 3: Pick one idea from your list; it will be your topic. Try to develop it by adding details. Get details by going back to your list for other ideas that fit your topic, by brainstorming for more ideas, and by listing new ideas.

Step 4: Group your related ideas by marking a list of your ideas and then putting all the ideas with the same mark into one category, all the ideas with the next mark into another category, and so on, or by mapping.

Step 5: Write a topic sentence and list your ideas below it.

Step 6: Draft your paragraph by writing the topic sentence and all the ideas on your list in paragraph form. Revise, draft, and edit until you are satisfied with your paragraph.

Step 7: Proofread your final draft; then prepare your good copy of your paragraph.

INSTRUCTOR'S NOTE:

The Peer Review Form on page 297 of this chapter can help students refine their drafts, and it can reinforce the importance of audience feedback and careful revision.

Writing Your Own Paragraph

When you write on any of these topics, be sure to go through the stages of the writing process in preparing your paragraph.

1. This assignment involves working with a group. First, pick a topic from the following list:

     bad drivers
     keeping secrets
     powerful music

   Next, join a group of other students who picked the same topic you did. Brainstorm in a group. Discuss questions that could be asked to get ideas for your paragraph.

   For the drivers topic, sample questions could include "What kind of driver is the worst?" or "How can you avoid being a bad driver?"

   For the secrets topic, sample questions could include "When is it permissible to reveal a secret?" or "Have you ever asked someone to keep your secret?"

   For the music topic, sample questions could include "When is music most powerful? At sad occasions or at happy ones?"

   As you brainstorm, write the questions down. Keep them flowing. Don't stop to answer the questions. Don't stop to say, "That's silly," or "I can't answer that." Try to gather at least twelve questions.

Twelve Brainstorming Questions

1. _____

2. _____

3. _____

4. _____

5. _____

6. _____

7. _____

8. _____

9. _____

10. _____

11. _____

12. _____

Once you have the questions, split up. Begin the thought lines step by answering as many questions as you can. You may also add more questions or freewrite. Then pick a specific topic, list the related details, and write a topic sentence.

Work through the outlines stage by developing an outline with sufficient details.

After you've written a draft of your paragraph, read it to your writing group, the same people who met to brainstorm. Ask each member of your group to make one positive comment and one suggestion for revision.

Finally, revise and edit your draft, considering the group's ideas for improvement. When you are satisfied with your revised draft, prepare a final copy of the paragraph.

2. Following are some topic sentences. Select one and use it to write a paragraph.

Parents should always remember that children need _____

and _____.

Learning a new language is hard because _____.

The two things that surprised me about college were

_____ and _____.

Some people enjoy _____ because it is an escape from

their problems.

3. This assignment requires you to interview a partner. Your final goal is to write a paragraph that will inform the class about your partner. Your paragraph should use this topic sentence:

_____ (fill in your partner's name) has had three significant experiences.

Step 1: Before you write the paragraph, prepare to interview a classmate. Make a list of six questions you want to ask. They can be questions such as, "Have you ever had any interesting experiences?" or "Have you ever been in danger?" Write at least six questions *before* you begin the interview. List the questions below, leaving room to fill in short answers later.

Interview Form

1. **Question:** _____

   Answer: _____

2. **Question:** _____

   Answer: _____

3. **Question:** _____

   Answer: _____

4. **Question:** _____

   Answer: _____

5. **Question:** _____

   Answer: _____

6. **Question:** _____

   Answer: _____

Additional questions and answers: _____

_____

_____

_____

Step 2: As you interview your partner, ask the questions on your list and jot down brief answers. Ask any additional questions you can think of as you are talking; write down the answers in the additional lines at the end of the interview form.

Step 3: Change places. Let your partner interview you.

Step 4: Split up. Use the list of questions and answers about your partner as the thought lines part of your assignment. Work on the outline and draft steps.

Step 5: Ask your partner to read the draft version of your paragraph, to write any comments or suggestions for improvement below the paragraph, and to mark any spelling or grammar errors in the paragraph itself.

Step 6: Revise your draft. When you have completed a final version of your paragraph, read the paragraph to the class.

4. Select one of the following topics. Narrow an aspect of the topic and write a paragraph on it. If you choose the topic of old movies, for example, you might want to narrow it by writing about your favorite old movie.

clothing styles	sports heroes	lies
holidays	college rules	habits
old movies	the Internet	recycling
working out	doctors	fears

5. Look carefully at photograph A. In it, a woman is using a popular piece of technology, a personal data assistant. Think about the technology you use regularly (computer, cell phone, DVD player, CD player, and so forth), and write about one item that is important in your daily life.

Photograph A

6. Study photograph B. Use this photo of a silhouette to write a paragraph about the most important relationship in your life.

Photograph B

Name: _____   **Section:** _____

PEER REVIEW FORM FOR A PARAGRAPH

After you have written a draft version of your paragraph, let a writing partner read it. When your partner has completed the following form, discuss it. Then repeat the same process for your partner's paragraph.

The topic sentence of this paragraph is _____

_____

_____

The detail that I liked best begins with the words _____

_____

The paragraph has enough/too many/too few [circle one] details to support the topic sentence.

A particularly good part of the paragraph begins with the words

_____

I have questions about _____

_____

Other comments on the paragraph: _____

_____

_____

_____

_____

_____

_____

_____

_____

_____

_____

_____

_____

Reviewer's name: _____

WRITING FROM READING

One Man's Kids

Daniel Meier

Daniel Meier graduated from the Harvard Graduate School of Education in 1984 and began teaching first grade at schools in Massachusetts. In 1987, he wrote this article about his work for the <u>New York Times Magazine.</u> In it, he explains how men and women react differently when they discover his job is "not traditional male work."

Words You May Need to Know (corresponding paragraph numbers are in parentheses)

dominated (1): ruled, controlled
flukes (4): a type of fish
complying (4): agreeing to a request
singular (5): remarkable, exceptional
pursuit (5): occupation
transact (5): conduct to a conclusion, settle
expertise (5): skill or knowledge
exult (6): rejoice
intellectual (7): related to knowledge rather than to emotions
hilarity (7): fun, cheerfulness

curriculum (9): a group of related courses or a course of study
merit pay (11): a system of pay based on the quality of a person's work as well as on his or her position
talking shop (11): talking about the details of a specific job
trappings (12): accessories, characteristics
complimentary (12): given free as a courtesy or to repay a favor
lull (13): a pause

1   I teach first graders. I live in a world of skinned knees, double-knotted shoelaces, riddles that I've heard a dozen times, stale birthday cakes, hurt feelings, wandering stories, and one lost shoe ("and if you don't find it, my mother'll kill me"). My work is dominated by six-year-olds.

2   It's 10:45, the middle of snack, and I'm helping Emily open her milk carton. She has already tried the other end without success, and now there's so much paint and ink on the carton from her fingers that I'm not sure she should drink it at all. But I open it. Then I turn to help Scott clean up some milk he has just spilled onto Rebecca's whale crossword puzzle.

3   While I wipe my milk-and-paint-covered hands, Jenny wants to know if I've seen that funny book about penguins that I read in class. As I hunt for it in a messy pile of books, Jason wants to know if there is a new seating arrangement for lunch tables. I find the book, turn to answer Jason, then face Maya, who is fast approaching with a new knock-knock joke. After what seems like the tenth "Who's there?" I laugh, and Maya is pleased.

4   Then Andrew wants to know how to spell "flukes" for his crossword. As I get to "u," I give a hand signal for Sarah to take away the snack. But just as Sarah is almost out the door, two children complain that "we haven't

even had ours yet." I stop the snack mid-flight, complying with their request for graham crackers. I then return to Andrew, noticing that he has put "flu" for 9 Down, rather than 9 Across. It's now 10:50.

5   My work is not traditional male work. It's not a singular pursuit. There is not a large pile of paper to get through or one deal to transact. I don't have one area of expertise or knowledge. I don't have the singular power over language of a lawyer, the physical force of a construction worker, the command over fellow workers of a surgeon, the wheeling and dealing transactions of a businessman. My energy is not spent in pursuing, climbing, achieving, conquering, or cornering some goal or object.

6   My energy is spent in encouraging, supporting, consoling, and praising my children. In teaching, the inner rewards come from without. On any given day, quite apart from teaching reading and spelling, I bandage a cut, dry a tear, erase a frown, tape a torn doll, and locate a long-lost boot. The day is really won through matters of the heart. As my students groan, laugh, shudder, cry, exult, and wonder, I do, too. I have to be soft around the edges.

7   A few years ago, when I was interviewing for an elementary-school teaching position, every principal told me with confidence that, as a male, I had an advantage over female applicants because of the lack of male teachers. But in the next breath, they asked with a hint of suspicion why I chose to work with young children. I told them I wanted to observe and contribute to the intellectual growth of a maturing mind. What I really felt like saying, but didn't, was that I loved helping a child to learn to write her name for the first time, finding someone a new friend, or sharing in the hilarity of Winnie the Pooh getting so stuck in a hole that only his head and rear show.

8   I gave that answer to those principals, who were mostly male, because I thought they wanted a "male" response. This meant talking about intellectual matters. If I had taken a different course and talked about helping children in their emotional development, it would have been seen as closer to a "female" answer. I even altered my language, not once mentioning the word "love" to describe what I do indeed love about teaching. My answer worked; every principal nodded approvingly.

9   Some of the principals also asked what I saw myself doing later in my career. They wanted to know if I eventually wanted to go into educational administration. Becoming a dean of students or a principal has never been one of my goals, but they seemed to expect me, as a male, to want to climb higher on the career stepladder. So I mentioned that, at some point, I would be interested in working with teachers as a curriculum coordinator. Again, they nodded approvingly.

10   If those principals had been female instead of male, I wonder whether their questions, and my answers, would have been different. My guess is that they would have been.

11 At other times, when I'm at a party or a dinner and tell someone that I teach young children, I've found that men and women respond differently. Most men ask about the subjects I teach and the courses I took in my training. Then, unless they bring up an issue such as merit pay, the conversation stops. Most women, on the other hand, begin the conversation on a more immediate and personal level. They say things like, "Those kids must love having a male teacher" or "That age is just wonderful; you must love it." Then, more often than not, they'll talk about their own kids or ask me specific questions about what I do. We're then off and talking shop.

12 Possibly, men would have more to say to me, and I to them, if my job had more of the trappings and benefits of more traditional male jobs. But my job has no bonuses or promotions. No complimentary box seats at the ball park. No cab fare home. No drinking buddies after work. No briefcase. No suit. (Ties get stuck in paint jars.) No power lunches. (I eat peanut butter and jelly, chips, milk, and cookies with the kids.) No taking clients out for cocktails. The only place I take my kids is to the playground.

13 Although I could have pursued a career in law or business, as several of my friends did, I chose teaching instead. My job has benefits all its own. I'm able to bake cookies without getting them stuck together as they cool, buy cheap sewing materials, take out splinters, and search just the right trash cans for useful odds and ends. I'm sometimes called "Daddy" and even "Mommy" by my students, and if there's ever a lull in the conversation at a dinner party, I can always ask those assembled if they've heard the latest riddle about why the turkey crossed the road. (He thought he was a chicken.)

 Exercise 4

Practice

Moving From General Statements to Specific Details in "One Man's Kids"

Daniel Meier uses specific details to support the general points he makes. To become more familiar with this technique, complete the following exercise by rereading "One Man's Kids" and paying attention to the specific details.

1. Daniel Meier says that his "work is dominated by six-year-olds." Give examples, from the essay, of the kind of work he did one morning between 10:45 and 11:00 a.m.

   a. He helps Emily open her milk carton.

   b. He helps Scott clean up some milk he has just spilled onto Rebecca's whale crossword puzzle.

   c. He finds a funny book about penguins for Jenny.

   d. He listens to Maya tell a knock-knock joke.

2. He says that his work is "not traditional male work."

   a. He doesn't have the control of language of a lawyer.

   b. He lacks the physical strength of a construction worker.

   c. He does not get involved in the deal-making of a businessman.

3. At job interviews with male principals, Meier knew what word to avoid and what word to use in a "male" response.

   a. The word he never mentioned was <u>love.</u>

   b. He knew he had to talk about <u>intellectual matters.</u>

4. When he talks to men and women about his work, they have different responses.

   a. Most men ask about the subjects he teaches and about <u>the courses he took in his training.</u>

   b. Men can't think of much say to say unless they bring up <u>an issue like merit pay.</u>

   c. Most women make comments like "those kids must love having a male teacher" or <u>"that age is just wonderful; you must love it."</u>

   d. Then they may talk about their own children or ask Meier specific questions about what he does.

WRITING FROM READING: "One Man's Kids"

When you write on any of the following topics, be sure to work through the stages of the writing process in preparing your paragraph.

1. Begin this assignment by brainstorming with a partner or group. Make lists of jobs that are traditionally considered "man's work" or "woman's work." Then, on your own, find one job on the lists that you (as a male or female) are traditionally not expected to do. Write a paragraph explaining why you would (or would not) want to do that job.

2. Write a paragraph explaining why Daniel Meier enjoys his work.

3. Write a paragraph explaining what you do during fifteen minutes of a busy day at your job. Begin by listing the kinds of actions you perform when your work is particularly hectic. For an example of how to develop your paragraph, see paragraphs 2, 3, and 4 of "One Man's Kids."

4. Write about the job you would like to have and the rewards it would bring you. Begin by asking yourself such questions as, What intellectual satisfaction would this job bring me? What emotional benefits does it offer? Could I grow in this job? What would the financial benefits be?

5. If you are working or have ever worked with children, write a paragraph describing the good (or bad) aspects of the job. You can first describe the job and responsibilities and then write about its good (or bad) points.

6. Dan Meier says that "In teaching, the inner rewards come from without"; he means that his satisfaction comes from seeing others grow and succeed. Write about someone you know who finds satisfaction in working with people: helping them grow and succeed, healing them, nurturing them, counseling them, coaching them, or teaching them.

When Words Get in the Way

Athlone G. Clark

Athlone G. Clarke, a native of Jamaica, soon discovered the language barrier that can exist between English-speaking people from different English-speaking countries. In exploring the differences in everyday words, he sometimes felt as if he were "looking in a mirror where everything appears the same, except it's reversed."

Words You May Need to Know (corresponding paragraphs are in parentheses)

face value (1): the surface meaning

pleasantries (2): polite social remarks

commonplace (3): ordinary, usual

deemed (3): considered, regarded

derogatory (3): belittling, degrading

profusely (4): freely and generously

context (4): background

dashed (8): broken to pieces

superfluous (8): unnecessary

excess (8): an amount over what is normal or sufficient

universal (9): effective everywhere

---

1   Coming from Jamaica, I have discovered that even among people who speak the same language, there can be artificial barriers. In my island home, greetings are usually informal and taken at face value. I assumed it to be the same here, but I soon discovered there are deep historical wounds hidden behind everyday words.

2   One evening, as I passed my elderly neighbor Mr. Gabinsky on the stairs, he greeted me with his usual thick accent: "Hey there, young boy, how is the family doing today?" We exchanged a few pleasantries and went our separate ways.

3   That same evening, another neighbor who lived in the apartment upstairs dropped by. "You shouldn't let that man from across the hall get away with calling you 'boy,'" Al said. "He is disrespecting you in a big way." This was news to me. Back home it was commonplace for elderly people to refer to younger adults as "boy" or "girl." Al, who is African American, explained that it was different here, that the "b" word has its roots in slavery and was to be deemed derogatory when used by my white neighbor.

4   So, the next time Mr. Gabinsky greeted me in such a manner, I quickly put a stop to it. He apologized profusely. As it turned out, he was from Hungary and, like myself, was not yet accustomed to choosing his words according to historical context.

5   And then there was the day I got lost trying to find a "shop" that sold milk. Many of us who grew up on the islands know what a vital link the "shop" is in the food chain. My journey would have been less complicated had I been looking for a "store" that sold milk. It is interesting to note that

if my mission had been to buy clothes instead of milk, then that would mean I was out "shopping."

6   Here I am, an English-speaking man living in an English-speaking country, but with the feeling of looking in a mirror where everything appears the same, except it's reversed.

7   One of most complex words I have had to work into my vocabulary is "minority." I had to learn what a "minority contract" was, and why someone like Mr. Gabinsky, who is white, could not qualify. The word is almost always used in the context of racial classification. It hardly matters that there may be fewer Hungarian Americans living here than African Americans or Asian Americans or Hispanic Americans.

8   Sports is a subject dear to my heart, and my hopes were cruelly dashed when I discovered there would be no African, European, or Asian nations competing in the "World Series." One of my favorite athletes is now an unrestricted free agent. The words "unrestricted" and "free" at first seemed a little superfluous, until I learned that there is no such thing as excess in American sports when it comes to words and salaries.

9   At least the language of business appears to be universal. The first time I passed a certain Persian rug establishment in Atlanta, there was a big sign out front that said, "Going out of business. Fifty percent off." Ten years later, the sign is still there, touched up with a fresh coat of paint.

 Exercise 5

Practice

Recognizing the Specific Examples in "When Words Get in the Way"

Athlone G. Clark gives examples of a language barrier that appears even between speakers of the same language. These examples fall into several categories. Complete the exercise below by rereading the essay and noting the examples and their categories.

1. For Clarke, one kind of misunderstanding developed over language related to race.

   a. He had to learn the meaning of "minority" and "minority contract."

   b. He and Mr. Gabinsky discovered the history of the word _"boy."_

2. Clarke also struggled over the difference between two words that have to do with buying something.

   a. When he wants to buy milk, he looks for a _shop._

   b. Later he learns he should have looked for a _store._

   c. If he had been looking for clothes instead of milk, he would have been performing the activity called _shopping._

3. Sports is another area in which the language confuses Clarke.

   a. He is surprised that the World Series has no players from

     _Africa_____, _Europe_____, or _Asia._____

b. He believes that one word, instead of two, could describe an

<u>unrestricted</u>, <u>free</u> agent.

4. The language of business, Clarke discovers, seems to be the same everywhere.

a. A Persian rug store in Atlanta has a sign that says <u>*"Going out of*</u>

<u>*business."*</u>

b. Ten years later, the sign is still there, and the store is still in business.

WRITING FROM READING: "When Words Get in the Way"

When you write on any of the following topics, be sure to work through the stages of the writing process in preparing your paragraph.

1. In a paragraph, explain what Clarke means when he says that, in America, the language seems to make him feel as if he is "looking in a mirror where everything appears the same except it's reversed." Include incidents Clarke describes when he discovers a word means something quite different from what he thought it did.

2. If you moved to the United States after you learned to speak English in another country, write a paragraph about four or five American words or phrases that confused you.

3. If you moved to the United States knowing no English, write about four or five English words or phrases that have no equivalent in your first language. Also, explain why these words or phrases cannot be translated into your language. Is it because the object, person, or situation they describe does not exist in your country?

If you prefer, you can write about four or five words or phrases in your first language that have no equivalent in English.

4. Choose an area that you once knew little about but that you now understand well. It can be some part of science, health, the restaurant business, the hospitality business, auto repair, law enforcement, fashion, computers, retail sales, sports, music, and so forth. In a paragraph, write about four or five words or terms that once were unknown or confusing to you. Explain how you learned their meaning.

5. Interview someone at least ten years older than you. Ask him or her to explain the meaning of three or four words or phrases that were popular slang when he or she was in high school. Write a paragraph about this slang. Explain what each word or term means and how it sounds to you today.

6. If you have ever traveled to another English-speaking country (for example, Jamaica, the Bahamas, England, Scotland, Ireland, Canada, Australia, or New Zealand), write about several words or phrases that were new to you.

CHAPTER 24

Writing a Narrative Paragraph

Paragraphs use different methods to make their point. One kind of paragraph uses narration.

WHAT IS NARRATION?

Narration means telling a story. Everybody tells stories; some people are better storytellers than others. When you write a **narrative** paragraph, you can tell a story about something that happened to you or to someone else, or about something that you saw or read.

A narrative covers events in a time sequence because it is always about happenings: events, actions, incidents. However, interesting narratives do more than just tell what happened. They help the reader become involved in the story by providing vivid details. These details come from your memory, your observation, or your reading. Using good details, you don't just tell the story; you *show* it.

Give the Narrative a Point

We all know people who tell long stories that seem to lead nowhere. These people talk on and on; they recite an endless list of activities and soon become boring. Their narratives have no point.

The difficult part of writing a narrative is making sure that it has a point. That point will be included in the topic sentence. The point of a narrative is the meaning of the incident or incidents you are writing about. To get to the point of your narrative, ask yourself questions like these:

What did I learn?
What is the meaning of this story?
What is my attitude toward what happened?

Did it change me?

What emotion did it make me feel?

Was the experience a good example of something (such as unfairness, or kindness, or generosity)?

The answers to such questions can lead you to a point. An effective topic sentence for a narrative is

INSTRUCTOR'S NOTE:

Students often need to be reminded that topic sentences should not be announcements. Some students may have developed the habit in speech classes, in informal presentations, or in high school classes where content counted more than structure.

not this: This paper will be about the time I found a wallet on the sidewalk. (This is an announcement; it does not make a point.)

but this: When I found a wallet on the sidewalk, my honesty was tested.

not this: Last week my car alarm wouldn't stop screeching. (This identifies the incident but does not make a point. It is also too narrow to be a good topic sentence.)

but this: I lost my faith in fancy gadgets when my car alarm wouldn't stop screeching.

Exercise 1

Practice

Recognizing Good Topic Sentences for Narrative Paragraphs

If a sentence is a good topic sentence for a narrative paragraph, write *OK* on the line provided.

1. _OK_   Losing my car keys sent me into a foolish panic.

2. _____   My twenty-first birthday will be the subject of this paragraph.

3. _____   Two kittens appeared on our doorstep yesterday.

4. _____   I want to tell you about my first day at boot camp.

5. _OK_   A bad car accident made me grateful to be alive.

6. _OK_   Winning the skateboard contest gave my brother more self-confidence.

7. _____   The discovery of a mouse in my closet will be discussed here.

8. _OK_   My father learned to watch his temper when he argued with a highway patrol officer.

9. _____   Last night, someone stole my mountain bike.

Exercise 2

👥 *Collaborate*

Writing the Missing Topic Sentences in Narrative Paragraphs

Below are three paragraphs. Working with a partner or group, write an appropriate topic sentence for each one. Be ready to share your answers with another group or with the class.

Answers Will Vary.

Possible topic sentences shown at right.

1. topic sentence: My plan for an afternoon in the sun taught me to

keep an eye on the weather.

Yesterday was my day off, so I decided to get some fresh air and sunshine in my back yard. I grabbed an old lawn chair, turned on my CD player, and stretched out in the hot sun. At first, the sun was strong, almost overpowering, and I resolved to go inside before I roasted. But soon I was dozing in the sun, and I felt the comfort of a breeze. Every few minutes, I woke up enough to glance at the sky and see clouds forming. After about a half hour of napping, I became conscious of a distant rumbling. Then the breeze developed into a wind. Suddenly I felt cooler, even cold. However, it felt so good to lie in the chilly current that I fell asleep again. Suddenly, I woke to what sounded like a gunshot right next to me. I jumped up, terrified. The tree two feet away from me had been torn in half by lightning. Shaking with fear, I ran into my house.

2. topic sentence: *Although it is hard to count on fun and*

entertainment, they can turn up in the most unexpected places.

My favorite television talk show was coming to my town, and the producers were giving away free tickets on a first-come, first-served basis. I was determined to get those tickets and be in the audience for a taping of the show. When I told my best friend about the show, he wanted to go, too. "Let's camp out in front of the theater overnight," he said, "and be the first in line to get tickets." We went to the theater at midnight, carrying our backpacks full of snacks, CDs, and video games. As we arrived, we were stunned to see that two hundred people had arrived before us, all with the same idea. We joined the end of the line and spent the night making friends, swapping music, and talking about our favorite parts of the show. The time went quickly because we were having so much fun. When morning came, the tickets ran out just before we got to the front of the line. It was a disappointment, but we didn't feel the night had been totally wasted.

3. topic sentence: *Saying goodbye to my old house meant saying*

goodbye to many childhood memories and looking ahead to new

experiences.

A year ago, I spent my last day in the house where I had grown up. As the day began, my mother and I hurried to pack the last boxes and load the car with our suitcases. Soon, my aunt and my two cousins came to say goodbye and to bring us a bag of sandwiches for the long drive to our new home. When they left, I took one last tour of my home. There was the old kitchen where my mother had cooked so many meals for me and my older brothers. Next was the living room with the worn floor boards, scratched and nicked by so many children jumping, bouncing, and kicking as they played. Finally, there was my little room with its sloping ceiling and so many memories. As I lingered there, my mother called to me. "Anton," she said, "it's time to go. Come on, now." I dried my eyes and joined my mother. It was time to move on.

HINTS FOR WRITING A NARRATIVE PARAGRAPH

Everyone tells stories, but some people tell stories better than others. When you write a story, be sure to

- Be clear.
- Be interesting.
- Stay in order.
- Pick a topic that is not too big.

1. Be clear. Put in all the information the reader needs in order to follow your story. Sometimes you need to explain the time, or place, or the relationships of the people in your story in order to make the story clear. Sometimes you need to explain how much time has elapsed between one action and another. This paragraph is not clear:

> Getting the right textbooks from the campus bookstore was a frustrating experience. First of all, I missed the first two days of classes, so Jose had to give me the list of books, and I really couldn't understand his writing. Then, when I got there, they didn't have all the books I needed. The book I needed the most, the workbook for my Intermediate Algebra class, wasn't on the shelves, and they said they had run out and wouldn't get more until next week. In addition, I couldn't use a Mastercard, only a Visa card, to pay, and I didn't have a Visa card. I left with only one of my required textbooks.

What is wrong with the paragraph? It lacks all kinds of information. Who is Jose? Is he a classmate? Someone who works in the bookstore? And what list is *the* list of books? The writer talks about getting "there," but is "there" the campus bookstore, or another bookstore, and who are "they"?

2. Be interesting. A boring narrative can make the greatest adventure sound dull. Here is a dull narrative:

TEACHER'S
DISCUSSION
QUESTIONS:

Ask students why the
paragraph is dull. What
words are vague? What
details could be added?

> Volunteering with the homebuilders club was great. Last weekend I helped the club members fix up an old house. First, we did some things outside. Then we worked on the inside and cleaned up the kitchen. We did a little painting, too. I particularly liked the end of the project, when the family who owned the house saw the improvements. They were happy.

Good specific details are the difference between an interesting story and a dull one.

3. Stay in order. Put the details in a clear order so that the reader can follow your story. Usually, time order is the order you follow in narration. This narrative has a confusing order:

> Celia was really upset with me yesterday. But that was before I explained about the car accident. Then she forgave me and felt guilty about being so mean. She was angry because I had promised to take her to the movies last night. When I didn't show up, she started calling my cell phone number. She claims she called seven times and never got an answer. What Celia didn't know was that on my way to her house, I skidded on a wet road and hit a tree. I wasn't badly hurt, but the paramedics insisted on taking me to the emergency room. My cell phone was in my car while I rode in an ambulance. By the time I left the hospital and made it to Celia's house, it was midnight, and Celia was not in a good mood.

There's something wrong with the order of events here. Tell the story in the order it happened. First, I promised to take Celia to the movies. Second, I had a car accident. Third, Celia tried to call many times. Fourth, I was taken to the emergency room and then released. Fifth, I went to Celia's house, where she was angry. Sixth, I told my story and she forgave me. A clear time sequence helps the reader follow your narrative.

4. Pick a topic that is not too big. If you try to write about too many events in a short space, you run the risk of being superficial. You cannot describe anything well if you cover too much. This paragraph covers too much:

> Visiting New York City was like exploring a new world for me. It started with a ride on the subway, which was both frightening and exciting. Then my cousin, a native New Yorker, introduced me to Times Square, where I saw people dressed like aliens in a science fiction movie and I learned to navigate through thousands of people all trying to cross the street. After that, we went to a famous New York deli where I ate Greek, Korean, and Italian food. The next day, we walked to Central Park and heard a free concert. That night, we went to a club where the music was modern and wild.

This paragraph would be better if it discussed one shorter time period in greater depth and detail. For example, it could cover one incident—the subway ride, the visit to Times Square, the deli meal, the concert, or the club—more fully.

Using a Speaker's Exact Words in Narrative

Some of the examples of narrative that you have already seen have included the exact words someone said. You may want to include part of a conversation in your narrative. To do so, you need to know how to punctuate speech.

A person's exact words get quotation marks around them. If you change the words, you do not use quotation marks.

> **exact words:** "You're acting strangely," he told me.
> **not exact words:** He told me that I was acting strangely.
>
> **exact words:** My father said, "I can get tickets to the soccer match."
> **not exact words:** My father said he could get tickets to the soccer match.

There are a few other points to remember about punctuating a person's exact words. Once you've started quoting a person's exact words, periods and commas generally go inside the quotation marks. Here are two examples:

> Marcelline said, "My car needs new tires."
> "Eat your breakfast," my grandmother told me.

When you introduce a person's exact words with phrases like "She said," or "The teacher told us," put a comma before the quotation marks. Here are two examples:

> She said, "Take your umbrella."
> The police officer told us, "This road is closed."

If you are using a person's exact words and have other questions about punctuation, check the section on punctuation in the grammar section of this book.

WRITING THE NARRATIVE PARAGRAPH IN STEPS

Thought Lines **Gathering Ideas: Narration**

Suppose your instructor asks you to write a narrative paragraph on this topic:

My Last _____

You might begin by *freewriting:*

Freewriting on My Last _____

> My last _____. My last what? Last chance? Last dance?
> My last chance at passing Algebra. My last cup of coffee. My last day of
> high school. That was wild. Seniors are crazy sometimes. Coffee—I love
> coffee. Quit it suddenly. Last cup of morning coffee. Needed my morning
> coffee.

You scan your freewriting and realize that you have three possible topics: My Last Day of High School, My Last Chance at Passing Algebra, and My Last Cup of Coffee. Since you do not have any details on passing algebra, and the last day of high school seems like a topic that many students might write about, you decide to be original and work with My Last Cup of Coffee.

Exercise 3

Practice

Finding Topics in Freewriting

Each of the freewriting examples that follow contains more than one possible topic for a paragraph. In the spaces below each freewriting, write the possible topics, and write the one that you think would be the best topic for a narrative a paragraph. Briefly explain why it would be the best topic: Is it the one with the most details? Is it the most original topic? Or is it the one that would be the easiest to develop with specific details?

TEACHING TIP:

Remind students that freewriting may contain phrases and conversational expressions.

1. **Freewriting on This Topic: My Only _____**

    My only. Only the lonely. Only what? My only afternoon in student
    detention. My only win at gambling. Those silly Lotto cards you scratch off
    and see the amount underneath. What a surprise. I never win anything. My
    only car accident. But it was minor. My only plane trip. Never again, after
    that experience. Too much waiting around.

    possible topics: afternoon in student detention, win at gambling, car

    accident, plane trip

    your choice of the best topic: plane trip

    reason for your choice: easiest to develop

Answers Will Vary.

Possible answers shown at right.

2. **Freewriting on This Topic: My Best _____**

    My best dress. A beautiful satin dress. Emerald green. My best day.
    The best day ever. Hard to tell. I guess the day I met Antonio. Antonio was
    so handsome. I miss him now. It's hard to break up. The day we met, he was

so funny. I thought he was wild. A friend. My best friend. I could write about how I met my best friend. My best birthday. The one when I got a surprise party was excellent. I was truly surprised.

possible topics: *best dress, best day (when I met Antonio), meeting* _____

my best friend, best birthday _____

your choice of the best topic: *best day (when I met Antonio)* _____

reason for your choice: *has the most details* _____

Listing Ideas

Now that you have a specific topic, you can scan your freewriting for all your ideas on that topic. You put all those ideas into a list:

My Last Cup of Coffee

I love coffee.
Quit it suddenly.
Last cup of morning coffee.
Needed my morning coffee.

Adding Specific Details by Brainstorming

To add ideas to your list, try brainstorming. Add questions that will lead you to more details. You can start with questions that are based on the details you already have. See where the questions—and their answers—lead you.

Question: **Why do you love coffee?**
Answer: I love the taste.

Question: **Is that the only reason?**
Answer: It picks me up. Gives me energy.

Question: **Why did you quit it suddenly?**
Answer: I figured quitting suddenly would be the best way. Don't drag it out.

Question: **Why was your last cup drunk in the morning? Why not the afternoon or evening?**
Answer: My first cup in the morning was the one I needed the most. To wake up.

Question: **Were there any other times you needed it?**
Answer: I needed it all day.

Question: **Can you be more specific?**
Answer: I craved coffee around 10:00 a.m., and then again around 3:00 or 4:00 p.m., and also after dinner.

Question: **How did you feel after you quit?**
Answer: I felt terrible at first. The next day I felt better.

Question: **What do you mean by saying you felt terrible?**
Answer: I was irritable. Shaky. I had bad headaches.

As you can see, questions can lead you to more details and can help you to decide whether you will have enough details to develop a paragraph on your topic, or whether you need to choose another topic. In this case, the details in the answers are sufficient for writing a paragraph.

Brainstorming for Details

Following are topics and lists of details. With a partner or group, brainstorm at least five questions and answers, based on the existing details, that could add more details. The first one is partly done for you.

1. **topic:** A Power Failure

The electricity went off.
It was a very hot day.
We had no air conditioning or fans.
The ice in the refrigerator was melting.
I tried to cool off.
I couldn't do a lot of things because there was no electricity.

Brainstorming Questions and Answers

Question 1: How long did the power stay off?

Answer 1: About four hours.

Question 2: What was the temperature?

Answer 2: Ninety degrees.

Question 3: How did you try to cool off?

Answer 3: I splashed my face and neck with water.

Question 4: What things couldn't you do?

Answer 4: Use my computer, watch television.

Question 5: What did you do instead?

Answer 5: I sat around, complaining.

2. **topic:** An Incident on the School Bus

The students were loud.
They were mean to the driver.
The driver yelled.
I was one of the smallest children.
I was afraid.
The driver stopped the bus.

Brainstorming Questions and Answers

Question 1: Were the students shouting?

Answer 1: Yes, and singing.

Question 2: How were they mean to the driver?

Answer 2: They called the driver names and threw things.

Question 3: What did they throw?

Answer 3: Pieces of paper. Gum.

Question 4: Why was the driver yelling?

Answer 4: To tell them to behave.

Question 5: Why were you afraid?

Answer 5: I was afraid the students would turn against me.

3. topic: A Special Gift

Dave gave it to me.
It was a framed picture.
He was very thoughtful.
The picture was special.
He really surprised me.
It happened a long time ago.

Brainstorming Questions and Answers

Question 1: Who is Dave?

Answer 1: My boyfriend.

Question 2: What was the picture?

Answer 2: A photograph of Dave and me.

Question 3: Why was it so special?

Answer 3: It was a picture of the day we met.

Question 4: Why else is it special?

Answer 4: In the photograph, we are at a wedding.

Question 5: How long ago did he give you the gift?

Answer 5: About a year ago.

Focusing the Thought Lines

To begin focusing your topic and details around some point, list your topic and all the details you have gathered so far. The list below includes all the details gathered from freewriting and brainstorming.

My Last Cup of Coffee

I love coffee.
Quit it suddenly.
Last cup of morning coffee.
Needed my morning coffee.
I love the taste of coffee.
It picks me up.
Gives me energy.
I figured quitting suddenly would be the best way.
Don't drag it out.
My first cup in the morning was the one
I needed the most.

To wake up.
I needed it all day.
I craved coffee around 10:00 a.m., and then again around 3:00 or 4:00
    p.m., and also after dinner.
I felt terrible at first.
The next day I felt better.
First I was irritable. Shaky. I had bad headaches.

Coherence: Grouping the Details and Selecting a Logical Order

If you survey the list, you can begin to group the details:

List of Details on My Last Cup of Coffee

Why I Love Coffee

I love the taste.
It picks me up.
Gives me energy.

The Morning I Quit

I quit it suddenly.
I figured quitting suddenly would be the best way.
Don't drag it out.
Drank my last cup in the morning.
My first cup in the morning was the one I needed most.
To wake up.

The Afternoon

I needed it all day.
Around 3:00 or 4:00 p.m. I craved coffee.
I felt terrible at first.
I was irritable and shaky.

The Evening

I craved coffee after dinner.
I was more irritable.
I had a bad headache.

The Next Day

I felt better.

Looking at these groups, you notice one, Why I Love Coffee, is background for your narrative. Three groups, The Morning I Quit, The Afternoon, and The Evening, tell about the *stages* of your quitting. And the last group tells how you felt *after* you had your last cup. These groups seem to lead to a *logical order* for the paragraph: a *time order*. A logical order will give your paragraph coherence.

Unity: Selecting a Topic Sentence

To give the paragraph unity, you need a point, a topic sentence. Surveying your topic and detail, you might decide on this topic sentence:

My last cup of coffee was in the morning.

To be sure that your paragraph has *unity*, check your topic sentence. It should (1) make a point, and (2) relate to all your details.

Does it make a point? No. It says your last cup of coffee was in the morning. That isn't much of a point. It is too narrow to develop into a paragraph. Does the topic sentence relate to all your details? No. You have details about why you love coffee, when you needed it, how you quit, and how you felt afterward. But with your topic sentence, you can talk only about the morning you quit.

You need a better topic sentence. To find it, ask yourself questions such as,

Did I learn anything from this experience?
Did the experience hurt me?
Did it help me?
Was it a sad experience?
Was it a joyful one?
Were the results good or bad?
Is there a lesson in this experience?

Surveying your details, you might realize that they tell of someone who drank a great deal of coffee, and who feels better after quitting. You might decide on a better topic sentence:

My last cup of coffee was the beginning of better health.

This topic sentence relates to many of the details you have. You can mention why you love coffee and when you drank it so you can give some background on how hard it was to quit. You can explain quitting and discuss how you felt afterward. This topic sentence will give your paragraph unity.

To check your topic sentence for unity, ask the following questions:

✔| Checklist

Unity and the Topic Sentence: A Checklist

✔ Does the topic sentence make a point?

✔ Is the point broad enough to cover all the details?

✔ Do the details relate to the topic sentence?

If the answer to these questions is yes, you are helping to unify your paragraph.

Now that you have a topic sentence and a list of details, you are ready to begin the outlines stage of writing.

Grouping Details

Practice

Below are topics and lists of details. Group the details of each list, writing them under the appropriate headings. Some details may not fit under any of the headings.

1. topic: A Day at the Beach
  details: I came home with a bad sunburn and thoughts of my new friend
  It had been raining for weeks last summer.
  I was dying to go to the beach.
  I set up my beach chair and unpacked my sunblock, water bottle, and CD player.

On my first vacation day, the sun suddenly shone, and I was off to the beach.
After listening to one song on my CD player, I fell asleep.
My friend Manny woke me up by sprinkling sand on my back.
Alex and I talked for hours.
Manny was with his handsome friend Alex.
Manny introduced Alex and left.
People on the beach were playing frisbee.
Alex and I didn't leave the beach until sundown.

List details about the background of the day: It had been raining for weeks. I was dying to go to the beach. On my first vacation day, the sun shone, and I was off to the beach.

List details about the first part of the day at the beach, when you were alone: I set up my beach chair and unpacked my sunblock, water bottle, and CD player. After listening to one song on my CD player, I fell asleep.

List details about Manny and Alex's arrival: My friend Manny woke me up by sprinkling sand on my back. Manny was with his handsome friend Alex. Manny introduced Alex and left.

List details about your time with Alex: Alex and I talked for hours.

_____

_____

List details about leaving: Alex and I didn't leave the beach until sundown.

2. **topic:** A True Friend's Courage
  details: Salvatore always lent me money.
  One day in my senior year, I was taken in for questioning about an armed robbery.
  I met Salvatore when we were both in the sixth grade.
  Sal was much smaller than any of the guys in the hall that day.
  We were friends through high school.
  The word of the police questioning got around at my school.
  The day after the police questioned me, I was in the hall at school.
  Some tough members of a school clique started taunting me, pushing me against the hallway wall.
  Salvatore came up to my tormentors.
  After Sal's challenge, no one threatened or teased me.

Salvatore came between me and the group and raised his fists.
He told them to back off.
A month later, when the real armed robbers were arrested, Sal's faith in me was justified.

List details about the writer's and Salvatore's background: I met

Salvatore when we were both in the sixth grade. We were friends

through high school. Salvatore always lent me money.

_____

_____

List details about the writer's trouble with the police and the

spread of the story at school: One day in my senior year, I was taken

in for questioning about an armed robbery. The word of the police

questioning got around at my school.

List details about the writer's confrontation with a group of students:

The day after the police questioned me, I was in the hall at school.

Some tough members of a school clique started taunting me,

pushing me against the hallway wall.

List details about what Salvatore did and its effects: Salvatore came

up to my tormentors. Salvatore came between me and the group and

raised his fists. He told them to back off. Sal was much smaller than

any of the guys in the hall that day. After Sal's challenge, no one

threatened or teased me.

List details about what happened a month after the incident in the

hall: A month later, when the real armed robbers were arrested, Sal's

faith in me was justified.

3. topic: A Pleasant Holiday
  details: We had a great picnic on Labor Day.
I boiled two dozen eggs for deviled eggs.
Charlie marinated chicken the night before.
We told old stories as we ate.
At the picnic, we danced to the radio.
To set up before the picnic, Teresa set up the picnic table outside.

Charlie grilled the chicken in the yard while we socialized.
I brought my special deviled eggs and potato salad.
Everyone brought his or her best recipes.
Everyone sang as we cleaned up and got ready to leave.
We left with a promise to do it again.

List details about the time before the picnic: *I boiled two dozen eggs*
for deviled eggs. Charlie marinated chicken the night before. Teresa
set up the picnic table outside.

List details about the time during the picnic: *We had a great picnic*
on Labor Day. We told old stories as we ate. At the picnic, we danced
to the radio. Charlie grilled the chicken in the yard while we socialized.
I brought my special deviled eggs and potato salad. Everyone brought
his or her best recipes.

List details about the time after the picnic: *Everyone sang as we*
cleaned up and got ready to leave. We left with a promise to do it
again.

Exercise 6

Collaborate

Creating Topic Sentences

Do this exercise with a partner or a group. Following are lists of details. For each list, write two appropriate topic sentences.

1. topic sentence 1: *I foolishly jumped to conclusions last week.*

_____

topic sentence 2: *Because of my temper, I ruined my own birthday*
surprise last week.

details: Last weekend my boyfriend and I nearly had a serious argument.
It started when he asked me if I wanted to go bowling on Sunday night.
I was furious because Sunday was my birthday.
I was expecting him to take me to a more romantic place for my special day.
I was also hurt because I thought he had forgotten my birthday.
My first reaction to his question was to say I hated bowling.
He said, "But you always want to go bowling. You're in a league."
Then I cried and called him inconsiderate.
He just said he couldn't figure me out.

He got up to leave.
Finally I said, "You are so selfish, you even forgot that Sunday is my birthday!"
That was when he told me he had planned a big surprise party for me at the bowling lanes.

2. topic sentence 1: The most boring work can be interesting if there

is a personal angle to it.

topic sentence 2: Cleaning a closet can be fun when it reveals

personal memories.

> **details:** Last week my mother decided to clean out her bedroom closet.
> Her first step was to get me to help her.
> As we started packing up old shoes, sweaters and dresses, I was counting the hours until I could escape this chore.
> Then we began clearing the shelves at the top of the closet.
> Pretty soon my mother was sighing over old pictures of my father and faded Valentine's Day cards he had given her.
> Now I was extremely bored.
> Next she pulled down a dusty shoe box.
> In it were hundreds of photos of an adorable baby and a handsome little boy.
> "Who's that?" I said, only half interested.
> "Why, it's you," my mother said.
> Suddenly I was extremely interested.
> As I looked through the photos, the minutes seemed to fly by.

3. topic sentence 1: I learned that smart shoppers look before they

buy.

topic sentence 2: Buying a new television may be cheaper than

buying a used one.

> **details:** My old television broke two days ago.
> Yesterday, I took it to a repair service and found out the repair would cost $150.
> I figured the television wasn't worth repairing.
> I could get a new one for a little more money, I thought.
> On my way to the discount stores to look at new televisions, I stopped to see my friend Jason.
> Jason offered to sell me his color television for $230.
> It seemed like a good deal.

His television was only a year old.

By the time I left Jason, I had nearly decided to buy his television but stopped at one electronics store just to be sure.

There were all kinds of televisions.

Some cost more than a thousand dollars, and others were bargain-priced but much too big or elaborate for my room.

Then I saw one just like Jason's.

It was on sale for $219.

Outlines Devising a Plan: Narration

Once you have a topic sentence and a list of details, you can write them in outline form. Below is an outline for a paragraph on My Last Cup of Coffee. As you read the outline, you will notice that some of the items on the earlier list have been combined and the details have been grouped into logical categories.

Outline on My Last Cup of Coffee

topic sentence: My last cup of coffee was the beginning of better health.
details:

why I love coffee	I love the taste of coffee. Coffee picks me up and gives me energy.
the morning I quit	I quit it suddenly. I figured quitting suddenly would be the best way. Don't drag it out. Drank my last cup in the morning. My first cup in the morning was the one I needed most. I needed it to wake up.
the afternoon	I needed it all day. Around 3:00 or 4:00 p.m. I craved coffee. I felt terrible at first. I was irritable and shaky.
the evening	I craved coffee after dinner. I was more irritable. I had a bad headache.
the next day	I felt better.

Once you prepare your outline, check it for these qualities, using the following checklist.

 **Checklist**

A Checklist for a Narrative Outline

✔ Do all the details connect to the topic sentence?

✔ Are the details in a clear order?

✔ Does the outline need more details?

✔ Are the details specific enough?

With a good outline, you are ready to write a rough draft of a narrative paragraph.

Exercise 7

Practice

Finding Details That Do Not Fit

Following are outlines. In each outline, there are details that do not relate to the topic sentence. Cross out the details that do not fit.

1. **topic sentence:** After one incident, I stopped buying clothes that need ironing.
   details: One day I had an important job interview.
   To look my best, I decided to wear a freshly ironed white shirt.
   I searched my closet, but everything I owned was wrinkled.
   ~~I hate ironing, so I often put it off.~~
   Desperate, I set up the ironing board and turned on the iron.
   I was frantically trying to press the creases out of a cotton shirt as the minutes ticked by.
   Then the phone rang.
   I put down the iron and dashed to the phone.
   I was stuck on the phone, arguing with my landlord, for ten minutes.
   When I hung up the phone, I noticed a strange smell.
   I realized I had placed the iron face down and it had burned a hole in my shirt and in the ironing board.
   Smoke was fogging the room.
   ~~Now there are irons with an automatic "off" switch for such emergencies.~~

2. **topic sentence:** Yesterday, my son's temper taught him a lesson.
   details: Last night, just before dinner, my five-year-old son Jimmy wanted a popsicle.
   ~~He likes orange popsicles best.~~
   When I told him he couldn't have a treat before dinner, he became angry.
   Soon he was screaming and crying.
   He even lay on the floor and kicked his legs.
   In his rage, he picked up one of his favorite toy trucks.
   He threw it across the room, where it broke in half.
   ~~The truck is made of a hard plastic, so it is easy to break.~~
   When Jimmy saw the truck in pieces, he was astonished.
   He suddenly realized that his anger had hurt him, not me.

3. topic sentence: Last Friday was one of those days when everything goes right.

       details: First, my computer class was cancelled, so I had some free time.

At work, I got paid.

After work, I met my friends at our favorite club.

~~There are three places I like to visit.~~

We listened to music and had a great meal.

After dinner, the place became crowded with people singing, dancing, flirting, and laughing.

~~There's a new dance I don't know yet.~~

~~Sometimes it seems Friday night is just as popular as Saturday night.~~

I could stay out late and dance because I didn't have class or work on Saturday.

I felt rich, carefree, and excited.

 Recognizing Details That Are Out of Order

Practice   Each outline below has one detail that is out of order. Indicate where it belongs by drawing an arrow from it to the place where it should go.

1. topic sentence: My brother's carelessness cost me my job yesterday.

       details: Tom was supposed to drive me to work.

I got up on time, but he overslept.

I had to rush him through breakfast so I would not be late.

He had forgotten to put the spare tire in the car.

We got in the car, and the gas gauge was on "Empty."

The night before, Tom had forgotten to put gas in the car.

We made it to the gas station, riding on gas fumes.

Getting gas made me fifteen minutes late for work.

A mile past the gas station, we had a flat tire.

I was ready to scream.

"No problem," said Tom.

Then he looked embarrassed.

Waiting for the tow truck took an hour.

I was so late, my boss fired me.

2. topic sentence: Davey's Halloween party was a little too scary for him and his friends.

       details: My sister invited three little friends for four-year-old Davey's Halloween party.

The party began as each child showed off his or her costume.

The final treat was a walk through a haunted house my sister had created in the basement.
One came as a firefighter; another was a little mermaid, and Davey and his best friend were ghosts.
Soon they were playing games and dancing to their favorite music.
Since the children were young, my sister had limited the haunting to some carved pumpkins with candles burning high in the dim basement, and some rubber spiders.
Suddenly, one of the children in the haunted house began to squeal much louder than the others.
"Ooh! The spider!" He screamed. "It's crawling up my arm!"
"It's just a rubber spider," my sister said, turning on the lights.
There, on the child's arm, was a real and very frightened spider.

3. **topic sentence:** Listening to the words "I dare you" can be foolish and dangerous.

details: When my brother was eighteen, he got his own car.
The first thing he did with his car was ride around, showing it to all his friends.
Then he decided to take three of his buddies for a ride.
Fortunately, no one was hurt when my brother learned a hard lesson.
"How fast can this car go?" his friend Leroy asked.
"Pretty fast," said my brother.
My brother pushed the gas pedal hard.
"Oh, come on," said Leroy. "That's nothing. Hit it hard. Come on. I dare you."
My brother didn't want to go any faster, but his two friends were watching and grinning.
They were waiting to see what he would do.
He hit the gas; the car swerved and skidded into a light pole.
The front end of the car was destroyed.

Exercise 8

Collaborate

Putting Details in the Correct Order

Do this exercise with a partner or a group. In each of the outlines below, the list of details is in the wrong order. Number the details in the correct order, writing *1* next to the detail that should be listed first, and so on.

1. **topic sentence:** Samantha's plan for giving a surprise birthday party showed her talent for organizing.

details:	_1_	She invited Tyrone, the guest of honor, for a quiet dinner at her house on the day she wanted to have the party.
	_2_	Once she knew Tyrone would come for dinner, she mailed the invitations, clearly marked "Surprise Party."
	_4_	When her guests arrived, she hid them all on the gaily decorated back porch.
	_6_	Tyrone entered the porch and saw all his friends in a room decorated for a party.
	_3_	On the day of the party, she called each guest to remind him or her to be early.
	_5_	When Tyrone arrived, Samantha led him to the porch.
	_7_	The guests and Tyrone had a wonderful time.

2. topic sentence: Getting my son to preschool yesterday morning was a terrible chore.

details:	_1_	My son had been up late the night before because I had taken him to a special children's show at the community center.
	_2_	He was very tired and cranky the next morning.
	_5_	I had to go back to his bedroom at least twice.
	_4_	He said "Yes" when I asked him if he was awake, but he buried his head under the covers.
	_3_	I came in early and woke him gently.
	_13_	He raced to my car but resisted wearing his seat belt.
	_7_	He wouldn't wear the clothes I put out for him.
	_9_	He came to breakfast wearing one green and one blue sneaker and a torn sweatshirt.
	_10_	At breakfast, he couldn't decide what to eat.
	_11_	I finally give him Cheerios, but he played with them.
	_6_	Once he was out of bed, we fought about his clothes.

_____8_____ I finally gave up and let him wear whatever he wanted; meanwhile I made breakfast.

_____12_____ It got late, so we rushed to leave.

3. topic sentence: Yesterday, I began learning how to make my own decisions.

details:

_____2_____ Enrique was out of town yesterday.

_____3_____ I was offered a new job at a higher salary than my current job.

_____5_____ I was forced to think for myself.

_____1_____ I usually get my boyfriend Enrique to make all my decisions.

_____4_____ The job offer was good for one day only.

_____8/9_____ I considered the advantages of the new job.

_____8/9_____ I thought about the drawbacks of the new position.

_____6_____ At first I was very anxious about thinking for myself and couldn't concentrate.

_____7_____ Then I calmed down and began to think.

_____10_____ Once I had made my own decision, I felt wonderful.

Rough Lines Drafting and Revising: Narration

Once you have a good outline, you can write a draft of your paragraph. Once you have a first draft, you can begin to think about revising and editing. The checklist below may help you revise your draft.

✔ Checklist

A Checklist for Revising the Draft of a Narrative Paragraph

✔ Is my narrative vivid?

✔ Are the details clear and specific?

✔ Does the topic sentence fit all the details?

✔ Are the details written in a clear order?

✔ Do the transitions make the narrative easy to follow?

✔ Have I made my point?

Transitions

Transitions are _words_, _phrases_, or even _sentences_ that link ideas. Sometimes they tell the reader what he or she has just read and what is coming next. Every kind of writing has its own transitions. When you tell a story, you have to be sure that your reader can follow you as you move through the steps of your story. Most of the transitions in narration have to do with time. Below is a list of transitions writers often use in writing narratives.

Info BOX

Transitions for a Narrative Paragraph

after	finally	now
again	first (second, etc.)	soon
always	frequently	soon after
at first	immediately	still
at last	in the meantime	suddenly
at once	later	then
at the same time	later on	until
before	meanwhile	when
during	next	while

Below is a draft created from the outline on My Last Cup of Coffee. As you read it, you will notice that it combines some of the short sentences from the outline, adds some details, and adds transitions.

A Revised Draft of a Paragraph on My Last Cup of Coffee

sentences combined
added details

sentences combined
added details
transition added

detail added
transition added

My last cup of coffee was the beginning of better health. It was hard for me to stop drinking coffee because I love the taste of coffee. In addition, coffee picks me up and gives me energy. I quit it suddenly because I figured that a sharp break from my habit would be better than dragging out the process. I drank my last cup in the morning. It was the cup I needed most, to wake up, so I decided to allow myself that cup. By afternoon, I saw how much I needed coffee all day. Around 3:00 or 4:00 p.m., I craved it. I felt terrible. I was shaky and irritable. After dinner, my coffee craving was worse. I was more irritable, and I had a pounding headache. The next day, I felt better.

Exercise 9 **Recognizing Transitions**

Practice

Underline all the transitions—words and phrases—in the paragraphs below.

1. Yesterday I learned the dangers of trying to perform two tasks at the same time. My girlfriend was coming over for dinner, and I had promised I would make the dinner myself. Of course, my idea of cooking is boiling water for spaghetti and throwing on a jar of sauce. I had just begun to heat a pot of water when I realized the kitchen was filthy.

Immediately, I rushed to mop the floor and clean the counters. While I frantically washed the floor, the water on the stove boiled over. Now I had to turn down the heat under the pot and clean the stove. Meanwhile, I was tracking dirty footsteps over the part of the floor I had just wiped clean. At the same time, I dumped some spaghetti into the pot and popped a jar of spaghetti sauce into the microwave. Then I went back to recleaning the floor and swabbing the remaining spills off the stove. Suddenly I heard a "pop" from the microwave. I had covered the jar of sauce too tightly. After a few seconds, the bubbling tomato mixture had exploded, coating the entire microwave with a hot, sticky red mess. While I struggled to clean up this latest disaster, my girlfriend arrived and quickly suggested that we call out for pizza.

2. My brother Billy has never been fond of cats, but a recent experience changed his mind. Billy was at a friend's house when he suddenly noticed a ball of fuzz with two green eyes peeking at him from under the sofa. At first this tiny creature only peered out at him suspiciously, but soon the kitten came a little closer. Soon after, the tiny cat was at Billy's feet, rolling over and begging to be petted. Billy reached to stroke the kitten's soft fur and heard a loud, blissful purring. Then, without warning, two tiny paws reached out and grabbed Billy's fingers, and tiny teeth nipped at his hand. Now Billy was in love. He had never seen such a feisty cat. Billy plans to adopt this kitten as soon as it is old enough to leave its mother. He plans to name it Rocky.

Exercise 10

Practice

Adding the Appropriate Transitions

In the paragraphs below, transitions are shown in parentheses. Circle the appropriate transitions.

1. An ordinary day for my father would be an impossible one for most people. His day starts at 5:30 a.m. (when/after) he wakes up and makes breakfast for me and my two sisters, Amber, two, and

Tiffany, four. (Soon after/At the same time), he helps the girls dress and checks that their backpacks have their favorite toys and school supplies. (Then/Until) he takes them to preschool and drives to his own classes at a school where he is studying to be a chef. (Later/Meanwhile), he picks up the girls, plays with them, and makes an early dinner for us all. (Finally/Suddenly), he leaves for work. My father has a night job as a security guard. (After/Immediately,) he puts in his eight hours at work, he comes home, grabs a few hours of sleep, and begins another day of family life, classes, and work.

2. After last weekend's experience, I will never again be a passenger in my Aunt Jennifer's car. (As soon as/At once,) we got in the car, Aunt Jennifer opened a pack of cigarettes. She backed out of the driveway with one hand (now/while) she was taking out a cigarette and lighting it. She waved this cigarette as she drove; (at last/meanwhile), she sat sideways, half facing me and maintaining a nonstop conversation. (Then/Still) her cell phone rang. She picked it up and talked, holding her cigarette in one hand and the phone in the other. (Before/During) this time she was steering the car with her elbows and even her knees. (Until/Frequently), she narrowly missed hitting a light pole or a street sign. (At the same time/Again), I prayed that we would arrive alive. (When/Soon) we finally reached our destination, I promised myself never again to get into an automobile with this distracted driver.

INSTRUCTOR'S NOTE:

Chapters 2 and 4 contain information on coordination and subordination, respectively. Both chapters provide practice in using effective transitional devices and in combining sentences.

Exercise 11

 *Collaborate*

Using Transitions

Do this exercise with a partner or a group. Write a sentence for each item below. Be ready to share your answers with another group or with the entire class.

1. Write a sentence with *frequently* in the middle of the sentence.

Harry has a demanding job; frequently, he works ten-hour shifts.

2. Write a sentence that begins with *Before*.

   Before it started to rain, I closed the car windows.

3. Write a sentence with *at last* in the middle of the sentence.

   Cory and I talked for hours; at last I had found a true friend.

4. Write a sentence that begins with *at first*.

   At first I thought that the class would be too difficult for me.

5. Write a sentence with *later on* in the middle of the sentence.

   The freeway was jammed at first; later on, it was less crowded.

6. Write a sentence with *when* in the middle of the sentence.

   You can call me when you are ready to leave for school.

7. Write a sentence with *always* in the middle of the sentence.

   If you can't reach me by phone, you can always send me an e-mail.

8. Write a sentence that begins with *Then*.

   Then the marching band made a right turn past the bleachers.

9. Write a sentence that begins with *Suddenly*.

   Suddenly, a siren wailed, and lights began flashing.

10. Write a sentence with *in the meantime* in the middle of the sentence.

    Brian called 911; in the meantime, I ran to the injured child.

Final Lines Polishing and Proofreading: Narration

The draft of the paragraph on My Last Cup of Coffee has some rough spots:

- One idea is missing from the paragraph: Why did you decide to give up coffee? How was it hurting your health?
- Added details could make it more vivid.
- The paragraph needs transitions to link ideas.
- To make its point, the paragraph needs a final sentence about better health.

Following is the final version of the paragraph on My Last Cup of Coffee. As you review the final version, you will notice several changes:

- A new idea, about why you wanted to stop drinking coffee, has been added.
- To avoid repetition, one use of the word "coffee" has been replaced by "it."
- More transitions have been added, including words, phrases, and clauses.
- Some vivid details have been added.

- The verbs in the first few sentences of the paragraph have been changed to the past tense, since those sentences talk about the time when you drank coffee.
- A final sentence about better health has been added.

A Final Version of a Paragraph on My Last Cup of Coffee
(Changes from the draft are underlined.)

My last cup of coffee was the beginning of better health. It was hard for me to stop drinking coffee because I <u>loved</u> the taste of <u>it</u>. In addition, I <u>thought that</u> coffee <u>picked</u> me up and <u>gave</u> me energy. <u>However, I decided to quit drinking coffee when I realized how much I needed it to keep going and to keep from feeling low</u>. I quit it suddenly because I figured that a sharp break from my habit would be better than dragging out the process. I drank my last cup in the morning. It was the cup I needed most, to wake up, so I decided to allow myself that <u>final</u> cup. By afternoon, I saw how much I needed coffee all day. Around 3:00 or 4:00 p.m., I craved it. I felt terrible. I was shaky, <u>nervous</u>, and irritable. After dinner, <u>when I used to have two or three cups of strong coffee,</u> my craving was worse. I was more irritable, <u>I was ready to snap at anyone who asked me a question</u>, and I had a pounding headache. <u>Soon, the worst was over, and</u> by the next day, I felt better. <u>Now, free of my coffee-drinking habit, I have a steady flow of energy, few crashing lows, and pride in my achievement.</u>

Before you prepare your final copy of your paragraph, check it for any places where grammar, word choice, and style need revision. Check also for any errors in spelling and punctuation.

Exercise 12

Practice

Correcting Errors in Final Lines

Proofread the following paragraphs. Correct any errors in spelling, punctuation, or word choice. There are eighteen errors in the first paragraph and eleven in the second paragraph. Write your corrections in the space above each error.

       through   *occasion*
    1. My last walk thru my old house was a sad yet happy ocassion.
         where   *whole*
I was leaving a place were I had spent my hole childhood, so the place
                     dining
had many pleasant memories. As I walked into the old dinning room,
         surprise   *chocolate*
I remembered the time I had a suprize birthday with a giant choclate

cake. Then I looked out the window and saw the empty lot where we
used   *games*
use to play softball and other game's all summer. After a while, I
   into   *brother's*
went in to my brother old room, and my heart hurt. I thought of the
         killed,   *mother's*
day my brother was kill and I recalled my Mother's face when she
                 shadows
heard the news. To me, this room was full of shadow's and sadness.

As I closed the front door of the old house and took one last look, I

didn't

was glad to leave. I din't know what the future would bring but I was
forward
looking foreward to starting over in a new home.

Wednesday

2. My boss can be very irritating some times, and last Wensday
asked
was one of those times. First, he called me and ask me if I could come
assistant
in early because Nikki, his assistent, had called in sick. I said I would
plans
come in two hours early, and then I made planes to skip my math class

and get a ride to work from my mother. After I had gone to all this trou-
called   *coming*
ble, my boss call me back and said to forget comming in early because
restaurant   *too*   *until*
the restaraunt wasn't to busy and he could manage untill I came at my

regular time. By the time he called, I had already missed my math class

and was about to get in the car with my mother. Now I had nothing to
off
do for two hours. Then, to top it all of, later that night, my boss asked
straight
me to stay an extra hour. I just wish he could get his scheduling strait

so I could plan my own time and stick by my plan.

Lines of Detail: A Walk-through Assignment

For this assignment, write a paragraph on My First _____.
(You fill in the blank. Your topic will be based on how you complete Step 1
below.)

> **Step 1:** To begin the thought lines part of writing this paragraph,
> complete the following questionnaire. It will help you think of
> possible topics and details.

Collaborative Questionnaire for Gathering Topics and Details

Answer the following questions as well as you can. Then read your answers
to a group. The members of the group should then ask you follow-up questions based on your answers. For example, if your answer is "I felt nervous," a group member might ask, "Why were you nervous?" or "What made
you nervous?" Write your answers on the lines provided; the answers will
add details to your list.

Finally, tear out the page and ask each member of your group to circle
one topic or detail that could be developed into a paragraph. Discuss the
suggestions.

Repeat this process for each member of the group.

Questionnaire

1. Have you ever been interviewed for a job? When? _____

_____

Write four details you remember about the interview:

a. _____

b. _____

c. _____

d. _____

Additional details to add after working with the group:

_____

_____

_____

2. Do you remember your first day of school (in elementary school, middle school, high school, or college?) Write four details about that day.

a. _____

b. _____

c. _____

d. _____

Additional details to add after working with the group:

_____

_____

_____

3. Do you remember your first visit to a special place? Write four details about that place. _____

a. _____

b. _____

c. _____

d. _____

Additional details to add after working with the group:

_____

_____

_____

Step 2: Select a topic from the details and ideas on the questionnaire. Brainstorm and list ideas about the topic.

Step 3: Group your ideas in time order.

Step 4: Survey your grouped ideas and write a topic sentence. Check that your topic sentence makes a point and is broad enough to relate to all the details.

Step 5: Write an outline of your paragraph, putting the grouped details below the topic sentence. Check your outline. Be sure that all the details relate to the topic sentence and that the details are in a clear and logical order.

INSTRUCTOR'S NOTE:

A Peer Review Form for students' exchange of drafts is on page 336.

Step 6: Write a first draft of your paragraph. Then revise and edit; check that you are sticking to your point, that all your details relate to your point, that your ideas are easy to follow, and that you are using effective transitions.

Step 7: In preparing the final copy of your paragraph, check for errors in punctuation, spelling, and word choice.

Writing Your Own Narrative Paragraph

When you write on any of the following topics, be sure to follow the stages of the writing process in preparing your paragraph.

1. Write about the best or the worst day of your life. Begin by freewriting. Then read your freewriting, looking for both the details and the focus of your paragraph.

   If your instructor agrees, ask a writing partner or a group to (a) listen to your freewriting, (b) help you focus it, (c) help you add details by asking you questions.

2. Interview a family member or friend who is older than you. Ask the person about a significant event in his or her childhood. Ask questions as the person speaks. You can ask questions such as, "Why do you think you remember this incident?" or "How did you feel at the time?" Take notes. If you have a tape recorder, you can tape the interview. But take notes as well.

   When you have finished the interview, review the information with the person you've interviewed. Would he or she like to add anything? If you wish, ask follow-up questions.

   Next, on your own, find a point to the story. Use that point in your topic sentence. In this paragraph, you will be writing about another person, not about yourself.

3. Write about a time when you were afraid. Begin by brainstorming questions about what frightened you, why you were afraid, how you dealt with the situation, and so forth. In the outlines stage, focus on some point about the incident: Did you learn from it? Did it change you? Did it hurt or help you? Answering such questions can help you come to a point.

4. Write about a time when you felt very lucky. Include details about the time before, during, and after your good luck.

5. Following are some topic sentences. Complete one of them and use it to write a paragraph.

When _____, I became angry because _____.

Saying good-bye to _____ was one of the hardest things I have ever done.

One day at _____ taught me _____.

My greatest success came when I _____.

The longest day of my life was the day I _____.

6. To write on this topic, begin with a partner. Ask your partner to tell you about a day that turned out unexpectedly. It can be a day that included a good or bad surprise.

   As your partner speaks, take notes. Ask questions. When your partner has finished speaking, review your notes. Ask your partner if he or she has anything to add.

   On your own, outline and draft a paragraph on your partner's day. Read your draft to your partner, adding comments and suggestions.

   Check the final draft of your paragraph for errors in punctuation, spelling, and word choice.

   Your partner can work through this same process to write a paragraph about a day that turned out unexpectedly for you.

7. Write a paragraph that tells a story based on photograph A. In the photo, a child is crying. Create an incident from this photo. What made the child cry? Is anyone with the child or watching him cry? What will happen next?

Photograph A

8. Write a paragraph that tells a story based on photograph B. The photo shows a mysterious castle. Write about an incident that took place in this castle.

Photograph B

Name: _____ Section: _____

PEER REVIEW FORM FOR A NARRATIVE PARAGRAPH

After you have written a draft of your paragraph, let a writing partner read it. When your partner has completed the following form, discuss the responses. Then repeat the same process for your partner's paragraph.

The topic sentence for this paragraph is _____

_____

I think the topic sentence (a) states the point well or (b) could be revised.

The part of the narrative I liked best begins with the words _____

_____

The part that could use more or better details begins with the words _____

One effective transition is _____

(Write the words of a good transition.)

I would like to see something added about _____

_____

I would like to take out the part about _____

_____

I think this paragraph is (a) easy to follow, (b) a little confusing [choose one].

Other comments: _____

_____

_____

_____

_____

_____

_____

_____

_____

_____

Reviewer's name: _____

WRITING FROM READING: Narration

The Baby Myna

Ved Mehta

Ved Mehta, blind since the age of four, grew up in India but was educated at Oxford University in England and Harvard University in the United States. He became a writer of essays and short stories and received many awards. In this selection from his autobiography, Mehta tells a story of his childhood.

Words You May Need to Know (corresponding paragraph numbers are in parentheses)

frenetically (5): frantically
surreptitiously (13): secretly
defiant (26): rebellious, disobedient
abrasive (26): rough

treble notes (26): high-pitched notes
harmonium (26): an organlike keyboard instrument
enticing (28): tempting, attractive
hillocks (29): little hills

---

1   One day, Sher Singh returned from leave in his village in the Kangara District, in the hills, with a baby myna for me. "I have brought you a friend," he said. "It's a baby myna. It's one of the only birds in the world that can talk. It's just the right age to learn to talk."

2   I was excited. I went with Sher Singh to the Mozang Chowk and bought a wire cage with a door, a metal floor, and a little swing. The cage had a hook at the top, and I hung it in my room. (We were temporarily living in our own house, at 11 Temple Road.) I got a couple of brass bowls—one for water, the other for grain—and filled them up and put them in the cage. I got a brush for cleaning out the cage. I named the myna Sweetie. The name came to me just out of the sky.

3   "How do you catch a baby myna?" I asked Sher Singh.

4   "It's difficult, Vedi Sahib. There are very few of them around, and you have to know where a baby myna is resting with her mother. You have to slip up on them in the middle of the night, when they are sleeping in their nest, and throw a cover over them and hope that you catch the baby, because only a baby myna can learn to talk. Sometimes the mother myna will nip at your finger, and there are people in my village who are constantly getting their fingers nipped at because they have been trying to catch a baby myna."

5   At first, Sweetie was so small that she could scarcely fly even a few inches. I would sit her on my shoulder and walk around the room. She would dig her nervous, trembling claws through my shirt and into my shoulder as she tried to keep her balance, fluttering around my ear and sending off little ripples of air. But Sweetie grew fast, and soon she was flying around my room. Before I opened her cage to fill up the bowls or clean the floor, I would have

to shut the door. She would often nip at my fingers and escape from the cage. She would go and perch on the mantelpiece. When I ran to the mantelpiece to catch her, she would fly up to the curtain rod. When I climbed up onto the windowsill and shook the curtain, she would fly back to the mantelpiece. Sometimes she would be so silent that I would wonder if she was still in the room. Other times, I would hear her flying all around the room—now she would be by the window, now by the overhead light, her wings beating against the pane and the lampshade. I would make kissing sounds, as I had heard Sher Singh make them. I would call to her—"Sweetie! Sweetie!" I would whistle affectionately. I would run frenetically from one end of the room to the other. I would scream with rage. But she wouldn't come to me. I would somehow have to summon Sher Singh through the closed door, and then give him a cue to come in when I thought she wasn't near the door, and he would have to prance around the room and somehow catch her with his duster.

6   "She's a real hill girl, all right, flying around like that," he would say.

7   When we had finally got her back in the cage, I would scold her roundly, but it didn't seem to do much good.

8   "Vedi Sahib, you'll lose her, like your eyes, if you don't keep her always in the cage," Sher Singh said.

9   "But then how can I feed her? How can I clean out her cage?"

10   "I will do all that, Vedi Sahib. And, because I can see, I can watch her."

11   "But I like looking after her," I said.

12   "You'll lose her, Vedi Sahib," he said. "And mind your finger. She's getting big."

13   I devised a way of filling her bowls and cleaning some of the cage's floor by surreptitiously sticking my fingers between the wires. But now and again I would want to feel her on her swing or take her out and hold her, and then she would nip at my finger and sometimes draw blood. She would escape and give me a real run around the room.

14   Every time I passed Sweetie's cage, I would say "Hello, Sweetie," and wait for her to talk. But she would only flutter in the cage or, at most, make her swing squeak.

15   "Are you sure Sweetie can talk?" I asked Sher Singh.

16   "All baby mynas from Kangara can learn to talk," he said.

17   "Are you sure she is from Kangara?"

18   "Only mynas from Kangara have a black patch on the throat. You can feel it, and you can ask anyone—it's as black as coal."

19   I took Sweetie out of her cage. I held her tight in one hand and tried to feel the patch on her throat with the other. She screamed and tried to bite my finger, but I finally found the patch. It was a little soft, downy raised circle that throbbed with her pulse.

20   "What do mynas sound like when they talk?" I later asked Sher Singh.

21   "They have the voice of the Kangara, of a Kangara hill girl."

22   "What is that?"

23   "The Punjab hills, the leaves in the wind, the waterfall on a mountain-side—you know, Vedi Sahib, it's the sound of a peacock spreading its wings in Kangara at dawn."

24   One day, I passed her cage and said, "Hello, Sweetie."

25   "Hello, Sweetie," she answered.

26   I jumped. I don't know how I had expected her voice to sound, but it was thin, sharp, and defiant—at once whiny and abrasive—like three treble notes on the harmonium played very fast. Her words assaulted my ears— "Sweetie" was something that film stars called each other on the screen, and sounded very naughty.

27   I had scarcely taken in the fact that Sweetie could really speak when she repeated "Hello, Sweetie." She kept on repeating it, hour after hour. "Hello, Sweetie" would suddenly explode into the air like a firecracker.

28   Try as I would, I couldn't teach her to say anything else. All the same, there was something thrilling and comforting in having my own film star in the cage, and I got so used to her enticing outbursts that I missed them when she kept quiet or was dozing.

29   Every evening, at the time when my big sisters and my big brother went to play hockey or some other game with their school friends, it was Sher Singh's duty to take me for a walk to Lawrence Gardens. There I would ride the merry-go-round—a big, creaky thing with wooden seats and a metal railing— while Sher Singh ran alongside. It would revolve and lurch, tipping this way and that way, filling me with terror and excitement. On the ground, I would throw off my shoes and run up and down the hillocks. They were covered with damp, soft grass and occasional patches of dead grass. The grass would caress, tickle, and prick my feet. All around, there were the light, cheerful sounds of sighted children running and playing and of birds flying and perching and calling. In the distance, there was the solitary, mournful song of a nightingale.

30   I felt sorry that Sweetie, shut up in the house, couldn't enjoy the company of other birds, and one evening I insisted that we take her along in her cage and let her enjoy the fresh air and the life of Lawrence Gardens, even if it was only through the wires of her cage.

31   "But don't let her out of the cage," Sher Singh said. "She is a spirit from the hills. She will fly back to Kangara."

32   "Fly all the way back to Kangara! She would die without food or water. Besides, she is my friend. She wouldn't leave me."

33   "Vedi Sahib, you know how loyal Kangara servants are?"

34   "No one could be more loyal than you, Sher Singh."

35   "Well, Kangara mynas are as disloyal as Kangara servants are loyal. You can love a beloved myna all you want to, give her all the grain to eat you want to, give her all the water to drink you want to, and at the first opportunity she will nip at your finger and fly away. But you can kick a servant from Kangara and he will still give you first-class service."

36   "Why is that?"

37   "Because servants from Kangara, like mynas, have breathed the Himalayan air and are free spirits. A Kangara servant is a servant by choice— but no myna is in a cage by choice."

38   I couldn't follow exactly what Sher Singh was saying, but I laughed. Anyway, I insisted that we take Sweetie with us.

39   At Lawrence Gardens, I had no intention of taking Sweetie out of her cage, but when she heard the other birds she set up such a racket that children and servants who usually took little notice of me wandered toward us to find out what I was doing to the poor myna. They said all kinds of things:

40   "She is lonely."

41   "He's keeping her a prisoner."

42   "Tch, tch! He can't play with other children, so he won't let his myna play with other birds."

43   "She'll fly away to Kangara!" I cried.

44   People laughed, hooted, and jeered. "She's so small she probably can't even fly up to that tree."

45   "Why are you pointing? He doesn't know how high that tree is."

46   I suddenly got an idea. I had with me a ball of strong, fortified string that Brother Om used for flying kites. I took Sweetie out of the cage and, while I held her screaming and biting in my hands, I had Sher Singh tie up her legs with the string. Then I caught hold of the ball and let her go, and the people about us clapped and cheered. I started giving her string, and she flew high up and pulled and tugged. I gave her more string and let her lead me where she would around the grass. I thought it was a wonderful game. Before I knew what had happened, her weight at the end of the string was gone, and the limp string had fluttered down on me.

47   "She's bitten through the string! Look, she's bitten through the string!" everyone shouted, running away.

48   "Sher Singh, catch her! Catch her!" I cried. "Bring Sweetie back!"

49   "I think I see her!" he called, running off.

50   A few minutes later, Sher Singh came back. "She's nowhere to be found, Vedi Sahib. She's gone, Sahib—gone straight back to Kangara. You will now have to get along without Sweetie."

51   Sher Singh and I looked for her all over Lawrence Gardens, calling "Sweetie! Sweetie!" until it was dark and everyone had left. Then Sher Singh and I walked home with the empty cage.

Exercise 13

Practice

Recognizing the Steps in "The Baby Myna"

Ved Mehta explains several stages in his ownership and loss of Sweetie. Complete the exercise below by rereading "The Baby Myna" and focusing on the steps.

    1. There were several stages in Sweetie's flying around the room.

        a. At first, she could barely fly a short distance.

        b. Then she would escape from the cage when Mehta tried to feed her.

    c. At that time, Mehta had to ask <u>Sher Singh</u> to catch Sweetie.

    d. Finally, Mehta devised a way to feed her and clean her cage without her escaping.

    e. But he would sometimes want to <u>feel her on her swing or hold her</u> and she would again <u>nip at his finger and escape.</u>

2. He followed several steps in getting her to talk.

    a. Every time he passed her cage, he said, <u>"Hello, Sweetie."</u>

    b. Then he asked Sher Singh if Sweetie <u>could really talk.</u>

    c. As part of his answer, Sher Singh told Mehta to feel <u>the black patch on Sweetie's throat.</u>

    d. Finally, one day, Sweetie said, <u>"Hello, Sweetie,"</u> and kept saying it, hour after hour.

3. On the day he lost Sweetie, Mehta took several steps that led to the loss.

    a. First, he took her to Lawrence Gardens in her cage.

    b. Then she began to set up a racket when she heard other birds.

    c. The children in the gardens convinced Mehta to let Sweetie out of her cage by saying things like <u>"She is lonely," "He's keeping her a prisoner,"</u> and <u>"He can't play with other children, so he won't let his myna play with other birds."</u>

    d. To keep Sweetie in his possession while she was out of her cage, Mehta did this: <u>had Sher Singh tie up her legs with string.</u>

    e. Sweetie got free when she <u>bit through the string.</u>

Exercise 14

Practice

Recognizing Mehta's Use of Sense Words in "The Baby Myna"

As Mehta tells his story of Sweetie, he does not write much about what someone or something *looks* like; instead, he relies on many words that describe a *sound* or *touch*. Complete this exercise using the exact words of the story.

1. Write some exact words that describe what Mehta's hand feels when Mehta holds Sweetie: <u>"she would nip at my finger and some-times draw blood."</u>

2. Write some exact words to describe what Sweetie's voice sounds like: <u>"thin, sharp, and defiant—at once whiny and abrasive—like three treble notes on the harmonium played very fast."</u>

3. Write some exact words that Mehta uses to describe the grass against his feet: "damp, soft grass," "The grass would caress, tickle, and prick my feet."

4. Write some exact words to describe what Sweetie, perched on Mehta's shoulder, felt like to Mehta: "She would dig her nervous, trembling claws through my shirt and into my shoulder as she tried to keep her balance."

5. Write the exact words that describe the feeling of the patch on Sweetie's throat: "a little, soft, downy, raised circle that throbbed with her pulse."

WRITING FROM READING: "The Baby Myna"

When you write on any of the following topics, be sure to work through the stages of the writing process in preparing your paragraph.

1. Write a paragraph about an incident with an animal. The incident may have happened to you, or you may have seen it happen to someone else. As a way of starting, list all the details of the incident and then put them in time order.

2. Write about a time when you tried to hold on to someone or something that wanted to be free. To begin, you can freewrite all your memories of this situation.

3. As Ved Mehta tells his story, we become aware of how his blindness affects what he does. For instance, because he is blind, he has a hard time catching Sweetie when she flies in his room. On the other hand, Mehta, being blind, seems very aware of every sound and of the textures of objects, animals, and nature. Write a paragraph about what it means to have a specific disability. To begin this assignment, you might want to interview a friend who is disabled and ask him or her to tell you about an incident related to the disability.

4. Write about a time in your childhood when other children pressured you to do something. To begin, you can ask a writing partner to interview you, asking questions like the following:

Did you give in to their pressure?
If so, why? Was it out of fear?
If you didn't give in, why didn't you?
How did you feel during and after the incident?

After the interview, you can interview your partner so he or she can collect ideas for his or her paragraph.

5. Write a paragraph about how you tried to train a pet. Focus on one specific skill or behavior (such as fetching a ball, walking on a leash) that you were trying to develop in your pet.

6. Write about a time you saw an animal in a cage. Focus on what you think the animal was feeling or on your own reaction to the scene.

7. Write a paragraph about what Ved Mehta learned from his experience of owning, training, and losing Sweetie.

I Fell in Love, or My Hormones Awakened

Judith Ortiz Cofer

Judith Ortiz Cofer, daughter of a Puerto Rican mother and a mainland United States father, was born in Puerto Rico. When she was four years old, Cofer and her family moved to the United States. There she earned both bachelor's and master's degrees in English, and she later completed further studies at Oxford University in England. Cofer has taught English in the South and is a well-known poet. This excerpt from her autobiography tells of the bittersweet experience of first love.

Words You May Need to Know (corresponding paragraph numbers are in parentheses)

Marlon Brando (1): a movie star who, in the 1950s and 1960s, often played rebels and loners

L&M's (4): a brand of cigarettes

adulation (6): adoration, excessive devotion

extravaganza (7): an elaborate drama

Paterson (7): a city in New Jersey

seamstress (8): a woman whose occupation is sewing

Michelangelo (8): an Italian sculptor and painter in sixteenth-century Italy

gluttonously (9): greedily

relished (9): enjoyed

ruddy (9): having a fresh, healthy color

sergeant-at-arms (9): an officer whose job is to keep order

disdain (9): arrogance, contempt

phantom (11): ghostly

1   I fell in love, or my hormones awakened from their long slumber in my body, and suddenly the goal of my days was focused on one thing: to catch a glimpse of my secret love. And it had to remain secret, because I had, of course, in the great tradition of tragic romance, chosen to love a boy who was totally out of my reach. He was not Puerto Rican; he was Italian and rich. He was also an older man. He was a senior at the high school when I came in as a freshman. I first saw him in the hall, leaning casually on a wall that was the border line between girlside and boyside for underclassmen. He looked extraordinarily like a young Marlon Brando—down to the ironic little smile. The total of what I knew about the boy who starred in every one of my awkward fantasies was this: that he was the nephew of the man who owned the supermarket on my block; that he often had parties at his parents' beautiful home in the suburbs which I would hear about; that this family had money (which came to our school in many ways)—and this fact made my knees weak: and that he worked at the store near my apartment building on weekends and in the summer.

2   My mother could not understand why I became so eager to be the one sent out on her endless errands. I pounced on every opportunity from Friday to late Saturday afternoon to go after eggs, cigarettes, milk (I tried to drink as much of it as possible, although I hated the stuff)—the staple items

that she would order from the "American" store.

3   One day I did see him. Dressed in a white outfit like a surgeon: white pants and shirt, white cap, and (gross sight, but not to my love-glazed eyes) blood-smeared butcher's apron. He was helping to drag a side of beef into the freezer storage area of the store. I must have stood there like an idiot because I remember that he did see me; he even spoke to me! I could have died. I think he said, "Excuse me," and smiled vaguely in my direction.

4   After that, I *willed* occasions to go to the supermarket. I watched my mother's pack of cigarettes empty ever so slowly. I wanted her to smoke them fast. I drank milk and forced it on my brother (although a second glass for him had to be bought with my share of Fig Newton cookies, which we both liked, but we were restricted to one row each). I gave my cookies up for love and watched my mother smoke her L&M's with so little enthusiasm that I thought (God, no!) that she might be cutting down on smoking or maybe even giving up the habit. At this crucial time!

5   I thought I had kept my lonely romance a secret. Often I cried hot tears on my pillow for the things that kept us apart. In my mind there was no doubt that he would never notice me (and that is why I felt free to stare at him—I was invisible). He could not see me because I was a skinny Puerto Rican girl, a freshman that did not belong to any group he associated with.

6   At the end of the year I found out that I had not been invisible. I learned one little lesson about human nature—adulation leaves a scent, one that we are all equipped to recognize, and no matter how insignificant the source, we seek it.

7   In June the nuns at our school would always arrange for some cultural extravaganza. In my freshman year, it was a Roman banquet. Our young, energetic Sister Agnes was in the mood for spectacle. She ordered the entire student body (it was a small group of under 300 students) to have our mothers make togas out of sheets. Then, as the last couple of weeks of school dragged on, the city of Paterson becoming a concrete oven, and us wilting in our uncomfortable uniforms, we labored like frantic Roman slaves to build a splendid banquet hall in our small auditorium.

8   On the night of the banquet, my father escorted me in my toga to the door of our school. I felt foolish in my awkwardly draped sheet (blouse and skirt underneath). My mother had no great skill as a seamstress. The best she could do was hem a skirt or a pair of pants. That night I would have traded her for a peasant woman with a golden needle. I saw other Roman ladies emerging from their parents' cars looking authentic in sheets of material that folded over their bodies like the garments on a statue by Michelangelo. How did they do it? How was it that I always got it just slightly wrong, and worse, I believed that other people were just too polite to mention it. "The poor little Puerto Rican girl," I could hear them thinking. But in reality, I must have been my worst critic, self-conscious as I was.

9   All during the program I was in a state of controlled hysteria. My secret love sat across the room from me looking supremely bored. I watched his every move, taking him in gluttonously. I relished the shadow of his eyelashes on his ruddy cheeks, his pouty lips smirking sarcastically at the ridiculous sight of our little play. Once he slumped down in his chair, and our sergeant-at-arms nun came over and tapped him on his shoulder. He drew himself up slowly, with disdain. I loved his rebellious spirit. I believed myself still invisible to him in my "nothing" status as I looked upon my beloved. But towards the end of the evening, he looked straight across the room and into my eyes! How did I survive the killing power of those dark pupils? I trembled in a new way. I was not cold—I was burning! Yet I shook from the inside out, feeling light-headed, dizzy.

10   The room began to empty, and I headed for the girls' lavatory. I wanted to relish the miracle in silence. I did not think for a minute that anything more would follow. I was satisfied with the enormous favor of a look from my beloved. I took my time, knowing that my father would be waiting outside for me, impatient. The others would ride home. I would walk home with my father. I wanted as few witnesses as possible. When I could no longer hear the crowds in the hallway, I emerged from the bathroom, still under the spell of those mesmerizing eyes.

11   The lights had been turned off in the hallway, and all I could see was the lighted stairwell, at the bottom of which a nun would be stationed. My father would be waiting just outside. I nearly screamed when I felt someone grab me by the waist. But my mouth was quickly covered by someone else's mouth. I was being kissed. My first kiss and I could not even tell who it was. I pulled away to see that face not two inches away from mine. It was he. He smiled down at me. Did I have a silly expression on my face? My glasses felt crooked on my nose. I was unable to move or speak. More gently, he lifted my chin and touched his lips to mine. This time I did not forget to enjoy it. Then, like the phantom lover that he was, he walked away into the darkened corridor and disappeared.

12   I don't know how long I stood there. My body was changing right there in the hallway of a Catholic school. My cells were tuning up like musicians in an orchestra, and my heart was a chorus. It was an opera I was composing, and I wanted to stand still and just listen. But, of course, I heard my father's voice talking to the nun. I was in trouble if he had had to ask about me. I hurried down the stairs, making up a story on the way about feeling sick. That would explain my flushed face, and it would buy me a little privacy when I got home.

 Exercise 15

Practice

Recognizing the Time Order of "I Fell in Love, or My Hormones Awakened"

"I Fell in Love, or My Hormones Awakened" tells a story that covers many months. Judith Ortiz Cofer is careful to indicate exactly what happened at what time. In the following spaces, list the incidents that happened at the following times.

1. One day in the supermarket, Cofer finally <u>saw her secret love.</u>

2. In June, Sister Agnes had all the high school students working on
<u>a Roman banquet.</u>

3. On the night of the banquet, Cofer looked at the other girls in their togas
and felt <u>foolish.</u>

4. During the banquet, Cofer watched <u>her secret love.</u>

5. Then she realized he was <u>looking at her.</u>

6. She stayed in the girls' lavatory because she <u>wanted to relish the</u>
<u>miracle of a look from her secret love.</u>

7. In the hallway, she received <u>her first and second kisses.</u>

8. Afterward, alone in the hallway, she felt <u>her body changing, cells tuning</u>
<u>up like an orchestra, heart like a chorus.</u>

9. Then she heard <u>her father's voice talking to a nun.</u>

10. As she hurried down the stairs, she made up a story about <u>feeling sick.</u>

Exercise 16

Practice

Recognizing Time Transitions in "I Fell in Love, Or My Hormones Awakened"

Cofer's story describes incidents that cover one school year. She uses many transitions to indicate time to be sure that her writing is coherent and smooth. In the following paragraph, underline all the words or phrases that are time transitions.

<u>All during</u> the program I was in a state of controlled hysteria. My secret love sat across the room from me looking supremely bored. I watched his every move, taking him in gluttonously. I relished the shadow of his eyelashes on his ruddy cheeks, his pouty lips smirking sarcastically at the ridiculous sight of our little play. <u>Once</u> he slumped down in his chair, and our sergeant-at-arms nun came over and tapped him on his shoulder. He drew himself up slowly, with disdain. I loved his rebellious spirit. I believed myself still invisible to him in my "nothing" status <u>as I</u> looked upon my beloved. But <u>towards the end</u> of the evening, he looked straight across the room and into my eyes! How did I survive the killing power of those dark pupils? I trembled in a new way. I was not cold—I was burning! Yet I shook from the inside out, feeling lightheaded, dizzy.

WRITING FROM READING: "I Fell In Love, or My Hormones Awakened"

When you write on any of the following topics, be sure to work through the stages of the writing process in preparing your paragraph.

1. Judith Ortiz Cofer says that her first experience with love taught her "one little lesson about human nature—adulation leaves a scent, one that we are all equipped to recognize, and no matter how insignificant the source, we seek it." Write a paragraph explaining what she means by these words and how she learned the lesson. You can begin by discussing her words with a group. First, remember that "adulation" means adoration or excessive devotion, and the source of the adulation is the person giving this excessive devotion and adoration. Then you might consider such questions as the following:

    Who is giving adulation? To whom?
    Who recognizes the "scent" of the adulation? That is, who recognizes that he or she is being given this adulation?
    Who feels insignificant?
    Who seeks out the source of the adulation?

2. Write a paragraph about a time when you suddenly felt older, more grown up. To begin, list all the details of the incident and then put them in time order.

3. Write a paragraph about a time when you were infatuated. To begin, you can freewrite, focusing on how you felt at each stage of the infatuation.

4. Write a paragraph about a time when someone was infatuated with you. To begin, you can freewrite about how you felt at each stage of the infatuation.

5. Write a paragraph from the boy's point of view in "I Fell in Love, or My Hormones Awakened." That is, imagine what he was feeling at different stages of the story: when he saw Judith at the supermarket, when he looked at her at the Roman banquet, and when he kissed her.

6. Write a paragraph about a secret—yours or someone else's—and how it was revealed. To begin, you can ask a writing partner to interview you, asking such questions as the following:

    Why did you or someone else feel the need to keep something secret?
    How was the secret revealed?
    Who revealed it?
    Why was it revealed?
    What were the effects of revealing it?

    After your interview, interview your partner so that he or she can collect ideas for his or her paragraph.

7. Cofer writes about a time when she felt insignificant. Write a paragraph about a time when you felt insignificant. Be sure to include the circumstances that led to your feeling that way: Did you feel like an outsider in your community? Did you feel physically unattractive, awkward, or unintelligent? Also discuss the result of such feelings: Were you able to overcome them? If so, how?

CHAPTER 25

Writing a Descriptive Paragraph

WHAT IS DESCRIPTION?

Description shows a reader what a person, place, thing, or situation is like. When you write description, you try to *show, not tell*, about something. You want to make the reader see that person, place, or situation, and then, perhaps, make the reader think about or act on what you have shown.

HINTS FOR WRITING A DESCRIPTIVE PARAGRAPH

Using Specific Words and Phrases

Your description will help the reader see if it uses specific words and phrases. If a word or phrase is *specific*, it is *exact and precise*. The opposite of specific language is language that is vague, general, or fuzzy. Think of the difference between specific and general in this way:

Imagine that your mother asks you what gift you want for your birthday.

"Something nice," you say.
"What do you mean by nice?" your mother asks.
"You know," you say. "Not the usual stuff."
"What stuff?" she asks.
"Like the usual things you always give me," you reply. "Don't give me that kind of stuff."
"Well, what would you like instead?" she asks.

The conversation could go on and on. You are being very general in saying that you want a "something nice." Your mother is looking for specific details: What do you mean by "nice"? What is "the usual stuff"? What are "the usual things"?

In writing, if you use words like "nice" or "the usual stuff," you will not have a specific description or a very effective piece of writing. Whenever you can, try to use a more precise word instead of a general term. To find a more explicit term, ask yourself such questions as, "What type?" or "How?" The examples below show how a general term can be replaced by a more specific one.

general word: sweater (Ask "What type?")
more specific words: pullover, vest, cardigan

general word: vegetables (Ask "What type?")
more specific words: broccoli, carrots, peas

general word: walked (Ask "How?")
more specific words: stumbled, strutted, strode

general word: funny (Ask "How?")
more specific words: strange, comical, entertaining

Exercise 1

Practice

Identifying General and Specific Words

Below are lists of words. Put an *X* by the one term in each list that is a more general term than the others. The first one is done for you.

List 1
- __X__ silverware
- _____ knife
- _____ soup spoon
- _____ teaspoon
- _____ fork

List 4
- _____ tire
- _____ steering wheel
- __X__ car parts
- _____ gas tank
- _____ windshield

List 2
- _____ shampoo
- _____ hair spray
- _____ hair conditioner
- _____ hair dye
- __X__ hair product

List 5
- _____ apples
- _____ strawberries
- _____ mangoes
- __X__ fruit
- _____ bananas

List 3
- _____ guitar
- _____ saxophone
- __X__ musical instrument
- _____ violin
- _____ flute

List 6
- _____ sports cars
- __X__ cars
- _____ convertibles
- _____ sedans
- _____ luxury cars

Exercise 2

Practice

Ranking General and Specific Items

Below are lists of items. In each list, rank the items, from the most general (*1*) to the most specific (*4*).

List 1
- __1__ movie
- __3__ film with an alien
- __2__ science fiction film
- __4__ *ET*

List 3
- __1__ medical worker
- __3__ surgeon
- __2__ physician
- __4__ brain surgeon

List 2

__1__ food
__3__ Thanksgiving food
__2__ holiday food
__4__ Thanksgiving Turkey

List 4

__2__ office furniture
__3__ computer furniture
__1__ furniture
__4__ printer stand

Exercise 3

Collaborate

Interviewing for Specific Answers

To practice being specific, interview a partner. Ask your partner to answer the questions below. Write his or her answers in the spaces provided. When you have finished, change places. In both interviews, your goal is to find specific answers, so you should both be as explicit as you can in your answers.

Interview Questions

1. What is your favorite breed of dog? _____

2. Name three objects that are in your wallet or purse right now.

_____

3. What is your favorite television commercial? _____

_____

4. What actor or actress do you most dislike? _____

_____

5. If you were buying a car, what color would you choose? _____

_____

6. What sound do you think is the most irritating? _____

_____

7. When you think of a beautiful woman or man, who comes to

mind? _____

_____

8. When you think of a glamorous place, what place do you

picture? _____

9. When you are at home and want to relax, what kind of chair do

you sit in? _____

_____

Exercise **4**

Practice

Finding Specific Words or Phrases

List four specific words or phrases beneath each general one. You may use brand names where they are appropriate. The first word on List 1 is done for you.

List 1

general word: green
specific word or phrase: olive green

light green

lime green

forest green

List 2

general word: bread
specific word or phrase: rye bread

whole wheat bread

pumpernickel bread

sourdough bread

List 3

general word: gun
specific word or phrase: revolver

rifle

pistol

shotgun

List 4

general word: happy
specific word or phrase: blissful

contented

pleased

glad

List 5

general word: tree
specific word or phrase: elm tree

pine tree

palm tree

oak tree

Exercise **5**

Practice

Identifying Sentences That Are Too General

Below are lists of sentences. Put an *X* by one sentence in each group that is general and vague.

1. a. __X__ Jose has some issues with his father.

b. _____ Jose and his father do not agree about Jose's decision to leave college.

c. _____ Jose's father dislikes Jose's wife.

2. a. _____ She constantly complains about her salary.

   b. _____ She loves to gossip about other people's misery.

   c. __X__ She is a negative person.

3. a. __X__ The trip cost a lot of money.

   b. _____ The plane fare was $700.

   c. _____ Our hotel room cost $100 a night.

4. a. _____ Most of the movie showed cars crashing.

   b. _____ There was no real plot.

   c. __X__ The movie I saw last night was stupid.

5. a. __X__ I want to be the best that I can be.

   b. _____ I want to work with disabled children.

   c. _____ I want to play in the Super Bowl.

Using Sense Words in Your Descriptions

One way to make your description specific and vivid is to use **sense words.** As you plan a description, ask yourself,

What does it **look** like?
What does it **sound** like?
What does it **smell** like?
What does it **taste** like?
What does it **feel** like?

The sense details can make the description vivid. Try to include details about the five senses in your descriptions. Often you can brainstorm sense details more easily if you focus your thinking.

Info BOX

Devising Sense Detail

For the sense of	think about
sight	colors, light and dark, shadows, or brightness.
hearing	noise, silence, or the kinds of sounds you hear.
smell	fragrance, odors, scents, aromas, or perfume.
taste	bitter, sour, sweet, or compare the taste of one thing to another.
touch	the feel of things: texture, hardness, softness, roughness, smoothness.

Brainstorming Sense Details for a Description Paragraph

With a partner or a group, brainstorm the following ideas for a paragraph. That is, for each topic, list at least six questions and answers that could help you find sense details. Be prepared to read your completed exercise to another group or to the class.

1. **topic:** Eric has the most cluttered work station in the office. Brainstorm questions and answers:

    Question: What makes it so cluttered?

    Answer: It's full of junk.

    Question: What kind of junk?

    Answer: Paper. Lots of paper he doesn't need.

    Question: Blank paper? Or documents?

    Answer: He has old letters, memos, scrap paper.

    Question: What else makes it cluttered?

    Answer: There are books piled all over the desk and on the floor.

    Question: Is there anything else on the desk?

    Answer: Old phone books, a calculator, framed photos, pencils.

    Question: Is there anything else on the floor?

    Answer: Old newspapers and empty coffee cups.

2. **topic:** The car hit by a truck was a total loss. Brainstorm questions and answers:

    Question: What was wrong with the car?

    Answer: The whole front end was smashed in.

    Question: What about the rest of the car?

    Answer: The rear was crumpled, and one side door was torn off.

    Question: How did all this happen?

    Answer: The car flipped over several times.

    Question: As a result of high speed or reckless driving?

    Answer: No, the impact of the truck sent the car flying.

    Question: Can't the car be rebuilt?

    Answer: The engine is destroyed, and the body is crushed.

Question: What kind of car is it?

Answer: A 1995 Corvette.

3. **topic:** The holiday parade created excitement and joy.
Brainstorm questions and answers:

Question: What holiday was this?

Answer: The Fourth of July.

Question: Where was the parade?

Answer: In a small town in Kentucky.

Question: Who was excited?

Answer: The people in the parade and the people watching it.

Question: Who was in the parade?

Answer: Two school marching bands, the volunteer firefighters.

Question: Who was watching?

Answer: Families and lots of small children. Teens. Older folks.

Question: Why was it so joyful?

Answer: It was a time for everyone to meet friends and celebrate.

Exercise 7

Practice

Answers Will Vary.

Possible answers shown at right.

Writing Sense Words

Write sense descriptions for the items below.

1. Write four words or phrases to describe what a tile floor feels like:

   smooth, cool, hard against bare feet, slippery when wet

2. Write four words or phrases to describe what a squirrel looks like:

   always startled, alert, quivering, waving an enormous tail

3. Write four words or phrases to describe the sounds of a basketball game:

   thuds, shouts, cheers, grunts

4. Write four words or phrases to describe the taste of pizza:

   rich, spicy, creamy, heavy with tomatoes

WRITING THE DESCRIPTION PARAGRAPH IN STEPS

Thought Lines **Gathering Ideas: Description**

Suppose your instructor asks you to write about this topic: An Outdoor Place. You might begin by *brainstorming*.

Sample Brainstorming on An Outdoor Place

Question: **What place?**
Answer: Outside somewhere.

Question: **Like the outside of a building?**
Answer: Maybe.

Question: **The beach?**
Answer: That would be OK. But everybody will write on that.

Question: **How about a park?**
Answer: Yes. A park would be good.

Question: **How about the park near your workplace—the city park?**
Answer: I could do that. I go there at lunchtime.

You scan your brainstorming and realize you have three possible topics: the outside of a building, the beach, or a city park. You decide that you can write the most about the city park, so you brainstorm further:

Brainstorming on a Specific Topic: A City Park

Question: **What does the park look like?**
Answer: It's small.

Question: **How small?**
Answer: Just the size of an empty lot.

Question: **What's in it?**
Answer: Some trees. Benches.

Question: **What else is in it?**
Answer: A fountain. In the middle.

Question: **Any swing sets or jungle gyms?**
Answer: No, it's not that kind of park. Just a green space.

Question: **Why do you like this park?**
Answer: I just like it. It's near the store where I work. I go there at lunchtime.

Question: **But why do you go there?**
Answer: It's nice and green. It's not like the rest of the city.

Question: **What's the rest of the city like?**
Answer: The rest of the city is dirty, gray, and noisy.

By asking and answering questions, you can (1) choose a topic, and (2) begin to develop ideas on that topic. Each answer can lead you to more questions and thus to more ideas.

Exercise 8

Practice

Identifying Topics in Brainstorming

Following are examples of early brainstorming. In each case, the brainstorming is focused on selecting a narrow topic from a broad one. Imagine that the broad topic is one assigned by your instructor. Survey each example of brainstorming and list all the possible narrower topics within it.

1. **broad topic:** Describe a party you attended.
   brainstorming:

   Question: **What kind of party?**
   Answer: I don't know. I don't go to many parties.

   Question: **When you were younger, you had a birthday party, didn't you?**
   Answer: Yes, that was fun. It was when I was six.

   Question: **Did you have friends come over, or just family?**
   Answer: Some friends from my first-grade class came.

   Question: **Or could you write about another party?**
   Answer: Maybe the office party last week.

   Question: **Was it fun?**
   Answer: Yes, but I don't know what I'd write about it.

   Question: **How about another kind of party?**
   Answer: Maybe I could write on my sister's graduation party.

   possible topics: <u>my sixth birthday party, the office party, my sister's</u>

   <u>graduation party</u>

Answers Will Vary.

Possible answers shown at right.

2. **broad topic:** Write about an attractive person.
   brainstorming:

   Question: **Who is attractive?**
   Answer: Maybe a movie star.

   Question: **Male or female?**
   Answer: I don't know. Maybe I could write about a model.

   Question: **What does attractive mean?**
   Answer: Beautiful. Handsome. Maybe it means attractive inside.
               Because of an attractive personality or warmth.

   Question: **So who is attractive inside?**
   Answer: My sister Lupe. She's not beautiful, but she's beautiful inside.

   possible topics: <u>a movie star, a model, a person who is attractive</u>

   <u>inside, my sister Lupe</u>

Exercise 9

👥 *Collaborate*

Developing Ideas Through Further Brainstorming

Following are examples of brainstorming. Each example brainstorms a single, narrow topic. Working with a group, write four further questions and answers based on the ideas already listed.

1. **topic:** My Bed
   brainstorming:

   Question: **What can you say about your bed?**
   Answer: It's comfortable.

Question: **Why is it comfortable?**
Answer: I sleep in it.

Question: **Everybody sleeps in beds. Why is *yours* so comfortable?**
Answer: It's broken in.

Question: **What do you mean?**
Answer: The mattress fits my body.

Question: **How?**
Answer: It's soft enough to fit around me.

Four additional questions and answers:

Question: What about your pillows?

Answer: I like soft pillows, too.

Question: How soft?

Answer: Very soft, so I can squish them around.

Question: Are they feather pillows?

Answer: Yes

Question: How many pillows?

Answer: Four. I like comfort when I sleep.

2. **topic:** My Favorite Meal: A Burger and Fries
   brainstorming:

Question: **Why do you like burgers and fries so much?**
Answer: I like crispy fries and juicy burgers.

Question: **Why? Is it the taste?**
Answer: Sure.

Question: **What do you like about the taste of a burger?**
Answer: I guess I like the pickles and onions and the chewy taste of
           ground meat.

Question: **What else?**
Answer: I like beef.

Four additional questions and answers:

Question: What was the best burger you ever ate?

Answer: A burger my uncle made.

Question: Why was it so good?

Answer: He grilled it on the barbecue grill.

Question: What else made it so good?

Answer: It was huge, about a half pound.

Question: What about the taste?

Answer: He put something in the meat, a special, spicy sauce.

Focusing the Thought Lines

To begin focusing your topic and details around some point, list the topic and all the details you've gathered so far. The following list includes all the details you've gathered from both sessions of brainstorming on A City Park.

> topic: A City Park
>
> park near my workplace
> I go there at lunchtime.
> It's small.
> just the size of an empty lot
> Some trees. Benches.
> A fountain. In the middle.
> a green space
> I like it.
> It's near the store where I work.
> It's nice and green.
> It's not like the rest of the city.
> The rest of the city is dirty, gray, and noisy.

Grouping the Details

If you survey the list, you can begin to group the details:

What It Looks Like
It's small.
just the size of an empty lot
It's nice and green.
a green space
Some trees. Benches.
A fountain.
In the middle.

Where It Is
park near my workplace
It's near the store where I work.

How I Feel About It
I like it.
I go there at lunchtime.
It's not like the rest of the city.
The rest of the city is dirty, gray, and noisy.

Surveying the details, you notice that they focus on the look and location of a place you like. You decide on this topic sentence:

> A small city park is a nice place for me because it is not like the rest of the city.

You check your topic sentence to decide whether it covers all your details. Does it cover what the park looks like and its location? Yes, the words "small" and "city" relate to what it looks like and its location. Does it cover how you feel about the park? Yes, it says the park is "a nice place for me because it is not like the rest of the city."

Now that you have a topic sentence and a list of details, you are ready to begin the outlines stage of writing.

Exercise 10   **Grouping Details**

Practice

Following are topics and lists of details. Group the details of each list, writing them under the appropriate headings. Some details may not fit under any of the headings.

1. **topic:** A Beautiful Flower Arrangement
   details: The roses smelled sweet and feminine.
   The small white carnations made the red roses seem brighter.
   The ferns had the scent of the woods.
   The vase was shaped like a tall column.
   There were small pink chrysanthemums among the roses.
   The vase was blue and white china.
   A huge white silk ribbon circled the vase.

List details about what the flowers looked like: The small white carnations made the red roses seem brighter. There were small pink chrysanthemums among the roses.

List details about the vase: The vase was shaped like a tall column. The vase was blue and white china. A huge white silk ribbon circled the vase.

List details about the smell of the flowers: The roses smelled sweet and feminine. The ferns had the scent of the woods.

2. **topic:** An Antique Book
   details: It had a green leather cover.
   The title of the book was pressed into the cover in faded gold letters.
   The pages were yellow.
   The book smelled musty.
   Several pages were loose.
   Two pages had stains.
   The corners of the leather cover were frayed.
   The title page was missing.

List details about the cover of the book: It had a green leather cover. The title of the book was pressed into the cover in faded gold letters. The corners of the leather cover were frayed.

List details about the inside of the book: The pages were yellow. Several pages were loose. Two pages had stains. The title page was missing.

3. **topic:** A Baby's Room
   details: Jamal and Alicia painted the ceiling of the room a pale green.
   The crib was made of white wood.
   A mobile with soft cloth fishes dangled from the ceiling light and danced above the crib.
   There was a white wooden rocking chair with striped yellow cushions.
   The walls were papered with green and yellow teddy bears.
   A big wooden toy chest sat in a corner of the room.

List details about the furniture: The crib was made of white wood.

There was a white wooden rocking chair with striped yellow cushions.

A big wooden toy chest sat in a corner of the room.

_____

List details about the walls: The walls were papered with green and

yellow teddy bears.

_____

List details about the ceiling: Jamal and Alicia painted the ceiling a

pale green. A mobile with soft cloth fishes dangled from the ceiling

light and danced above the crib.

_____

Exercise 11

👥 *Collaborate*

Writing Appropriate Topic Sentences

Do this exercise with a partner or a group. Following are lists of details. For each list, write two appropriate topic sentences.

1. **topic sentence 1:** The old house had its drawbacks and

advantages.

_____

topic sentence 2: The old house needed work, but it had a low price

and possibilities.

INSTRUCTOR'S NOTE:

Remind students to survey *all* the details before devising possible topic sentences.

details: The living room of the old house had faded, peeling wallpaper.
The fireplace was full of dirt and dust.
The carpet was spotted with mildew.
In the hall, the wooden floor was rotted.
The stairs creaked and groaned.
The upstairs bedrooms were shabby.
Yet all the rooms were spacious.
The price of the house was a bargain.
The architecture was elegant.

2. topic sentence 1: The man in the dentist's waiting room was extremely nervous.

topic sentence 2: Terror filled the man in the dentist's waiting room.

details: The man in the dentist's waiting room had sweat trick-ling down his face.
His jaw was clenched.
He sat on the edge of his chair.
He kept looking at the clock.
His eyes were full of misery.
His hands trembled as he tried to flip through a magazine.
When the nurse called his name, he jumped.

3. topic sentence 1: The frozen dinner was as bad as it first looked.

topic sentence 2: The frozen dinner was an icy surprise.

details: Ice crystals covered the frozen dinner.
The ice made the meatballs look gray.
The meal came out of the carton as a solid block of ice.
As it cooked in the microwave, the frozen dinner began to look edible.
The meatballs began to darken.
The noodles separated into golden strips.
When the microwave timer went off, I tasted the dinner.
It was a wet, icy mess inside.

4. topic sentence 1: The powerful storm hit trees, buildings, and people.

topic sentence 2: The storm transformed the ordinary scene into chaos.

details: The thunder roared while the lightning crashed and crackled, coming closer and closer.
Rain gushed into the streets.
The wind became stronger.
Leaves and tree branches flew in the air.
Doors blew shut and windows flew open.
Cars pulled over to the side of the road.
Pedestrians ran for cover.

Outlines Devising A Plan: Description

Once you have a topic sentence, a list of details, and some grouping of the details, you can write them in outline form. Before you write your details in outline form, check their order. Remember, when you write a description, you are trying to make the reader *see*. It will be easier for the reader to imagine what you see if you put your description in a simple, logical order. You might want to put descriptions in order by **time sequence** (first to last), by **spatial position** (for example, top to bottom, right to left, or outside to inside), or by **similar types** (for example, all about the flowers, then all about the trees in a garden).

If you are describing a house, for instance, you may want to start with the outside of the house and then describe the inside. You do not want the details to shift back and forth, from outside to inside and back to outside. If you are describing a person, you might want to group all the details about his or her face before you describe the person's body. You might want to describe a meal from the first course to dessert.

Look again at the grouped list of details on a city park. To help make the reader see the park, you decide to arrange your details in *spatial order:* First, describe where the park is located; second, describe the edges and the middle of the park. The final lines of your paragraph can describe your feelings about the park. The following outline follows this order.

Outline for a Paragraph on A City Park

topic sentence: A small city park is a nice place for me because it is not like the rest of the city.

details:

location	It is near the store where I work.
appearance	It is just the size of an empty lot.
from edges	It is nice.
	It is a green space.
to the middle	It has some trees and benches.
	It has a fountain in the middle.
how I feel	I like it.
about it	I go there at lunchtime.
	It is not like the rest of the city.
	The rest of the city is dirty, gray, and noisy.

Once you have an outline, you can begin writing a description paragraph.

 Putting Details in Order

Practice

Following are lists that start with a topic sentence. The details under each topic sentence are not in the right order. Put the details in the right order by labeling them, with *1* being the first detail, *2* the second, and so forth.

1. **topic sentence:** The play turned out to be a great success.
   (Arrange the details in time order.)
   details: ___4___ Everyone applauded loudly when the curtain fell for the last time.

   ___2___ From the first scene, the audience was quiet, listening to every word of dialogue.

_____3_____ At the intermission, people were saying how much they liked the play.

_____1_____ Every seat was filled ten minutes before the play started.

2. **topic sentence:** The old house had been well cared for. (Arrange the details from outside to inside.)

details:

_____1_____ The white wooden fence was freshly painted.

_____4_____ The front hall had a gleaming tile floor.

_____2_____ Every tree in the front yard had been trimmed.

_____3_____ The front door had a polished door knob.

_____5_____ Not a speck of dust could be found in the living room.

3. **topic sentence:** My little sister looked like a model. (Arrange the details from head to foot.)

details:

_____1_____ Her carefully tinted hair gleamed with gel.

_____6_____ The heels on her silver sandals were three inches high.

_____5_____ She wore a platinum ankle bracelet.

_____2_____ Around her neck was a shimmering red scarf.

_____4_____ She wore a red leather skirt.

_____3_____ The scarf fell onto a blouse of silver sequins.

Exercise 13

👥 *Collaborate*

Creating Details Using a Logical Order

The following lists include a topic sentence and indicate a required order. With a partner or group, write five sentences of details in the required order.

1. **topic sentence:** The medicine cabinet in my bathroom is full of everything except medicine.
(Describe the contents of the cabinet from top shelf to bottom shelf.)

a. The top shelf, the tallest, has tall shampoo bottles.

b. It also has tall bottles of mouthwash.

c. The next shelf has a collection of hair gels and mousse.

d. Deodorants, skin lotions, and shaving cream come next.

e. The bottom shelf is crammed with after shave and cologne.

2. **topic sentence:** The movie was filled with suspenseful encounters.
(Describe these encounters from the beginning of the movie to the end.)

a. It started with a dramatic escape by parachute.

b. This was followed by a car chase on a winding road.

c. The chase led to a scene at a drug dealer's hideout.

d. Later, the hero was caught in a burning building.

e. Finally, he had to swim in a lagoon full of sharks.

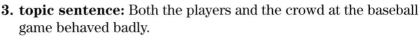

3. **topic sentence:** Both the players and the crowd at the baseball game behaved badly.
(First describe the players' behavior; then describe the crowd's behavior.)

a. ___One player threatened an umpire.___

b. ___Another spat at a member of the opposing team.___

c. ___The crowds in the stands booed.___

d. ___People in the stands began to throw cans and bottles.___

e. ___A few spectators were escorted out by police.___

4. **topic sentence:** The painting of the old man's face showed an angry person.
(Describe the face in the painting from the forehead to the chin.)

a. ___The wrinkles on the forehead led to scowling eyebrows.___

b. ___The old man's eyes were dark slits.___

c. ___There were deep lines around the sides of his nose.___

d. ___These lines extended below his mouth, pulling downward.___

e. ___His chin jutted out, defiantly.___

Rough Lines Drafting and Revising: Description

After you have an outline, the next step is creating a rough draft of the paragraph. Once you have the first draft, look it over, using the following checklist:

✔ Checklist

A Checklist for Revising a Descriptive Paragraph

✔ Are there enough details?

✔ Are the details specific?

✔ Do the details use sense words?

✔ Are the details in order?

✔ Is the description easy to follow?

✔ Have I made my point?

If you look at the outline for A City Park, you'll notice that it has some problems:

- The details are not very specific. Words like "nice" do not say much, and "nice" is used twice, in the topic sentence and in the details.
- There are some parts of the outline that need more support. The description of the inside of the park needs more details.

- The description would also be easier to follow if it had some effective transitions.

These weak areas can be improved in the drafting and revising stage of the writing process.

Transitions

As you revise your description paragraph, you may notice places in the paragraph that seem choppy or abrupt. That is, one sentence may end, and another may start, but the two sentences don't seem to be connected. Reading your paragraph aloud, you may sense that it is not very smooth. Good transitions can help to make smooth connections between your ideas. Here are some transitions you may want to use in writing a description:

Info BOX

Transitions for a Descriptive Paragraph

To show ideas brought together

and	also	in addition	next

To show a contrast

although	however	on the contrary	unlike
but	in contrast	on the other hand	yet

To show a similarity

all	each	like	similarly
both			

To show a time sequence

after	first	next	then
always	second (etc.)	often	when
before	meanwhile	soon	while

To show a position in space

above	between	in front of	over
ahead of	beneath	inside	there
alongside	beyond	near	toward
among	by	nearby	under
around	close	next to	up
away	down	on	underneath
below	far	on top of	where
beside	here	outside	

There are many other transitions you can use, depending on what you need to link your ideas.

Below is a revised draft of the paragraph on A City Park. When you read it, you will notice the added details and more precise words. You will also notice that some short, choppy sentences have been combined and that transitions have been added. In addition, a final sentence of details has been added to the end of the paragraph.

A Revised Draft of a Paragraph on A City Park

specific detail	A small city park is a <u>pleasant</u> place for me because it is not like the rest of the city. The park is near the store
added details	where I work; <u>in fact, it is only a ten-minute walk</u>. <u>It is</u>
sentences combined	
specific detail	<u>just the size of an empty lot, yet it is an attractive green</u>
sense detail	
transition added,	<u>space ringed with maple trees</u>. <u>Under</u> the trees are
transition	
added details	<u>weathered wooden</u> benches <u>where people of every age</u>
sense detail	
specific details	<u>sit and enjoy the calm</u>. The only sound is the <u>splash</u> of
sentences combined	the fountain at the center of the park. <u>I enjoy the park</u>
	<u>and visit it at lunchtime</u>. It is not like the rest of the city,
sense words and	<u>which is dirty, gray, and filled with the noise of screech-</u>
specific detail	
final sentence	<u>ing brakes, rumbling trucks, and blaring horns</u>. <u>The park</u>
transition	
sense details	<u>is a clean, quiet spot, where the sun filters through the</u>
	<u>leaves of trees.</u>

Although it is important to work on specific details and sense words in each stage of your writing, it is easiest to focus on revising for details in the drafting stage, when you have a framework for what you want to say. With that framework, you can concentrate on the most vivid way to express your ideas.

 Exercise 14

Practice

Recognizing Transitions

Underline the transitions in the paragraph below.

My sister's one-room apartment was a college student's dream. It was <u>on</u> the second floor of an old house converted into small apartments. <u>Inside</u> the door was a small room painted a cheerful yellow. The walls were covered with black-and-white photographs in red, yellow, and blue frames. My sister, who was majoring in photography, had placed bookcases made of bricks and boards <u>below</u> the photos. <u>On</u> every bookshelf, piles of books about famous photographers and their works mixed with cameras, lenses, and photographic prints. <u>Between</u> two bookcases my sister had placed an old single bed disguised to look like a sofa. <u>Nearby</u> was an old oak table; <u>on top of</u> the table, shiny green plants reached out to the sun coming from a large window above the table. Two old oak stools <u>under</u> the table completed

the room. <u>Beyond</u> this room were a tiny kitchen alcove and a small bath-

room. <u>When</u> I, a sixteen-year-old, saw my older sister's college apartment, I

couldn't wait to finish high school and have my own sophisticated place.

Exercise 15

Practice

Adding the Appropriate Transitions

In the paragraph below, transitions are shown in parentheses. Circle the
appropriate transitions.

Cleavon and Daniella decorated the banquet room in a distinctive style.

(First/Soon) Cleavon draped the walls with gold and purple streamers.

(Often/Meanwhile,) Daniella tied clusters of small purple balloons, made to

look like bunches of grapes, (above/toward) the doors. (Before/Soon) the

two began decorating the banquet tables. They covered them with white

linen tablecloths; (on top of/underneath) the cloths they placed baskets of

gold and purple flowers. (Then/Always,) they placed the silverware.

(Toward/Next to) each place setting they put a single gold rose. With their

decorations, Cleavon and Daniella made the dinner a royal banquet.

Exercise 16

Practice

Revising for Specific Details or Sense Words

In the following paragraph, replace each underlined word or phrase with
more specific details or sense words. Write your changes in the space above
each underlined item.

My boyfriend cooked his first Thanksgiving dinner last week, and it was

a great success. Michael is a cook at an Italian restaurant, but he had never

cooked a traditional Thanksgiving dinner. However, when his mother got

the flu, Michael volunteered to cook for his family for the holiday. He had

twelve   *7:00 a.m.*
<u>a lot of</u> people to feed, so he began early. At <u>an early time</u> on Thanksgiving

        six apple pies   *green linen*
day, Michael made <u>some desserts</u>. Then he set the table. He used a <u>pretty</u>

        an autumn leaves   *gold and white china*
tablecloth and a <u>nice</u> centerpiece with some <u>good</u> dishes. When he was fin-

            elegant   *impressive*
ished, the tablecloth looked <u>pretty</u> and the centerpiece was <u>nice</u>. Later, he

cooked the fifteen-pound turkey, the sausage and onion stuffing, and <u>some</u>

sweet potatoes, a green bean casserole, and corn
<u>vegetables.</u> By the time the family sat down to dinner, they were thrilled by

the smells of crispy roast turkey and candied yams *hearty taste*   *creaminess*

all the good smells. They loved the taste of the turkey and the texture of the

sighed their ooh's and ah's

mashed potatoes. All across the room, people eating made sounds of pleasure.

stuffed

By the time people had finished the meal, they felt full but happy.

Final Lines   Focus on Support and Details

Before you prepare the final copy of your paragraph, check it again for any problems in support and details, and for any places where grammar, word choice, and style need revision. Check also for any errors in spelling and punctuation.

Following is the final version of the paragraph on A City Park. As you review it, you'll notice several changes:

- The name of the park has been added, to make the details more specific.
- There were too many repetitions of "it" in the paragraph, so "it" has frequently been changed to "the park," "Sheridan Park," and so forth.
- An introductory sentence has been added to make the beginning of the paragraph smoother.

A Final Version of a Paragraph on A City Park

(Changes from the draft are underlined.)

> Everyone has a place where he or she can relax. A small city park is a pleasant place for me because it is not like the rest of the city. Sheridan Park is near the store where I work; in fact, it is only a ten-minute walk. The park is just the size of an empty lot, yet it is an attractive green space ringed with maple trees. Under the trees are weathered wooden benches where people of every age sit and enjoy the calm. The only sound is the splash of the fountain at the center of the park. I enjoy the park and visit it at lunchtime. This special place is not like the rest of the city, which is dirty, gray, and filled with the noise of screeching brakes, rumbling trucks, and blaring horns. The park is a clean, quiet spot, where the sun filters through the leaves of trees.

Exercise 17   Correcting Errors in the Final Lines

Practice

Proofread the following paragraphs. Correct any errors in spelling, punctuation, or word choice. There are ten errors in the first paragraph and thirteen in the second. Write your corrections in the space above each error.

vacation

1. Yesterday I found a brochure for a vaccation in the Bahamas,

and I immediately entered a beautiful fantasy. I pictured turquoise

waters   *sands*   *strolling*

water's and pale sand's. I could see myself stroling down the beach

imagined

where the sand would feel like sugar between my toes. I imagine the

rhythm

soft rhythmn of the tide and the louder beat of reggae music. In my

brought

dream, an island girl brout me a foamy drink filled with pineapple mango' papaya, and guava juice. I sipped the drink from a bowl

carved out of half a coconut. I felt that I was drinking in paradise,

                 only
but unfortunately, my paradise was onely a dream.

              father   *an*
    2. When my Father goes to work each morning, he carries a old
                        family history
leather bag with a famly hisstory. The bag is made of worn black

                                  torn
leather, and some of the leather is cracked and tore. The tarnished
     buckles
brass buckle's can barely be closed because the bag is stretched to
                       father's
the bursting point with my father necessities. He has filled the bag

with papers, folders, a calculator, tape measures, brochures, and

sample products. Since my father is a salesperson for a tile company,

the old bag is really too small for all the items my father takes on his
           .   *insists*
sales calls However, he insist on using this bag because it belonged
          grandfather   *forty*
to my grand father. My grandfather worked in an office for fourty

years and never went to work without that leather briefcase. Now
                       different
my father, who is in an entirely diffrent line of work, remembers his
          carrying
father by carrin the same bag.

Lines of Detail: A Walk-Through Assignment

For this assignment, write a paragraph about your classroom, the one in which you take this class.

Step 1: To begin, freewrite on your classroom for ten minutes. In your freewriting, focus on how you would *describe* your classroom.

Step 2: Next, read your freewriting to a partner or a group. Ask your listener(s) to write down any ideas in your freewriting that could lead to a specific topic for your paragraph. (For example, maybe your freewriting has several ideas about what you feel when you are in the classroom, or how others behave, or how the furniture and decor of the room create a mood.)

Step 3: With a specific topic in mind, list all the ideas in your freewriting that might fit that main topic.

Step 4: Now, brainstorm. Write at least ten questions and answers based on your list of ideas.

Step 5: Group all the ideas you've found in freewriting and brainstorming. Survey them and write a topic sentence for your paragraph. Your topic sentence may focus on the atmosphere of the classroom, the look of the classroom, how you feel in the classroom, the activity in the classroom, and so forth.

Step 6: Write an outline. Be sure that your outline has enough supporting points for you to write a paragraph of seven to twelve sentences.

Step 7: Write and revise your paragraph. Check each draft for support and work on using specific details and sense words.

Step 8: Share your best draft with a partner or the group. Ask for suggestions or comments. Revise once more.

Step 9: Prepare the final copy of your paragraph, checking for errors in punctuation, spelling, or word choice.

INSTRUCTOR'S NOTE:

A Peer Review Form for students' exchange of drafts is on page 374.

Writing Your Own Descriptive Paragraph

When you write on any of the following topics, be sure to follow the stages of the writing process in preparing your paragraph.

1. Write about a memorable meal. It can be a meal that you remember because it was great, or one that you remember because it was terrible. In describing the meal, try to use sense words that connect to smell, sight, texture (touch), and even sound, as well as taste.

2. Write about your most comfortable piece of clothing. In your topic sentence, focus on what makes it so comfortable.

3. Interview a partner so that you and your partner can gather details and write separate paragraphs with the title, "My Dream Vacation."

   First, prepare a list of at least six questions to ask your partner. Write down your partner's answers and use these answers to ask more questions. For example, if your partner says she wants a trip to the Caribbean, ask her what part of the Caribbean she would like to visit. If your partner says he would like to go to the Super Bowl, ask him what teams he would like to see.

   When you have finished the interview, switch roles. Let your partner interview you.

   Finally, give your partner his or her interview responses, take your own responses, and use them as the basis for gathering as many details as you can. In this way, you are working through the thought lines stage of your paragraph. Then go on to the other stages. Be prepared to read your completed paragraph to your partner.

4. Write a paragraph that describes one of the following:
   the contents of your wastebasket
   the contents of your refrigerator
   people riding the subway
   people in the express lane at the supermarket
   children riding the school bus
   a toddler in a car seat or stroller
   the contents of your medicine cabinet
   what you ate for breakfast
   Be sure to focus your paragraph with a good topic sentence.

5. Write a paragraph about the messiest room you've ever seen.

6. Imagine a place that would bring you a sense of peace. In a paragraph, describe that place.

7. Following are some topic sentences. Complete one of them and use it to write a paragraph.

   The happiest place I know is _____.

   _____ is the most comfortable place in my home.

   Whenever I visit _____, I feel a sense of _____.

   Between classes, the halls of the college seem _____.

   I like to spend time alone at _____ because _____.

8. Write about the sensations of being caught in rush hour traffic. You might begin by brainstorming all the details you recall.

9. Look carefully at photograph A or photograph B. In a paragraph, describe the face in either photograph. In order to write this description, consider how you can use specific details and sense description to express what you see and what impression it conveys.

Photograph A

Photograph B

10. Write a paragraph about photograph C. Describe the scene; be sure to include the different types of people at the scene as well as the vehicles.

Photograph C

Name _____ Section _____

PEER REVIEW FORM FOR A DESCRIPTIVE PARAGRAPH

After you have written a draft version of your paragraph, let a writing partner read it. When your partner has completed the following form, discuss the responses. Then repeat the same process for your partner's paragraph.

The part of this paragraph that I like best begins with the words _____

_____

This paragraph uses some sense words and phrases. Among these sense words and phrases are

_____

The part of the paragraph that could use more specific details or sense words begins with the words _____

The topic sentence of this paragraph is _____

_____

_____

I think there is (enough/too little) [circle one] support for the topic sentence.

I have questions about _____

_____

Other comments on the paragraph: _____

_____

_____

_____

_____

_____

_____

_____

_____

_____

_____

_____

_____

Reviewer's name _____

WRITING FROM READING: Description

I Wish

Lillian Gwin

When Lillian Gwin wrote this, in 1970, she was a high school senior at Flandreau Indian School in South Dakota, a high school run by the Bureau of Indian Affairs. Her writing won a contest and was published in an anthology of prose and poetry by young Native Americans. Gwin, a member of the Gros Ventre-Arika tribe, writes of her sadness in the white man's world and her hopes for the future.

Words You May Need to Know

tanning: converting an animal hide or skin into leather

deer hide: deer skin

muck: filth, dirt

I wish I could see the campsite of my ancestors and hear the laughter of children playing Indian games, and men talking about the last hunt, or see the women sitting quietly on the ground tanning a fresh deer hide. I wish I could sit by a clear pool of water, see my reflection in its purity, and let my horse drink. Instead, I look into the pond at a shoe, a piece of paper, cans, old tires, and I say to myself, "My great-grandfather wouldn't have watered his horse in this muck!" I sometimes wish I could ride, ride, ride, and never see another white man's building. But at night when I lie down on the white man's bed, I look out the window and up to the stars twinkling merrily, and I know that the Great Spirit, who put them there, also planned the Indians' new pathway. I promise myself that I will face the white man's tomorrow with a prayer in my heart for the unity of man. He would want it that way.

Exercise 18

Practice

Identifying Sense Words and Specific Words in "I Wish"

Lillian Gwin uses many sense words and specific words. To become aware of her writing techniques, reread "I Wish" and complete the following exercise.

1. Gwin uses several words or phrases that describe what someone can see. Write the exact words of two examples of sight words or phrases from her writing.

   a. "a clear pool"

   b. "see my reflection in its purity"

2. Gwin also uses several words or phrases describing what someone can hear. Write the exact words of two examples of sound words or phrases from her writing.

   a. "the laughter of children playing Indian games"

   b. "men talking about the last hunt"

3. Instead of writing that she sees "junk" in a pond, Gwin uses very specific words to describe what is in the pond. Write the specific words:

"A shoe, a piece of paper, cans, old tires"

4. Instead of saying, "I wish I could run away from white society," Gwin uses very specific words to make the same point. Write the specific words:

"I sometimes wish I could ride, ride, ride, and never see another white man's building."

WRITING FROM READING: "I Wish"

When you write on any of the following topics, be sure to work through the stages of the writing process in preparing your paragraph.

1. Lillian Gwin uses many details to describe a world she dreams about. Write a paragraph in which you use many details to describe an environment or lifestyle you dream about.

2. Write a description of a place in nature. It might be a beach, a forest, a field, a mountain, a lake, and so on. In your description, try to be very specific and to use sense words.

3. Imagine yourself in another time and place. Write a paragraph giving details about your life in that time and place.

4. Write a paragraph called "I Wish." Write about whatever you wish for. Concentrate on using specific details and sense words.

5. Interview someone who is much older than you. Ask the person to describe a part of his or her life that is gone now. It could be something like a family routine, or a way of traveling, shopping, working, or enjoying leisure time. Ask questions and take notes, looking for specific details. Write a paragraph about this person's description.

6. Write a paragraph about a situation that saddened you and about how you learned to cope with that situation. Describe the situation with specific details and sense words.

Death Row (from *The Chamber*)

John Grisham

John Grisham, a Mississippi lawyer, is a best-selling author of legal thrillers. Many of his novels, including A Time to Kill, The Firm, and The Rainmaker, have been made into movies. In this selection from his novel The Chamber, he describes Sam, a convicted murderer on death row at the State Penitentiary in Parchman, Mississippi.

Words You May Need to Know (corresponding paragraph numbers are in parentheses)

the Delta (1): in Mississippi, a flat plain of land between branches of a river
linger (1): remain, stay on in a place
boundless (3): unlimited

ventilation (3): facilities for providing fresh air
dank (3): unpleasantly moist or humid
penal facility (3): prison

1   A loud thunderstorm rolled across the Delta before dawn, and Sam was awakened by the crack of lightning. He heard raindrops dropping hard against the open windows above the hallway. Then he heard them drip and puddle against the wall under the windows not far from his cell. The dampness of his bed was suddenly cool. Maybe today would not be so hot. Maybe the rain would linger and shade the sun, and maybe the wind would blow away the humidity for a day or two. He always had these hopes when it rained, but in the summer a thunderstorm usually meant soggy ground which under a glaring sun meant nothing but more suffocating heat.

2   He raised his head and watched the rain fall from the windows and gather on the floor. The water flickered in the reflected light of a distant yellow bulb. Except for this faint light, the Row was dark. And it was silent.

3   Sam loved the rain, especially at night and especially in the summer. The State of Mississippi, in its boundless wisdom, had built its prison in the hottest place it could find. And it designed its Maximum Security Unit along the same lines as an oven. The windows to the outside were small and useless, built that way for security reasons, of course. The planners of this little branch of hell also decided that there would be no ventilation of any sort, no chance for a breeze getting in or the dank air getting out. And after they built what they considered a model penal facility, they decided they would not air condition it. It would sit proudly beside the soybeans and cotton, and absorb the same heat and moisture from the ground. And when the land was dry, the Row would simply bake along with the crops.

4   But the State of Mississippi could not control the weather, and when the rains came and cooled the air, Sam smiled to himself and offered a small

prayer of thanks. A higher being was in control after all. The state was help-less when it rained. It was a small victory.

5   He eased to his feet and stretched his back. His bed consisted of a piece of foam, six feet by two and a half, four inches thick, otherwise known as a mattress. It rested on a metal frame fastened securely to the floor and wall. It was covered with two sheets. Sometimes they passed out blankets in the winter. Back pain was common throughout the Row, but with time the body adjusted and there were few complaints. The prison doctor was not considered to be a friend of death row inmates.

6   He took two steps and leaned on his elbows through the bars. He lis-tened to the wind and thunder and watched the drops bounce along the windowsill and splatter on the floor. How nice it would be to step through that wall and walk through the wet grass on the other side, to stroll around the prison grounds in the driving rain, naked and crazy, soaking wet with water dropping from his hair and beard.

 Exercise 19

Practice

Identifying Sense Words and Specific Details in "Death Row"

In describing death row, Grisham uses many sense words and specific words. To become more aware of his writing techniques, reread "Death Row" and complete the following exercise.

1. Grisham uses many words or phrases that describe sounds. Write the exact words of two examples of sound words or phrases from his writing:

a. "the crack of lightning"

b. "raindrops dropping hard against the open windows"

2. Grisham uses many words or phrases that describe how some-thing feels (temperature, texture, etc.) to the touch. Write the exact words of two examples of touch words or phrases from his writing:

a. "The dampness of his bed was suddenly cool."

b. "suffocating heat"

3. Grisham uses several words or phrases that describe what Sam can see. Write the exact words of two examples of sight words or phrases from his writing:

a. "watched the rain fall from the windows"

b. "The water flickered in the reflected light."

4. Instead of saying that Sam had a small, uncomfortable bed, Grisham uses very specific words to describe the bed. Write those exact words:

"His bed consisted of a piece of foam, six feet by two and a half, four inches thick, otherwise known as a mattress. It rested on a metal frame fastened securely to the floor and wall."

5. Instead of saying that Sam would like to be free, Grisham uses very specific words to describe Sam's wish. Write those exact words:

"How nice it would be to step through that wall and walk through the wet grass on the other side, to stroll around the prison grounds in the driving rain, naked and crazy, soaking wet with water dropping from his hair and beard."

WRITING FROM READING: "Death Row"

When you write on any of the following topics, be sure to work through the stages of the writing process in preparing your paragraph.

1. To begin this paragraph, sit in one room for fifteen minutes. During that time, list what you see, hear, smell, feel, and even taste. Use this list as the basis for a paragraph describing morning, afternoon, or night in the room.

2. Describe a time when you felt free. Begin your assignment by brainstorming. Prepare at least seven questions such as, "Where was I at the time?" "What was I seeing?" Use the questions, answers, and follow-up questions and answers to gather ideas. Focus your questions and answers on sense words and specific words.

3. Write a paragraph that uses one of the following topic sentences. Be sure that you support the topic sentence with specific words and sense words.

   Topic Sentences
   Even in a depressing place, a person can feel hope.

   Nature can bring pleasure when a person is feeling low.

   Hope kept me going when _____

4. Grisham writes about what one person, a prisoner in a cell, sees, hears, and feels. Write a paragraph describing what one of the following people sees, hears, and feels (and perhaps even smells or tastes):

   a baby in a playpen
   a toll collector in a toll booth
   a puppy or kitten left alone in the kitchen
   an umpire at a baseball game
   a truck driver on an interstate highway
   a model on the runway at a fashion show

5. Write about a time when you were confined in one place for longer than you wanted to be. To begin this assignment, have a writing partner interview you. Your partner should begin with at least six questions such as, "How did you feel?" "What did the place look like?" "Why were you there?"

   Your partner should write down your answers and use these answers to form more questions. For example, if you say you felt bored, your partner might ask, "What bored you?"

   When you have been interviewed, switch roles. Interview your partner with your own prepared list of questions.

   At the end of both interviews, give your partner his or her responses and take your own. Use them as the basis for the thought lines part of your paragraph. Focus on using specific words and sense words.

My Childhood: Skips and Stoops, Sisters and Saturdays

Al Roker

In this selection, Al Roker, the weatherman and feature reporter for NBC's Today Show, *remembers the childhood games he played in Queens, New York. Although he was never a great athlete and never had "the winning moment" in any game, today he cherishes "the wonderful moments in between."*

Words You May Need to Know (corresponding paragraph numbers are in parentheses)

momentum (1): the force of speed or movement
ultimate (3): maximum, highest
Oxfords (3): a low, sturdy shoe that laces over the instep
wheedled (3): persuaded, coaxed

inquisitive (6): curious
simplicity (8): freedom from confusion or complications
stoop (10): a small porch, platform, or staircase leading to the entrance of a house
ruffians (10): tough, rowdy men or boys

1   I wasn't a great athlete growing up. I never threw the winning touchdown pass, and I never cleared the bases with the game on the line. I did have a garbage hook shot, but I was counted on more to clog up the middle and break up the other team's momentum. I guess everyone has a role. Growing up in Queens, mine was definitely not that of all-star.

2   But that was fine. For me it was never really about the game. I was just happy to be out there. Maybe that's why my memories aren't of *the* winning moment; they are of the wonderful moments in between.

3   I remember my mother sending me out to play in a pair of Skips. Skips were a no-name pair of sneakers that were sold at stores such as Sears. Wearing those on the playgrounds was the ultimate in uncool. I would show up wearing my Oxfords. I could say my mother accidentally threw out my sneakers, or something, anything. I could also blame the shoes on missed shots or bad plays. But I begged and whined and wheedled until finally my Skips were magically replaced by a pair of Converse: Now there were no more excuses.

4   But I recall a fate worse than Skips: having to take my sisters along to play. I'm the oldest of six, three boys, three girls. The girls—well, they were girls, and they ruined everything. I can still hear my mom calling out as I'd break for the door: "Al, take your sisters with you."

5   I'd mumble "Ah, geez, Mom. Do I hafta?"

6   Mom would answer in that famous maternal tone. You know the one, half inquisitive and half irritated. "What's that, Al?"

7   "Nothing."

8   Life had a certain simplicity. Our parents didn't have to keep an eye on us because there was always a parent in the community within eyeshot or at least earshot. We knew that if they saw us, the Parent Network would go into effect. Chances were, by the time I got home my parents would be lying in wait for me. They knew what I did; they had it chapter and verse. I couldn't even lie about it because they had the facts: "At 10:19 a.m., you were seen scaling the fence. . . ." "All right, I did it, I did it. You got me. I confess." I hated the Parent Network.

9   We lived in this little part of Queens. To me, that's what New York City really was—a collection of little neighborhoods. It still is. Today, people think New York City is what they see on TV. But Queens or Brooklyn, Staten Island or the Bronx—they're just like anyplace else. We just had different accents.

10   Everything started on the stoop. Not on our stoop. A good stoop had to have the right "feel." It maximized the number of guys who could fit into a small area through combined vertical and horizontal seating. Ours had my mother's fairly extensive plantings: it wasn't a place for what she called "young ruffians." So we'd usually go next door to the Segrees' house and hang out on their stoop.

11   We spent more time deciding "what to do" than actually "doing." It always went the same way:

"What do you want to play today?"

"I dunno. What do you want to play?"

"Wanna go up to the park?"

"I dunno."

We would blow up an hour just trying to figure out whether we were going to play in the street or go up to the park. That was before the long debate even started on what we were actually going to play. Most times we would get tired of talking about it, and somebody would finally say, "Let's just . . ." and everybody else would say, "Fine."

12   But we only had to make it through the morning, because Saturdays were special: The afternoons were reserved for dads. That's when fathers and sons would mix it up. When we were kids, it was fun to have our fathers playing punch ball or touch football for an entire afternoon. My dad was a good athlete. In fact, we used to pile into the family station wagon and drive to Brooklyn to watch him play softball. But what I always admired about my father was that even though he was very athletic and his son wasn't, he never pressured me.

13   My dad and I watched sports together. The first time I ever saw a game live was when my dad, my uncle Champ, my cousin, and I took the subway to Yankee Stadium. I had watched many games on television, and Yankee Stadium looked big, even on my small black and white television set. But that was nothing like being there.

14   I'll never forget coming out of the dark tunnel into brilliant sunshine—it was amazing. But what I really remember is being most interested in what we were going to eat. Uncle Champ asked me, "Did you come here to eat or to watch baseball?" and I thought, "Is this a trick question?"

15   But most of all, I remember that I loved being a kid. Everything about it. Yeah, even the Skips and my sisters. But do me a favor—don't tell my sisters.

Practice

Identifying Specific Words and Phrases in "My Childhood: Skips and Stoops, Sisters and Saturdays"

In this childhood remembrance, Al Roker uses many specific terms to create a picture of growing up. To become more aware of his writing techniques, complete the following exercise.

1. Roker does not simply say he lived in New York City; he says he lived in a "little part of Queens_____."

2. Roker tells us the specific brand of sneakers that he hated. What was that brand? Skips_____.

3. Roker gives a name to the neighborhood parents who keep an eye on each other's children; he calls this group the Parent Network____ .

4. Roker does not say he and his friend used to gather on the neighbors' stoop; he names the neighbors. They are the Segrees____ .

5. When Roker's family used to drive out of the neighborhood to see his father play a game, what game did his father play? softball____

6. What specific kind of transportation did Roker's father drive?
station wagon_____

7. What specific place did they drive to? Brooklyn_____

8. Roker was excited to finally visit a stadium he had seen often on television. Name the stadium: Yankee Stadium_____

9. Roker visited the stadium with his father and his uncle. What was his uncle's name? Champ_____

10. What day of the week was the special day when fathers joined their children in play? Saturday_____

WRITING FROM READING: "My Childhood: Skips and Stoops, Sisters and Saturdays"

When you write on any of the following topics, be sure to work through the stages of the writing process in preparing your paragraph.

1. To begin this essay, list as many childhood games as you can remember. They do not have to be athletic games; they can also include card games, video games, or fantasy games. Once you have this list, write your memories of each: who played with you, where and when you played, which games you loved, hated, and so forth.

Then pick one of the games and write a paragraph describing your experiences with that game.

2. Roker writes about a pair of sneakers that he wouldn't wear because he felt they were "the ultimate in uncool." Write a paragraph about a piece of clothing that you hated. You can describe what it looked like, where it came from, what you felt like when you wore it, and what eventually happened to it.

3. Roker mentions his excitement on first seeing Yankee Stadium. Describe your first visit to a special place. To begin the assignment, freewrite for ten minutes. Then ask a writing partner to read your freewriting, identify some good specific details, and ask you further questions about the place. Use your partner's comments and questions to lead you to more specific details and sense descriptions.

   When your partner has surveyed your freewriting and questioned you, switch roles and review your partner's freewriting. When both reviews are complete, use your ideas and your partner's reactions as the basis for a descriptive paragraph on your first visit to a special place.

4. Was there a period in your life when you felt that a brother, sister, cousin, or other close relative was a nuisance? If so, write a paragraph describing how that person looked and acted in those days. You can also describe how you reacted.

5. In a paragraph, describe a neighborhood. It must be a neighborhood you know well: one you used to live in or one you live in now. You can describe the buildings, streets, people, traffic, trees and plants, and so forth. Just be sure to be specific, so that this neighborhood becomes not just any area but one with a distinct identity or a special atmosphere.

CHAPTER 26

Writing an Illustration Paragraph

WHAT IS ILLUSTRATION?

Illustration uses specific examples to support a general point. In your writing, you often use illustration since you frequently want to explain a point with a specific example.

HINTS FOR WRITING AN ILLUSTRATION PARAGRAPH

Knowing What Is Specific and What Is General

A *general* statement is a broad point. The following statements are general:

College students are constantly short of money.
Bronson Avenue is in a bad neighborhood.
Pictures can brighten up a room.

You can support a general statement with specific examples:

general statement:	College students are constantly short of money.
specific examples:	They need gas money, bus or subway fare. They need cash for snacks, lunch, or dinner.
general statement:	Bronson Avenue is in a bad neighborhood.
specific examples:	It has burned out and abandoned buildings. There are drug dealers on the corners.
general statement:	Pictures can brighten up a room.
specific examples:	I love to look at my grandmother's family photos which cover a whole living room wall. My dentist has framed cartoons on the walls of his waiting room.

When you write an illustration paragraph, be careful to support a general statement with specific examples, not with more general statements:

not this: general statement:	Essay tests are difficult.
~~**more general statements:**~~	~~I find essay tests to be hard.~~
	~~Essay tests present the most~~
	~~challenges.~~
but this: general statement:	Essay tests are difficult.
specific examples:	They test organizational skills.
	They demand a true understanding
	of the subject.

If you remember to illustrate a broad statement with specific examples, you will have the key to this kind of paragraph.

Exercise 1

Practice

Recognizing Broad Statements

Each list below contains one broad statement and three specific examples. Underline the broad statement.

1. On Thanksgiving, there are football games on many television channels.
   If the weather is good, my cousins and I play hockey.
   <u>Thanksgiving means sports to me.</u>
   Everyone talks sports as we eat our turkey.

2. Puppies like to chew on shoes, furniture, and carpets.
   <u>Puppies require a great deal of patience.</u>
   Young dogs have accidents on the carpet.
   Jumping on human beings is a puppy's favorite activity.

3. <u>People in this town are friendly to newcomers.</u>
   The mail carrier said "hi" to me when I picked up my mail.
   My neighbor offered to help carry my furniture into my new apartment.
   Another neighbor came over and introduced himself.

4. I called the cable company and was put on hold for ten minutes.
   <u>Trying to get information from my cable television company was a frustrating experience.</u>
   The person at the end of the line told me she would not answer a question about my bill.
   She said I had to come to the cable office in person, even though the office is open only from 9:00 a.m. to 5:00 p.m., when I work.

5. My sister spends sixty percent of her salary on child care.
   I pay less, but my child's babysitter is an untrained teen.
   There is a waiting list for subsidized preschool care.
   <u>Parents are desperate for quality, affordable child care.</u>

Exercise 2

Practice

Distinguishing the General Statement from the Specific Example

Each general statement is supported by three items of support. Two of these items are specific examples; one is too general to be effective. Underline the one that is too general.

TEACHING TIP:

Ask students to give
examples of some typical
conversational greetings
or questions (e.g.,
"How's it going?" or
"How're you doing?" or
"What's up?") Put some
of their responses on the
board and circle all the
vague terms. Students
will see that since we
use general statements
so often, we think that
we're being specific.

1. general statement: More people than ever are experimenting with hair color.

support: Twelve-year-old boys are frosting the tips of their short hair.
Cellophane-red color streaks through brown or black hair.
<u>You would never see so much hair dye twenty years ago.</u>

2. general statement: We should think of what our bodies can do, not what they look like.

support: <u>The appearance of our bodies isn't as important as the way our bodies function.</u>
A person may not have a perfectly shaped body but may be in great physical condition.
As we age, we may look older than we would like, but we can stay as fit as many young people.

3. general statement: A night at the movies is an expensive one.

support: A movie ticket can cost ten dollars or more.
<u>Going to the movies isn't cheap.</u>
Popcorn and a coke can cost as much as a movie ticket.

4. general statement: Summer and certain foods seem to go together.

support: Ice cream tastes better in the summer.
<u>People associate summer with specific foods.</u>
Hot dogs on the grill are a summer treat.

5. general statement: I rarely use stamps these days.

support: I write my friends by e-mail.
<u>I don't buy stamps very often.</u>
I pay my bills on-line.

Exercise 3

👥 *Collaborate*

Adding Specific Examples to a General Statement

With a partner or group, add four specific examples to each general statement below.

1. general statement: High school cafeteria food can be awful.

Answers Will Vary.

Possible answers shown
at right.

examples: The salads are wilted and brown.

The bread is stale.

The burgers are made from mystery meat.

The pudding comes out of a can.

2. general statement: Children are used in many television food advertisements.

examples: Children are seen eating breakfast cereal.

They love a certain brand of pudding.

They are often munching cookies.

In the summer, children are in ice cream ads.

3. **general statement:**   People perform many activities while they drive a car.

   examples: Many talk on cell phones.

   Some drink coffee.

   Some smoke cigarettes.

   Some brush their hair.

4. **general statement:**   Today's drugstores sell more than medicine and toothpaste.

   examples: They sell makeup.

   Many sell milk, soft drinks, and snacks.

   They sell videos.

   They sell toys.

WRITING THE ILLUSTRATION PARAGRAPH IN STEPS

Thought Lines **Gathering Ideas: Illustration**

Suppose your instructor asks you to write a paragraph about some aspect of **cars.** You can begin by listing ideas about your subject to find a focus for your paragraph. Your first list might look like the following.

Listing Ideas About Cars

cars in my neighborhood

my brother's car

car prices

drag racing

cars in the college parking lot

parking at college

car insurance

This list includes many specific ideas about cars. You could write a paragraph about one item or about two related items on the list. Reviewing the list, you decide to write your paragraph on cars in the college parking lot.

Adding Details to an Idea

Now that you have a narrowed topic for your paragraph, you decide to write a list of ideas about cars in the college parking lot:

Cars in the College Parking Lot: Some Ideas

vans

cars with strollers and baby seats

beat-up old cars, some with no bumpers

few new sports cars, gifts from rich parents

some SUVs

older people's cars, Volvos and Cadillacs

racing cars, modified, brightly striped

elaborate sound systems

bumper stickers

some stickers have a message

some brag

Creating a Topic Sentence

If you examine this list and look for *related ideas*, you can create a topic sentence. The ideas on the list include (1) details about the kind of cars, (2) details about what is inside the cars, and (3) details about the bumper stickers. Not all the details fit into these categories, but many do.

Grouping the related ideas into the three categories can help you focus your ideas into a topic sentence.

Kinds of Cars

beat-up old cars, some with no bumpers
vans
few new sports cars, gifts from rich parents
some SUVs
older people's cars, Volvos and Cadillacs
racing cars, modified, brightly striped

Inside the Cars

elaborate sound systems
strollers and baby seats

Bumper Stickers

bumper stickers
some stickers have a message
some brag

You can summarize these related ideas in a topic sentence:

Cars in the college parking lot reflect the diversity of people at the school.

Check the sentence against your details. Does it cover the topic? Yes. The topic sentence begins with "Cars in the college parking lot." Does it make some point about the cars? Yes. It says the cars "reflect the diversity of people at the school."

Since your details are about old and new cars, what is inside the cars and on the bumper stickers, you have many details about differences in cars and some hints about the people who drive them.

 Exercise 4

Practice

Finding Specific Ideas in Lists

Following are two lists. Each is a response to a broad topic. Read each list, and then underline any words that could become a more specific topic for a paragraph.

Topic: business

big business success	computers in business
running a business	<u>business law class</u>
working for yourself	business ethics
the stock market	<u>collecting unemployment</u>
<u>the dress code at a bank</u>	<u>writing a good resume</u>

Topic: entertainment

<u>free concerts in our town</u>	entertainment around the world
<u>children's video games</u>	<u>cable sports channels</u>
<u>call-in radio programs</u>	blockbuster movies in history
<u>local night spots</u>	fads in entertainment
<u>reality television</u>	actors and actresses

Exercise 5

Practice

Grouping Related Ideas in Lists of Details

Following are lists of details. In each list, circle the items that seem to fit into one group; then underline the items that seem to fit into a second group. Some items may not fit into either group.

1. **topic:** having a large family
   <u>special warmth</u>   (great expense)
   (being forced to share)   companionship always available
   sense of belonging   (lack of privacy)
   (little individual attention)   big family dinners
   <u>ready-made support system</u>   (rivalries among the children)

2. **topic:** a true friend
   won't betray a confidence   (laughs at your jokes)
   (listens to your worries)   hard to find
   never gossips about you   (gives honest advice)
   (respects your dreams)   (celebrates your success)
   like a family member   <u>doesn't hold a grudge</u>

3. **topic:** ways to exercise
   hire a personal trainer   (walk in your neighborhood)
   join a private health club   (jog on the beach)
   (run in a park)   buy expensive equipment
   burning calories   (ride a bike to work)
   (play basketball with friends) (take the stairs, not elevators)

4. **topic:** fighting the flu
   wads of tissue   chicken soup
   (aspirin)   (antibiotics)
   tea with lemon and honey   high fever and body aches
   (cough medicine)   orange juice
   (decongestant tablets)   (cough drops)

Exercise 6

Practice

Writing Topic Sentences for Lists of Details

Following are lists of details that have no topic sentences. Write an appropriate topic sentence for each one.

1. **topic sentence:** *The car for sale is not a bad buy, but it has some problems.*

    details: The car for sale has a perfectly clean engine.
It also has low mileage.
The interior is well-maintained.
It has air bags.
The tires have very little tread left.
There is a dent in the driver's side door.
The car radio is broken.
The car needs a new battery.

2. **topic sentence:** *Carla's mother seems determined to destroy her daughter's confidence.*

    details: Carla's mother is always pushing her to go on a diet.
She is also critical of Carla's intelligence and ability.
She says Carla shouldn't go to college because it will be wasted on her.
Her mother thinks Carla should just get a job and bring home some money.
Her mother has never liked Carla's friends.
And when Carla has a boyfriend, her mother manages to find something wrong with him.
She makes jokes about Carla's bad choice in men.

3. **topic sentence:** *My Uncle Tomás is every child's dream of an uncle.*

    details: When I was suspended from kindergarten, my Uncle Tomas brought me a gift to console me.
He said I was just an independent child.
When Uncle Tomás was my babysitter, he let me stay up late and watch scary movies on television.
He also let me eat ice cream just before dinner.
He said it was full of calcium and other nutrients.
He took me to my first professional baseball game.
When I was a teenager, he took me to big empty parking lots and taught me how to drive.
At my high school graduation, he was in the front row, cheering for me.

4. **topic sentence:** *My family is committed to giving something back to the community.*

    details: Each week, my parents go to the hospital to hold and comfort newborn babies with AIDS.
My brother is a volunteer with Habitat for Humanity.
I volunteer at the Boys and Girls Club, teaching the elementary school students how to use computers.
My grandfather is part of a motorcycle club that rides together to aid Toys for Tots, a charity for children.
Even my sister's dog is a trained therapy dog.
My sister and her dog Sky visit nursing homes, and Sky lets people pet and cuddle him.

Choosing the Better Topic Sentence

Following are lists of details. Each list has two possible topic sentences. Underline the better topic sentence for each list.

1. possible topic sentences:
   a. All kinds of flowers appear almost everywhere in our lives.
   b. <u>The important times in our lives, happy and sad, are marked with flowers.</u>

   details: A lover sends a single rose to hint at love.
   Every bride carries a bouquet.
   Wreaths are found at many funerals.
   People also leave flowers on the graves of loved ones.
   Millions of flowers are sold on Valentine's Day.
   Even more appear on Mother's Day.
   Proms involve corsages and a flower for each man's button hole.

2. Possible topic sentences:
   a. <u>Humor can hide a person's dark side.</u>
   b. The ability to make people laugh is a true talent.

   details: Sean was always the joker in our group.
   He was lively, cheerful, and quick with a witty comment.
   He could make me break into laughter during the most serious movie.
   His smart remarks caused me to laugh in many classes.
   When I got scolded for laughing, Sean would sit, looking very serious.
   His expression made me laugh even more.
   Sean was always the center of fun and good times.
   Then one day I saw him sitting alone in the college cafeteria.
   He didn't know anyone was looking at him.
   His expression was sad and lonely.

3. possible topic sentence:
   a. It's impossible to know what a person will like for a gift.
   b. <u>A perfect gift starts with thoughtfulness, not money.</u>

   details: Mrs. Garcia knew that her sons would give her gifts on her birthday.
   She wasn't surprised when her older son, Mike, handed her a beautifully wrapped box of expensive chocolates.
   Covered in pale blue velvet ribbon and pink silk flowers, the box was almost too pretty to open.
   When she opened it, she saw two layers of the finest chocolates: dark chocolate, milk chocolate, and white chocolate.
   She knew that two pounds of this chocolate must have cost Mike at least thirty dollars.
   Then Danny, her younger son, gave her a small box, badly wrapped in wrinkled tissue paper.
   Inside the box was a cheap plastic frame with a faded snapshot in it.
   It was an old photo of Mrs. Garcia as a beautiful young girl.

The chocolates were the same gift that Mike gave her every
year on her birthday and on Mother's Day.
They were available in every luxury mall.
The picture was one Mrs. Garcia had stashed away years ago
and forgotten.
It became her favorite gift.

Outlines Devising a Plan: Illustration

When you plan your outline, keep your topic sentence in mind:

> Cars in the college parking lot reflect the diversity of people at
> the school.

Remember the three categories of related details:

> Kinds of Cars
> Inside the Cars
> Bumper Stickers

These three categories can give you an idea for how to organize the outline.
Below is an outline for a paragraph on cars in the college parking lot.
As you read the outline, you will notice that details about the insides of the
cars and about bumper stickers have been added. Adding details can be
part of the outlining stage.

Info BOX

An Outline on Cars in the College Parking Lot

topic sentence:	Cars in the college parking lot reflect the diversity of people at the school.
details: kinds of cars	There are beat-up old cars. Some have no bumpers. There are vans. There are a few new sports cars. Maybe these are gifts from rich parents. There are some SUVs. Older people's cars, like Volvos and Cadillacs, are there. There are a few racing cars, modified and brightly striped.
inside the cars	Some cars have elaborate sound systems. Some have a baby stroller or baby seat. Some have empty paper cups and food wrappers.
bumper stickers	Some have stickers for a club. There are stickers with a message. There are stickers that brag.

As you can see, the outline used the details from the list and included other
details. You can add more details, combine some details to eliminate repetition, or even eliminate some details as you draft your essay.

Exercise 8

Collaborate

Adding Details to an Outline

Below are three partial outlines. Each has a topic sentence and some details. Working with a partner or group, add more details that support the topic sentence.

Answers Will Vary.

Possible answers shown at right.

1. **topic sentence:** There are many foods that we eat without knives, forks, or spoons.
   details:
   a. Fruits like apples and grapes are finger foods.
   b. You don't need a knife and fork for doughnuts.
   c. Many people eat fried chicken without utensils.
   d. Hot dogs on buns are always finger foods.
   e. Hamburgers are hand-held foods.
   f. Popcorn is never eaten with a spoon.
   g. Potato chips are eaten right out of the bag.

2. **topic sentence:** People watch football on television for a number of reasons.
   details:
   a. They are cheering for their favorite team.
   b. It is a good way to relieve stress.
   c. They like the sports commentators.
   d. They have placed a bet on the game.
   e. Everyone else in the house is watching.
   f. They like the cheerleaders.
   g. They can talk about the game at work.

3. **topic sentence:** Many college students have the same complaints.
   details:
   a. The cafeteria food is terrible.
   b. They can't get into the classes they want.
   c. There are not enough holidays.
   d. There are not enough close parking spaces.
   e. The registration process is disorganized.
   f. Financial aid doesn't arrive on time.
   g. Tuition is too expensive.

Exercise 9

Practice

Eliminating Details That Are Repetitive

In the following outlines, some details use different words to repeat an example given earlier in the list. Cross out the repetitive details.

1. **topic sentence:** The cheapest product is not always the best buy.
   details: I bought cheap cellophane tape, but it never held anything together.
   Cheap dishwashing liquid is weaker than the more expensive, concentrated kind.
   My cheap umbrella lasted through one rainy day.
   ~~Expensive cellophane tape is more effective than the low-priced brand.~~
   Big bags of bargain cookies can taste dry and stale.
   I bought a pack of sale-priced ballpoint pens and they leaked ink all over my clothes.
   I was proud of my $2.99 shirt, but it fell apart after one washing.
   ~~What good is a bargain umbrella that turns inside out when the weather turns breezy?~~

2. topic sentence: My father has more courage than anyone else I know.

details: He fought against cancer and survived.

He never complained about chemotherapy.

He calmed his family's fears before his surgery.

When he was in the military, he was a Navy Seal.

He endured rigorous training under miserable and dangerous conditions.

He lost his job at age forty-five.

He had the courage to go back to school and train for a new career.

He was terrified of computers.

Now he is learning to use technology as part of his training.

~~My father faced a life-and-death cancer operation.~~

~~He survived some of the U.S. Navy's most challenging physical tests to become a Navy Seal.~~

3. topic sentence: The hair products industry has something for everyone.

details: You can lighten your hair.

You can darken it.

You can straighten your hair.

You can curl it.

You can mousse it.

You can thicken it.

You can make it shine.

~~You can turn it a shade lighter.~~

You can condition it.

~~You can go from blonde to brunette.~~

You can give it an oil treatment.

Rough Lines **Drafting and Revising: Illustration**

Review the outline on cars in the college parking lot on page 392. You can create a first draft of this outline in the form of a paragraph. At this point, you can combine some of the short, choppy sentences of the outline, add details, and add transitions to link your ideas. You can revise your draft using the following checklist.

> **✓ Checklist**
>
> **A Checklist for Revising an Illustration Paragraph**
>
> ✔ Should some of the sentences be combined?
>
> ✔ Do I need more or better transitions?
>
> ✔ Should I add more details to support my points?
>
> ✔ Should some of the details be more specific?

Transitions

As you revise your illustration paragraph, you may find places where one idea ends and another begins abruptly. This problem occurs when you forget to add **transitions,** the words, phrases, or sentences that connect one idea to another. When you write an illustration paragraph, you will need some transitions that link one example to another and other transitions to link one section of your paragraph to another section. Here are some transitions you may want to use in writing an illustration paragraph.

Transitions for an Illustration Paragraph

another example	one instance
a second example	other examples
for example	other kinds
for instance	such as
in addition	the first instance
in the case of	another instance
like	to illustrate
one example	

Look carefully at the following draft of the paragraph on cars in the college parking lot, and note how it combines sentences, adds details, and uses transitions to transform the outline into a clear and developed paragraph.

An Outline for a Paragraph on Cars in the College Parking Lot

topic sentence	Cars in the college parking lot reflect the diversity
sentences combined	of people at the school. <u>There are beat-up old cars,</u>
details added	<u>some with no bumpers, near several vans. There are</u>
sentences combined	<u>one or two new sports cars,</u> <u>like BMWs; they might</u>
transition added	<u>belong to the few lucky students with rich and gener-</u>
details added	<u>ous parents.</u> Other kinds include SUVs and older peo-
transition added	ple's cars <u>such as</u> Volvos and Cadillacs. <u>In addition,</u>
transition added	the parking lot holds a few racing cars, modified and
transition added	brightly striped. Some cars have elaborate sound
details added	systems <u>for music lovers. Others must belong to par-</u>
details added	<u>ents</u> because they have a baby stroller or baby seat
	inside. Many are filled with empty paper cups or food
details added	wrappers <u>since busy students have to eat on the run</u>.
transition, details	Many cars also have bumper stickers; some are for
added	clubs, <u>like Morristown Athletic Club,</u> while others
transition, details	have a message <u>such as "Give Blood: Save Lives"</u> or
added	"Animals: It's Their World, Too." Some stickers brag
details added	<u>that the driver is the "Proud Parent of an Honor</u>
details added	<u>Student at Grove Elementary School" or is "Single—</u>
	<u>and Loving It."</u>

Revising a Draft by Combining Sentences

Practice

The paragraph following has many short, choppy sentences, which are underlined. Wherever you see two or more underlined sentences clustered next to each other, combine them into one clear, smooth sentence. Write your revised version of the paragraph in the spaces above the lines.

My aunt's back yard is ideal for someone like me. <u>First of all, it has plenty of</u> ~~First of all, it has plenty~~

~~of shade, which is essential on hot summer days in our state~~
<u>shade. Shade is essential on hot summer days in our state.</u> Three large, leafy trees

are clustered near the house. <u>They block the rays of the afternoon sun. They</u> ~~Blocking the rays of the afternoon sun, they lower the~~

~~temperature about ten degrees~~
<u>lower the temperature about ten degrees.</u> Another pleasant feature of this yard is

the patio. <u>I love to sit outside. I like to read there. I also like to sleep. In addition,</u> ~~I love to sit outside and read, sleep, or listen to music there~~

<u>I love to listen to music.</u> My aunt's large, paved patio is the perfect place to relax.

Finally, this back yard appeals to my lazy nature. <u>Most of the yard is filled by the</u> ~~Since most of the yard is filled~~

~~by the patio, trees, and plants, it has barely any lawn~~
<u>patio. It is also filled by trees and plants. It has barely any lawn.</u> This is my ideal

yard because there is hardly any lawn to mow.

Exercise 11

Practice

Revising a Draft by Adding Transitions

The paragraph below needs some transitions. Add appropriate transitions (words or phrases) to the blanks.

<u>Answers Will Vary.</u>

Possible answers shown at right.

Sometimes I feel that I have too many choices and that they only confuse me.

_____*In one instance,*_____ my brother wanted a sweater for his birthday. When I

asked him what color he wanted, he said blue. At my local mall, I found sweaters

in many shades of blue. _____*For example,*_____ there were navy blue, powder blue,

royal blue, turquoise blue, and gray blue sweaters. *In another instance*, my

mother asked me to pick up some milk at the store. But did she want skimmed

milk, low fat milk, acidophilus milk, chocolate milk, or whole milk? I didn't

know what to buy. _____*Another example*_____ of too much variety occurred when

I had to pick a long-distance calling plan. I was trapped in a maze of plans

_____*such as*_____ Cingular, Sprint, MCI, and AT&T. I know I should value my

freedom to choose, but all these choices are cutting into my free time.

Exercise 12

 *Collaborate*

Adding Details to a Draft

The paragraph below lacks the kind of details that would make it more interesting. Working with a partner or group, add details to the blank spaces provided. When you are finished, read the revised paragraph to the class.

Different occasions are associated with different snacks. For example, people

in a movie theater tend to snack on _____,

_____, and _____. Baseball games call for

food like _____ and _____, while snow ski-

ing or ice hockey makes people crave _____ or

_____. When parents have their friends over, they are likely to

enjoy snacks such as _____ and _____

before dinner. In contrast, when teens stay up late and get hungry, they are likely

to go out for _____. On a long car trip, families pack snacks

like _____. Between classes, students rely on

_____, _____, or _____ for

energy. Snacks have become our old friends: there whenever and wherever we

need them.

Final Lines Proofreading and Polishing: Illustration

As you prepare the final version of your illustration paragraph, make any changes in word choice or transitions that can refine your writing. Following is the final version of the paragraph on cars in the college parking lot. As you read it, you will notice a few more changes:

- Some details have been added
- Several long transitions have been added. The paragraph needed to signal the shift in subject from the kinds of cars to what was inside the cars; then it needed to signal the shift from the interior of the cars to bumper stickers.
- A concluding sentence has been added to reinforce the point of the topic sentence: A diverse college population is reflected in its cars.

A Final Version of a Paragraph on Cars in the College Parking Lot
(Changes from the draft are underlined.)

Cars in the college parking lot reflect the diversity of people at the school. There are beat-up old cars, some with no bumpers, near several vans. There are one or two new sports cars, like BMWs; they might belong to the few lucky students with rich and generous parents. Other kinds include SUVs and older people's cars such as Volvos and Cadillacs. In addition, the parking lot holds a few racing cars, modified and brightly striped. <u>What is inside the cars is as revealing as the cars themselves</u>. Some cars have elaborate sound systems for music lovers <u>who can't drive without pounding sound</u>. Others must belong to parents because they have a baby stroller or baby seat inside. Many are filled with empty paper cups or food wrappers, since busy students have to eat on the run. <u>Bumper stickers also tell a story</u>. Many cars have stickers; some are for clubs, like Morristown Athletic Club, while others have a message, such as "Give Blood: Save Lives" or "Animals: It's Their World, Too." Some stickers brag that the driver is the "Proud Parent of an Honor Student at Grove Elementary School" or is "Single—and Loving It." <u>A walk through the parking lot hints that this college is a place for all ages, backgrounds, and interests.</u>

Before you prepare the final version of your illustration paragraph, check your latest draft for errors in spelling or punctuation and for any errors made in typing and copying.

Exercise 13   **Proofreading to Prepare the Final Version**

Practice

Following are two illustration paragraphs with the kind of errors it is easy to overlook when you prepare the final version of an assignment. Correct the errors by writing above the lines. There are fourteen errors in the first paragraph and thirteen errors in the second paragraph.

1. Ever since my elementry *(elementary)* school years, Iv'e *(I've)* known I wanted to be a law enforcement. When I was seven I seen *(in)* *(,)* *(saw)* a sherriff's *(sheriff's)* deputy rescue the lady next door, whose husband had been beating her. After I saw the look on her face when the officer help *(helped)* her out of the house, I knew I wanted to help people, too. Later, I played softball in the Police athletic *(Athletic)* League, and I make friend's *(made friends)* with one officer. He kep *(kept)* his eye on me for years and encouraged me to stay in school. In High School *(high school)*, I did volunteer work for a group that helps crime victims *(,)* Today, I am a criminal justice major and look forward to protecting and serving my community.

2. There is no rite *(right)* age to marry, but there is the rite *(right)* kind of committment *(commitment)*. My cousin Jim, for example, marryed *(married)* when he and his bride were nineteen. Every one *(Everyone)* told them to wait a few years and predicted the marriage would never last, but they have been happilly *(happily)* married for fifteen years. They had times when they were so broke they were nearly homeless. They also lost a child in a terrible accident *(,)* but they fought to stay close and to support each other. In another instant *(instance)*, my aunt married for the first time at thirty-five. Her husband was fourty *(forty)*, financially successful, and active in the community. Their marriage lasted ten month's *(months)*. They had all ready *(already)* been quarreling and criticizing each other before the wedding and had

separated twice before they divorced. People can be immature at

fifty or sixty, or they can be grown up in there teens. Its their ability

their   *It's*

to make a mature commitment that counts.

Lines of Detail: A Walk-Through Assignment

Your assignment is to write an illustration paragraph about change.

Step 1: List all your ideas on this broad topic for ten minutes. You can list ideas on any aspect of change such as a change of attitude, changing schools, a new job, a change in a daily routine, and so forth.

Step 2: Review your list. Underline any parts that are specific ideas related to the broad topic, change.

Step 3: List all the specific ideas. Choose one as the narrowed topic for your paragraph.

Step 4: Add related ideas to your chosen, narrowed topic. Do this by reviewing your list for related ideas and by brainstorming for more related ideas.

Step 5: List all your related ideas and review their connection to your narrowed topic. Then write a topic sentence and an outline for your paragraph.

Step 6: Write a first draft of your paragraph.

Step 7: Revise your first draft. Be sure it has enough details and clear transitions. Combine any choppy sentences.

A Peer Review Form for students' exchange of drafts is on page 402.

Step 8: After a final check for any errors in punctuation, spelling, and word choice, prepare the final version of the paragraph.

Writing Your Own Illustration Paragraph

When you write on any of these topics, be sure to work through the stages of the writing process in preparing your paragraph.

1. Select one of the topics listed. Narrow the topic and write a paragraph on it. If you choose the topic of money, for example, you might narrow it by writing about credit cards for college students or about paying bills.

basketball	money	jobs
driving	exercise	sleep
the Internet	movies	apartments
photographs	mail	rumors
crime	weather	fashion
books	celebrities	boxing
science fiction	lies	compliments

2. Following are topic sentences. Select one and use it to write a paragraph.

The best advice I've ever been given is _____.

There are several parts of my daily routine that I dislike.

There are several parts of my daily routine that I enjoy.

The most hurtful word in the language is _____.

The most beautiful word in the language is _____.

An empty room makes me think of _____.

Three teams represent the best in _____ (baseball, football, basketball, hockey, soccer—choose one.)

Several people illustrate what it means to be a hero.

3. If you were asked to give the motto you live by, what would it be? For example, do you live by the words, "Treat other people the way you would like to be treated" or "Always do your best"? Write a paragraph that illustrates why you believe that your motto is a good one. You can begin with a topic sentence like

I live by the motto, "_____" because it has been

proven true many times.

In the paragraph, give examples of times when this motto has been shown to be true.

4. Look carefully at photos A, B, and C. Use them as a way to begin thinking about a paragraph with this topic sentence: Popular pets are not just cats and dogs. When you write the paragraph, your examples do not have to come from the photographs, but can come from your own experiences and observations.

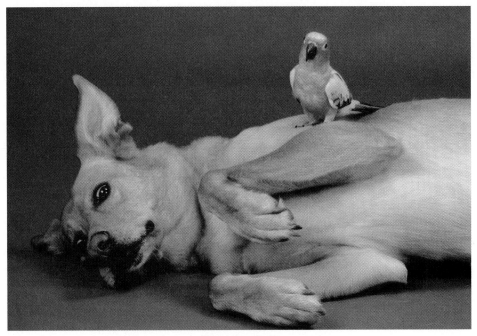

Photograph A

Photograph B

Photograph C

Photograph D

5. Look carefully at photograph D. Notice the students and their styles of clothing. You do not have to describe the students in the photo; instead use the photo to think about this topic: Styles in student clothing change quickly. Support it with your own examples.

Name: _____ **Section:** _____

PEER REVIEW FORM FOR AN ILLUSTRATION PARAGRAPH

After you have written a draft version of your paragraph, let a writing partner read it. When your partner has completed the following form, discuss the responses. Then repeat the same process for your partner's paragraph.

The topic sentence of the paragraph is _____

_____

_____

The details that I liked best begin with the words _____

_____

The paragraph has _____ (enough, too many, too few) details to support the topic sentence.

A particularly good part of the paragraph begins with the words _____

_____

I have questions about _____

_____

_____

Other comments on the paragraph: _____

_____

_____

_____

_____

_____

_____

_____

_____

_____

_____

_____

_____

Reviewer's Name: _____

WRITING FROM READING: Illustration

A Different Mirror

Ronald Takaki

Ronald Takaki, born in Honolulu, is a historian known for his books on history, race, and multiculturalism. The following excerpt is from his book A Different Mirror. In the book, Takaki argues that in studying America's history, we must study all the groups who have created America, so that we "see ourselves in a different mirror." This excerpt focuses on specific details that support the idea of America's diversity.

Words You May Need to Know

ethnic diversity: variety of people, races, and cultures
discerned: recognized, perceived
Ellis Island: an island off the shore of New York City, where many immigrants first landed in America
Angel Island: an island off San Francisco

Chinatown, Harlem, South Boston, the Lower East Side (of New York City): places associated with a variety of ethnic groups and races
derived: originated from
Forty-Niners: people who joined the Gold Rush of 1849, when gold was discovered in California
Vaqueros: cowboys

The signs of America's ethnic diversity can be discerned across the continent: Ellis Island, Angel Island, Chinatown, Harlem, South Boston, the Lower East Side, places with Spanish names like Los Angeles and San Antonio or Indian names like Massachusetts and Iowa. Much of what is familiar in America's cultural landscape actually has ethnic origins. The Bing cherry was developed by an early Chinese immigrant named Ah Bing. American Indians were cultivating corn, tomatoes, and tobacco long before the arrival of Columbus. The term *okay* was derived from the Choctaw word *oke*, meaning "it is so." There is evidence indicating that the name *Yankee* came from Indian terms for the English—from *eankke* in Cherokee and *Yankwis* in Delaware. Jazz and blues as well as rock and roll have African-American origins. The "Forty-Niners" of the Gold Rush learned mining techniques from the Mexicans; American cowboys acquired herding skills from Mexican *vaqueros* and adopted their range terms—such as *lariat* from *la reata*, *lasso* from *lazo*, and *stampede* from *estampida*. Songs like "God Bless America," "Easter Parade," and "White Christmas" were written by a Russian-Jewish immigrant named Israel Baline, more popularly known as Irving Berlin.

Recognizing Takaki's Use of Specific Details

To illustrate his point about the diversity of America's history, Ronald Takaki gives many specific examples of the sources of our language and heritage. Fill in those examples below.

1. What fruit did a Chinese immigrant develop?

   the Bing cherry

2. Where did the term *Yankee* come from?

   Indian term for the English

3. Who taught the "Forty-Niners" mining techniques?

   the Mexicans

4. What kinds of music have African-American origins?

   jazz, blues, and rock and roll

5. Who first grew corn, tomatoes, and tobacco?

   American Indians

6. What American word grew out of the Choctaw word *oke*?

   okay

7. What was the background of the person who wrote "God Bless America"?

   Israel Baline (Irving Berlin) was a Russian-Jewish immigrant.

8. Name one American state that has an Indian name.

   Massachusetts or Iowa

9. Name one American city that has a Spanish name.

   Los Angeles or San Antonio

10. What American word came from the Mexican word *estampida*?

    stampede

WRITING FROM READING: A Different Mirror

When you write on any of the following topics, be sure to work through the stages of the writing process in preparing your paragraph.

1. Interview three people in your class. Ask each to tell you about his or her family background. Before you begin, prepare a list of at least six questions, such as "Were you born in this country?" or "Do you know how long your family has been in America?" Use the answers as the basis for a paragraph on diversity in your classroom. You may discover a wide range of backgrounds or a similarity of backgrounds. In either case, you have details for a paragraph about your classmates and their origins.

2. Write a paragraph about the many foods that are considered American but that really originated in another country or culture. Give specific examples.

3. Takaki gives examples of words Americans use, such as *Yankee*, that originated in another language. Write a paragraph on words or expressions that Americans use that originated in another language. (For example, many Americans who are not Spanish use the word *adios*.)

4. Write a paragraph on the place names in America that came from one or more other languages. You might write about only Spanish place names, for example, and group them into states and cities. Or you could write about names from several languages and group them into Spanish names, Indian names, French names, and so forth.

5. Write a paragraph about what one ethnic group has contributed to American life and culture. You can use specific examples of contributions to language, music, dance, food, clothing, customs, and so forth.

Brotherhood

Clifton L. Taulbert

An internationally acclaimed speaker and best-selling writer, Clifton L. Taulbert is famous for his memoirs about growing up in the segregated South. One of his works, <u>When We Were Colored</u>, became the basis for the critically acclaimed movie <u>Once Upon a Time When We Were Colored.</u> In this excerpt from another of his works, <u>Eight Habits of the Heart</u>, Taulbert writes about his childhood in Glen Allan, Mississippi, when "the social structure between whites and blacks seemed to be carved in stone." In spite of this divide, he says, there were still people who crossed the divide and practiced brotherhood.

Words You May Need to Know (corresponding paragraph numbers are in parentheses)

stir (2): excitement, fuss
evoked (2): suggested, called up
charge (3): responsibility, duty
slights (4): insults, poor treatment
apt (4): likely
admonished (5): cautioned
shoo (6): scare away, or request or force a person to leave
ungodly (7): wicked, sinful
prohibited (7): forbidden
Old Testament (7): the first of the two main divisions of the

Christian Bible, regarded as the complete Bible of the Jews
dispelled (7): driven off, scattered
a kosher cook (7): one who follows the Jewish dietary laws
speak ill of (9): criticize
mores (10): the fundamental moral views of a group
persistence (11): perseverence
embittered (12): hardened

---

1   In the 1950's the social structure between whites and blacks seemed to be carved in stone. Everyone knew what to expect, and nearly everyone practiced the rules, which had been passed down for generations. Nevertheless, there were still those who reached beyond their comfortable traditional relationships and practiced brotherhood.

2   I especially recall the stir in Glen Allan when Mr. Freid, a Jewish merchant, hired Miss Maxey, a colored schoolteacher, to work part-time in his store serving both whites and coloreds. Many people now might think, So what? But at the time this was far from an acceptable practice. Mr. Freid's store was big, with large plate-glass windows and huge ceiling fans that evoked the feel of New Orleans. It was our general department store. Hardware and dry goods, nails and dresses, fertilizer and underwear all were there, strategically placed in separate sections. The floor was hardwood, spotless, and seemed to have been oiled daily. But there was only one long counter with one cash register to serve the entire store. We all had to meet at the same spot to pay. And as long as I could remember, only Mr. Freid or his mother had worked the cash register.

3   Hiring Miss Maxey stirred things up. This just wasn't done, giving a colored person a job up front, with the charge to handle money and wait on both coloreds and whites. It was a small break in our rigid social structure, but it gave some members of the white community offense. The colored community was pleased because we knew Miss Maxey to be as smart as anyone. Yet it was hard for many whites to acknowledge that, for their belief in her inferiority was based on lies that they had come to cherish as fact.

4   Still, Miss Maxey's hiring wasn't the first of its kind in Glen Allan. Years earlier Mr. Youngblood, another Jewish merchant who had owned a department store in town, had hired Miss Hester Rucker to help him out, when hiring black people into a job reserved for whites was never done. But then the Jews in our community had suffered their own slights, and thus were apt to come down on the side of injustice when they had their chance. The Freids, like Mr. Youngblood, practiced brotherhood to the extent they could within our system. Miss Maxey worked there for only a short time, but as long as she did, it was she who rang up the penny nails and the materials for farming.

5   I also recall the relationship that existed between the senior Mrs. Freid and her colored cook, the same Miss Hester who had worked in Mr. Youngblood's store when she was young. Glen Allan was a town of maids, my mother being one of them, and they all worked hard. Miss Hester, however, displayed a special attitude toward her job. I remember the way she held up her head and the respectful way that she and Mrs. Freid spoke to each other. Not only did Miss Hester hold her head high, but she also admonished the colored kids never to look down, telling us, "There's no need to count the rocks!"

6   During pecan season Mrs. Freid would graciously let us kids pick as many pecans as we wished from her yard. While others would shoo us away, she never did. She always acknowledged our presence and spoke to us, and Miss Hester, her cook, never seemed nervous or bothered that we were there. One day, after spending all morning picking up as many pecans as I could, I was very hungry. Miss Hester, though, seemed to know when my stomach began tightening and talking, which happened as the aroma of her good cooking invaded the yard. The more intense the smell, the closer to the kitchen I picked. Finally Miss Hester came to the door and asked if I was hungry. Of course I was, but I should have said no, as I had been taught. Yet the equality that existed in that house allowed me to say yes. Because Miss Hester felt comfortable asking me in to eat, I had no problem about dropping my task and walking in.

7   The Jewish families were still somewhat of an oddity in our small community, and we had been taught to look upon their eating habits as somehow mysterious and ungodly. Of course, we were the ones who ate every piece of pork available, which was clearly prohibited by the Old Testament that the entire community embraced. However, rumors of ungodliness were

soon dispelled by Miss Hester, who had learned to be a kosher cook—producing stuffed cabbage rolls, a meat dish called kreplach, potato knishes, and other foods that gave off exotic smells.

8   Often she gave me a sandwich of spicy salami spread with brown mustard, a taste I still recall. She also wanted me to eat matzoh ball soup, but I found the pale, spongy matzoh ball in its pool of broth unexciting next to a salami sandwich and her angel food cake. Because of the brotherhood of mutual respect that was practiced in that house, I was able to pick pecans and enjoy a snack in a house on the white side of town. Miss Hester and Mrs. Freid built community in front of me, and I'll always remember how it tasted, looked, and felt.

9   Dr. Mary Hogan and Nurse Callie Mae were Glen Allan's health professionals. One white and the other black, they worked as a team. They took care of the sick and delivered the babies, often going into less than desirable dwellings to attend to all kinds of people's needs, but I never heard a colored person in our town speak ill of our doctor or say that she had two standards of treatment. When called, Dr. Hogan and Nurse Callie Mae both came. Their names were always said together, and the service they delivered was always welcomed. Working together, they healed the sick, but I now know that what they showed me also fed my soul.

10   Even though our educational system was legally segregated, a wonderful relationship nevertheless developed between Dr. Norma C. O'Bannon and Mrs. Ann Briton, the supervising educators for Washington County, Mississippi. Dr. O'Bannon was white and the superintendent. Mrs. Britton was the supervisor of the colored teachers. I remember them as a team, riding side by side as they came from Greenville to our small town. I am sure they spent their time together on the road, in gentle defiance of the social mores of our day, discussing teaching and our welfare as well as other challenges that faced our principal, Mr. Moore.

11   Like most students, we looked for ways not to be studying. The visits these ladies paid to our school gave us that, but they gave us more besides. It was rare to see a black woman and a white one dressed equally well and working together as professionals, but they did. They would barely have parked out front when you'd hear Mr. Powell, our janitor, announce that they had arrived. "Hey, y'all!" the welcome cry would come. "Here come Miss O'Bannon and Miss Ann!" And then he would proudly hold the door to let them in. Mrs. Britton's title—Miss Ann—recognized that she was one of us. But both ladies were welcomed, moving from classroom to classroom to deliver short motivational talks, always reminding us that persistence would pay off. They taught by example; after all, both Dr. O'Bannon and Mrs. Britton had reached high and had seized the same professional star.

12   Brotherhood is such a powerful habit of the heart that even when only one person reaches out to do right, the impact can be lifelong. If I had not

encountered this habit of the heart when I was young, I could have left the South embittered and hurt. Instead, I left with purpose and a plan. I could not have done so without the memory of all these acts of brotherhood. I needed to see them practiced in front of me to believe that they could happen.

Exercise 15

Practice

Recognizing Taulbert's Use of Specific Detailss

In "Brotherhood," Clifton L. Taulbert supports general statements with specific details and examples. Fill in those details and examples below.

1. Taulbert says that Mr. Freid's store was a general department store. Give six examples of the kinds of things it sold.

hardware, dry goods, nails, dresses, fertilizer, underwear

2. Taulbert got his first taste of kosher food at the Freid's house. Name two of the foods he learned about at the Freid's house.

A spicy salami sandwich with brown mustard, matzoh ball soup

3. Give the names of the medical team that took care of the sick in Glen Allan.

Dr. Mary Hogan and Nurse Callie Mae

4. What was unusual about this team?

One was white, and the other was black.

5. Taulbert talks about a "wonderful relationship" between Dr. Norma C. O'Bannon and Mrs. Ann Britton. What profession brought these two together?

education

6. Taulbert says he is sure that, as they took car trips together, Dr. O'Bannon and Mrs. Britton must have shared conversations about specific subjects. Name one of the subjects they talked about.

teaching, or the student's welfare, or other challenges for the school's

principal, Mr. Moore

7. Taulbert concludes that the specific acts of brotherhood between black and white that he witnessed as a child gave him a "purpose and a plan." List four pairs of black and white people which showed him the meaning of brotherhood.

a. Dr. Norma C. O'Bannon and Mrs. Ann Britton

b. Dr. Mary Hogan and Nurse Callie Mae

c. Mrs. Freid and Miss Hester Rucker

d. Mr. Freid and Miss Maxey or Mr. Youngblood and Miss Hester Rucker

WRITING FROM READING: "Brotherhood"

When you write on any of the following topics, be sure to work through the stages of the writing process in preparing your paragraph.

1. Clifton L. Taulbert writes about a lesson he learned from observing people in his community. Write a paragraph about a lesson you learned from your community and give examples of people and actions that taught you this lesson.

2. In his hometown of Glen Allan, Taulbert noticed a few pairings and friendships that others in the town might have disapproved of. Yet to Taulbert, these relationships were examples of brotherhood. Write a paragraph in which you give examples of relationships (work relationships, school relationships, friendships, and so forth) that you have observed and that show a kind of brotherhood.

3. Taulbert learned about Jews partly through eating kosher food. Write about what you learned about a culture, race, or ethnic group through its food.

4. The kindness of Mrs. Freid in letting him pick pecans had a lasting effect on Taulbert. Write a paragraph giving examples of two or more small acts of kindness that have had a lasting effect on you.

5. Write a paragraph about two of the rules (spoken or unspoken) in your community, and give examples of how these rules are observed or broken. For example, Taulbert says that in the 1950s Glen Allan, white storekeepers did not allow black people to handle money and to serve both races at the cash register. He also says that most black and white women did not travel in a car together as equals. Then he gives examples of people who broke these rules. Think of two such rules in your community, and write about how they are observed or violated by specific people.

Why Not Real Awards for Real Achievements?

Ben Stein

Ben Stein is a writer, an attorney, and an actor. He is also known as the host of the television quiz show Win Ben Stein's Money. *In this essay, Stein talks about a different kind of awards show.*

Words You May Need to Know (corresponding paragraph numbers are in parentheses)

Evian (1): a brand of bottled water

Winnebago (1): a make of recreational vehicle

Ron Howard (2): the producer of Backdraft, a movie about firefighters.

garner (2): collect

apathy (3): lack of interest or concern

wrenched (4): painfully strained or twisted

casting illusions (6): creating what is not real

---

1   Strange. We have an Oscars ceremony to tell wildly pampered people (the kind who demand and get Evian water for their Winnebago showers while on location) how great they are for daring to stand in front of a camera for thousands of dollars per day, playing the role of, say, a brave cop. Yet we have no TV award show that gives recognition to real cops who really do risk their lives year in and out to keep other people safe. Why not have a nationally broadcast presentation of prizes for officers who deserve some thanks from society?

2   Or maybe firefighters. Ron Howard and others have made fine movies about firefighters, and these sometimes garner Oscars. But we have hundreds of thousands of real firefighters who day in and night out risk their lives in the most dangerous job in America. Why not have a show that recognizes these brave men and women for the lives they save?

3   Michelle Pfeiffer starred in a fine movie about teaching kids in the inner city, but she was just acting. In real life, there are men and women who struggle against danger, apathy, and shortages of material and money to teach children and give them hope. Sometimes these teachers are even injured in their classrooms, as recently happened here in Los Angeles. Why not acknowledge this?

4   Movie-viewers and TV-watchers are used to seeing heroics and tears in emergency rooms. But those scenes are just pretend, staged by people paid thousands of dollars a week to do it. In America, actual nurses and doctors get exposed to HIV and spat upon and wrenched emotionally while trying to save the lives of people they don't even know. They often make the difference between life and death. Why don't they have an award? Why aren't they ever called before national cameras?

5   We have a million military men and women living in bitter cold in Korea, mud in Bosnia, wretched heat in Cuba and Haiti, separated from their families for six months at a time while on submarines, landing jets on aircraft carriers at night—as frightening an exercise as exists on earth—all in order to protect us and keep us free. We have Marines at Parris Island, sailors on the water, and pilots flying over Iraq who live modestly, train, fight, and sometimes die with no day-to-day TV recognition. Why not fix that?

6   Why not put before America the best real men and women we produce, instead of only showing the folks who are good at casting illusions? I'm an actor myself and am happy to give actors their due. But actors are not true heroes or stars. Why not give a stage to the real thing once a year? That would be an awards ceremony worth watching.

 Exercise 16

Practice

Identifying Ben Stein's Use of Examples

To illustrate his point about America's true heroes, Ben Stein uses many specific examples. Fill in those examples below.

1–5. Name the five groups that Stein believes deserve an awards ceremony of their own.

    a. firefighters

    b. police officers

    c. teachers

    d. doctors and nurses

    e. military men and women

6. Name the specific places where, Stein says, members of the military work: Korea, Bosnia, Cuba, Haiti, Parris Island, Iraq

7. What actress played a heroic teacher in the inner city?

Michelle Pfeiffer

8. What specific physical dangers and stresses do doctors and nurses suffer?

They are "exposed to HIV and spat upon and wrenched emotionally while trying to save the lives of people they don't even know."

9. Who, according to Stein, has the most dangerous job in America?

firefighters

10. What group, according to Stein, is not made up of true heroes or stars?

actors

WRITING FROM READING: "Why Not Real Awards for Real Achievements?"

When you write on any of the following topics, be sure to work through the stages of the writing process in preparing your paragraph.

1. Working with a partner or group, brainstorm all the television awards shows you can remember. Then discuss which one was the worst. It may have been the worst because it was too long, gave the awards to the wrong people, seemed phony, and so forth. After your group work, write individual paragraphs on the worst awards show you have seen. Be sure to include many specific examples of its defects.

2. Think of a film you saw that was meant to be a realistic picture of some group such as police, soldiers, sailors, nurses, teachers, students, gangs, and so forth, or of some issue such as drug abuse, poverty, terrorism, crime, and so forth. Write a paragraph about how realistic or unrealistic this film was. Be sure to use many specific examples.

3. Write a paragraph that gives specific examples of people you know (not celebrities) who deserve recognition for one of these qualities:

   bravery
   compassion
   kindness
   sacrifice for others

4. Write a paragraph with one of the following topic sentences:

   The most unappreciated group in America is _____.

   My childhood heroes had several common characteristics.

   Many cartoons have heroes that children can admire and parents can approve of.

   Three people have become heroes for today's teens.

   Be sure to develop and support your thesis with specific examples.

5. Interview a teacher, police officer, medical worker, firefighter, or member of the armed forces. Before the interview, prepare a list of at least ten questions to ask about the person's job. You can include questions about the stresses, dangers, and rewards of the job. Write and/or tape the answers during the interview and ask follow-up questions. Finally, ask the person to add any comments he or she would like to make. Use this information to write a paragraph about the good and bad aspects of this work.

Writing a Process Paragraph

WHAT IS PROCESS?

A **process** writing explains how to do something or describes how something happens or is done. When you tell the reader how to do something (a **directional process**), you speak directly to the reader and give him or her clear, specific instructions about performing some activity. Your purpose is to explain an activity so a reader can do it. For example, you may have to leave instructions telling a new employee how to close the cash register or use the copy machine.

When you describe how something happens or is done (an **informational process**), your purpose is to explain an activity, without telling a reader how to do it. For example, you can explain how a boxer trains for a fight or how the special effects for a movie were created. Instead of speaking directly to the reader, an informational process speaks about "I," "he," "she," "we," "they," or about a person by his or her name. A directional process uses "you" or, in the way it gives directions, the word "you" is understood.

A Process Involves Steps in Time Order

Whether a process is directional or informational, it describes something that is done in steps, and these steps are in a specific order: a **time order.** The process can involve steps that are followed in minutes, hours, days, weeks, months, or even years. For example, the steps in changing a tire may take minutes, whereas the steps taken to lose ten pounds may take months.

You should keep in mind that a process involves steps that *must follow a certain order*, not just a range of activities that can be placed in any order.

This sentence *signals a process:*

> Planting a rose garden takes planning and care.
> (Planting a rose garden involves following steps in order; that is, you cannot put a rose bush in the ground until you dig a hole.)

This sentence *does not signal a process:*

> There are several ways to build your confidence.
> (Each way is separate; there is no time sequence here.)

Telling a person in a conversation how to do something or how something is done gives you the opportunity to add important points you may have overlooked or to throw in details you may have skipped at first. Your listener can ask questions if he or she does not understand you. Writing a process, however, is more difficult. Your reader is not there to stop you, to ask you to explain further, or to question you. In writing a process, you must be organized and very clear.

HINTS FOR WRITING A PROCESS PARAGRAPH

1. In choosing a topic, find an activity you know well. If you write about something familiar to you, you will have a clearer paragraph.

2. Choose a topic that includes steps that must be done in a specific time sequence.

> **not this:** I find lots of things to do with old photographs.
> **but this:** I have a plan for turning an old photograph into a special gift.

3. Choose a topic that is fairly small. A complicated process cannot be covered well in one paragraph. If your topic is too big, the paragraph can become vague, incomplete, or boring.

> **too big:** There are many steps in the process of an immigrant becoming an American citizen.
> **smaller and manageable:** Persistence and a positive attitude helped me through the stages of my job search.

4. Write a topic sentence that makes a point. Your topic sentence should do more than announce. Like the topic sentence for any paragraph, it should have a point. As you plan the steps of your process and gather details, ask yourself some questions: What point do I want to make about this process? Is the process hard? Is it easy? Does the process require certain tools? Does the process require certain skills, like organization, patience, endurance?

> **an announcement:** This paragraph is about how to change the oil in your car.
> **a topic sentence:** You do not have to be a mechanic to change the oil in your car, but you do have to take a few simple precautions.

5. Include all the steps. If you are explaining a process, you are writing for someone who does not know the process as well as you do. Keep in mind that what seems clear or simple to you may not be clear or simple to the reader, and be sure to tell what is needed before the process starts. For

TEACHING TIPS:

(1) Tell students they can be objective "reporters" as they analyze the steps they or others undertake to complete a process.
(2) If students have difficulty elaborating on a step, tell them they can emphasize the importance of each step in a process by examining what would happen (or go wrong) if the step is neglected or not completed correctly.

instance, what ingredients are needed to cook the dish? Or what tools are needed to assemble the toy?

6. Put the steps in the right order. Nothing is more irritating to a reader than trying to follow directions that skip back and forth. Careful planning, drafting, and revision can help you get the time sequence right.

7. Be specific in the details and steps. To be sure you have sufficient details and clear steps, keep your reader in mind. Put yourself in the reader's place. Could you follow your own directions or understand your steps?

If you remember that a process explains, you will focus on being clear. Now that you know the purpose and strategies of writing a process, you can begin the thought lines stage of writing one.

Exercise 1

Practice

Recognizing Good Topic Sentences for Process Paragraphs

If a sentence is a good topic sentence for a process paragraph, put OK on the line provided. If a sentence has a problem, label that sentence with one of these letters:

A This is an announcement; it makes no point.
B This sentence covers a topic that is too big for one paragraph.
S This sentence describes a topic that does not require steps.

1. __OK__ I've found a system for doing the laundry that saves me time and stress.

2. __A__ How I learned to install a ceiling fan is the subject of this paragraph.

3. __S__ There are quite a few reasons for buying old furniture.

4. __B__ The steps involved in liver transplants are complicated.

5. __OK__ Finding a bargain on a digital camera means knowing where to look and what to look for.

6. __A__ This paper shows the method of deep-frying a turkey.

7. __B__ The Constitution of the United States evolved in several stages.

8. __S__ There are many things to remember when you play the drums.

9. __OK__ If you learn just a few techniques, you can paint a room as well as the professionals do.

10. __OK__ Gabriella discovered the correct way to repair a tear in wallpaper.

Exercise 2

👥 *Collaborate*

Including Necessary Materials in a Process

Below are three possible topics for a process paragraph. For each topic, work with a partner or a group and list the items (materials, ingredients, tools, utensils, supplies) the reader would have to gather before beginning the process. When you've finished the exercise, check your lists with another group to see if you've missed any items.

1. **topic:** barbecuing hamburgers

   needed items: _a gas grill or charcoal grill with charcoal and charcoal_

   lighter, a metal burger flipper, hamburger patties and a platter

2. **topic:** waxing a car

   needed items: _wax, a heavy cloth to apply the wax, a soft cloth to_

   buff the car

3. **topic:** washing a dog

   needed items: _a large tub to place the dog in, warm water, dog_

   shampoo, a washcloth, water to rinse the dog, lots of towels

WRITING THE PROCESS PARAGRAPH IN STEPS

Thought Lines **Gathering Ideas: Process**

The easiest way to start writing a process paragraph is to pick a small topic, one that you can cover well in one paragraph. Then you can gather ideas by listing or freewriting or both.

If you decided to write about how to adopt a shelter dog, you might begin by freewriting.

Then you might check your freewriting, looking for details that have to do with the process of adopting a shelter dog. You can underline those details, as in the example that follows.

Freewriting for a Process Paragraph

Topic: How to Adopt a Shelter Dog

What kind of dog do you want? It's difficult to walk through an animal shelter and see all those dogs begging for a home. Be realistic. A purebred or a mixed breed? A puppy? Can you afford it? There's a fee at the shelter. You have to be willing to take care of a dog for a long time.

Next, you can **put what you've underlined into a list, in correct time sequence:**

before you decide on any dog
Can you afford it?
You have to be willing to take care of a dog for a long time.

considering the right dog
What kind of a dog do you want?
A purebred or a mixed breed. A puppy?
Be realistic.

at the shelter
It's difficult to walk through a shelter.
A fee at the shelter.

Check the list. Are some details missing? Yes. A reader might ask, "How do you decide what kind of dog is best for you? What's so expensive about getting a dog at a shelter? And how much does it cost to own a dog, anyway?" Answers to questions like these can give you the details needed to write a clear and interesting informational process.

Writing a Topic Sentence for a Process Paragraph

Freewriting and a list can now help you focus your paragraph by identifying the point of your process. You already know that the subject of your paragraph is how to adopt a shelter dog. But what's the point? Is it easy to adopt a shelter dog? Is it difficult? What does it take to find the right dog?

Looking at your list of steps and details, you notice that most of the steps come before you actually select a dog. Maybe a topic sentence could be

> You have to do your homework if you want to find the shelter dog that's right for you.

Once you have a topic sentence, you can think about adding details that explain your topic sentence and you can begin the outlines stage of writing.

Exercise 3

Practice

Finding the Steps of a Process in Freewriting

Read the following freewriting, then reread it, looking for all the words, phrases, or sentences that have to do with steps. Underline all those items. Then once you've underlined the freewriting, put what you've underlined into a list in a correct time sequence.

How I Fought a Cold: Freewriting

Felt it coming on. Scratchy throat, bad headache, really tired on Tuesday. You just know something is going to hit you, the flu or a cold. You need to rest. Just sit, watch television, look out the window, or sleep. <u>Tuesday at dinner, I took extra Vitamin C and aspirin.</u> Wednesday morning, I could barely get out of bed, <u>so I decided to call in sick</u> and fight this cold or whatever it was. Felt better Thursday morning and went to work. On Wednesday after I called in sick, <u>I drank some juice, took more aspirin and Vitamin C,</u> and went back to sleep. <u>I slept til 3:00 p.m.</u> <u>Then I ate some toast and had tea with honey.</u> <u>I kept drinking more fluids all afternoon</u>: water, juice, chicken soup. Mainly, <u>I lay on the couch with my tea or juice and dozed off.</u> <u>I went back to bed at 8:00 p.m. and slept right through until 7:00 a.m.</u> I rested myself out of a bad cold.

Your List of Steps in Time Sequence

1. I took extra Vitamin C and aspirin on Tuesday at dinner.

2. Called in sick on Wednesday.

3. Drank some juice, took more aspirin and Vitamin C.

4. Slept until 3:00 p.m.

5. Ate some toast and drank some tea with honey.

6. Kept drinking fluids throughout the afternoon.

7. Dozed off on the couch.

8. Returned to bed at 8:00 p.m.

9. Slept until 7:00 on Thursday morning.

_____

_____

Outlines **Devising a Plan: Process**

Using the freewriting and topic sentence on how to adopt a shelter dog, you could make an outline. Then you could revise it, checking the topic sentence and improving the list of details where you think they could be better. A revised outline on adopting a shelter dog is shown below.

An Outline for a Paragraph on How to Adopt a Shelter Dog

topic sentence: You have to do your homework if you want to find the shelter dog that's right for you.

details:

before you decide on any dog
Decide whether you can afford a dog.
Dogs cost money for food, regular veterinary care, and grooming.
Decide if you are willing to take care of a dog for a long time.
Dogs can live ten to fifteen years.
They need exercise, attention, and training.

considering the right dog
Think carefully about what kind of dog you want.
You have to decide whether you want a purebred or mixed breed.
You can get both types at a shelter.
Puppies are adorable and fun.
They need more training and attention.
The size and temperament of the dog are important, too.
Do some research and talk to friends who own dogs.

at the shelter
It is difficult to walk through an animal shelter and see all the dogs begging for a home.
But remember the kind of dog you've decided to adopt.
Look around carefully.
Make your selection, pay the adoption fee, and look forward to giving your dog the best years of its life.

You probably noticed that the outline follows the same stages as the list but has many new details. These details can be added as you create your plan.

The following checklist may help you revise an outline for your own process paragraph.

> **Checklist**
>
> **A Checklist for Revising a Process Outline**
>
> ✔ Is my topic sentence focused on some point about the process?
>
> ✔ Does it cover the whole process?
>
> ✔ Do I have all the steps?
>
> ✔ Are they in the right order?
>
> ✔ Have I explained clearly?
>
> ✔ Do I need better details?

Exercise 4

Practice

Revising the Topic Sentence in a Process Outline

The topic sentence below doesn't cover all the steps of the process. Read the outline several times; then write a topic sentence that covers all the steps of the process and has a point.

topic sentence: You can buy a unique gift at a flea market if you look around.

details: First, decide what you're looking for: a dish, a framed poster, candle holders.
Decide how much you are willing to pay.
At the market, survey all the stalls before you make a choice.
Even if you see the perfect gift at the first stall, keep looking.
If you show too much interest too soon, the price may go up.
On the second tour of the market, return to the objects you liked and narrow your choice to one.
Casually ask the price.
Then offer much less.
If your offer is not accepted, act as if you are leaving. You will most likely get a new price, and the bargaining will begin.
When you and the seller can reach a compromise, you have your gift.

Answers Will Vary.

Possible answer shown at right.

revised topic sentence: You can buy a unique gift at a flea market if you arrive with a goal and know how to bargain for what you want.

Exercise 5

Practice

Revising the Order of Steps in a Process Outline

The steps in each of these outlines are out of order. Put numbers in the spaces provided, indicating what step should be first, second, and so forth.

1. topic sentence: Every night, my dog Captain Crunch has the same bedtime routine.

details: ___1___ At first he stretches out on the living room rug while I lie on the couch and watch television.

___2___ Captain Crunch is not a night person, so he doesn't want to spend too much time in front of the television.

___6___ He follows me into my bedroom.

___8___ When I am nearly asleep, Captain Crunch jumps on my bed and sleeps on my feet.

___7___ He settles on the bedroom carpet while I climb into bed.

___3___ To signal me it is time for bed, he starts to yawn in front of the television.

___4___ When the yawns don't work, he starts to sigh.

___5___ Then I feel a wet nose under my hand, and I finally get up and turn off the television.

2. topic sentence: In less than ten minutes, I can make my room look clean.

details: ___10___ I now have a clean-looking room with a new pillow, full of garbage, on my bed.

___1___ First, I take all the major junk (like a basketball, a bunch of smelly sneakers) and throw it in the closet.

___5___ I want to cram all this food garbage into a big bag.

___6___ Suddenly I realize I have no bag.

___7___ I have a sudden inspiration for a bag substitute.

___8___ I snatch a pillow case off one of the pillows on my newly made bed.

___2___ Once the major junk is in the closet, I take the smaller junk, like dirty socks and shirts, and put them under the sheets of my bed.

___3___ I proceed to make my bed, concealing all the dirty clothes.

___4___ Last comes the minor food garbage: Pepsi cans, candy wrappers, leftover cookies.

___9___ I fill the pillow case with the cans, wrappers, and cookies.

3. topic sentence: When my five-year-old son Mark wants something from his grandmother, he has a foolproof system for getting it.

details: ___6___ His grandmother doesn't know my son uses this weather talk as a way to introduce what he really wants.

    4   After she tells him how she is, he talks about the weather.

    5   His grandmother thinks the weather talk is cute because it is what grown-ups talk about.

    1   He starts with a phone call to his grand-mother.

    2   She loves to talk to him, so he has already set the stage for his plan.

    3   He always begins by saying, "Hi Grandma. How are you?"

    7/8   If it's raining, Mark will say, "I can't go outside today, so I'd sure like you to come over and read me a story."

    7/8   If it's sunny, he'll say, "It's such a nice day, you and I should go to the park."

    9   His grandmother falls for his scheme every time.

Exercise 6

Practice

Listing All the Steps in an Outline

Following are three topic sentences for process paragraphs. Write all the steps needed to complete an outline for each topic sentence. After you've listed all the steps, number them in the correct time order.

Answers Will Vary.

Possible answers shown at right.

1. **topic sentence:** There are a few simple steps for buying your college textbooks.

   steps: 1. Go to class to find out what books are needed.

   2. Write down the title, author, edition, and publisher of each book.

   3. Take the list with you to the college bookstore.

   4. Look for each book in the right section (math, art, etc.)

   5. Write down the price of each book, new or used.

   6. Leave the bookstore and compare the prices at off-campus book-stores and in student advertisements.

   7. Once you have the best prices, buy your books immediately.

2. **topic sentence:** Anyone can make a delicious salad.

   steps: 1. You will need lettuce, tomatoes, and cucumbers, and any other vegetables you like. Also get a bottle of salad dressing, a large bowl, a large fork, a large spoon, and a sharp knife.

2. Rinse the lettuce, tomatoes, and the cucumbers, if needed.

3. Gently dry the lettuce and tear it into bite-size pieces.

4. Place it in the bowl.

5. Slice the tomatoes and cucumber.

6. Add them to the lettuce.

7. Pour a small quantity of the bottled dressing on the salad.

8. Use the large fork and spoon to toss the salad and serve.

3. topic sentence: At registration time, you can develop a plan for getting the classes you want.

steps: 1. Meet with a counselor before registration begins and make

a list of the courses you need to take.

2. Get the class schedule on the day it is published.

3. Study it carefully.

4. Using your counselor's list of required courses, circle the classes

and times you want.

5. Now circle alternative times and classes.

6. Check the schedule for the day you are eligible to register.

7. Be the first one in line on that day.

Rough Lines Drafting and Revising: Process

You can take the outline and write it in paragraph form, and you'll have a first draft of the process paragraph. As you write the first draft, you can combine some of the short sentences from the outline. Then you can review your draft and revise it for organization, details, clarity, grammar, style, and word choice.

Using the Same Grammatical Person

Remember that the *directional* process speaks directly to the reader, calling him or her "you." Sentences in a directional process use the word "you," or they imply "you."

> **directional:** *You* need a good skillet to get started.
> Begin by cleaning the surface. ("You" is implied.)

Remember that the *informational* process involves somebody doing the process. Sentences in an informational process use words such as "I" or "we" or "he" or "she" or "they" or a person's name.

> **informational:** *Dave* needed a good skillet to get started.
> First, *I* can clean the surface.

TEACHER'S DISCUSSION QUESTION:

Ask students to give reasons why shifting to "you" is so common a practice. See if anyone starts referring to "you" in his or her answer. A humorous discussion of this shift in persons can help students understand how easy it is to shift to an illogical use of "you" in writing.

One problem in writing a process is shifting from describing how **some**body did something to telling the reader how to do an activity. When **that** shift happens, the two kinds of processes get mixed. That shift is **called a shift in person.** In grammar, the words "I" and "we" are considered **to be in the** first person, "you" is the second person," and "he," "she," "it," **and "they"** are in the third person.

If these words refer to one, they are *singular;* if they **refer to** more than one, they are *plural.* The following list may help.

Info BOX

A List of Persons

1st person singular:	I
2nd person singular:	you
3rd person singular:	he, she, it, or a person's name
1st person plural:	we
2nd person plural:	you
3rd person plural:	they, or the names of more than one person

---

In writing your process paragraph, decide whether your **process will be** directional or informational, and stay with one kind.

Below are two examples of a shift in person. Look at **them carefully** and study how the shift is corrected.

shift in person: After *I* preheat the oven to 350 degrees, *I* mix **the egg** whites and sugar with an electric mixer set **at high** speed. *Mix* until stiff peaks form. Then *I* put the mixture in small mounds on an ungreased **cookie sheet.** ("Mix until stiff peaks form" is a shift to the **"you"** person.)

shift corrected: After *I* preheat the oven to 350 degrees, *I* mix **the egg** whites and sugar with an electric mixer set **at high** speed. *I* mix until stiff peaks form. Then *I* **put the** mixture in small mounds on an ungreased **cookie** sheet.

shift in person: A *salesperson* has to be very careful when **a cus**tomer tries on clothes. *The clerk* can't hint **that a** suit may be a size too small. *You* can insult a **customer** with a hint like that. (The sentences shifted **from** "salesperson" and "clerk" to "you.")

shift corrected: A *salesperson* has to be very careful when **customers** try on clothes. *The clerk* can't hint that a **suit may** be a size too small. *He or she* can insult a **customer** with a hint like that.

Using Transitions Effectively

As you revise your draft, you can add transitions. Transitions **are particu**larly important in a process paragraph because you are trying **to show** the steps in a *specific sequence,* and you are trying to show the *connections* between steps. Good transitions will also keep your paragraph **from sound**ing like a choppy, boring list.

Following is a list of some of the transitions you can use in writing a process paragraph. Be sure that you use transitional words and phrases only when it is logical to do so, and try not to overuse the same transitions in a paragraph.

Info BOX

Transitions for a Process Paragraph

after	during	last	the second step, etc
afterward	eventually	later	then
as	finally	meanwhile	to begin
as he/she is	first	next	to start
as soon as	second, etc.	now	until
as you are	first of all	quickly	when
at last	gradually	sometimes	whenever
at the same time	in the beginning	soon	while
before	immediately	suddenly	while I am
begin by	initially	the first step	

When you write a process paragraph, you must pay particular attention to clarity. As you revise, keep thinking about your audience to be sure your steps are easy to follow. The following can help you revise your draft.

Checklist

A Checklist for Revising a Process Paragraph

✔ Does the topic sentence cover the whole paragraph?

✔ Does the topic sentence make a point about the process?

✔ Is any important step left out?

✔ Should any step be explained further?

✔ Are the steps in the right order?

✔ Should any sentences be combined?

✔ Have I used the same person throughout the paragraph to describe the process?

✔ Have I used transitions effectively?

 **Exercise 7**

Practice

Correcting Shifts in Person in a Process Paragraph

Below is a paragraph that shifts from being an informational to a directional process in several places. Those places are underlined. Rewrite the underlined parts, directly above the underlining, so that the whole paragraph is an informational process.

Eddie has an efficient system for sorting and organizing his mail. As soon as

he picks up his mail, he begins sorting it. Any junk mail such as advertisements and offers for credit cards or phone plans never reaches the kitchen table. ~~You~~ *He*

immediately ~~toss~~ *tosses* it into the garbage. Then Eddie sits at the table and sorts the

remaining mail. Eddie opens all the bills. He puts the ones that ~~you need~~ *he needs* to pay

right away in one stack; he places the ones he can pay later in another stack.

Next, Eddie places each stack in its own compartment in a plastic tray. Finally, he

looks at what mail is left: cards from friends, a reminder from the dentist about

his next appointment, a bank statement. By sorting his mail every day, Eddie

never has to face a mountain of old mail that can take ~~you~~ *him* hours to sort.

Exercise 8

Practice

Revising Transitions in a Process Paragraph

The transitions in this paragraph could be better. Rewrite the underlined transitions, directly above each one, so that the transitions are smoother.

When you make your bed with clean sheets and pillowcases, you can take a

few quick steps to a luxurious sleep. ~~First,~~ *To begin,* strip the bed of its old sheets and pil-

lowcases, tossing them in a laundry basket. ~~Second,~~ *Then* take the pillows off the bed,

so that the bed surface is empty and clear. ~~Third,~~ *As soon as the bed has been stripped,* bring in the clean sheets and

pillowcases. ~~Fourth,~~ *Now* take the bottom sheet and tuck the edges under all sides of

the mattress. Be sure the surface is flat and smooth. If you are using a fitted

sheet, this step is easy; if you are using a flat bottom sheet, this step is more diffi-

cult. ~~Fifth,~~ *When the bottom sheet is smooth,* spread the top sheet over the bed, with the stitched border edge near

the head of the bed. ~~Sixth,~~ *At the same time,* position this sheet so that there is enough sheet to

overlap both sides of the bed and to fold down the top border. ~~Seventh,~~ *Quickly* tuck in

the top sheet at the bottom corners. ~~Eighth,~~ *Finally,* plump the pillows and put them

snugly into their cases. When you put the pillows at the head of the bed and add a

bedspread or comforter, you have the pleasure of a crisp, clean night's sleep

ahead of you.

Exercise 9

Practice

Combining Sentences in a Process Paragraph

The paragraph below has many short, choppy sentences which are under-lined. Wherever you see two or more underlined sentences clustered next to each other, combine them into one clear, smooth sentence. Write your revised version of the paragraph in the spaces above the lines.

My uncle has come up with a smart way to avoid standing in line at popular

His first step was to do a little research into which restaurants issue pagers

restaurants. His first step was to do a little research. He looked into which restau-

to their waiting customers.

rants issue pagers to their waiting customers. Next, he drove around town and

He was looking for the ones near a bookstore or a

surveyed those restaurants. He was looking for specific ones. He wanted ones

discount store.

near a bookstore. He also wanted ones near a discount store. Once he was famil-

iar with these restaurants, he began to put his plan into action. When he wants to

If there is a long wait

eat at a restaurant, he always chooses one on his new list. If there is a long wait

at the restaurant, my smart uncle takes the pager and leaves for the nearby

at the restaurant, my uncle knows what to do. He takes the pager. He leaves for

bookstore or discount store.

the nearby bookstore. Sometimes he leaves for the nearby discount store. He

browses in the bookstore or picks up a few items at the discount store. When his

pager tells him his table is ready, he walks a few steps and has a good dinner.

The Draft

Below is a draft of the process paragraph on adopting a shelter dog. This draft has more details than the outline on page 419. Some short sentences have been combined, and transitions have been added.

A Draft of a Paragraph on How to Adopt a Shelter Dog

transition added
details added

transition added
sentences combined
detail added
transition added

sentences combined
transition sentence added
sentences combined

transition added,
sentences combined
transition added

You have to do your homework if you want to find the shelter dog that's best for you. Begin by deciding whether you can afford a dog. Most shelters spay and neuter their animals, but dogs cost money for food, regular veterinary care, and grooming. Then decide if you are willing to take care of a dog for the ten or fifteen years that is its likely life span. Remember that dogs need regular exercise, attention, and training. If you are ready to make the personal and financial commitment of owning a pet, you can begin thinking carefully about the kind of dog you want. You have to decide whether you want a purebred or a mixed breed, for you can get both types at a shelter. At the same time, think about the age of the dog you want. Puppies are adorable and fun, but they need more training and attention. The size and temperament of the dog are important, too. Do some research and talk to friends who own dogs. It is difficult to walk through an animal shelter and see all the dogs begging for a home. When you make your adoption visit, remember the kind of dog you've decided to adopt and look around carefully. Finally, make your selection, pay the adoption fee, and look forward to giving your dog the best years of its life.

Final Lines **Proofreading and Polishing: Process**

Before you prepare the final copy of your process paragraph, you can check your latest draft for any places in grammar, word choice, and style that need revision.

Following is the final version of the process paragraph on adopting a shelter dog. You'll notice that it contains several changes from the draft on page 427:

- A sentence of introduction has been added; it begins the paragraph and creates a smoother opening.
- Two more transitions have been added.
- The second use of "carefully " has been changed to "thoroughly," to avoid repetition.
- "Look around" has been changed to "look" to emphasize that this is not a quick or casual glance but an examination.

A Final Version of a Paragraph on How to Adopt a Shelter Dog
(Changes from the draft are underlined.)

Most people who love animals and have big hearts have thought about adopting a dog with no home, a shelter dog. However, you have to do your homework if you want to find the shelter dog that's best for you. Begin by deciding whether you can afford a dog. Most shelters spay and neuter their animals, but dogs cost money for food, regular veterinary care, and grooming. Then decide if you are willing to take care of a dog for the ten or fifteen years that is its likely life span. Remember that dogs need regular exercise, attention, and training. If you are ready to make the personal and financial commitment of owning a pet, you can begin thinking carefully about the kind of dog you want. You have to decide whether you want a purebred or a mixed breed, for you can get both types at a shelter. At the same time, think about the age of the dog you want. Puppies are adorable and fun, but they need more training and attention. The size and temperament of the dog are important, too. To make all these decisions, do some research and talk to friends who own dogs. Later, as you prepare to go to the shelter, be aware that it is difficult to walk through an animal shelter and see all the dogs begging for a home. When you make your adoption visit, remember the kind of dog you've decided to adopt and look thoroughly. Finally, make your selection, pay the adoption fee, and look forward to giving your dog the best years of its life.

Before you prepare the final copy of your process paragraph, check your latest draft for errors in spelling and punctuation, and for any errors made in typing or recopying.

Proofreading to Prepare the Final Paragraph

Practice

Following are two process paragraphs with the kind of errors it is easy to overlook when you prepare the final version of an assignment. Correct the errors, writing above the lines. There are eight errors in the first paragraph and ten in the second paragraph.

1. There's an easy way to make a healthy pizza. When you order a pizza from a popular pizza chain, you get a pizza loaded with fat ' but you can make a tasty, low-fat one in a few _minutes_ minute. Start with a ready-made crust; you can find a variety of them in any _supermarket_ supper-market. Next, you can cover the crust with a jar of pizza sauce, or, if you want a white pizza, you can skip this step. Your second _topping_   _where_   . toping is cheese, and here is wear you can cut back on the fat You can use a low-fat mozzarella, Swiss, or Parmesan cheese. Once you _ready_ have the cheese base, you are readdy to add toppings. Healthy toppings include delicious ones like peppers, mushrooms, onions, sundried tomatoes, and olives. After you pile on the toppings, _pop_ Pop your creation into the oven. In minutes, you will have your personal, healthy pizza.

learned   _used_
2. I finally learn to say "no," and it changed my life. I use to _someone_ say "yes" to every favor some one asked for and every invitation I _got_ get. After years of being stuck doing things I hated and resenting people who asked me to do them, I decided to change. I began by _him or her_ making up stories. If someone asked me to drive them to the airport for the third time in a month, I said I couldn't because my grandmother was sick. Nobody challenged me, so I kept making _until_ phony excuses untill I got a little braver. Then, when my cousin asked me to come to a painting party and help paint his garage, I said, "I can't." When he asked me why I couldn't, I just said, "I have _wasn't_   _no comma_ plans." It wasnt really a lie, because I did have plans to sleep late and watch football. After saying "no" and "I have plans" eight or ten times, I became bolder. Now I say "no," and if someone asks me why, I simply say, "It's not possible. Sorry." I'm not as angry as I _choose_ used to be because I can now chose how I spend my time instead of letting others take up all my time.

Lines of Detail: A Walk-Through Assignment

Your assignment is to write an informational process paragraph on how you found the perfect gift for your best friend or parent. Follow these steps:

Step 1: Decide whether to write about a gift for your friend or for your parent. Then think about a time when you found a gift that made that person very happy.

Step 2: Now freewrite. Write anything you can remember about the gift, how you decided what to give, how you found it and gave it.

Step 3: When you've completed the freewriting, read it. Underline all the details that refer to steps in planning that event. List the underlined details in time order.

Step 4: Add to the list by brainstorming. Ask yourself questions that can lead to more detail. For example, if an item on your list is, "I realized my mother likes colorful clothes," ask questions such as, "What colors does she like?" "What is her favorite color?" or "What kind of clothes does she like to wear?"

Step 5: Survey your expanded list. Write a topic sentence that makes some point about your finding this gift. To reach a point, think of questions such as, "What made the gift perfect?" or "What did I learn from planning to find and give this gift?"

Step 6: Use the topic sentence to prepare an outline. Be sure that the steps in the outline are in the correct time order.

Step 7: Write a first draft of the paragraph, adding details and combining short sentences.

INSTRUCTOR'S NOTE:

A Peer Review Form for students' exchange of drafts is on page 433.

Step 8: Revise your draft. Be careful to use smooth transitions, and check that you have included all the necessary steps.

Step 9: Prepare and proofread the final lines copy of your paragraph.

Writing Your Own Process Paragraph

When you write on one of these topics, be sure to work through the stages of the writing process in preparing your process paragraph.

1. Write a **directional** or **informational process** about one of these topics:

cleaning out a closet
setting a fancy table
painting a chair
training for a marathon
coloring your hair
choosing a roommate
saving on CDs
avoiding morning traffic jams
handling a customer's complaint
getting ready for moving day

proposing marriage to a partner
getting children to eat vegetables
fixing a leaky pipe
installing speakers in a car
buying airline tickets online
quitting a job gracefully
getting hair extensions
fighting a traffic ticket
making a telemarketing call
getting to school on time

2. Write about the wrong way to do something, or the wrong way you (or someone else) did it. You can use any of the topics in the list above, or you can choose your own topic.

3. Imagine that a friend is about to register for classes at your college. This will be your friend's first term at the college. Write a paragraph giving your friend clear directions for registering. Be sure to have an appropriate topic sentence.

4. Interview one of the counselors at your college. Ask the counselor to tell you the steps for applying for any available scholarships. Take notes or tape the interview, get copies of any forms that may be included in the application process, and ask questions about these forms.

　　After the interview, write a paragraph explaining the process of applying for one specific scholarship. Your explanation is directed at a current student who has never applied for a scholarship.

5. Interview someone who always seems to be organized at school or at work. Ask that person to tell you how he or she manages to be so efficient. Narrow the question to something such as how the person always manages to get all his work done at the store, or how she always gets her assignments in on time. Ask whether the person has developed a system and what steps are involved in that system. Take notes or tape the interview.

　　After the interview, write a paragraph about that system, explaining how to be organized for a particular task at college or at work. Your paragraph will explain the process to someone who needs to be more organized.

6. Look carefully at the people in photograph A. They are socializing and having fun. Write a process paragraph on this related topic: how to get to know people you have just met.

Photograph A

7. The children in photograph B are playing hopscotch. Use the photograph to think about a childhood game you used to play. Now write a paragraph on how to play that game.

Photograph B

Name: _____   Section: _____

PEER REVIEW FORM FOR A PROCESS PARAGRAPH

After you've written a draft of your process paragraph, let a writing partner read it. When your partner has completed the form below, discuss. Repeat the same process for your partner's paragraph.

The steps that are most clearly described are _____

_____

_____

I'd like more explanation about this step: _____

_____

Some details could be added to the part that begins with the words _____

A transition could be added to the part that begins with the words _____

I have questions about _____

_____

The best thing about this paragraph is _____

_____

Other comments on the paragraph: _____

_____

_____

_____

_____

_____

_____

_____

_____

_____

_____

_____

_____

_____

Reviewer's Name:_____

WRITING FROM READING: Process

Say Yes to Yourself

Joseph T. Martorano and John P. Kildahl

As therapists, Joseph T. Martorano and John P. Kildahl are familiar with the way we can damage ourselves through negative inner speech. In this excerpt from their book, Beyond Negative Thinking, they offer a way to stop sending ourselves the "silent broadcast" that can destroy our confidence.

Words You May Need to Know (corresponding paragraph numbers are in parentheses)

churns (1): becomes agitated or upset

sabotage (2): secretly attack, undermine

M.B.A. (4): a Master of Business Administration degree

flukes (5): accidents

foreboding (6): strong inner feelings of disaster

squandering (6): wasting

tenacious (11): stubborn, persistent

immobilized (12): kept him from moving

accentuate (13): emphasize

exorcized (17): gotten rid of

demons (17): evil spirits

---

1   It's the classic story with a twist: a traveling salesman gets a flat tire on a dark lonely road and then discovers he has no jack. He sees a light in a farmhouse. As he walks toward it, his mind churns: "Suppose no one comes to the door." "Suppose they don't have a jack." "Suppose the guy won't lend me a jack even if he has one." The harder his mind works, the more agitated he becomes, and when the door opens, he punches the farmer and yells, "Keep your lousy jack!"

2   That story brings a smile because it pokes fun at a common type of self-defeatist thinking. How often have you heard yourself say, "Nothing *ever* goes the way I planned," "I'll *never* make that deadline," or "I *always* screw up"? Such inner speech shapes your life more than any other single force. Like it or not, you travel through life with your thoughts as navigator. If those thoughts spell gloom and doom, that's where you're headed, because put-down words sabotage confidence instead of offering support and encouragement.

3   Simply put, to *feel* better, you need to *think* better. Here's how:

4   **1. Tune in to your thoughts.** The first thing Sue said to her new therapist was, "I know you can't help me, Doctor. I'm a total mess. I keep spoiling things at work, and I'm sure I'm going to be fired. Just yesterday, my boss told me I was going to be transferred. He called it a promotion. But if I was doing a good job, why would they transfer me?" Then, gradually, Sue's story moved past the put-downs. She had received her M.B.A. two years before and was making an excellent salary. That didn't sound like failure.

5   At the end of their first meeting, Sue's therapist told her to jot down her thoughts, particularly at night if she was having trouble falling asleep. At her next appointment Sue's list included, "I'm not really smart. I got ahead by a bunch of flukes," "Tomorrow will be a disaster. I've never chaired a meeting before," and "My boss looked furious this morning. What did I do?" She admitted, "In one day alone, I listed twenty-six negative thoughts. No wonder I'm always tired and depressed."

6   Hearing her fears and forebodings read out loud made Sue realize how much energy she was squandering on imagined catastrophes. If you've been feeling down, it could be you're sending yourself negative messages, too. Listen to the words churning inside your head. Repeat them aloud or write them down, if that will help capture them.

7   With practice, tuning in will become automatic. As you're walking or driving down the street, you can hear your silent broadcast. Soon your thoughts will do your bidding, rather than the other way around. And when that happens, your feelings and actions will change, too.

8   **2. Isolate destructive words and phrases.** Fran's inner voice kept telling her she was "only a secretary." Mark's reminded him he was "just a salesman." With the word *only* or *just*, they were downgrading their jobs and, by extension, themselves. By isolating negative words and phrases, you can pinpoint the damage you're doing to yourself.

9   **3. Stop the thought.** Short-circuit negative messages as soon as they start by using the one word command, *stop!*

10   "What will I do if . . . ?" *Stop!*

11   In theory, stopping is a simple technique. In practice, it's not as easy as it sounds. To be effective at stopping, you have to be forceful and tenacious. Raise your voice when you give the command. Picture yourself drowning out the inner voice of fear.

12   Vincent, a hard-working bachelor in his twenties, was an executive in a large company. Although attracted to a woman in his department, he never asked her for a date. His worries immobilized him: "It's not a good idea to date a co-worker," or, "If she says no, it'll be embarrassing." When Vincent stopped his inner voice and asked the woman out, she said, "Vincent, what took you so long?"

13   **4. Accentuate the positive.** There's a story about a man who went to a psychiatrist. "What's the trouble?" asked the doctor.

14   "Two months ago my grandfather died and left me $75,000. Last month, a cousin passed away and left me $100,000."

15   "Then why are you depressed?"

16   "This month, *nothing!*"

17   When a person is in a depressed mood, everything can seem depressing. So once you've exorcized the demons by calling a stop, replace them with good thoughts. Be ready with a thought you've prepared in advance.

Think about the promotion you got or a pleasant hike in the woods. In the words of the Bible, "whatever is honorable, . . . whatever is lovely, whatever is gracious . . . think about these things."

18   **5. Reorient yourself.** Have you ever been feeling down late in the day, when someone suddenly said, "Let's go out"? Remember how your spirits picked up? You changed the direction of your thinking, and your mood brightened. Practice this technique of going from painful anxiety to an active, problem-solving framework.

19   By reorienting, you can learn to see yourself and the world around you differently. If you think you can do something, you increase your chances of doing it. Optimism gets you moving. Depressing thoughts bog you down because you are thinking, "What's the use?"

20   Make it a habit to remember your best self, the one that you want to be. In particular, remember things for which you have been complimented. That's the real you. Make this the frame of reference for your life—a picture of you at your best. You'll find that reorienting works like a magnet. Imagine yourself reaching your goals, and you will feel the tug of the magnet pulling you toward them.

21   Over the years, we've discovered that when people *think* differently, they *feel*—and *act*—differently. It's all in controlling your thoughts. As the poet John Milton wrote, "The mind . . . can make a heaven of hell, a hell of heaven."

22   The choice is yours.

Exercise 11   **Identifying Details and Examples in the Steps of "Say Yes To Yourself"**

Practice   Joseph Martorano and John F. Kildahl say that "to *feel* better, you need to *think* better." They offer simple steps for thinking better, and they explain each step with clear details and examples. To become more familiar with the steps and the details, reread "Say Yes to Yourself" and complete the following exercise.

1. The first step is to tune in to your thoughts.

   a. Listen to the messages you send to yourself.

   b. To help capture these messages, you can repeat them, or
   write them down. _____

2. Next, isolate destructive words and phrases.

   a. One woman's inner voice told her she was only _a secretary._
   _____

   b. One man's voice told him he was just a salesman. _____
   _____

   c. Once you zero in on such negative messages, you can fight them.

3. After you identify a negative thought, stop the thought.

   a. You must fight the negative thoughts with one word: Stop! _____.

   b. Doing this is not as easy as it appears.

    c. To silence the inner voice, you must be _____*forceful*_____ and *tenacious.*

  4. Once you have learned to get rid of the inner statements that cause fear and anxiety, you can accentuate the positive.

    a. Replace the bad thought with a good one.

    b. For instance, think about _____*your promotion*_____ or *a pleasant hike in the woods*, the authors say.

  5. Finally, reorient yourself.

    a. To brighten your mood, *change the direction of your thinking.*

    b. Doing this will help you to see yourself and your life differently.

    c. Keep focused on _*your best self*_ , the person you want to become.

    d. You will be motivated by this picture of you at your best.

| WRITING FROM READING: "Say Yes to Yourself"

When you write on any of the following topics, be sure to work through the stages of the writing process in preparing your paragraph.

  1. In a paragraph, explain what Joseph Martorano and John P. Kildahl mean by "self-defeatist thinking" and how they believe a person can overcome this thinking in several steps.

  2. For one day, jot down all your negative thoughts. Pick out the ones that are the most unrealistic and, in a paragraph, write about one of those unrealistic thoughts. First, explain the thought. Then explain the steps you would take to challenge it. These steps can be based on Martorano and Kildahl's article but should be specifically applied to your thought and how you would deal with it.

  3. Write a paragraph about the steps you take to comfort or support a friend who is depressed or anxious.

  4. Pretend that you have suffered a great blow to your confidence. Maybe you have lost a job, failed a test, broken up with a partner—you pick the circumstance. Write a paragraph explaining the steps you would take to regain your confidence. Include the ways in which you would refocus your thinking.

  5. Interview someone (a friend, relative, co-worker, teacher) who always seems positive and optimistic. Ask this person to describe how he or she copes with a setback or disappointment. You can ask such questions as

      Do you ever feel defeated or sad?
      What's your first reaction to bad news?
      What do you do to cope?
      How do you try to think positive thoughts?

Prepare at least seven questions before the interview. At the interview, take notes. Use these notes to write a paragraph about how this person copes with a setback.

How to Buy a New Car

Amy Dacyczyn

Amy Dacyczyn believed she could fulfill her dream of having a large family and buying a house without both partners earning full-time incomes. Later, she became "a crusader for the causes of thrift and frugality." Years later, she and her husband had six children and a farmhouse in New England. She did it, she says, by "saving more rather than earning more," and by starting a national newsletter, The Tightwad Gazette, which had 100,000 subscriptions within two years. This selection is Dacyczyn's reply to a reader's question.

Words You May Need to Know (corresponding paragraph numbers are in parentheses)

ammo (1): ammunition; in this case, information which a car buyer can use to bargain for the price of a car

meticulously (2): carefully

frigid (3): very cold

pertains (4): is related to, refers to

bearing in mind (6): remembering

specifications (7): a detailed description of requirements

quota (8): a required share

Dear Amy,

1   I am interested in finding out how your husband purchased a new car and saved so much money. I am desperate for some ammo when dealing with car dealers. It's a jungle out there!

Judith Perry

Lee, Massachusetts

Dear Judith,

2   Purchasing a new car can only be considered economical if you plan to own it for more than ten years, you maintain it meticulously, and you buy it with cash. The exception would be if your cash is invested in a safe plan that has a higher interest rate than the interest rate you could get for a car loan. At least try to pay off the loan quickly.

3   Figuring that you expect to own this vehicle for ten or more years, plan ahead. Don't buy a compact car if you are planning a family. Carefully consider the options you want. When purchasing our Horizon, we decided to save $250 and not get the rear window wiper and defogger. However, there were many frigid mornings of frost scraping when we wished we had gotten it.

4   The ammo to which you refer can be found in bookstores: a new car buyer's guide. Find one that pertains to the type of vehicle you want, tells you the suggested list price and dealer's cost. The dealer's cost is broken down by models and options.

5   After you decide on the model you want, visit a dealer to learn the codes for options and which options go together.

6   Make up a list of options with the codes, dealer's cost, and the suggested list price. Total up the prices. From this determine what you feel is an allowable profit, bearing in mind that the dealer will get further discounts below the dealer cost. A $200 to $500 profit will be adequate.

7   Start making the rounds of dealers and tell them what you would be willing to pay. If they do not want to meet your price, go elsewhere. To speed up the process, you can mail copies of your specifications and the price you are willing to pay to other area dealers. Also check on buying clubs or organizations that can get you a group discount.

8   In general, remember that sometimes at the end of the month, dealers become desperate to make a sales quota. Don't let dealers talk you into buying something other than what you have decided you want. Avoid trading in. You'll get a better price for your old car through a private sale. Ignore sales and rebates. These are designed to confuse you.

9   If you buy off-the-lot, you will likely pay for options you didn't really want and not get ones you really wanted. The dealer has money tied up in a lot car and won't give you as good a deal.

10   In general, dealerships will not sell any car at a loss. They don't operate like grocery stores, which sell one item at a loss to get you to buy several more. You will buy only one car from them. However, they will cut their profits to the bone. Your only consideration should be the bottom line. How much you "save" is not as important as how much you spend. Using this method, my husband has gotten roughly 20 percent off the sticker price of two vehicles.

 12

Practice

Identifying Details and Examples in the Steps of "How to Buy a New Car"

Amy Dacyczyn offers simple steps for saving money on a new car and explains each step with clear details and examples. To become more familiar with the steps and the details, reread "How to Buy a New Car" and complete the following exercise.

1. Before you begin shopping, do some preliminary work.

    a. Plan ahead; imagine that you will keep your new car for ten or more years.

    b. Think carefully about the _options_ you will want on the car.

    c. In a bookstore, find _a new car buyer's guide_ _____

        _____ about the type of car you want.

2. Visit one dealer to research the options for the kind of car you want.

    a. Learn the codes for the _options._

    b. Learn the dealer's cost.

c. Learn the *suggested list price.*

d. Also learn which options go together.

3. Then start looking, exploring all possibilities as you bargain.

a. Make the rounds of dealers.

b. You can also mail *copies of your specifications and the price you are willing to pay* to other dealers.

c. Check ___*buying clubs*___ or ___*organizations*___ that can get you a group discount.

4. As you make a deal, keep several tips in mind.

a. At the end of the month, dealers may become *desperate to make a sales quota.*

b. Don't get talked into *buying anything except what you decided you want.*

c. If you buy a car off the lot, you may *pay for options you didn't want* and may not *get the options you really wanted.*

Above all, remember that how much you are spending is the most important consideration.

WRITING FROM READING: "How to Buy a New Car"

When you write on any of the following topics, be sure to work through the stages of the writing process in preparing your paragraph.

1. In a paragraph, explain Amy Dacyczyn's method for buying a new car. Break the steps into the planning part, the research part (at a bookstore and at one dealer), and the bargaining part.

2. If you recently found a good deal on an item, write a paragraph explaining how another person could get the same kind of deal. For example, you can write on one of the following topics:

   how to find good furniture at a low price
   how to get the best deals on clothes
   how to find the best wedding dress (or bridesmaid's gown, prom dress, tuxedo) at a reasonable price
   how to save on a DVD player or home entertainment unit

   You can choose any "how to buy" topic with which you have some experience.

3. Amy Dacyczyn says that you can buy a new car economically if you keep it for more than ten years, pay cash for it, and maintain it meticulously. In a paragraph, explain the steps of one regular maintenance task such as rotating and balancing the tires, changing the oil, or replacing filters or belts.

4. Write a paragraph explaining how to sell your car privately.

5. Write a paragraph for someone who knows nothing about cars. Teach this person how to find a good automobile mechanic.

CHAPTER 28

Moving from Paragraphs to Essays

WHAT IS AN ESSAY?

You write an essay when you have more to say than can be covered in one paragraph. An **essay** can consist of one paragraph, but in this book, we take it to mean a writing of more than one paragraph. An essay has a main point, called a *thesis*, supported by subpoints. The subpoints are the *topic sentences*. Each paragraph in the *body*, or main part, of the essay has a topic sentence. In fact, each paragraph in the body of the essay is like the paragraphs you've already written because each one makes a point and then supports it.

COMPARING THE SINGLE PARAGRAPH AND THE ESSAY

Read the paragraph and the essay that follow; both are about sharing happy moments. You will notice many similarities.

A Single Paragraph

When I am happy, I want to share my happiness. When my wife gave birth to our son, for example, I couldn't wait to tell everyone. I started by calling my parents, my wife's parents, and every other relative I could think of. After I had run out of family members, I told friends, coworkers, and even a few total strangers. In another instance, I had to share the news about my dream of getting a college education. As soon as I opened the letter announcing my college loan, I wanted to spread the information. Just seeing the look on my wife's face increased my happiness. Later, telling my best friend, who had encouraged me to apply for the loan, was a pleasure. When good comes into my life, I figure, why not share it?

An Essay

Everybody has special moments of pure joy when a dream suddenly becomes a reality or a goal is finally in sight. These rare times mark the high points in life, and some people like to experience them alone. However, I am not one of these people. When I am happy, I want to share my happiness.

When my wife gave birth to our son, for example, I couldn't wait to tell everyone. I started by calling my parents, my wife's parents, and every other relative I could think of. By the time I found myself calling my second cousin in New Zealand, I realized I had run out of relatives. I prolonged my happiness by calling all my friends, the people at the bakery where I work, and even a few strangers. One poor man nearly tripped when I ran into him as he tried to get out of the hospital elevator. "Oh, I'm so sorry," I said, "but I've just had a baby boy." I even told the mail carrier on my street.

In another instance, I had to share the news about my dream of getting a college education. As soon as I opened the letter announcing my college loan, I wanted to spread the information. Just seeing the look on my wife's face increased my happiness. She knew what I was thinking: with the loan, I wouldn't have to take a second job in order to attend college. Later, telling my best friend, who had encouraged me to apply for the loan, was a pleasure. My getting the loan was his victory, too, for without him, I would have given up on going to college.

I suppose I could have told my friend about my financial aid a few days later over lunch. As for the birth of my son, I could have saved hefty long-distance phone charges by sending birth announcements to aunts, uncles, and cousins who live far away. But I chose not to hold back. When good comes into my life, I figure, why not share it?

If you read the two selections carefully, you noticed that they make the same main point, and they support that point with two subpoints.

> **main point:** When I am happy, I want to share my happiness.
> **subpoints: 1.** When my wife gave birth to our son, I couldn't wait to tell everyone.
> **2.** I had to spread the news about my dream of getting a college education.

You noticed that the essay is longer because it has more details and examples to support the points.

ORGANIZING AN ESSAY

When you write an essay of more than one paragraph, the **thesis** is the focus of your entire essay; it is the major point of your essay. The other important points that relate to the thesis are in topic sentences.

TEACHING TIP:

Tell students that the thesis statement is the controlling idea for the essay, much as the topic sentence is the controlling idea for a paragraph.

Thesis: Working as a salesperson has changed my character.

> **Topic sentence:** I have had to learn patience.
> **Topic sentence:** I have developed the ability to listen.
> **Topic sentence:** I have become more tactful.

Notice that the thesis expresses a bigger idea than the topic sentences below it, and it is supported by the topic sentences. The essay has an introduction, a body, and a conclusion.

1. **Introduction:** The first paragraph is usually the introduction. The thesis goes here.
2. **Body:** This central part of the essay is the part where you support your main point (the thesis). Each paragraph in the body of the essay has its own topic sentence.
3. **Conclusion:** Usually one paragraph long, the conclusion reminds the reader of the thesis. It can be shorter than a body paragraph.

WRITING THE THESIS

INSTRUCTOR'S NOTE:

Throughout this chapter, the term "thesis" is synonymous with "thesis statement" and "thesis sentence."

There are several characteristics of a thesis:

1. It is expressed in a sentence. A thesis is *not* the same as the topic of the essay, or as the title of the essay:

   topic: learning to ski
   title: Why I Learned to Ski
   thesis: I learned to ski because all my friends ski, I needed more exercise in the winter, and I wanted to meet girls.

2. A thesis **does not announce;** it makes a point about the subject.

   announcement: This essay will explain the reasons why street racing is popular with teens.
   thesis: Street racing is popular with teens because it gives them a sense of power and identity.

3. A thesis **is not too broad.** Some ideas are just too big to cover well in an essay. A thesis that tries to cover too much can lead to a superficial or boring essay.

   too broad: The world would be a better place if everyone would just be more tolerant.
   acceptable thesis: The diversity celebration at our school spread good feeling among many groups.

4. A thesis **is not too narrow.** Sometimes, writers start with a thesis that looks good because it seems specific and precise. Later, when they try to support such a thesis, they can't find anything to say.

   too narrow: Yesterday I spent five hours in a hospital emergency room, waiting for help.
   acceptable thesis: Because I have no health insurance, illness is always a crisis for me.

HINTS FOR WRITING A THESIS

1. Your thesis can **mention the specific subpoints** of your essay. For example, your thesis might be

Boundaries are important because they make children feel safe, connected, and loved.

With this thesis, you have indicated the three subpoints of your essay: (1) Boundaries make children feel safe, (2) Boundaries make children feel connected, and (3) Boundaries make children feel loved.

2. Another way to write your thesis is to **make a point** without listing your subpoints. For example, you can write a thesis like the following:

Children need boundaries in order to grow.

With this thesis, you can still use the subpoints stating that boundaries make children feel safe, boundaries make children feel connected, and boundaries make children feel loved. You just don't have to mention all your subpoints in the thesis.

Exercise 1

Practice

Recognizing Good Thesis Sentences

TEACHING TIP:

Ask students if they can spot which statements are actually fragments and thus not suitable for thesis statements.

Following is a list of thesis statements. Some are acceptable, but others are too broad or too narrow. Some are announcements; others are topics, not sentences. Put a *G* next to the good thesis sentences.

1. _____ What to do if a tornado threatens will be discussed in this essay.

2. _____ Rainfall last month was less than five inches.

3. _____ Communication is the basis of all relationships.

4. _____ Why coffee has become a growth industry in America.

5. _____ Organized crime is an evil force today.

6. __*G*__ Male college students are choosing a wide range of hair styles.

7. __*G*__ Cameras should be installed at busy intersections to photograph drivers who run red lights.

8. _____ St. Paul is the capital of Minnesota.

9. _____ The disadvantages of marrying in your thirties.

10. __*G*__ Traveling by bus can be an eye-opening adventure.

Exercise 2

Practice

Selecting a Good Thesis Sentence

In each pair of thesis statements below, put a *G* next to the good thesis sentence.

1. a. _____ The effects of music on young children.

   b. __*G*__ Music is an effective tool for teaching young children.

2. a. __*G*__ A high-speed train would take some of the traffic off our local highway.

   b. _____ Something must be done to solve the international crisis of overdevelopment and overloaded highways.

3. a. _____ The difficulties of learning English as a second language will be discussed in this essay.

b. ___G___ Students learning English as a second language have difficulties with fast-talking native speakers and confusing grammar rules.

4. a. _____ The need for a new high school in Homeville.

   b. ___G___ Homeville's high school is falling apart.

5. a. ___G___ I quit my job because the working conditions were terrible.

   b. _____ The terrible working conditions and what I did about them will be the subject of this essay.

6. a. ___G___ Obedience training can help a young dog in several ways.

   b. _____ What obedience training can do to help a young dog grow into a valued pet.

7. a. _____ The similarities between an SUV and a light truck in federal fuel economy standards.

   b. ___G___ In federal fuel economy standards, there are significant similarities between an SUV and a light truck.

8. a. ___G___ Fresh pizza has a better smell, taste, and texture than frozen pizza.

   b. _____ Why fresh pizza is better than frozen pizza.

9. a. _____ Cable television service and its drawbacks.

   b. ___G___ There are three problems for subscribers to cable television.

10. a. _____ Last year, Fernwood got its own suicide hotline.

    b. ___G___ Fernwood's suicide hotline is helping to save lives.

Exercise 3   **Writing a Thesis That Relates to the Subpoints**

Practice   Following are lists of subpoints that could be discussed in an essay. Write a thesis for each list. Remember that there are two ways to write a thesis: you can write a thesis that includes the specific subpoints, or you can write one that makes a point without listing the subpoints. As an example, the first one is done for you, using both kinds of topic sentences.

1. **one kind of thesis:** Children need to leave their computers and televisions and play some outdoor sports.

   another kind of thesis: For children playing sports outdoors burns more energy, creates more friendships, and stimulates more interest than playing indoors.

   subpoints:

   a. Sitting at a computer or in front of a television burns very little energy; playing sports burns more energy.

   b. Playing indoors is often solitary; sports involve other children and may lead to friendships.

   c. Children playing indoors can easily become bored, but outdoor sports require more involvement.

2. **thesis:** *Grandparents can help their grandchildren in two significant ways.*

   subpoints:

   a. Grandparents can be good listeners when grandchildren have a problem.

   b. Grandparents can be generous with their time when grandchildren need help.

3. **thesis:** *Grandparents can be both irritating and helpful to their grandchildren.*

   subpoints:

   a. Grandparents can be intolerant of grandchildren's appearance or lifestyle.

   b. Grandparents can be too free with their opinions and advice.

   c. Grandparents can be good listeners when grandchildren have a problem.

   d. Grandparents can be generous with their time when grandchildren need help.

4. **thesis:** *People interviewing for a job should dress appropriately, appear confident, and express their enthusiasm.*

   subpoints:

   a. People interviewing for a job should be appropriately dressed.

   b. Interviewers want people who are confident.

   c. People who are enthusiastic about the job are more likely to impress interviewers.

5. **thesis:** *There are three occasions when I overspend.*

   _____

   subpoints:

   a. I overspend to cheer myself up.

   b. I overspend to celebrate a success.

   c. I overspend to impress a friend with a fancy gift.

WRITING THE ESSAY IN STEPS

In an essay, you follow the same steps you learned in writing a paragraph—thought lines, outlines, rough drafts, and final version—but you adapt them to the longer essay form.

Thought Lines **Gathering Ideas: An Essay**

Often you begin by *narrrowing a topic*. Your instructor may give you a large topic so you can find something smaller, within the broad one, that you would like to write about.

Some students think that because they have several paragraphs to write, they should pick a big topic, one that will give them enough to say. But big topics can lead to boring, superficial, general essays. A smaller topic can challenge you to find the specific, concrete examples and details that make an essay effective.

If your instructor asked you to write about student life, for instance, you might *freewrite* some ideas as you narrow the topic:

Narrowing the Topic of Student Life

Student activities—how boring!
Maybe how to meet people at college, except, how *do* you meet people? I don't really know. I have my friends, but I'm not sure how I met them.
The food on campus. Everyone will do that topic.
The classrooms in college. The tiny chairs and the temperature. Yes!

In your freewriting, you can consider your *purpose*—to write an essay about some aspect of student life—and *audience*—your instructor and classmates. Your narrowed topic will appeal to this audience since both college teachers and students spend a good part of their time in classrooms.

Listing Ideas

Once you have a narrow topic, you can use whatever process works for you. You can brainstorm by writing a series of questions and answers about your topic, you can freewrite on the topic, you can list ideas on the topic, or you can do any combination of these processes.

Following is a sample *listing of ideas* on the topic of classrooms.

College Classrooms: A List

the tiny chairs	the temperature
the awful desks	all the graffiti
the carving in the desks	too hot in the room
freezing on some days	cramped rooms
blinds on windows don't close	teacher's desk
no one cares	

By *clustering* related items on the list, you'll find it easier to see the connections between ideas. The following items have been clustered (grouped), and they have been listed under subtitles.

College Classrooms: Ideas in Clusters

the furniture	**student damage**
the tiny chairs	the carving in the desks
the awful desks	all the graffiti
teacher's desk	

the temperature

freezing on some days
too hot in the room
blinds on the windows don't close

When you surveyed the clusters, you probably noticed that some of the ideas from the original list were left out. These ideas, on the cramped rooms and no one caring, could fit into more than one place and might not fit anywhere. You might come back to them later.

When you name each cluster by giving it a subtitle, you move toward a focus for each body paragraph of your essay. And by beginning to focus the body paragraphs, you start thinking about the main point, the thesis of the essay. Concentrating on the thesis and on focused paragraphs helps you to *unify* your essay.

Reread the clustered ideas. When you do so, you'll notice that each cluster is about a different kind of problem in the college classroom. You can incorporate that concept into a thesis with a sentence such as this:

> The typical classroom at my college is unwelcoming because of its tiny furniture, uncomfortable temperature, and student damage.

Once you have a thesis and a list of details, you can begin working on the outlines part of your essay.

TEACHING TIP:

This is a good place to remind students that not all thesis statements are segmented. However, they should be aware that some writing instructors require a segmented thesis statement because it provides students with the direction and organization of the essay's body paragraphs.

Exercise 4

 *Collaborate*

Answers Will Vary.

Possible answers shown at right.

Narrowing Topics

Working with a partner or a group, narrow these topics so that the new topics are related, but smaller, and suitable for short essays between four and six paragraphs long. The first topic is narrowed for you.

1. **topic:** health
   smaller, related topics:
   a. fighting a cold
   b. the right vitamins to take
   c. getting a good night's sleep

2. **topic:** law enforcement
   smaller, related topics:
   a. salaries for sheriff's deputies
   b. speed traps in our town
   c. majoring in criminal justice

3. **topic:** television
   smaller, related topics:
   a. wrestling on television
   b. plasma screen televisions
   c. home shopping channels

4. **topic:** homes
   smaller, related topics:
   a. do-it-yourself plumbing repairs
   b. my favorite place in the house
   c. our basement apartment

5. **topic:** athletes
   smaller, related topics:
   a. my career in high school football
   b. running a marathon
   c. amateur boxing in my neighborhood

Exercise 5

Practice

Clustering Related Ideas

Below are two topics, each with a list of ideas. Mark all the related items on the list with the same number (*1*, *2*, or *3*). Some items might not get any number. When you've finished marking the list, write a title for each number that explains the cluster of ideas.

1. topic: what makes a relationship thrive

_____ experts disagree on the importance of children

__1__ the partners are friends as well as lovers

__3__ there is a safe and pleasant home

__1__ the partners are mature

__3__ there is money coming in to pay the bills

__2__ friends provide a support system

__1__ the partners share mutual goals

__2__ family members accept and act kindly towards the partners

__3__ there are no major health problems

__2__ no friends or family try to control the partners' decisions

The ideas marked *1* can be titled _partners' relationship_

The ideas marked *2* can be titled _their link to friends and family_

The ideas marked *3* can be titled _their secure existence_

Answers Will Vary.

Possible answers shown at right.

2. topic: the first day of a new job

__3__ go home, breathe a sigh of relief, and relax

__1__ leave early for work

__3__ tell yourself you've just survived the hardest day of your new job

__2__ watch others carefully to see how things are done

__1__ get up extra early

__1__ don't lose any sleep worrying about how the day will go

_____ lunch is an awkward time

__2__ keep your energy level up with your manager and co-workers

__2__ tune in to the rhythm and style of the workplace

__1__ lay your clothes out on the night before your first day

__2__ ask about anything you don't understand or know how to do

The items marked *1* can be titled _before work_

The items marked *2* can be titled _during work_

The items marked *3* can be titled _after work_

Outlines Devising a Plan: An Essay

In the next stage of writing your essay, draft an outline. Use the thesis to focus your ideas. There are many kinds of outlines, but all are used to help a writer organize ideas. When you use a **formal outline,** you show the difference between a main idea and its supporting detail by *indenting* the supporting detail. In a formal outline, Roman numerals (numbers) and capital letters are used. Each Roman numeral represents a paragraph, and the letters beneath the numeral represent supporting details.

TEACHING TIP:

Tell students that the thesis will be only one sentence (statement) and that they should expect to develop some general statements to lead into the thesis. Later in this chapter, you will find instruction on writing the introductory paragraph, on pages 455 to 458.

The Structure of a Formal Outline

first paragraph	I. Thesis
second paragraph	II. Topic sentence
details	A.
	B.
	C.
	D.
	E.
third paragraph	III. Topic sentence
details	A.
	B.
	C.
	D.
	E.
fourth paragraph	IV. Topic sentence
details	A.
	B.
	C.
	D.
	E.
fifth paragraph	V. Conclusion

HINTS FOR OUTLINING

Developing a good, clear outline now can save you hours of confused, disorganized writing later. The extra time you spend to make sure your outline has sufficient details and that *each paragraph stays on one point* will pay off in the long run.

1. Check the topic sentences. Keep in mind that each topic sentence in each body paragraph should support the thesis sentence. If a topic sentence is not carefully connected to the thesis, the structure of the essay will be confusing. Here are a thesis and a list of topic sentences; the topic sentence that does not fit is crossed out:

thesis:	I. Designing a CD of a person's favorite songs is a creative act and a thoughtful gift.
topic sentences:	II. Selecting the songs takes insight.
	III. Assembling the CD requires imagination.
	IV. ~~CD players are getting cheaper all the time~~.
	V. Whoever receives the CD will be flattered that someone took the time to design such a personal gift.
	VI. A personally crafted CD challenges the mind of the giver and opens the heart of the receiver.

Since the thesis of this outline is about the creative challenge of designing a personal CD as a gift and the pleasure of receiving one, topic sentence IV doesn't fit: it isn't about making the gift *or* receiving it. It takes the essay off track. A careful check of the links between the thesis and the topic sentences will help keep your essay focused.

2. Include enough details. Some writers believe that they don't need many details in the outline. They feel they can fill in the details later, when they actually write the essay. Even though some writers do manage to add details later, others who are in a hurry or who run out of ideas run into problems.

For example, imagine that a writer has included very few details in an outline such as in this outline for a paragraph:

II. Vandalism of cars takes many forms.

    A. Most cars suffer external damage.

    B. Some are hit in their interiors.

The paragraph created from that outline might be too short and lack specific details, like this:

> Vandalism of cars takes many forms. First of all, most cars suffer external damage. However, some are hit in their interiors.

If you have difficulty thinking of ideas when you write, try to tackle the problem in the outline. The more details you put into your outline, the more detailed and effective your draft essay will be. For example, suppose the same outline on the burglary topic had more details, like this:

        II. Vandalism of cars takes many forms.

more details about exterior damage
    A. Most cars suffer external damage.
    B. The most common damage is breaking off the car antenna.
    C. "Keying" a car, scratching its surface with a key, is also widespread.
    D. Some vandals slash or take the air out of the tires.
    F. Others pour paint on the body of the car.

more details about interior damage
    G. Some are hit in their interiors.
    H. Interior damage ranges from ripped upholstery to torn carpet.

You will probably agree that the paragraph can be more detailed, too.

3. Stay on one point. It is a good idea to check the outline of each body paragraph to see if each paragraph stays on one point. Compare each topic sentence, which is at the top of the list for the paragraph, against the detail indented under it. Staying on one point gives each paragraph unity.

Below is the outline for a paragraph that has problems staying on one point. See if you can spot the problem areas.

        III. Charles is a fun-loving and cheerful person.

        A. Every morning at work, he has a new joke for me.

        B. He even makes our boss, who is very serious, smile.

    C. One day when a customer was extremely rude to him, he kept his temper.

    D. On weekends, when our job gets hectic, Charles never gets irritated.

    E. Most of our customers love him because he always greets them with, "How are you on this beautiful day?"

    F. When we all took a pay cut, he looked on the positive side.

    G. "At least we still have our jobs," he said.

The topic sentence of the paragraph is about Charles' love of fun and cheerfulness. But sentences C and D talk about Charles' ability to remain calm. When you have a problem staying on one point, you can solve the problem two ways:

1. Eliminate details that do not fit your main point.
2. Change the topic sentence to cover all the ideas in the paragraph.

For example, you could cut out sentences C and D about Charles' calm nature, getting rid of the details that do not fit. As an alternative, you could change the topic sentence in the paragraph so that it relates to all the ideas in the paragraph. A better topic sentence is "Charles is a fun-loving, even-tempered, and cheerful person."

Revisiting the Thought Lines Stage

Writing an outline can help you identify skimpy places in your plan, places where your paragraphs will need more details. You can get these details in two ways:

1. Go back to the writing you did in the thought lines stage. Check whether items on a list or ideas from freewriting can lead you to more details for your outline.
2. Brainstorm for more details by using a question-and-answer approach. For example, if the outline includes "My little sister is greedy," you might ask, "When is she greedy? How greedy is she?" Or if the outline includes "There is nothing to do in this town," you might ask, "What do you mean? Sports? Clubs? Parties?"

The time you spend writing and revising your outline will make it easier for you to write an essay that is well developed, unified, and coherently structured. The checklist below may help you to revise.

 **Checklist**

A Checklist for Revising the Outline of an Essay

1. **Unity:** Do the thesis and topic sentences all lead to the same point? Does each paragraph make one, and only one, point? Do the details in each paragraph support the topic sentence? Does the conclusion unify the essay?
2. **Support:** Do the body paragraphs have enough supporting details?
3. **Coherence:** Are the paragraphs in the most effective order? Are the details in each paragraph arranged in the most effective order?

     A sentence outline on college classrooms follows. It includes the thesis in the first paragraph. The topic sentences have been created from the titles of the ideas clustered earlier. The details have been drawn from ideas in the clusters and from further brainstorming. The conclusion in this outline has just one sentence that unifies the essay.

An Outline for an Essay

paragraph 1

I. Thesis: The typical classroom at my college is unwelcoming because of its tiny furniture, uncomfortable temperature, and student damage.

paragraph 2

topic sentence

details

II. Child-size furniture makes it difficult to focus on adult-level classes.

    A. The student chairs are tiny.

    B. I am six feet tall, and I feel as if I am crammed into a kindergarten chair.

    C. They are attached to miniature desks which are just slightly enlarged armrests.

    D. I cannot fit my legs under the desk.

    E. I cannot fit my textbook and a notebook on the surface of the desk.

    G. In some classrooms, the teacher has no desk and is forced to use one of the miniature student versions.

paragraph 3

topic sentence

details

III. The temperature in the classrooms is anything but pleasant.

    A. I have been at the college for both the fall and winter terms.

    B. In the early fall, the rooms were too hot.

    C. The air conditioning feebly pumped hot air.

    D. The sun beat through the glass windows because the blinds were broken.

    E. On some days in the winter, we froze.

    F. Two of my teachers have reported the problems to maintenance, but nothing changed.

    G. It is hard to concentrate when you are sweating or shivering.

paragraph 4

topic sentence

details

IV. Student damage to the classrooms makes them seedy and ugly.

    A. There is graffiti all over the desks.

    B. There are messages, slogans, and drawings.

    C. They are all childish.

    D. Half the desks and chairs have gum stuck to their undersides.

    E. Some students carve into the desks and chairs.

    F. Others have stained the carpet with spilled coffee or soft drinks.

G. It's depressing to think that my fellow students enjoy damaging the place where they come to learn.

paragraph 5
conclusion

V. When I started college, I knew I would face many challenges, but I didn't expect them to include squeezing into the chairs, dressing for a blizzard or a heat wave, and picking the gum off my desk.

Exercise 6

Practice

Completing an Outline for an Essay

Following is part of an outline that has a thesis and topic sentences, but no details. Add the details and write in complete sentences. Write one sentence for each capital letter. Be sure that the details are connected to the topic sentence.

I. **Thesis:** Money has a different meaning for different people.

II. When some people think of money, they think of the freedom to spend it on whatever they want for themselves.

Answers Will Vary.

Possible answers shown at right.

A. On payday, some go out and celebrate in clubs and bars.

B. Others spend their money on their cars.

C. Some spend their cash on fancy wardrobes.

D. Some like jewelry.

E. Some spend their money at casinos.

III. To others, money means security.

A. They can pay off their credit cards.

B. They can buy health insurance.

C. They can fill the refrigerator with food.

D. They can afford to heat their homes.

E. They can save for an emergency.

IV. Some people think of money as something to share.

A. Many people send money to family in another country.

B. Parents pay their child's tuition.

C. Some people support elderly or sick family members.

D. Many give money to their church, temple, or mosque.

E. Many give to charity.

V. The way people perceive money reveals what matters to them.

Exercise 7

Practice

Focusing an Outline for an Essay

The outline below has a thesis and details, but it has no topic sentences for the body paragraphs. Write the topic sentences.

I. **Thesis:** My first visit to the Movieland Movie Theater will also be my last.

II. It was hard to watch the film in a filthy, dilapidated place, with an incompetent staff and nonfunctioning equipment.

   a. The place smelled moldy and sour.
   b. The first seat I tried to sit in had no back.
   c. The second one had no arms.
   d. When I finally found an intact seat, my shoes stuck to the floor as I sat down.
   e. The floor was coated with dried up soda and candy.
   f. The projectionist forgot to start the movie.
   g. Someone from the audience had to find and remind him.
   h. Two of the speakers were broken.

III. The audience was rude and inconsiderate.

   a. People from the audience talked throughout the movie.
   b. Several talked on their cell phones.
   c. Four people sitting in the front row shouted to their friends, who had just arrived at the back of the theater.
   d. Two children ran up and down the aisles for an hour during the movie.
   e. Some teens started throwing popcorn.
   f. One man near me couldn't hear the dialogue on the screen, so his wife shouted it to him.

IV. I never want to repeat the experience I had at Movieland.

Rough Lines   Drafting and Revising: An Essay

When you are satisfied with your outline, you can begin drafting and revising the essay. Start by writing a first draft of the essay, which includes these parts: introduction, body paragraphs, and conclusion.

WRITING THE INTRODUCTION

Where Does the Thesis Go?

The **thesis** should appear in the introduction of the essay, in the first paragraph. But most of the time it should not be the first sentence. In front of the thesis, write a few (three or more) sentences of introduction. Generally, the thesis is the *last sentence* in the introductory paragraph.

Why put the thesis at the end of the first paragraph? First of all, writing several sentences in front of your main idea gives you a chance to lead into it, gradually and smoothly. This will help you build interest and gain the reader's attention. Also, by placing the thesis after a few sentences of introduction, you will not startle the reader with your main point.

Finally, if your thesis is at the end of the introduction, it states the main point of the essay just before that point is supported in the body paragraphs. Putting the thesis at the end of the introduction is like putting an arrow pointing to the supporting ideas in the essay.

Hints for Writing the Introduction

There are a number of ways to write an introduction.

1. You can **begin with some general statements** that gradually lead to your thesis:

general statements

My mother has two framed pictures in the living room. They are sketches of a town square. In the pictures, people are sitting and talking, shopping in the small stores around the square, and strolling through the friendly looking streets. I envy the people in these scenes, for they seem to enjoy a calm, central gathering place, far from busy highways and enormous parking lots. Unfortunately, my community has no such place.

thesis at end   My town needs a neighborly, accessible town center.

2. You can **begin with a quote** that leads smoothly to your thesis. The quote can be a quote from someone famous, or it can be an old saying. It can be something your mother always told you, or it can be a slogan from an advertisement, or the words of a song.

quotation

A song tells us, "It's a small, small, small, small world." There are days when I wish my world were smaller. Sometimes I get sick of driving to a huge supermarket for my groceries, then dashing to a giant mall for new shoes, and finally making a quick stop at a drive-through restaurant for a hamburger. As I make this journey, I rarely meet anyone I know. At these times, I wish my life were different: I'd like to get off the highway, forget the fast food and the huge malls, and run into a few friends as I do my errands. Then I realize that

thesis at end   my town needs a neighborly, accessible town center.

(Note: You can add transition words or phrases to your thesis, as in the sample above.)

3. You can **tell a story** as a way of leading into your thesis. You can open with the story of something that happened to you or to someone you know, a story you read about or heard on the news.

story

Yesterday my best friend called, and we got into a lengthy conversation. After we had talked for half an hour, we realized we wanted to continue our conversation face-to-face. "Let's meet for coffee," my friend said. He suggested a coffee shop near the interstate highway. I suggested another place which he said was "in the middle of nowhere." Then we ran out of ideas. There was no easy, central place. At that moment, it **thesis at end** occurred to me that <u>my town needs a neighborly, accessible town center</u>.

4. You can **explain why this topic is worth writing about.** Explaining could mean giving some background on the topic, or it could mean discussing why the topic is an important one.

explain Almost everyone feels lonely at some time. Teens feel left out by the many cliques that make up high school society. Older people, often suffering the loss of a spouse, need human contact. Singles try to find a comfortable place in what seems to be a world of married couples. As for those couples, each partner needs to feel part of a world outside of marriage. In my community, there is no friendly place where all types of people can **thesis at end** feel accepted. <u>My town needs a neighborly, accessible town center.</u>

5. You can **use one or more questions** to lead into your thesis. You can open with a question or questions that will be answered by your thesis, or you can open with a question or questions that catch the reader's attention and move towards your thesis.

question Have you ever seen an old movie called "It's a Wonderful Life"? It's about George Bailey, a small-town husband and father whose life changes on Christmas Eve when an angel visits to teach George a lesson. Although I enjoy the plot of the movie, what I like most about the film is the small town George lives in, where everyone seems to know everyone else and life centers on a few streets of stores, homes, and businesses. I sometimes wish that I had a little of that simple life.

thesis at end   Then I conclude that <u>my town needs a neighborly, accessible town center.</u>

6. You can **open with a contradiction** of your main point as a way of attracting the reader's interest and leading to your thesis. You can begin with an idea that is the opposite of what you will say in your thesis. The opposition of your opening and your thesis creates interest.

contradiction   My town appears to have every shopping and entertainment attraction of an ideal community. It has two giant malls, a movie theater with sixteen screens and stadium seating, cafes, restaurants, popular clubs, a water park, a skating rink, and a bowling alley. However, it doesn't offer what people want most: the comfort of a small-town gathering place that invites shoppers, strollers, people with their dogs, and people who like to **thesis at end**   sit, talk, and drink coffee. <u>My town needs a neighborly, accessible town center.</u>

Exercise 8

Practice

Writing an Introduction

Below are five thesis sentences. Pick one. Then write an introductory paragraph on the lines provided. Your last sentence should be the thesis sentence. If your instructor agrees, read your introduction to others in the class who wrote an introduction to the same thesis, or read your introduction to the entire class.

Thesis Sentences

1. What men wear makes a statement about the image they want to convey.

2. Technology has revolutionized the music industry.

3. Today's tattoos can be art, fashion, or a personal statement.

4. Many parents try to give their children what the parents never had.

5. A million dollars would/would not change the way I live my life.

(Write an introduction) _____

_____

_____

_____

_____

_____

_____

WRITING THE BODY OF THE ESSAY

In the body of the essay, the paragraphs *explain, support, and develop* your thesis. In this part of the essay, each paragraph has its own topic sentence. The topic sentence in each paragraph does two things:

1. It focuses the sentences in the paragraph.
2. It makes a point connected to the thesis.

The thesis and the topic sentences are ideas that need to be supported by details, explanations, and examples. You can visualize the connections among the parts of an essay like this:

Introduction with Thesis

	Topic Sentence
	Details
Body	Topic Sentence
	Details
	Topic Sentence
	Details

Conclusion

When you write topic sentences, you can help to organize your essay by referring to the checklist below.

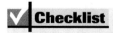

Checklist

A Checklist for the Topic Sentences of an Essay

✔ Does the topic sentence give the point of the paragraph?

✔ Does the topic sentence connect to the thesis of the essay?

How Long Are the Body Paragraphs?

Remember that the body paragraphs of an essay are the place where you explain and develop your thesis. Those paragraphs should be long enough to explain, not just list, your points. To do this well, try to make your body paragraphs *at least seven sentences* long. As you develop your writing skills, you may find that you can support your ideas in fewer than seven sentences.

Developing the Body Paragraphs

You can write well-developed body paragraphs by following the same steps you used in writing single paragraphs for the earlier assignments in this course. By working through the stages of gathering ideas, outlining, drafting, revising, editing, and proofreading, you can create clear, effective paragraphs.

To focus and develop the body paragraphs, ask the questions below as you revise:

✔ Checklist

A Checklist for Developing Body Paragraphs for an Essay

✔ Does the topic sentence cover everything in the paragraph?

✔ Do I have enough details to explain the topic sentence?

✔ Do all the details in the paragraph support, develop, or illustrate the topic sentence?

Creating Topic Sentences

Practice

Following are thesis sentences. For each thesis, write topic sentences (as many as indicated by the numbered blanks). The first one is done for you.

1. **Thesis:** Many families have traditions for celebrating special occasions.

   Topic sentence 1: Family birthdays can involve special rituals.

   Topic sentence 2: At weddings, many family traditions appear.

   Topic sentence 3: Some families have customs for celebrating New Year's Day.

2. **Thesis:** The student center in the daytime is different from the student center in the evening.

   Topic sentence 1: During the day, the center is full of students and noisy.

   Topic sentence 2: The few students at the center in the evening do not make much noise.

Answers Will Vary.

Possible answers shown at right.

3. **Thesis:** It is easy to spot the student who is falling behind in class.

   Topic sentence 1: This student is frequently absent or late.

   Topic sentence 2: He or she often asks questions about material the instructor covered in previous classes.

   Topic sentence 3: He or she often tries to borrow another student's notes or homework assignment.

4. **Thesis:** My closest friends have several characteristics in common.

   Topic sentence 1: They have a great sense of humor.

   Topic sentence 2: They are outgoing.

   Topic sentence 3: They are extremely loyal.

5. **Thesis:** Starting a new job has its good and bad points.

   Topic sentence 1: It is a chance to learn new skills.

   Topic sentence 2: It can lead to advancement.

   Topic sentence 3: It is stressful to work with strangers.

   Topic sentence 4: It means working extra hard to prove oneself.

WRITING THE CONCLUSION

The last paragraph in the essay is the **conclusion.** It does not have to be as long as a body paragraph, but it should be long enough to tie the essay together and remind the reader of the thesis. You can use any of these strategies in writing the conclusion:

1. You can **restate the thesis, in new words.** Go back to the first paragraph of your essay and reread it. For example, this could be the first paragraph of an essay:

introduction

I recently moved to a city that is a thousand miles from my home town. I drove the long distance with only one companion, my mixed-breed dog Casey. Casey was a wonderful passenger: he kept me company, never asked to stop or complained about my driving, and was happy to observe the endless stretches of road. By the end of our trip, I loved Casey even more than I had when we started. Unfortunately, I found that landlords do not appreciate the bonds between dogs and their owners. <u>In fact, renting a</u>

thesis at

end

<u>decent apartment and keeping a dog is nearly</u> <u>impossible.</u>

The thesis, underlined above, is the sentence that you can restate in your conclusion. Your task is to *keep the point but put it in different words.* Then work that restatement into a short paragraph, like this:

Most dogs can adapt to apartment living. They will not bark too much, destroy property, or threaten the neighbors. They can adjust to being alone indoors as long as their owners provide time for fun, exercise, and affection. But most landlords refuse to give dogs the benefit of the

restating the

doubt. <u>The landlords pressure dog owners to</u>

thesis

<u>make a choice between an apartment or a pet.</u>

2. You can **make a judgment, valuation, or recommendation.** Instead of simply restating your point, you can end by making some comment on the issue you've described or the problem you've illustrated. If you were looking for another way to end the essay on finding an apartment that allows pets, for example, you could end with a recommendation.

I understand that landlords need to make a profit on their property and that some dogs and dog owners damage that property. However, not all dogs go wild, and not all dog owners let their

ending with a

pets destroy an apartment. <u>If landlords made an</u>

recommendation

<u>individual judgment about each applicant with</u> <u>a pet, instead of following a hard, cold policy,</u> <u>they might realize that dogs can be model apart-</u> <u>ment dwellers.</u>

3. You can conclude by framing your essay. You can tie your essay together neatly by *using something from your introduction* as a way of concluding. When you take an example, or a question, or even a quote from your first paragraph and refer to it in your last paragraph, you are "framing" the essay. Take another look at the introduction to the essay on finding an apartment that will allow a dog. The writer talks about driving a thousand miles away from home, about his or her dear companion Casey. The writer also mentions the difficulties of finding a decent place to live when landlords will not allow dogs. Now consider how the ideas of the introduction are used in this conclusion:

frame

When <u>I drove into this city a thousand miles</u>

frame

<u>from my home, I brought my dear friend and</u>

frame	loyal companion with me. That friend, <u>my dog</u>
frame	<u>Casey</u>, made me smile as he sat in the passen-
	ger seat, a tall, proud traveler. He fell asleep on
frame	my feet when I stopped at a lonely rest stop.
frame	<u>Many cruel landlords told me I would have to</u>
frame	<u>give Casey up if I wanted a comfortable place to</u>
	<u>live.</u> But I refused, for Casey brings me more
	comfort than any fancy apartment ever could.

Exercise 10   **Choosing a Better Way to Restate the Thesis.**

Practice   Following are five clusters. Each cluster consists of a thesis sentence and two sentences that try to restate the thesis. Each restated sentence could be used as part of the conclusion to an essay. Put **B** next to the sentence in each pair that is a better restatement. Remember that the better choice repeats the same idea as the thesis but does not rely on too many of the same words.

1. thesis: If you want to eat healthy food, avoid sugar and sweets.

restatement 1: _____   Sweets and sugar are not healthy foods.

restatement 2: _B_   Controlling a sweet tooth is one way to a healthy diet.

2. thesis: The way you fill out a job application says a great deal about the kind of worker you will be.

restatement 1: _B_   How you fill out your job application gives an employer a glimpse of your work habits.

restatement 2: _____   The way you fill out a job application form says a lot about the kind of worker you will be.

3. thesis: Martin has a gift for meeting people, putting them at ease, and convincing them to support his plans.

restatement 1: _____   What Martin does best is meet people, put them at ease, and convince them to support his plans.

restatement 2: _B_   Martin knows how to talk to strangers, relax their doubts, and persuade them to back his projects.

4. thesis: Every job has its drawbacks.

restatement 1: _B_   No job is perfect.

restatement 2: _____   There are drawbacks to every job.

5. thesis: Winter days can make some people sad, tired, and hopeless.

restatement 1: _B_   For some people, winter is a season without happiness, energy, and hope.

restatement 2: _____   Sad, tired, and hopeless are what some people become on winter days.

Revising the Draft

Once you have a rough draft of your essay, you can begin revising it. The following checklist may help you to make the necessary changes in your draft.

✔ Checklist

Checklist for Revising the Draft of an Essay

✔ Does the essay have a clear, unifying thesis?

✔ Does the thesis make a point?

✔ Does each body paragraph have a topic sentence?

✔ Is each body paragraph focused on its topic sentence?

✔ Are the body paragraphs roughly the same size?

✔ Do any of the sentences need combining?

✔ Do any of the words need to be changed?

✔ Do the ideas seem to be smoothly linked?

✔ Does the introduction catch the reader's interest?

✔ Is there a definite conclusion?

✔ Does the conclusion remind the reader of the thesis?

Transitions within Paragraphs

In an essay, you can use two kinds of transitions: those within a paragraph and those between paragraphs.

Transitions that link ideas **within a paragraph** are the same kinds you've used earlier. Your choice of words, phrases, or even sentences depends on the kind of connection you want to make. Here is a list of some common transitions and the kind of connection they express.

Info BOX

Common Transitions within a Paragraph

To join two ideas

again	another	in addition	moreover
also	besides	likewise	similarly
and	furthermore		

To show a contrast or a different opinion

but	instead	on the other hand	still
however	nevertheless	or	yet
in contrast	on the contrary	otherwise	

To show a cause-and-effect connection

accordingly	because	for	therefore
as a result	consequently	so	thus

To give an example

for example	in the case of	such as	to illustrate
for instance	like		

To show time

after	first	recently	subsequently
at the same time	meanwhile	shortly	then
before	next	soon	until
finally			

Transitions between Paragraphs

When you write something that is more than one paragraph long, you need transitions that link each paragraph to the others. There are several effective ways to link paragraphs and remind the reader of your main idea and of how the smaller points connect to it. Here are two ways:

1. Restate an idea from the preceding paragraph at the start of a new paragraph. Look closely at the two paragraphs below and notice how the second paragraph repeats an idea from the first paragraph and provides a link.

transition restating an idea

Buying clothes for their designer labels is expensive. A tee shirt marked with the name of a popular designer can cost twenty or thirty dollars more than a similar tee shirt without the name. More expensive items like fleece jackets can be as much as seventy or eighty dollars higher if they carry a trendy name. For each designer jacket a person buys, he or she could probably buy two without a trendy logo or label. If a person decides to go all the way with fashion, he or she can spend a hundred dollars on designer socks and underwear.

Creating a wardrobe of designer clothes is not only expensive; it is also silly. While designers want buyers to think the designer label means quality, many trendy clothes are made in the same factories as less fashionable ones. And after all, how much "design" can go into a pair of socks to make them worth four times what an ordinary pair costs? The worst part of spending money on designer labels has to do with style. The hot designer of today can be out of style tomorrow, and no one wants to wear that name across a shirt, a jacket, or a pair of socks.

2. Use synonyms and repetition as a way of reminding the reader of an important point. For example, in the two paragraphs below, notice how certain repeated words, phrases, and synonyms all remind the reader of a point about kindness and generosity. The repeated words and synonyms are underlined.

Often the kindest and most generous people are the ones who don't have much themselves. When I was evicted from my apartment, my Aunt Natalie, who has three children under ten, took me in to her two-room apartment. Her heart was too big for her to leave me homeless. Another giving person is my best friend. He is a security guard trying to pay for college, but he regularly donates his time and money to the local Police Athletic League. One of the most compassionate people I know is a grandmother living on social security. Every day, she gets up at 5:00 a.m. to make sandwiches at the local food bank. She swears she isn't doing anything special, that she gets more than she <u>gives by taking care of others</u>.

Not everyone can be a hero working in a food bank at 5:00 a.m. But everyone can perform small acts of <u>generosity</u> and <u>humanity</u>, and most people do. Many are <u>thoughtful</u> and <u>caring</u> enough to leave a large tip for the server who lives on tips. Most people are <u>decent</u> on the highways; they let desperate drivers merge lanes. In the mall, shoppers routinely help lost children, hold the door for the shoppers behind them, and give directions to strangers. Without feeling at all heroic, people give blood at the blood drive, walk in the walk-a-thon, take in lost pets, and sell candy bars for their children's school. But even if they are not thinking about it, these people are <u>acting for others</u> and <u>giving to others</u>.

A Draft Essay

TEACHING TIP:

For additional revision practice, ask students to jot down the actual changes. Having them spot examples of transitional words or phrases can help them see the effectiveness of using sentence variety.

Below is a draft of the essay on college classrooms. As you read it, you'll notice many changes from the outline on pages 453–454:

- An introduction has been added, phrased in the first person, "I," to unify the essay.
- Transitions have been added within and between paragraphs.
- Sentences have been combined.
- Details have been added.
- General statements have been replaced by more specific ones.
- Word choice has been improved.
- A conclusion has been added. The conclusion uses one of the ideas from the lead-in, the idea that the outside and inside of National College are different. In addition, one of the other ideas in the conclusion, the point that no one seems to care about the condition of the classrooms, comes from the original list of ideas about the topic of college classrooms. It did not fit in the body paragraphs, but it works in the conclusion.

A Draft of an Essay (Thesis and topic sentences are underlined.)

National College, which I attend, has impressive buildings of glass and concrete. It has covered walkways, paved patios, and large clusters of trees and flowers. From the outside, the college looks great. However, on the inside, National College has some problems. The most important rooms in the institution do not attract the most important people in the institution, the students. <u>The typical classroom at my college is unwelcoming because of its tiny furniture, uncomfortable temperature, and student damage.</u>

First of all, <u>child-size furniture makes it difficult to focus on adult-level classes.</u> The student chairs are tiny. They are too small for anyone over ten years old, but for large or tall people, they are torture. For example, I am six feet tall, and when I sit on one of the classroom chairs, I feel as if I am crammed into a kindergarten chair. They are attached to miniature desks which are the size of slightly enlarged armrests. As I sit in class, I cannot fit my legs under the desk. I cannot fit my textbook and a notebook on the surface of the desk. Something always slips off and makes a noise that disrupts the class. In some classrooms, the instructor has no desk and is forced to use one of the miniature student versions.

As students twist and fidget in their tiny desks, they face another problem. <u>The temperature in the classroom is anything but pleasant</u>. I have been at the college for both fall and winter terms, and I have seen both extremes of temperature. In the early fall, the rooms were hot. The air conditioner feebly pumped hot air, which, of course, made the heat worse. Meanwhile, the sun beat through the glass windows because the blinds were broken. Winter did not bring any relief because in winter we froze. On some days, we wore our winter coats during class. Two of my teachers reported the problems to the maintenance department, but nothing changed. I wish the maintenance manager understood how hard it is for students to concentrate when they are sweating or shivering.

Heat and cold create an uncomfortable learning place, but students create a shabby one. <u>Student damage to the classrooms makes them seedy and ugly</u>. Graffiti covers the desks with childish messages, slogans, and drawings. In addition, half the desks have gum stuck to their undersides. Some students even hack their initials and artwork into the plastic and wood of the desks and chairs. Others have stained the carpet with spilled coffee or soft drinks. Sometimes I have to be careful where I walk so that my shoes don't stick to the mess. It's depressing to think that my fellow students enjoy damaging the place where they come to learn.

National College is impressive outside, but no one seems to care about the problems inside. The classrooms seem to be designed without a thought for adult learners who need to sit in adult-size seats and take lecture notes at adult-size desks. The maintenance department does not maintain a comfortable temperature so that students can learn, and students do not respect their learning environment. These problems surprise me. <u>When I started college, I knew I would face many challenges, but I didn't expect them to include squeezing into the chairs, dressing for a blizzard or heat wave, and picking the gum off my desk.</u>

Exercise 11

Practice

Identifying the Main Points in the Draft of an Essay

Below is the draft of a four-paragraph essay. Read it; then reread it and underline the thesis and the topic sentences in each body paragraph and in the conclusion.

During my high school years, I held several part-time jobs that involved dealing with the public. I once worked as an activities director for an after-school program where ten-year-olds started giving me orders. In my senior year, I worked at a local sandwich shop and learned how to smile at hungry, impatient customers waiting for their twelve-inch submarine orders. I am now a sophomore in college and work at Cook's Place, a small but popular family restaurant. <u>I have learned much while working at this family establishment, first as a waiter and now as the restaurant's first night manager.</u>

The restaurant's owner, Dan Cook, hired me a year ago to be a waiter for what he humorously calls "the dinner crowd shift." <u>I learned several essential business skills in a short time.</u> Although the restaurant has only ten tables (each seating four), I quickly learned how to keep track of multiple orders, how to work the computerized cash register, how to verify active credit card numbers, and how to use certain abbreviations while taking orders. Dan also showed me how to fill out weekly orders for our food and beverage suppliers. Many of our customers are regulars, and I also learned that maintaining a positive attitude and friendly manner can make my job enjoyable, even on slow nights. After a few weeks, I felt confident about my skills as a waiter and looked forward to going to work.

After I had been a waiter for five months, Dan told me he'd like to start spending more time visiting his grown children who live in another state. He asked me if I would like to become the restaurant's "first official night manager." I accepted his offer immediately, and I have acquired even more business skills in this position. I now manage the restaurant three nights each week and one Saturday evening each month. I plan the dinner specials with the cook, negotiate with suppliers to get the best bulk-order prices, and make calls to customers who fill out an evaluation form Dan and I devised. I have learned that if I treat people respectfully, they will usually treat me professionally. Over the past year, I've had to interview applicants whenever a server position became available, and I've learned how important it is to be tactful and encouraging even when I've had to turn someone down. Finally, I've even met with Dan's accountant several times. She showed me the forms various business owners have to fill out, and I've learned about the importance of accurate records for tax purposes. Dan says he's proud of my progress and jokes that I "work well with people and work the numbers well."

At Cook's Place, I was fortunate to have on-the-job training that was both educational and enjoyable. I've gained many business skills, but most importantly, I've learned the value of encouragement, teamwork, respect, and friendship. They are my ingredients for success in any relationship.

Exercise 12

Practice

Adding Transitions to an Essay

The essay below needs transitions. Add the transitions where indicated, and add the kind of transition—word, phrase, or sentence—indicated.

I have always liked math and done well in my math classes, so I planned

to major in math once I finished my required courses in college. However, I am

thinking of changing my major because of a course I signed up for almost by

accident. When I registered, the course was the only one left open that would

fit into my schedule. The course was Business Law, and I love it. It is a great

course because the teacher makes it clear, interesting, and lively.

_____ _____ (add a phrase), Mr. Morales, the instructor,

makes the subject easy to follow. When I started the class, I knew nothing

about business law; _____ *however,* _____ (add a word or phrase), I now

understand the basics. Mr. Morales has a very structured, simple plan for covering the class material. He doesn't just talk to us. _____Instead,_____

(add a word or phrase), he provides outlines and study guides. He uses

class discussion to make sure that we understand each new concept.

_____Moreover,_____ (add a word or phrase), he gives us practice quizzes

before we take any major tests.

_____Our instructor makes sure that we understand the material in the

class, and he also makes sure that we remain involved._____

(add a sentence). Business law is an interesting class because Mr. Morales

constantly links the lessons to current events or current legal issues. We

read and study newspaper articles on business fraud and lawsuits.

_____In addition,_____ (add a word or phrase) we watch tapes of television

programs on scandals in the stock market. I never thought I'd be enjoying

reading about accounting or insurance, but they're fascinating subjects when

they tell of crime in high places or billionaires gone wrong. In class we read,

discuss, and watch tapes about issues in business law, and we also get

to meet people in the field._____

(add a sentence). Sometimes Mr. Morales invites guest speakers to the class.

They are people like forensic accountants, who investigate accounting fraud,

or local detectives, who investigate insurance crimes.

_____The class is never dull, and it's never slow, either._____

(add a sentence). Business law is the one class that always keeps me

alert. Mr. Morales is a very active teacher. He walks around the room,

sits on his desk for a few minutes, then jumps off and paces back and

forth. He is always telling jokes. Even though most of the jokes are

corny, they vary the rhythm of the class and stimulate the students.

_____As a result,_____ (add a word or phrase) they put everyone at ease

and make it easy for students to ask questions. _____Furthermore,_____

(add a phrase) Mr. Morales makes the students move around, putting

them in small groups or splitting the class in two so that each half can argue one side of an issue. <u>With all this activity,</u>

(add a word or phrase), the class time seems to fly by.

I still like my math classes, but I love my business law class. Math is my

strength, _____ but _____ (add a word or phrase) the legal side of

business intrigues me. Whatever major I choose, I am sure of one thing. I

will always remember Mr. Morales' class.

Exercise 13   **Recognizing Synonyms and Repetition Used to Link Ideas in an Essay**

Practice   In the following essay, underline all the synonyms and repetition (of words or phrases) that help remind the reader of the thesis sentence. (To help you, the thesis is underlined.)

Some people have artistic talent. They become famous painters, musicians, or actors. Others are known for their athletic abilities, and they are seen on television in tournaments, matches, games, or other sports contests. My brother will never be on stage or in a tournament, yet he has a special talent. <u>My brother Eddie has a gift for making friends.</u>

Our family has moved six times in the past ten years, and every time, Eddie was the first to <u>get acquainted with the neighbors</u>. There is <u>something about his smile and cheerful attitude</u> that <u>draws strangers to him</u>. On one of our moves, Eddie had <u>met our neighbors</u> on both sides of the house and directly across the street by the time we unloaded the van. Within a week, Eddie had <u>made the acquaintance</u> of almost every family on the block. Eddie's <u>ability to connect with others</u> helped our whole family to feel comfortable in a new place. As Eddie <u>formed links</u> within the area, he introduced us to the community. Thanks to my brother, we all got to know Mrs. Lopez next door, the teenagers down the street, and even the mail carrier. Soon familiarity turned to deeper friendships.

One of the most amazing examples of <u>Eddie's talent</u> occurred when he and I took a long bus trip. Twenty-four hours on a bus can be exhausting and depressing, but Eddie made the trip fun. He began by talking to the man seated across from us. Soon the couple behind us joined in. When Eddie passed around a bag of potato chips, he <u>drew four more passengers</u> into this <u>cluster of newfound buddies</u>. Eddie and I didn't sleep during the entire trip. We were too busy <u>talking, laughing, and swapping life stories with the other travelers</u>. Some of the toughest-looking passengers turned out to be the kindest, warmest companions.

Only Eddie could transform a dreary bus ride into a cheerful trip with <u>new friends</u>. And thanks to Eddie, our family's many moves became <u>opportunities to meet new people</u>. If I am with my brother, I know we will never be lonely, for <u>Eddie's real talent is his ability to draw others to him</u>.

Final Lines **Proofreading and Polishing: An Essay**

Creating a Title

When you are satisfied with the final draft of your essay, you can begin preparing a good copy. Your essay will need a title. Try to think of a short title that is connected to your thesis. Since the title is the reader's first con-

TEACHING TIP:

Tell students that an essay title should be a phrase and not a sentence. Many students are tempted to reuse their thesis statement for the title.

tact with your essay, an imaginative title can create a good first impression. If you can't think of anything clever, try using a key phrase from your essay.

The title is placed at the top of your essay, about an inch above the first paragraph. Always capitalize the first word of the title and all other words *except* "the," "an," "a," prepositions (like "of," "in," "with"), and coordinating conjunctions (and, but, or, nor, for, yet, so). *Do not* underline or put quotation marks around your title.

The Final Version of an Essay

Following is the final lines version of the essay on college classrooms. When you compare it to the draft on pages 466-67, you will notice some changes:

- A title has been added.
- Transitions have been added: one is a phrase, and one is a sentence.
- The word choice has been changed so descriptions are more precise and repetition (of the word "problems") is avoided.
- Specific details have been added.

A Final Version of an Essay (Changes from the draft are underlined.)

A Look Inside College Classrooms

INSTRUCTOR'S NOTE:

Remind students that this sample essay is reduced to fit within a textbook and that in their essays, the title should be about three lines above the first paragraph.

National College, which I attend, has impressive buildings of glass and concrete. It has covered walkways, paved patios, and large clusters of trees and flowers. From the outside, the college looks <u>distinguished.</u> However, on the inside, National College has some problems. The most important rooms in the institution do not <u>appeal to</u> the most important people in the institution, the students. The typical classroom at my college is unwelcoming because of its tiny furniture, uncomfortable temperature, and student damage.

First of all, child-size furniture makes it difficult to focus on adult-level classes. The student chairs are tiny. They are too small for anyone over ten years old, but for large or tall people, they are torture. For example, I am six feet tall, and when I sit on one of the classroom chairs, I feel as if I am crammed into a kindergarten chair. They are attached to miniature desks which are the size of slightly enlarged armrests. As I sit in class, I cannot fit my legs under the desk. I cannot fit my textbook and a notebook on the surface of the desk. Something always slips off and makes a noise that disrupts the class. <u>The child-like atmosphere even affects the instructors</u>. In some classrooms, the instructor has no desk and is forced to use one of the miniature student versions.

As students twist and fidget in their tiny desks, they face another problem. The temperature in the classroom is anything but pleasant. I have been at the college for both fall and winter terms, and I have seen both extremes of temperature. In the early fall, the rooms were <u>sweltering</u>. The air conditioner feebly pumped hot air, which, of course, made the heat worse. Meanwhile, the sun beat through the glass windows because the blinds were broken. Winter did not bring any relief because in winter we froze. On some days, we wore our winter coats during class. <u>At different times during the semester</u>, two of my teachers reported the problems to the maintenance department, but nothing changed. I wish the maintenance manager understood how hard it is for students to concentrate when they are sweating or shivering.

Heat and cold create an uncomfortable learning place, but students create a shabby one. <u>Student damage to the classrooms makes them seedy and ugly</u>. Graffiti covers the desks with childish messages, slogans, and drawings. In addition, half the desks have gum stuck to their undersides. Some students even hack their initials and artwork into the plastic and wood of the desks and chairs. Others have stained the carpet with spilled coffee or soft drinks <u>and left crumbs and ground-in food behind</u>. Sometimes I have to be careful where I walk so that my shoes don't stick to the mess. It's depressing to think that my fellow students enjoy damaging the place where they come to learn.

National College is impressive outside, but no one seems to care about the <u>flaws</u> inside. The classrooms seem to be designed without a thought for adult learners who need to sit in adult-size seats and take lecture notes at adult-size desks. The maintenance department does not maintain a comfortable temperature so that students can learn, and students do not respect their learning environment. These problems surprise me. <u>When I started college, I knew I would face many challenges, but I didn't expect them to include squeezing into the chairs, dressing for a blizzard or heat wave, and picking the gum off my desk.</u>

Before your prepare the final copy of your essay, check your latest draft for errors in spelling and punctuation, and for any errors made in typing or recopying.

<table>
<tr><td>**Exercise 14**</td><td>**Proofreading to Prepare the Final Version**</td></tr>
<tr><td>*Practice*</td><td></td></tr>
</table>

Following are two essays with the kinds of errors it is easy to overlook when you prepare the final version of an assignment. Correct the errors, writing above the lines. There are twenty errors in the first essay, and sixteen in the second.

My Three Treasures (No quotation marks)
"My Three Treasures"

equipment
1. My room is filled with CDs, sports equiptment, audio equipment,

,
and a computer. I like having all these items but I could live without them.

things
The three thing's that are most valuable to me don't take up much room. The

a
things I value most are a photograph, a medal, and ticket.

.
The photograph reminds me of how lucky I am It is a photo of my girl-

friend Lucy on her birthday. In the picture, she is happy and beautiful, but

Every time
not as beautiful as she is on the inside. Everytime I look at this photograph,

remember
I remeber how fortunate I am to have a woman like Lucy love me. Her face

reminds me of all the happiness we have shared and promises we will have

,
more good times together. If there were a fire in my house I would run into

the blaze to save my picture of Lucy.

treasure
One tresure, Lucy's photograph, reminds me of my present and future happiness, but another is a memory of the past. It is an army medal that connects me to my grandfather. He was in the Vietnam War, and when he was wounded, he got a medal. I am the *only grandson* onely granson in the family, so when I turned eighteen, my grandfather gave me his medal. My grandfather *passed* past away last year, so the medal is even more special to me now. I carry it in my wallet to remember my *grandfather* grand father, the *hero* heroe.

The last treasure is another gift. It is a ticket stub from the first professional baseball game I ever saw. The ticket represents the first time my *father* Father took me into the world he loves so much. My father is a baseball fanatic, and even when I was a toddler, I used to *sit* set in front of the television with him and watch the games. But he never took me along to the real games; he always said I was too little. Then, on my *eighth* eight birthday, he gave me a big surprise. He and I went to a professional game. The game was exciting, but the best part of it was being with my father, sharing his favorite place. I kept the ticket to prove that I had passed the little boy stage of my life.

An old ticket, a medal, and a photograph *aren't* arent worth any money. However, they are worth the world to me. *They* they all connect me to the most important people in my past, present, and future.

My Dog Trained Me (count as one error)
How my dog trained me

2. When my aunt moved to Texas, she had to leave her dog behind. I told her I would take the dog because I figured he would be no trouble. After all, he was two years old and already housebroken and trained. I *didn't* did'nt know that I was the one who would receive the training.

Rocket, the dog, had very strong beliefs about *walks* walk's. He liked to go for a walk the first thing in the *morning* mourning. However, I liked to sleep late, so I just assumed Rocket would change his ways and learn to sleep longer. One day with my pet *opened* open my eyes to my new morning routine. At 7:00 a.m., Rocket

ignored

began to whine softly. When I ignore him, he began licking my face. To sum

up, I can only say that an early walk was better than endless licking by a dog.

Now that I had learned to take early walks, Rocket moved on to the

lesson   *little harder (no comma)*

next lessen. This one was a little, harder for me to figure out. Every night

p. m.

about 11:00 p m, Rocket would get up from his place on the couch and

stand by the kitchen cabinets. He would first look at the cabinets, and then

stare

stair at me. I didn't understand. I checked Rocket's bowls. He had clean

water in his water bowl and dry food in his food bowl. But Rocket contin-

ued to stand and stare. Even when I went to bed Rocket would still be in his

Finally   *aunt*

spot in the kitchen. Finely, I called my Aunt in Texas to see if Rocket had a

problem with kitchen cabinets. My aunt informed me that Rocket was

accustomed to getting a dog biscuit every night at bedtime, and that he

biscuits

could not sleep without his biscits, which she kept in a box in the kitchen.

learned

So now I have learn to read my dog's signal and to obey it by giving him his

nightly snack.

Rocket is a wonderful dog, and he's smart, too. I just never thought he'd

be smart enough to teach *me* how to behave. I only hope that my dog isn't

planning any new tricks for me to learn

Lines of Detail: A Walk-Through Assignment

Write a five-paragraph essay about three things in your life you would like
to get rid of. These things must be tangible objects like an old car, a bicycle, a uniform, and so forth. They cannot be people or personal qualities
like fear or insecurity. To write the essay, follow these steps:

Step 1: Freewrite a list of all the things you would like to get rid of in
your life. To get started, think about what is in your room, car,
purse, wallet, house, apartment, garage, basement, and so forth.

Step 2: Select the three items you would most like to toss out. Then
prepare a list of questions you can ask yourself about these
three items. You can ask questions such as the following:

> Why do I want to get rid of this item?
> Is it useless to me?
> Does it remind me of an unpleasant part of my life?
> Is it ugly? Broken? Out of style?

Does it remind me of a habit I'd like to break?

Can I get rid of it? If so, why don't I get rid of it? If not, why can't I get rid of it?

Answer the questions. The answers can lead you to details and topic sentences for your essay. For instance, you might hate the uniform you have to wear because it represents a job you would like to leave. However, you might not be able to get rid of the uniform because you need the job. Or maybe you'd like to toss out your cigarettes because you want to stop smoking.

Step 3: Survey your answers. Begin by listing the three things you would like to get rid of. Then list the details (the answers to your questions) beneath the item they relate to. For example, under the item "uniform," you could list the reason you hate it and the reason you cannot get rid of it.

Step 4: Once you have clustered the three items and the details related to each, you have the beginnings of a five-paragraph essay. Each item will be the focus of one of the body paragraphs, and its details will develop the paragraph.

Step 5: Focus all your clusters around one point. To find a focus, ask yourself whether the things you want to throw away have anything in common. If so, you can make that point in your thesis. For instance, you could write a thesis like one of these:

The things I would like to get rid of in my life are all related

to a _____ part of my life.

My weaknesses are reflected in three items I would like to get rid of in my life.

If I could get rid of _____, _____, and

_____, I would be _____.

If the things you would like to be rid of are not related, then you can use a thesis like one of the following:

Three items I'd like to throw out reflect different aspects of

my life.

I'd like to get rid of _____ because it _____

_____, of _____ because it _____,

and _____ because it _____.

INSTRUCTOR'S NOTE:

A Peer Review Form for students' exchange of drafts is on page 481.

Step 6: Once you have a thesis and clustered details, draft your outline. Then revise your outline until it is unified, expresses the ideas in a clear order, and has enough supporting details.

Step 7: Write a draft of your essay. Revise the draft, checking it for a smooth lead-in, balanced paragraphs, relevant and specific details, a strong conclusion, and smooth transitions.

Step 8: Before you prepare the final version of your essay, check for spelling, word choice, punctuation, and mechanical errors.

Writing Your Own Essay

When you write on any of these topics, be sure to work through the stages of the writing process in preparing your essay.

1. Take any paragraph you wrote for this class and develop it into an essay of four or five paragraphs. If your instructor agrees, read the paragraph to a partner or group, and ask your listener(s) to suggest points inside the paragraph that can be developed into paragraphs of their own.

2. Narrow one of the following topics, and then write an essay on it.

parents	teens	crime	cities
small towns	war	fashion	country life
pleasures	worries	relationships	shopping malls
fitting in	accidents	goals	the workplace

3. Write an essay on any one of the following topics:

   My Three Favorite Places
   Three Pets I Have Known and Loved
   Three Movies That Were/Were Not Worth Seeing
   Three Songs I Will Always Remember
   Three Mistakes That Drivers Make
   My Three Best/Worst Experiences Playing _____
   (Name a sport.)

4. Write a four-paragraph essay about a dream you had. In your first body paragraph, describe the dream in detail. In your second paragraph, explain what you think the dream means: Does it connect to one of your fears or hopes? Is it related to a current problem in your life? Does it suggest an answer to a problem? What does the dream tell you about yourself?

5. Examine your place in your family. Are you an only child? The oldest child? The youngest? A middle child? Do you have brothers? Sisters? Both? Write an essay on the advantages (or disadvantages) of your place in the family.

6. Study photograph A of the happy little girls playing basketball. Use it to think about this topic for an essay: The three best sports for children under ten.

Photograph A

7. Write a five-paragraph essay about photograph B. In the first body paragraph, describe one of the people in the photo. Describe what the person looks like, the expression on his or her face, and what the person is doing. In the second body paragraph, describe the other person in the photograph. In the third body paragraph, write about the relationship of the two people. Are they married? Brother and sister? In love? Use the details of the photograph to support your ideas about their connection.

Photograph B

8. The cat in photograph C seems determined to get the fish, even if it means snorkeling in a fish tank. Write an essay about three people who were willing to do ridiculous things to get what they wanted. You can write about people you know, or people you've read about or seen on television.

Photograph C

Topics for a Narrative Essay

1. Write about a time when you were surprised. It can be a good or bad experience.

2. Write about the most frustrating experience of your life.

3. Write about how you met your current boyfriend, girlfriend, partner, or spouse.

4. Write about the time you lost something or someone.

5. Write about your first day at a college or school.

Topics for a Description Essay

1. Imagine your ideal home or apartment. In a five-paragraph essay, describe the three rooms that would be most important to you. Describe their appearance and their contents, such as furniture, accessories, equipment, and appliances.

2. Describe the best social event you ever attended. It can be a wedding, a dance, a holiday party, a graduation celebration, or any other special event. Describe the people at the event, the place where it took place, and the food and refreshments served.

3. Write an essay describing any of the following:

> your two favorite childhood toys
> your two (or three) favorite pieces of clothing
> three beautiful animals
> any scene at sunset

4. Go to a place you visit regularly, but on this visit, study the place carefully. You may choose to visit a supermarket, service station, coffee shop, convenience store, and so forth. As soon as you leave, take notes about what you noticed. Then write an essay describing that place.

5. Imagine that someone who has never seen you (a distant relative, someone you've been corresponding with) is coming to visit. You will be meeting this person at the airport or train station. In an essay, describe yourself to this person. You can describe your face, body, clothes, walk, voice, or any other distinguishing characteristic.

Topics for an Illustration Essay

1. Make a statement about yourself and illustrate it with examples. You can use a thesis like one of the following:

When faced with a problem, I am a person who _____

Everyone who knows me thinks I am too _____

I have always felt satisfied with my _____

My greatest strength is _____

My greatest weakness is _____

2. Write about a person who has been kind to you. In the body paragraphs, give examples of this person's kindness to you.

3. Here are some general statements that you may have heard:

> The college years are the best in a person's life.
> Teenage marriages never work out.
> Hard work will get you where you want to be.
> Children these days are too spoiled.
> When their children grow up and leave home, many parents feel lost.
> Old people have an easy life; all they do is sit around all day.

Pick one of these statements and, in an essay, give examples (from your own experience and observation) of the truth or falseness of the statement.

4. Complete this statement:

The best part of living in _____ (name your city,

town or neighborhood) is its _____.

Then write an essay supporting this statement with examples.

5. Write a thesis that sums up your social life in high school. In an essay, support that thesis with examples.

Topics for a Process Essay

1. Think of some process you perform often. It could be something as simple as doing the laundry or setting your VCR to record a program while you are not home. Now, pretend that you must explain this process to someone who has no idea how to perform it. Write an essay explaining the process to that person.

2. Observe someone perform a task you've never looked at closely. You can watch your boss close up the store, for instance, or watch a friend braid hair. Then write an essay on how the person works through the steps of that process.

3. Interview a law enforcement officer, asking him or her what steps a person should take to protect a home from crime. Use the information you learned from the interview to write an essay on how to protect a home from crime.

4. Write an essay on a common legal or business procedure such as taking the driver's test, filling out a job application, applying for a passport or visa, applying for a loan, or establishing residency to get lower tuition rates. Write an essay about the steps of that process.

5. Write an essay about how to train for a specific sport.

Name: _____ **Section:** _____

PEER REVIEW FORM FOR AN ESSAY

After you have completed a draft of your essay, let a writing partner read it. When your partner has completed the form below, discuss the comments. Then repeat the same process for your partner's paragraph.

The thesis of this essay is _____

_____

The topic sentences for the body paragraphs are _____

_____

_____

_____

The topic sentence in the conclusion is _____

_____

The best part of the essay is the _____ (first, second, third, etc.) paragraph.

I would like to see details added to the part about _____

_____

I would take out the part about _____

_____

Additional comments: _____

_____

_____

_____

_____

_____

_____

_____

_____

_____

_____

Reviewer's Name: _____

CHAPTER 29

Writing from Reading

WHAT IS WRITING FROM READING?

One way to find topics for writing is to draw from your ideas, memories, and observations. Another way is to write from reading you've done. You can react to something you've read; you can agree or disagree with it. You can summarize what you've read. Many college assignments ask you to write about an assigned reading such as an essay, a chapter in a textbook, an article in a journal. This kind of writing requires an active, involved attitude toward your reading. Such reading is done in steps:

1. Preread.
2. Read.
3. Reread with a pen or pencil.

Attitude

Before you begin the first step of this reading process, you have to have a certain *attitude*. That attitude involves thinking of what you read as half of a conversation. The writer has opinions and ideas; he or she makes points just as you do when you write or speak. The writer supports his or her points with specific details. If the writer were speaking to you in conversation, you would respond to his or her opinions or ideas. You would agree, disagree, or question. You would jump into the conversation, linking or contrasting your ideas with those of the other speaker.

The right attitude toward reading demands that you read the same way you converse: you *become involved*. In doing this, you talk back as you read, and later, you may react in your own writing. Reacting as you read will keep you focused on what you are reading. If you are focused, you will remember more of what you read. With an active, involved attitude, you can begin the step of prereading.

Prereading

Before you actually read an assigned essay, a chapter in a textbook, or an article in a journal, magazine, or newspaper, take a few minutes to look it over, and be ready to answer the following questions.

▼ Checklist

A Prereading Checklist

✔ How long is this reading?

✔ Will I be able to read it in one sitting, or will I have to schedule several time periods to finish it?

✔ Are there any subheadings in the reading? Do they give any hints about the reading?

✔ Are there any charts? Graphs? Is there boxed information? Are there any photographs or illustrations with captions? Do the photos or captions give any hints about the reading?

✔ Is there any introductory material about the reading or the author? Does the introductory material give me any hints about the reading?

✔ What is the title of the reading? Does the title hint at the point of the reading?

✔ Are there any parts of the reading underlined or emphasized in some other way?

✔ Do the emphasized parts hint at the point of the reading?

Why Preread? Prereading takes very little time, but it helps you immensely. Some students believe it's a waste of time to scan an assignment; they think they should just jump right in and get the reading over with. However, spending just a few minutes on preliminaries can save hours later. And most important, prereading helps you become a *focused* reader.

If you scan the length of an assignment, you can pace yourself. And if you know how long a reading is, you can alert yourself to its plan. For example, a short reading has to come to its point soon. A longer essay may take more time to develop its point and may use more details and examples.

Subheadings, charts, graphs, boxed or other highlighted materials are important enough that the author wants to emphasize them. Looking over that material *before* you read gives you an overview of the important points the reading will contain.

Introductory material or introductory questions will also help you know what to look for as you read. Background on the author or on the subject may hint at ideas that will come up in the reading. Sometimes the title of the reading will give you the main idea.

You should preread so that you can start reading the entire assignment with as much *knowledge* about the writer and the subject as you can get. When you then read the entire assignment, you will be reading *actively,* for more knowledge.

Forming Questions Before You Read If you want to read with a focus, it helps to ask questions before you read. Form questions by using the information you gained from prereading.

Start by noting the title and turning it into a question. If the title of your assigned reading is "Causes of the Civil War," ask, "What were the causes of the Civil War?"

You can turn subheadings into questions. If you are reading an article about self-esteem, and one subheading is "Influence of Parents," you can ask, "How do parents influence a person's self-esteem?"

You can also form questions from graphics and illustrations. If a chapter in your economics textbook includes a photograph of Wall Street, you can ask, "What is Wall Street?" or "What is Wall Street's role in economics?" or "What happens on Wall Street?"

You can write down these questions, but it's not necessary. Just forming questions and keeping them in the back of your mind help you read actively and stay focused.

An Example of the Prereading Step Take a look at the article that follows. Don't read it; *preread* it.

Part-Time Job May Do Teenagers More Harm Than Good

Gary Klott

Gary Klott is a personal finance consultant for the National Newspaper Syndicate. In this article, he explores the effects of part-time jobs on high school students.

Words You May Need to Know (Corresponding paragraph numbers are in parentheses.)

extracurricular activities (2): activities outside the regular academic course, like clubs and sports
assume (3): suppose, take for granted

menial (4): of a low level, degrading
instant gratification (4): immediate satisfaction

1   Given today's high cost of auto insurance, dating, video games, music CDs and designer clothing, it shouldn't come as any surprise that a growing number of high school students are taking part-time jobs during the school year. Most parents have done little to discourage their children from working after school. In fact, many parents figure that part-time jobs can help teach their children about responsibility and the value of a dollar and better prepare them for life in the adult workaday world. But there is growing evidence to suggest that parents ought to sharply restrict the number of hours their children work during the school year.

2   Academic studies over the past decade have found that high school students who work—particularly those who work long hours during the school week—tend to do less well in school, miss out on the benefits of extracurricular activities and have more behavioral problems. Most recently, a study of twelfth-graders by Linda P. Worley, a high school counselor in

Marietta, Georgia, indicated that grades suffer when students work more than ten hours during the school week. The highest grade-point averages were found for students who worked only on weekends, 3.07, and for those who baby-sat or did yard work, 3.13. Students who didn't work at all had an average GPA of 3.02, while those who worked up to ten hours a week earned an average GPA of 2.95. Students working ten to twenty hours a week averaged 2.77, twenty to thirty hours per week 2.53 and 30 or more hours 2.10.

3　　　Even if a student manages to maintain good grades, parents shouldn't automatically assume that long work hours aren't harming their child's education. Several studies found that many students kept up their grades by choosing easier courses. A 1993 study of 1,800 high-school sophomores by researchers at Temple University and Stanford University found that students who worked more than twenty hours a week spent less time on homework, cut class more often, cheated more on tests and assignments, had less interest in formal education, had a higher rate of drug and alcohol use, and had lower self-esteem.

4　　　Researchers also note that some of the perceived benefits of after-school jobs are often overrated. For example, many of the jobs high school students take on are menial and provide few skills that will prove useful after high school. And many students learn the wrong lessons about the value of a dollar since they tend to spend all of their job earnings on cars, clothes, and other purchases that provide instant gratification without saving a penny.

By prereading the article, you might notice the following:

- The title of the article is "Part-Time Job May Do Teenagers More Harm Than Good."
- The article is short and can be read in one sitting.
- The author writes about money, and he writes for newspapers.
- The introductory material says the article is about teenagers with part-time jobs.
- There are several vocabulary words you may need to know.

You might begin reading the article with these questions in mind:

- Why are part-time jobs harmful to teens?
- What are the harmful effects?
- Why is a writer who writes about money arguing that it is bad for teens to make money?
- Should teens have full-time jobs instead of part-time ones?

Reading

The first time you read, try to *get a sense of the whole piece* you are reading. Reading with questions in mind can help you do this. If you find that you are confused by a certain part of the reading selection, go back and reread that part. If you do not know the meaning of a word, check the vocabulary list to see if the word is defined for you. If it isn't defined, try to figure out the meaning from the way the word is used in the sentence.

If you find that you have to read more slowly than usual, don't worry. People vary their reading speed according to what they read and why they are reading it. If you are reading for entertainment, for example, you can read quickly; if you are reading a chapter in a textbook, you must read more slowly. The more complicated the reading selection is, the more slowly you will read it.

An Example of the Reading Step

Now read "Part-Time Job May Do Teenagers More Harm Than Good." When you've completed your first reading, you will probably have some answers to the prereading questions that you formed.

Answers to Prereading Questions:
Part-time jobs can hurt teens' grades and other areas of their lives such as their behavior and attitudes.
The writer, who writes about money, says part-time jobs give students bad spending habits.
Full-time work would be worse than part-time work.

Rereading with Pen or Pencil

The second reading is the crucial one. At this point, you begin to think on paper as you read. In this step, you make notes or write about what you read. Some students are reluctant to do this because they are not sure what to note or write. Think of *making these notes as a way of learning, thinking, reviewing, and reacting.* Reading with a pen or pencil in your hand keeps you alert. With that pen or pencil, you can

- mark the main point of the reading,
- mark other points,
- define words you don't know,
- question parts of the reading that seem confusing,
- evaluate the writer's ideas,
- react to the writer's opinions or examples,
- add ideas, opinions, or examples of your own.

There is no single system for marking or writing as you read. Some readers like to underline the main idea with two lines and to underline other important ideas with one line. Some students like to put an asterisk, a star, next to important ideas, while others like to circle key words.

Some people use the margins to write comments such as, "I agree!" or "Not true!" or "That's happened to me." Sometimes readers put questions in the margin; sometimes they summarize a point in the margin next to its location in the essay. Some people list important points in the white space above the reading, while others use the space at the end of the reading.

Every reader who writes as he or she reads has a personal system; what these systems share is an attitude. *If you write as you read, you concentrate on the reading selection, get to know the writer's ideas, and develop ideas of your own.*

As you reread and write notes, don't worry too much about noticing the "right" ideas. Instead, think of rereading as the time to jump into a *conversation* with the writer.

An Example of Rereading with Pen or Pencil

For "Part-Time Job May Do Teenagers More Harm Than Good," your marked article might look like the following:

Part-Time Job May Do Teenagers More Harm Than Good

Gary Klott

I agree!

Given today's high cost of auto insurance, dating, video games, music CDs and designer clothing, it shouldn't come as any surprise that a growing number of high school students are taking part-time jobs during the school year. Most parents have done little to dis-

what parents believe

courage their children from working after school. In fact, many parents figure that part-time jobs can help teach their children about responsibility and the value of a dollar and better prepare them for life in the adult workaday world. But there is growing evidence to suggest that parents

what parents should do

ought to sharply restrict the number of hours their children work during the school year.

*

Academic studies over the past decade have found that high school students who work—particularly those who work long hours during the school week—tend to do less well in school, miss out on the benefits of extracurricular activities and have more behavioral problems. Most recent-

example

ly, a study of 12th-graders by Linda P. Worley, a high school counselor in Marietta, Georgia, indicated that grades suffer when students work more

the more you work, the lower the grades

than ten hours during the school week. The highest grade-point averages were found for students who worked only on weekends, 3.07, and for those who baby-sat or did yard work, 3.13. Students who didn't work at all had an average GPA of 3.02, while those who worked up to ten hours a week earned an average GPA of 2.95. Students working ten to twenty hours a week averaged 2.77, twenty to thirty hours per week 2.53 and 30 or more hours 2.10.

Even if a student manages to maintain good grades, parents shouldn't automatically assume that long work hours aren't harming their child's education. Several studies found that many students kept up their grades by

other harm to education

choosing easier courses. A 1993 study of 1,800 high-school sophomores by researchers at Temple University and Stanford University found that students who worked more than twenty hours a week spent less time on homework, cut class more often, cheated more on tests and assignments, had less interest in formal education, had a higher rate of drug and alcohol

self-respect, pride

use and had lower self-esteem.

bad spending habits

Researchers also note that some of the perceived benefits of afterschool jobs are often overrated. For example, many of the jobs high school students take on are menial and provide few skills that will prove useful after high school. And many students learn the wrong lessons about the value of a dollar since they tend to spend all of their job earnings on cars, clothes, and other purchases that provide instant gratification without saving a penny.

What the Notes Mean

In the sample above, much of the underlining indicates sentences or phrases that seem important. The words in the margin are often summaries of what is underlined. In the first paragraph, for example, the words "what parents believe" and "what parents should do" are like subtitles in the margin.

An asterisk in the margin signals an important idea. When "example" is written in the margin, it notes that a point is being supported by a specific example. Sometimes, what is in the margin is the reader's reaction, such as, "I agree!" One item in the margin is a definition. The word "self-esteem" is circled and defined in the margin as "self-respect, pride."

The marked-up article is a flexible tool. You can go back and mark it further. You may change your mind about your notes and comments and find other, better, or more important points in the article.

You write as you read to involve yourself in the reading process. Marking what you read can help you in other ways, too. If you are to be tested on the reading selection or are asked to discuss it, you can scan your markings and notations at a later time for a quick review.

Exercise 1

Practice

Reading and Making Notes for a Selection

Following is a paragraph from "Part-Time Job May Do Teenagers More Harm Than Good." First, read it. Then reread it and make notes on the following:

1. Underline the first eight words of the most specific example in the paragraph.

2. Circle the phrase "formal education" and define it in the margin.

3. At the end of the paragraph, summarize its main point.

Paragraph from "Part-Time Job May Do Teenagers More Harm Than Good"

Even if a student manages to maintain good grades, parents shouldn't automatically assume that long work hours aren't harming their child's education. Several studies found that many students kept up their grades by choosing easier courses. A 1993 study of 1,800 high-school sophomores and juniors by researchers at Temple University and Stanford University found that students who worked more than twenty hours a week spent less time on homework, cut class more often, cheated more on tests and assignments, has less interest in (formal education), had a higher rate of drug and alcohol use and had lower self-esteem.

education acquired in school

Main point of the paragraph (in your own words): Students who manage

to work long hours and make good grades may still be cheating themselves

of the best education.

Answers Will Vary.

Possible answers shown at right.

WRITING A SUMMARY OF A READING

One way to write about a reading is to write a summary. A *summary* of a reading tells the important ideas in brief form and in your own words. It includes (1) the writer's main idea, (2) the ideas used to explain the main idea, and (3) some examples or details.

Thought Lines ## Marking a List of Ideas: Summary

When you preread, read, and make notes on the reading selection, you have already begun the thought lines stage for a summary. You can think further, on paper, by *listing the points* (words, phrases, sentences) you've already marked on the reading selection.

To find the main idea for your summary and the ideas and examples connected to the main idea, you can *mark related ideas on your list*. For example, the list below was made from "Part-Time Job May Do Teenagers More Harm Than Good." Three symbols are used to mark the following:

S   the effects of part-time jobs on **schoolwork**

O   **other** effects of part-time jobs

P   what **parents** think about part-time jobs

Some items on the list don't have a mark since they do not relate to any of the categories.

A Marked List of Ideas for a Summary of "Part-Time Job May Do Teenagers More Harm Than Good"

high cost of car insurance, dating, video games, music CDs and designer clothing

P   parents think part-time jobs teach responsibility, money and job skills

parents should restrict teens' work hours

S   working students do less well in school

S   study of twelfth graders by Linda P. Worley said grades suffer if students work more than ten hours in school week

S   students who work long hours choose easier courses

S   they spend less time on homework

S   they cut class more

S   they cheat

S   they are less interested in school

O   they use drugs and alcohol more

O   they have lower self-esteem

some perceived benefits are overrated

O   students spend money foolishly

The marked list could then be reorganized, like this:

the effects of part-time jobs on school work

- working students do less well in school
- study of twelfth graders by Linda P. Worley said grades suffer if students work more than ten hours in the school week
- students who work long hours choose easier classes
- they spend less time on homework
- they cut class more
- they cheat
- they are less interested in school

other effects of part-time jobs

- if they work over twenty hours, they use drugs and alcohol more
- they have lower self-esteem
- working students spend money foolishly

what many parents think about part-time jobs

- parents think part-time jobs teach responsibility, money and job skills

Selecting a Main Idea

The next step in the process is to select the idea you think is the writer's *main* point. If you look again at the list of ideas, you see one category that has only one item: what many parents think about part-time jobs. In this category, the only item is that parents think part-time jobs teach responsibility, money and job skills.

Is this item the main idea of the article? If it is, then all the other ideas support it. But the other ideas contradict this point.

It is not the main idea, but it *is* connected to the main idea. The author is saying that parents *think* part-time jobs are good for high school students, but they may not be, especially if students work long hours.

You can write a simpler version of this main idea:

Parents should know that working long hours at part-time jobs is not good for teens.

Once you have a main idea, check it to see if it fits with the other ideas in your organized list. *Do the ideas in the list connect to the main idea?* Yes. The ideas about the effects of jobs on school work show the negative impact of part-time work. So do the ideas about the other effects. And even the part about what some parents think can be used to contrast with what jobs *really* do to teens.

Now that you have a main point that fits an organized list, you can move to the *outlines* stage of a summary.

Exercise 2

Practice

Marking a List and Finding the Main Idea for a Summary

Following is a list of ideas from an article called "Binge Nights: The Emergency on Campus" by Michael Winerip. It tells the true story of Ryan Dabbieri, a senior at the University of Virginia who nearly died from binge drinking at tailgating party before a football game. Read the list, and then mark each item with one of these symbols:

L **lessons learned** from the experience
P **personal background** on the binge drinker
S **steps** leading to the emergency
E the life-and-death **emergency**

After you've marked all the ideas, survey them, and think of one main idea. Try to focus on a point that connects to what Ryan Dabbieri, the binge drinker, learned.

_____P_____ Ryan Dabbieri was a 22-year-old senior at the University of Virginia.

_____P_____ Ryan did not think he was a binge drinker.

_____P_____ About once a week, he would drink five to seven drinks in two hours.

_____S_____ Before one big football game, he drank five or six very big shots of bourbon in fifteen minutes at a party.

_____S_____ At the stadium, he straightened up to get by security.

_____S_____ Inside, he passed out.

_____S_____ His friends carried him outside.

_____S/E_____ They couldn't revive him.

_____E_____ In the emergency room, he stopped breathing for four minutes.

_____E_____ His friends were terrified.

_____E_____ The doctors did a scan for brain damage.

_____E_____ Ryan's father flew in from Atlanta.

_____E_____ Ryan awoke the next day in intensive care.

_____L_____ Ryan says he won't drink again.

_____L_____ He says he is lucky to be alive.

main idea: A person may need to face a crisis to learn the dangers of binge drinking.

_____

_____

Outlines **Summary**

Below is an outline for a summary of "Part-Time Job May Do Teenagers More Harm Than Good." As you read it, you'll notice that the main idea of the thought lines stage has become the topic sentence of the outline, and most of the other ideas have become details.

***Outline for a Summary of "Part-Time Job May
Do Teenagers More Harm Than Good"***

topic sentence: Parents should know that working long hours at part-time jobs is not good for teens.

details:

effects on schoolwork

> Working students do less well in school.
> A study of twelfth graders by Linda P. Worley showed this.
> It showed that grades suffer if students work more than ten hours in the school week.
> Students who work long hours choose easier classes.
> They spend less time on homework.
> They cut class more.
> They are less interested in school.

other effects

> They use drugs and alcohol more.
> They have lower self-esteem.
> They spend money foolishly.

In the outline, the part about what many parents think about part-time jobs has been left out. Since it was an idea that contrasted with the topic sentence, it didn't seem to fit. That kind of selecting is what you do in the outlines stage of writing a summary. In the rough lines stage, you may change your mind and decide to use the idea later.

Rough Lines Drafting and Revising: Attributing Ideas in a Summary

The first draft of your summary paragraph is your first try at *combining* all the material into one paragraph. The draft is much like the draft of any other paragraph, with one exception: *When you summarize another person's ideas, be sure to say whose ideas you are writing.* That is, *attribute* the ideas to the writer. Let the reader of your paragraph know

INSTRUCTOR'S NOTE:

Since your students will not have had much experience with proper attribution, this may be a good time to tell them that giving proper credit to authors/sources is an integral part of many college credit courses.

1. the author of the selection you are summarizing.
2. the title of the selection you are summarizing.

You may want to *attribute ideas by giving your summary paragraph a title*, such as

> A Summary of "Part-Time Job May Do Teenagers More Harm Than Good" by Gary Klott

Note that you put the title of Klott's article in quotation marks.

Or you may want to *put the title and author into the paragraph itself.* Below is a draft version of a summary of "Part-Time Job May Do Teenagers More Harm Than Good" with the title and the author incorporated into the paragraph.

***A Draft of a Summary of "Part-Time Job May
Do Teenagers More Harm Than Good"***

"Part-Time Job May Do Teenagers More Harm Than Good" by Gary Klott says that parents should know that working long hours at part-time jobs is not good for teens. Working students do less well in school. A study of twelfth graders by Linda P. Worley showed that grades suffer if students work more than ten hours during the school week. Students who work long hours choose easier courses, spend less time on homework, cut class more often, and cheat. They are less interested in school. They use drugs and alcohol more and have less self-esteem. They spend money foolishly.

When you look this draft over and read it aloud, you may notice a few problems:

- The draft is very choppy; it needs transitions.
- In some places, the word choice could be better.
- The beginning of the paragraph could use an introduction.
- Linda P. Worley did a study about grades and working students. But the other information about effects on schoolwork came from other studies. This difference should be made clear.
- The paragraph ends abruptly.

Final Lines Summary

Look carefully at the final version of the summary. Notice how the idea about what parents think has been added to an introduction, and how transitions and word choice have improved the summary. Also notice how one phrase, "Other studies indicate that," clarifies the ideas in the summary, and how an added conclusion clinches the paragraph.

A Final Version of a Summary of "Part-Time Job May Do Teenagers More Harm Than Good" (Changes from the draft are underlined.)

<u>Many parents think part-time jobs teach their children responsibility, money and job skills, but they may be wrong.</u> An article called "Part-Time Job May Do Teenagers More Harm Than Good" by Gary Klott says that parents should know that working long hours at part-time jobs is not good for teens. <u>First of all,</u> working students do less well in school. A study of twelfth graders by Linda P. Worley showed that grades suffer if students worked more than ten hours during the school week. <u>Other studies indicate that</u> students who work long hours choose easier courses, spend less time on their homework, <u>and are likely to cheat and cut classes. In addition, such students</u> are less interested in school. <u>Their problems extend outside of school, too, where</u> they use drugs and alcohol <u>more than other students</u> and have less self-esteem. <u>Finally,</u> they <u>do not learn financial responsibility from their jobs since</u> they spend money foolishly. <u>Parents must consider all these drawbacks before they allow their teens to work long hours.</u>

Writing summaries is good writing practice, and it also helps you develop your reading skills. Even if your instructor does not require you to turn in a polished summary of an assigned reading, you may find it helpful to summarize what you have read. In many classes, midterms or other exams cover many assigned readings. If you make short summaries of each reading as it is assigned, you will have a helpful collection of focused, organized material to review.

WRITING A REACTION TO A READING

A summary is one kind of writing you can do after reading, but there are other kinds. Your instructor might ask you to *react* by writing about some idea you got from your reading. If you read "Part-Time Job May Do Teenagers More Harm Than Good," your instructor might have asked you to react by writing about this topic:

> Gary Klotz says that parents may have the wrong idea about their children's jobs. Write about another part of teen life which parents may not understand.

You may begin to gather ideas by freewriting.

Thought Lines **Reaction to a Reading: Freewriting**

You can freewrite in a reading journal, if you wish. This kind of journal is a special journal in which you write about selections that you've read. To freewrite, you can

- write key points made by the author,
- write about whatever you remember from the reading selection,
- write down any of the author's ideas that you think you might want to write about someday,
- list questions raised by what you've read,
- connect the reading selection to other things you've read, heard, or experienced.

A freewriting that reacts to "Part-Time Job May Do Teenagers More Harm Than Good" might look like this:

Freewriting for a Reaction to a Reading

"Part-Time Job May Do Teenagers More Harm Than Good"—Gary Klott

Jobs can be bad for teens. Author says parents should stop teens from working too many hours. But how? Most parents are afraid of their teens. Or they don't want to interfere. They figure teens want to be independent. I know I wanted to be independent when I was in high school. Did I? I'm not so sure. I think I wanted some attention from my folks. Maybe parents don't know this. Why didn't I say anything?

Thought Lines **Selecting a Topic, Listing and Developing Ideas**

Once you have your freewriting, you can survey it for a topic. You might survey the freewriting above and decide you can write about how parents don't know their teens want attention. To gather ideas, you begin a list:

> *teens want attention and parents don't know*
> *sometimes teens look independent*
> *they act smart*
> *no real self-confidence*
> *friends aren't enough*
> *I wanted my father's approval*
> *teens can't say what they need*

to get attention, they break rules
I would have liked some praise

Next, you organize, expand, and develop this list until you have a main point, the topic sentence, and a list of details. You decide on this topic sentence:

Some parents are unaware that their teenage children need attention.

With a topic sentence and a list of details, you are ready to begin the outlines stage of writing.

Outlines Reaction to a Reading

An outline might look like the one following. As you read it, notice that the topic sentence and ideas are *your* opinions, not the ideas of the author of "Part-Time Job May Do Teenager More Harm Than Good." You used his ideas to come up with your own. Also notice how it builds on the ideas on the list and organizes them in a clear order.

An Outline of a Reaction to a Reading

topic sentence: Some parents are unaware that their teenage children need attention.

details: **what parents see**	Teens act independent. They act smart. They break rules. Parents think that rule-breaking means teens want to be left alone.
what teens want	Teens do it to get attention. Teens can't say what they need. They have no real self-confidence. Their friends aren't enough.
personal example	I wanted my father's approval. I would have liked some praise.

Rough Lines Reaction to a Reading

If your outline gives you enough good ideas to develop, you are on your way to a paragraph. If you began with the ideas above, for example, you could develop them into a paragraph like this:

A Draft of a Reaction to a Reading

Some parents are unaware that their teenage children need attention. Teens act independent and smart. They break their parents' rules, so their parents think teenage rule-breaking is a sign the children want to be left alone. Teens break rules to get attention. They can't say what they need; therefore, they act out their needs. Teens have no real self-confidence. Friends aren't enough. I wanted my father's approval. I would have liked some praise.

Final Lines Reaction to a Reading

When you read the draft version of the paragraph, you probably noticed some places where it could be revised:

- The word choice could be better.
- There is too much repetition of words like "need" or "needs" or "their parents" or "children."
- The paragraph needs many transitions.
- Since the ideas are reactions related to a point by Gary Klott, he needs to be mentioned.
- The ending is a little abrupt.

Following is the final version of the same paragraph. As you read it, notice how the changes make it a clearer, smoother, more developed paragraph.

A Final Version of a Reaction to a Reading

(Changes from the draft are underlined.)

> Gary Klott says that many parents do not understand the impact of their teenagers' part-time jobs. There is another part of teen life that parents may not understand. Some parents are unaware that their teenage children need attention. Teens act independent and self-assured. They will break their parents' rules, so their parents think the rulebreaking is a sign the children want to be left alone. However, adolescents break rules to get attention. They can't say what they crave; therefore, they act out their needs. Teens have no real self-confidence. While friends help adolescents develop self-confidence, friends aren't enough. My own experience is a good example of what adolescents desire. I wanted my father's approval. I would have liked some praise, but I couldn't ask for what I needed. My father was a parent who was unaware.

WRITING ABOUT AGREEMENT OR DISAGREEMENT

Thought Lines Agree or Disagree Paragraph

Another way to write about a reading selection is to find a point in it and *agree or disagree with that point*. To begin writing about agreement or disagreement, you can review the selection and jot down any statements that provoke a strong reaction in you. You are looking for statements with which you can agree or disagree. If you reviewed "Part-Time Job May Do Teenagers More Harm Than Good," you might list these statements as points of agreement or disagreement:

Points of Agreement or Disagreement from a Reading

> "Grades suffer when students work more than ten hours during the school week."—agree
>
> High school students who work many hours "have less interest in formal education"—disagree

Then you might *pick one of the statements and react to it in writing*. If you disagreed with the statement that high school students who work many hours "have less interest in formal education," you might begin by brainstorming.

Brainstorming for an Agree or Disagree Paragraph

Question: Why do you disagree that high school students who work long hours "have less interest in formal education"?

Answer: I worked long hours. I was interested in getting a *good* education.

Question: If you were interested in school, why were you so focused on your job?

Answer: To make money.

Question: Then wasn't money more important than school?

Answer: No. I was working to make money to pay for college. Working was the only way I could afford college.

Question: Do you think it <u>looked</u> as if you didn't care about education?

Answer: Yes, sure.

Question: Why?

Answer: I used to be so tired from working I would fall asleep in class.

Once you have some ideas from brainstorming, you can list them, group them, and add to them by more brainstorming. Your topic sentence can be a way of stating your disagreement with the original point, like this:

> Although Gary Klott says that high school students who work long hours tend to lose interest in school, my experience shows the opposite.

With a topic sentence and details, you can work on the outlines stage of your paragraph.

Outlines **Agree or Disagree Paragraph**

An outline might look like the following. Notice that the topic sentence is your opinion, and that the details are from your experience.

Outline for an Agree or Disagree Paragraph

topic sentence: Although Gary Klott says that high school students who work long hours may lose interest in school, my experience shows the opposite.

details:
my experience
- While I was in high school, I worked long hours.
- I was very interested in getting a good education.
- I wanted to graduate from college.
- To save money for college, I was working long hours.
- Working was the only way I could pay for college.

why I appeared uninterested
- I probably looked as if I didn't care about school.
- I fell asleep in class.
- I was tired from working.

Rough Lines **Agree or Disagree Paragraph**

Once you have a good outline, you can develop it into a paragraph:

A Draft of an Agree or Disagree Paragraph

> Although Gary Klott says that high school students who work long hours lose interest in school, my experience shows the opposite. When I was in high school, I worked long hours. I endured my job and even increased my hours because I was interested in getting a good education. I wanted to graduate from college. I was working long hours to save money for college. Working was the only way I could pay tuition. I know that, to my teachers, I probably looked as if I didn't care about school. I was tired from working. I fell asleep in class.

Final Lines **Agree or Disagree Paragraph**

When you surveyed the draft of the paragraph, you probably noticed some places that need revision:

- The paragraph could use more specific details.
- Some sentences could be combined.
- It needs a last sentence, reinforcing the point that students who work long hours may be very interested in school.

As you read the final version of the paragraph, notice how the revisions improve the paragraph.

A Final Version of an Agree or Disagree Paragraph

(Changes from the draft are underlined.)

> Although Gary Klott says that high school students who work long hours lose interest in school, my experience shows the opposite. When I was in high school, I worked long hours. Sometimes I worked twenty-five hours a week at a fast-food restaurant. I endured my job and even increased my hours because I was interested in getting a good education. I wanted to graduate from college. I was working long hours to save money for college since working was the only way I could pay tuition. I know that, to my teachers, I probably looked as if I didn't care about school. I was so tired from working I came to school in a daze. I fell asleep in class. But my long, hard hours at work made me determined to change my life through education.

WRITING FOR AN ESSAY TEST

Another kind of writing from reading involves the essay test. Most essay questions require you to write about an assigned reading. Usually, an essay test requires you to write from memory, not from an open book or notes. Such writing can be stressful, but breaking the task into steps can eliminate much of the stress.

Before the Test: The Steps of Reading

If you work through the steps of reading days before the test, you are halfway to your goal. Prereading helps to keep you focused, and your first reading gives you a sense of the whole selection. The third step, rereading with a pen or pencil, can be particularly helpful when you are preparing for a test. Most essay questions will ask you to either summarize or react to a reading selection. In either case, you must be familiar with the reading's main idea, supporting ideas, examples, and details. If you note these by marking the selection, you are teaching yourself about the main point, supporting ideas, and structure of the reading selection.

Shortly before the test, review the marked reading assignment. Your notes will help you focus on the main point and the supporting ideas.

During the Test: The Stages of Writing

Answering an essay test question may seem very different from writing at home. After all, on a test, you must rely on your memory and write within a time limit, and these restrictions can make you feel anxious. However, by following stages of the writing process, you can meet that challenge calmly and confidently.

Thought Lines Essay Test

Before you begin to write, think about these questions: Is the instructor asking for a summary of a reading selection? Or is he or she asking you to react to a specific idea with examples or by agreeing or disagreeing? For example, in an essay question about the article, "Part-Time Job May Do Teenagers More Harm Than Good," by Gary Klott, you might be asked (1) to explain why Klott thinks a part-time job can be bad for a teenager (a summary), (2) to explain what Klott means when he says that students who work long hours may keep their grades up but still miss out on the best education (a reaction, in which you develop and explain one part of the reading, or (3) to agree or disagree that afterschool jobs teach the wrong lesson about the value of money (a reaction, so you have to be aware of what Klott said on this point).

Once you have thought about the question, list or freewrite your first ideas; at this time, do not worry about how "right" or "wrong" your writing is; just write your first thoughts.

Outlines Essay Test

Your writing will be clear if you follow a plan. Remember that the audience for this writing is your instructor and that he or she will be evaluating how well you stick to the subject, make a point, and support it. Your plan for making a point about the subject and supporting it can be written in a brief outline.

First, reread the question. Next, survey your list or freewriting. Does it contain a main point that answers the question? Does it contain supporting ideas and details?

Next, write a main point, and then list supporting ideas and details under the main point. Your main point will be the topic sentence of your answer. If you need more support, try brainstorming.

Rough Lines Essay Test

Write your point and supporting ideas in paragraph form. Remember to use effective transitions and to combine short sentences.

Final Lines Essay Test

You will probably not have time to copy your answer, but you can review it, proofread it, and correct any errors in spelling, punctuation, or word choice. The final check can produce a more polished answer.

Organize Your Time

Some students skip steps: they immediately begin writing their answer to an essay question, without thinking or planning. Sometimes they find themselves stuck in the middle of a paragraph, panicked because they have no more ideas. At other times, they find themselves writing in a circle, repeating the same point over and over. Occasionally, they even forget to include a main idea.

You can avoid these hazards by spending time on each of the stages. Planning is as important as writing. For example, if you have half an hour to write an essay, you can divide your time like this:

> 5 minutes thinking, freewriting, listing
> 10 minutes planning, outlining
> 10 minutes drafting
> 5 minutes reviewing, proofreading

Writing from Reading: A Summary of Options

Reading can give you many opportunities for your own writing. You can summarize a writer's work, use it as a springboard for your own related writing, or agree or disagree with it. However you decide to write from reading, you must still work through the same writing process. Following the steps of thought lines, outlines, rough lines, and final lines will help you develop your work into a polished paragraph.

Lines of Detail: A Walk-Through Assignment

Here are three ideas from "Part-Time Job May Do Teenagers More Harm Than Good":

    a. Students who work long hours miss out on extracurricular activities at school.
    b. Parents should prevent their teenage children from working long hours.
    c. Teens who work spend their money foolishly.

Pick *one* of these ideas with which you agree or disagree. Write a paragraph explaining why you agree or disagree. To write your paragraph, follow these steps:

Step 1: Begin by listing at least three reasons or examples why you agree or disagree. Make your reasons or examples as specific as you can, using your experiences or the experiences of friends and family.

Step 2: Read your list to a partner or group. With the help of your listener(s), add reasons, examples, and details.

Step 3: Once you have enough ideas, transform the statement you agreed or disagreed with into a topic sentence.

Step 4: Write an outline by listing your reasons, examples, and details below the topic sentence. Check that your list is in a clear and logical order.

INSTRUCTOR'S NOTE:

A Peer Review Form for students' exchange of drafts is on page 503.

Step 5: Write a draft of your paragraph. Check that you have attributed Gary Klott's statement, you have enough specific details, you have combined any choppy sentences, and you have used good transitions. Revise your draft until the paragraph is smooth and clear.

Step 6: Before you prepare the final copy, check your draft for errors in spelling, punctuation, and word choice.

WRITING YOUR OWN PARAGRAPH

Writing from Reading: "Part-Time Job May Do Teenagers More Harm Than Good"

When you write on any of these topics, be sure to work through the stages of the writing process in preparing your paragraph.

1. Klott talks about high school students who work to pay for car insurance, dates, video games, music CDs, and designer clothes. However, students might not have to work so hard if they learned to do without things they don't really need: the latest clothes, the newest CD, their own car, and so forth. Write a paragraph about the many things high school students buy that they don't really need.

2. Work can interfere with high school. Write about something else that interferes with high school. You can write about social life, extracurricular activities, sports, family responsibilities, or any other part of a student's life that can prevent him or her from focusing on school.

   As you plan this paragraph, think about details that could fit these categories:

   Why students choose this activity/responsibility over school
   The effects on students' schoolwork
   How to balance school and other activities or responsibilities

3. Many parents believe that a part-time job is good for high school students, but the job can be harmful. Write a one-paragraph letter to parents, warning them about some other part of teen life (not jobs) that parents may think is good but may be harmful. You can write about the dangers of their child being popular, or having a steady boyfriend or girlfriend, or always being number one in academics.

   Once you've chosen the topic, brainstorm with a partner or group: ask questions, answer them, add details. After you've brainstormed, work by yourself and proceed through the stages of preparing your letter to parents.

4. Some parents have misconceptions (incorrect ideas) about their teenage children; for instance, they may believe the teen with a part-time job is automatically learning how to handle money. On the other hand, teenage children have misconceptions about their parents. Write about some misconception that teens have about

their parents. You might, for instance, write about teens' mistaken belief that

the best parents are the ones who give their children the most freedom,

or

parents who love you give you everything you want,

or

parents do not remember what it is like to be young.

To begin, freewrite on one mistaken idea that teens might have about their parents. Focus on your own experiences, memories, and so forth—as a teen or as a parent of teenagers. Use your freewriting to find details and a focus for your paragraph.

5. Klott writes about parents' need to restrict teens' work hours. Write about a family rule that you hated when you were a child or teen. Include your feelings about that rule today.

Name: _____   **Section:** _____

PEER REVIEW FORM FOR WRITING FROM READING

After you have written a draft version of your paragraph, let a writing partner read it. When your partner has completed the following form, discuss the comments. Then repeat the same process for your partner's paragraph.

This paragraph (circle one) (1) summarizes, (2) agrees or disagrees, (3) reacts to an idea connected to a reading selection.

I think this paragraph should include (circle one) (1) both the title and author of the reading selection, (2) the author of the reading selection, (3) neither the title nor the author of the reading selection.

The topic sentence of this paragraph is _____

_____

_____

The best part of this paragraph starts with the words _____

_____

One suggestion to improve this paragraph is to _____

_____

Other comments on the paragraph: _____

_____

_____

_____

_____

_____

_____

_____

_____

_____

_____

_____

_____

_____

Reviewer's Name: _____

WRITING FROM READING

To practice the skills you've learned in this chapter, follow the steps of prereading, reading, and rereading with a pencil as you read the following selections.

New Directions

Maya Angelou

Maya Angelou was born Marguerite Johnson in St. Louis, Missouri, in 1928. She survived many hardships to become one of the most famous and beloved writers in America. Although she is best known for her autobiographical books, Angelou is also a political activist, singer, and performer on stage and screen. Her achievements include best-selling books, literary awards, and the reciting of her poetry at the inauguration of President William Clinton. In this essay, Angelou tells the story of a woman who cut a new path for her life.

Words You May Need to Know (corresponding paragraph numbers are in parentheses)

burdensome (1): troublesome, heavy
conceded (2): admitted
domestic (3): a household worker
meticulously (4): very carefully
cotton gin (4): a factory with a machine for separating cotton fibers from seeds
brazier (6): a container that holds live coals, covered by a grill, used for cooking

savors (6): food that smells and tastes good
lint (6): cotton fibers
specters (6): ghosts
balmy (9): mild and soothing
hives of industry (9): a place swarming with busy workers
looms (11): rises in front of us
assess (11): evaluate, judge
ominous (11): threatening
resolve (11): determination
unpalatable (11): not acceptable

1   In 1903 the late Mrs. Annie Johnson of Arkansas found herself with two toddling sons, very little money, a slight ability to read and add simple numbers. To this picture add a disastrous marriage and the burdensome fact that Mrs. Johnson was a Negro.

2   When she told her husband, Mr. William Johnson, of her dissatisfaction with their marriage, he conceded that he too found it to be less than he expected, and had been secretly hoping to leave and study religion. He added that he thought God was calling him not only to preach but to do so in Enid, Oklahoma. He did not tell her that he knew a minister in Enid with whom he could study and who had a friendly, unmarried daughter. They parted amicably, Annie keeping the one-room house and William taking most of the cash to carry himself to Oklahoma.

3   Annie, over six feet tall, big-boned, decided that she would not go to work as a domestic and leave her "precious babes" to anyone else's care. There was no possibility of being hired at the town's cotton gin or lumber mill, but maybe there was a way to make the two factories work for her. In

other words, "I looked up the road I was going and back the way I come, and since I wasn't satisfied, I decided to step off the road and cut me a new path." She told herself that she wasn't a fancy cook but that she could "mix groceries well enough to scare hungry away and from starving a man."

4   She made her plans meticulously and in secret. One early evening to see if she was ready, she placed stones in two five-gallon pails and carried them three miles to the cotton gin. She rested a little, and then, discarding some rocks, she walked in the darkness to the sawmill five miles farther along the dirt road. On her way back to her little house and her babies, she dumped the remaining rocks along the path.

5   That same night she worked into the early hours boiling chicken and frying ham. She made dough and filled the rolled-out pastry with meat. At last she went to sleep.

6   The next morning she left her house carrying the meat pies, lard, an iron brazier, and coals for a fire. Just before lunch she appeared in an empty lot behind the cotton gin. As the dinner noon bell rang, she dropped the savors into boiling fat and the aroma rose and floated over to the workers who spilled out of the gin, covered with white lint, looking like specters.

7   Most workers had brought their lunches of pinto beans and biscuits or crackers, onions and cans of sardines, but they were tempted by the hot meat pies which Annie ladled out of the fat. She wrapped them in newspapers, which soaked up the grease, and offered them for sale at a nickel each. Although business was slow, those first days Annie was determined. She balanced her appearances between the two hours of activity.

8   So, on Monday if she offered hot fresh pies at the cotton gin and sold the remaining cooled-down pies at the lumber mill for three cents, then on Tuesday she went first to the lumber mill presenting fresh, just-cooked pies as the lumbermen covered in sawdust emerged from the mill.

9   For the next few years, on balmy spring days, blistering summer noons, and cold, wet, and wintry middays, Annie never disappointed her customers, who could count on seeing the tall, brown-skin woman bent over her brazier, carefully turning the meat pies. When she felt certain the workers had become dependent on her, she built a stall between the two hives of industry and let the men run to her for their lunchtime provisions.

10   She had indeed stepped from the road which seemed to have been chosen for her and cut herself a brand-new path. In years that stall became a store where customers could buy cheese, meal, syrup, cookies, candy, writing tablets, pickles, canned goods, fresh fruit, soft drinks, coal, oil, and leather soles for worn-out shoes.

11   Each of us has the right and the responsibility to assess the roads which lie ahead, and those over which we have traveled, and if the future road looms ominous or unpromising, and the roads back uninviting, then we need to gather our resolve and, carrying only the necessary baggage, step off that road into another direction. If the new choice is also unpalatable, without embarrassment, we must be ready to change that as well.

Exercise 3 Completing an Outline of "New Directions"

Practice

After you've read "New Directions," read the following exercise. Then reread "New Directions," looking for the details that will complete this outline.

Maya Angelou tells the story of a woman whose determination and hard work helped her make a new direction for her life.

Mrs. Annie Johnson's husband left her to become a _preacher_

_____ in Enid, Oklahoma.

She was left with little money, _two young sons,_ _____

_____ and a one-room house.

She decided not to work as _a domestic_ _____;

instead, she planned to use her cooking skills.

To test her plan, she practiced walking a total of _sixteen_ _____

miles, from her home to the cotton gin and sawmill, and back again.

To practice carrying a heavy load, she carried _stones in two five-gallon_

pails _____.

The same night, she cooked chicken and ham and made pastry.

The next morning, she carried her meat pies and cooking equipment

to the cotton gin and sawmill.

Although the men had brought their lunch, they were attracted by _the_

smell of the meat pies cooking .

For years, Annie Johnson sold the pies in two locations, in all weather.

Eventually, she _set up a stall between the locations_ and let the men

come to her.

Later, she sold not only food but also _writing tablets, coal, oil, and_

leather soles.

_____

She is proof that we must all _assess the roads which lie ahead of us_

and the ones which lie behind us, and if they both look unpromising, we

must choose a new direction.

WRITING FROM READING: "New Directions"

When you write on any of the following topics, be sure to work through the stages of the writing process in preparing your paragraph.

1. Using the ideas and examples you gathered in Exercise 3, write a summary of "New Directions."

2. Write about someone who had many strikes against him or her but who succeeded. Be sure that you include some of the difficulties this person faced.

3. Maya Angelou says, "Each of us has the right and responsibility to assess the roads which lie ahead, and those over which we have traveled," and if an old road or a future road looks dark, we must "step off that road into another direction."

   Write a paragraph that agrees or disagrees with that statement.

   Begin by working with a group. First, discuss what you think the statement means. Then ask at least six questions about the statement. You may ask such questions as, "Does everyone have the courage or talent to choose a new road?" or "What keeps some people from choosing a new direction?" or "Do you know anyone who has done what Angelou advises?"

   Use the questions and answers to decide whether you want to agree or disagree with Angelou's statement.

4. There is an old saying, "When the going gets tough, the tough get going," and Mrs. Annie Johnson's story seems to prove the saying is true. She was faced with poverty, lack of job opportunities, raising two children alone, and yet through hard work, creativity, and determination, she triumphed.

   Write a paragraph that tells a story and proves the truth of another old saying. You can use a saying such as, "Take time to stop and smell the roses," or "You never know what you can do until you try," or any other saying.

   Begin by freewriting about old sayings and what they mean to you. Then pick one that connects to your experience or the experience of someone you know. Use that saying as the focus of your paragraph.

Home Away from Home

Beth Nieman

Beth Nieman is a home daycare provider in Phoenix, Arizona. In this essay, she explains what parents should understand about her role in her children's life.

Words You May Need to Know (corresponding paragraph numbers are in parentheses)

accredited (2): certified that it meets requirements
seminars (2): meetings for exchanging information and study
breezily (3): carelessly, casually

held in reserve (4): saved
ideal (6): perfect
displeasure (6): disapproval
specifications (7): requirements
upscale (8): upper class
aired (9): expressed

---

1   I'm a home day-care provider—the person who opens my home and family to other people's children for 20 to 50 hours a week while they are at work. I provide food, toys, activities, companionship and encouragment to the youngsters in their parents' absence. I know from the smiles on the little ones' faces that they enjoy themselves while in my care, and they've come to expect me to be kind and helpful. However, I'm not always sure what their parents expect from me.

2   I try hard to be professional. I'm accredited by the National Association for Family Child Care, and I attend seminars on everything from safety and nutrition to planning kids' crafts and summer activities. I encourage the children's efforts, no matter how small. I help Junior to help himself, to take responsibility for his belongings, to learn counting and the alphabet, to feed himself and to share. In return, I am offered a small hand as we cross the street. I'm asked to tie a shoe, dress a doll or examine an invisible wound. We share a laugh, a story . . . a childhood.

3   Parents should understand that I, like themselves, need to earn a living. As a self-employed person, it's up to me to keep myself busy. I am legally permitted to have a certain number of children in my home, and if I don't have them, I'll feel it in the wallet. Therefore, when a mother fails to arrive as scheduled, or breezily calls two hours late on Monday morning and announces that little Arlene won't be coming to day care this week because her great-aunt from Rhode Island has just arrived and will be caring for her instead (for free), I have two choices. I can swallow hard and say, "Oh, OK. Well, thanks for letting me know" (which is what I used to do), or I can have parents sign a contract at the beginning of our business relationship, stating that they will pay me a fixed amount per week each Monday, whether they bring their child or not. This is what my son's preschool does, because the school doesn't have a paying customer temporarily to fill my son's slot if he can't go to school due to family vacation or illness.

4   That brings to mind another problem. It's just not reasonable for parents to expect me to care for a sick child. I don't have the facilities or an extra person to handle the job, and it starts an exhausting cycle among myself and the children of passing germs back and forth. When I call parents and say that their child is feverish or vomiting or has diarrhea, I expect the mother or father to come and get him, not ask, "Well, what do you want me to do?" I realize that illness is unpleasant and inconvenient, but it is for me, too, and for the other children in my care. Surely I can't be expected to send the other kids home when one child is sick. I would like to suggest to parents that they make some backup arrangements or a few vacation days should be held in reserve should someone need to stay home with a sick child.

5   I had to laugh the other day when a friend dropped by at lunchtime. She looked around the table and smiled to see the little ones eating their nutritionally balanced lunches, complete with milk to drink and fruit for dessert. "You've really got it made," she said. "I would love to be able to work from home the way you do. I work with greedy, selfish people all day long, and I hate it!" Just as I was about to respond, a fight broke out. "That's my bunch of grapes!" "I had it first!" "Aaaugh!" "She hit me!"

6   "OK, OK," laughed my friend. "Point taken." Yes, I work in conditions that are sometimes less than ideal. I vacuum two or three times daily. I wipe noses and bottoms, repair broken toys and hurt feelings, and occasionally I'm spit on by my clients (though usually not intentionally). It's surprising, though, what an odd idea parents sometimes have of what I do all day long (though they are most emphatic in saying that they, themselves, could never do it). I'm sure they don't mean to be hurtful when they remark with displeasure at a fresh bandage ("What happened? Weren't you watching him?"), a ketchup stain ("This was a new outfit!"—then why did she wear it to day care?) or glance around, silently disapproving of the scattered toys, cookie crumbs and books (or so I imagine). It is always delightful to hear a compliment or a word of thanks at the end of a 10-hour day instead of a complaint.

7   I bring these issues to light because I've had the distinct impression that I'm thought to be a nanny, "the help," if you will. I'm not. I am a self-employed businesswoman. If I'm selected as a day-care provider, the child will receive excellent care and individual attention, will watch no television, will be served nutritious meals and have a variety of activities, both active and quiet, that are appropriate for his age. If I were a nanny, employed to watch a child to exact specifications, that would be one thing. But working parents can't afford to spend that much money on day care and bring their children to a group caregiver instead. At my house, I make the rules, set the policies, decide what I will and will not do. I would like my clients to respect my needs and accept the fact that outside of hiring Alice from "The Brady Bunch," they're going to have to meet me halfway. I'll try to be flexible, too. Otherwise, I'll be out of business! There are, after all, plenty of home day-care providers to choose from.

8   Sometimes I envy these mothers. I see someone drive up to my home in a car much newer than the one I drive (Is it paid for?). Their work clothes are fabulous compared with my home-issue sweats and tennis shoes (Do you have to dry-clean that?). Most parents have a more upscale address than I do. But I wonder who really does have it all? I am inclined to think it's me. The person who answers my child's questions is me; I have lots of time to hug him, tell him stories and listen to his naptime prayers.

9   I have thought of escaping to corporate America on days when yet another area on my rug absorbs a spill, yet another complaint is aired by a picky eater, or a parent arrives 30 minutes late and doesn't call me. But I have learned one very important lesson as a day-care provider that prevents me from leaving my children with sitters while I work away from home: love is not for sale.

 Exercise   4

Practice

Completing an Outline of "Home Away from Home"

After you've read "Home Away from Home," read the following exercise. Then reread "Home Away from Home," looking for details that will complete the outline.

Beth Nieman wants the parents of the children she cares for to understand her role.

She is a professional who provides specific services and items. (List some of these services and items) *food, toys, activities, companion-*

ship, and encouragement.

_____

_____

Yet some parents act as if she didn't need to make money.

(Give one example.) *Parents fail to arrive as scheduled or cancel the*

day or week at the last minute, and then expect not to pay.

_____

Others don't understand why she can't care for a sick child.

(Explain why she can't.) *She or the other children should not be*

exposed to germs.

She works under tough conditions. (Explain some of the conditions.)

She vacuums two or three times a day, wipes noses and bottoms,

repairs broken toys and hurt feelings, and is sometimes spit on by chil-

dren. She works ten hours a day.

She is not a nanny. (Explain the difference.) <u>A nanny is "the help," liv-</u>

<u>ing by another family's rules. Nieman is a self-employed businesswoman</u>

<u>who sets her own rules.</u>

In spite of the drawbacks of her job, Nieman likes working at home,

near her own children.

WRITING FROM READING: "Home Away from Home"

When you write on any of the following topics, be sure to work through the stages of the writing process in preparing your paragraph.

1. Using the ideas and examples you gathered in Exercise 4, write a summary of "Home Away from Home."

2. Beth Nieman says her job has taught her a lesson: love is not for sale. Write about a lesson you learned at a job. You can begin by freewriting about the job. Try recalling any problems or achievements on the job, and think about what the difficulties or successes taught you.

3. Write an agree or disagree paragraph about one of the following statements:

Day-care workers have it made.
Working mothers do not have it all.
Day-care workers should not be expected to care for sick children.
Parents should pay a fixed amount at the beginning of each week, whether they bring their child to day care or not.

4. Write a paragraph about what you love—or hate—about your job. Begin the thought lines part of writing with an interview. Have a writing partner interview you. Your classmate should prepare at least six questions before the interview. They may be questions such as, "What's the best part of your job?" "What's the worst part?" "How do you cope with the bad parts?" At the interview, let your partner jot down your answers and ask follow-up questions.

After you have been interviewed, switch roles. Interview your partner, with your own prepared list of questions.

At the end of both interviews, give your partner his or her responses and take your own. Use them to develop a focus and details for your paragraph.

5. Write a letter to your boss or to the customers, clients, patients, or children you serve at your job. Explain how they misunderstand your job and your role. You may include what they could do to make your life easier.

Grammar for ESL Students

NOUNS AND ARTICLES

A ***noun*** names a person, place, or thing. There are *count nouns* and *noncount nouns*.

> **Count nouns** refer to persons, places, or things that can be counted.
>
> three *cookies*, two *dogs*, five *suitcases*
>
> **Noncount nouns** refer to things that can't be counted.
>
> *luggage, employment, attention*

Here are some more examples of count and noncount nouns.

count	noncount
joke	humor
movie	entertainment
dream	inspiration
automobile	transportation

One way to remember the difference between count and noncount nouns is to put the word *much* in front of the noun. For example, if you can say *much entertainment*, then *entertainment* is a noncount noun.

Practice

Identifying Count and Noncount Nouns

Put **count** or **noncount** next to each word below.

1. _count_   housewife   **3.** _noncount_   equipment

2. _noncount_   fuel   **4.** _count_   carrot

5. noncount	interest	**8.** count	school
6. noncount	dignity	**9.** noncount	jewelry
7. noncount	rain	**10.** count	goal

Using Articles with Nouns

Articles point out nouns. Articles are either **indefinite** (*a, an*) or **definite** (*the*). There are several rules for using these articles.

Use *a* in front of consonant sounds; use *an* before vowel sounds.

a filter	an orphan
a room	an apple
a bench	an event
a thought	an issue
a necklace	an umbrella

Use *a* or *an* in front of singular count nouns. *A* or *an* mean *any one.*

I saw *an* owl.
She rode *a* horse.

Do not use *a* or *an* with noncount nouns.

not this: I need a̶ money.
but this: I need money.

not this: Selena is passing a̶n̶ arithmetic.
but this: Selena is passing arithmetic.

Use *the* before both singular and plural count nouns whose specific identity is known to the reader.

The dress with the sequins on it is my party dress.
Most of *the* movies I rent are science fiction films.

Use *the* before noncount nouns only when they are specifically identified.

not this: He wants t̶h̶e̶ sympathy. (Whose sympathy? What sympathy? The noncount noun *sympathy* is not specifically identified.)
but this: I need *the sympathy* of a good friend. (Now *sympathy* is specifically identified.)

not this: G̶e̶n̶e̶r̶o̶s̶i̶t̶y̶ of the family who paid for my education was remarkable. (The nouncount noun *generosity* is specifically identifed, so you need *the.*)
but this: *The generosity* of the family who paid for my education was remarkable.

Exercise 2 **Using *a* or *an***

Practice

Put *a* or *an* in the spaces where it is needed. Some sentences are correct as they are.

1. Robert filled the tank with _____ gasoline.

2. The fortuneteller gave me __a__ warning.

3. Sometimes __a__ rumor can spread lies.

4. Christina went to the market to buy _____ milk.

5. The thief stole __a__ sandwich and __an__ orange.

6. Last week, Sammy fell in _____ love.

7. Our house is __an__ example of __a__ home without _____ beauty.

8. __A__ parrot and __a__ toddler may not get along well.

9. _____ food costs more than it used to.

10. If you want to lose _____ weight, you should go on __a__ diet.

<table>
<tr><td>Exercise 3</td></tr>
<tr><td>Practice</td></tr>
</table>

Using _the_

Put _the_ in the spaces where it is needed. Some sentences are correct as they are.

1. My husband gave me __the__ support I needed.

2. Isaac has _____ faith in __the__ honesty of ordinary people.

3. Teresa is filled with _____ kindness.

4. With __the__ help of my best friend, I managed to repair the roof.

5. I was __the__ last one in __the__ class to finish __the__ test.

6. __The__ magazines I like best write about _____ sports.

7. __The__ conference in _____ Washington educated me about __the__

difficulties facing single parents.

8. My dog has __the__ courage of a much larger dog.

9. Giselle likes to walk near __the__ ocean.

10. One of these days, he will take __the__ advice I gave him.

<table>
<tr><td>Exercise 4</td></tr>
<tr><td>Connect</td></tr>
</table>

Correcting a Paragraph with Errors in Articles

Correct the eleven errors with _a_, _an_, or _the_ in the following paragraph. You may need to add, change, or eliminate articles. Write the corrections in the space above the errors.

Traveling

~~The~~ traveling can be a frustrating experience. Last week, I spent four

the   the

hours at airport, waiting for plane that would take me to Atlanta. The per-

a

son at the check-in counter did not announce ~~an~~ delay until one hour after

the plane was supposed to take off. One hour later, we finally boarded the plane, only to sit for another two hours. During those two hours, the air

                     a   *a*

conditioning was turned off, and no one offered me the drink or the snack.

The pilot   *news*

Pilot kept coming on the loudspeaker to say he had a news of bad weather

ahead and had to wait. Sitting in the tiny seat, sweltering in the heat, I felt

       anger   *impatience*   *the*

the anger and an impatience. I experienced bad side of travel.

NOUNS OR PRONOUNS USED AS SUBJECTS

A noun or a **pronoun** (a word that takes the place of a noun) is the subject of each sentence or dependent clause. Be sure that all sentences or dependent clauses have a subject.

> **not this:** Cooks breakfast on weekends.
> **but this:** *He* cooks breakfast on weekends.

> **not this:** My cousin was hurt when fell down the stairs.
> **but this:** My cousin was hurt when *he* fell down the stairs.

Be careful not to *repeat* the subject.

> **not this:** The lieutenant she said I was brave.
> **but this:** The lieutenant said I was brave.

> **not this:** The cat that bit me it was a Siamese.
> **but this:** The cat that bit me was a Siamese.

 Correcting Errors with Subjects

Practice

Correct any errors with subjects in the sentences below. Write your corrections in the space above the errors.

         Leah never
1. Your sister Leah she never stops arguing.

                     roof started
2. When the rain began, my roof it started to leak.

                  on taste
3. French fries with their skins on they taste the best.

              it
4. Occasionally on a cold night feels good to sit by a fire.

           they
5. Books make a great gift; can be enjoyed by more than one person.

     Geraldo likes
6. My rabbit Geraldo he likes to be petted.

                  phone was
7. Last week the battery in my cell phone it was dead.

   Larry
8. Wants to rent an apartment near the college.

  he
9. After leaves his girlfriend, he calls her and talks all night.

               town was
10. The most dangerous intersection in town it was near my house.

VERBS

Necessary Verbs

Be sure that a main verb isn't missing from your sentences or dependent clauses.

> **not this:** Carlos extremely talented.
> **but this:** Carlos *is* extremely talented.

> **not this:** Bill called the police when saw the robbery.
> **but this:** Bill called the police when *he* saw the robbery.

-s Endings

Be sure to put the *-s* on present tense verbs in the third person singular.

> **not this:** She ~~take~~ a break in the afternoon.
> **but this:** She *takes* a break in the afternoon.

> **not this:** The plane ~~arrive~~ at 7:00 p.m.
> **but this:** The plane *arrives* at 7:00 p.m.

-ed Endings

Be sure to put *-ed* endings on the past participle form of a verb. There are three main forms of a verb:

> **present:** Today I walk.
> **past:** Yesterday I walked.
> **past participle:** I *have* walked. He *has* talked.

The past participle form is also used after *were, was, had,* and *has.*

> **not this:** We have ~~talk~~ about this plan for several weeks.
> **but this:** We have *talked* about this plan for several weeks.

> **not this:** The baby was ~~amuse~~ by the new toy.
> **but this:** The baby was *amused* by the new toy.

Do not add *-ed* endings to infinitives. An infinitive is the verb form that uses *to* plus the present form of the verb:

> to suggest, to revise,

> **not this:** My husband wanted me to ~~suggested~~ a family party.
> **but this:** My husband wanted me to *suggest* a family party.

> **not this:** I finally learned how to ~~revised~~ a draft.
> **but this:** I finally learned how to *revise* a draft.

Practice

Correcting Errors in Verbs: Necessary Verbs, Third Person Present Tense, Past Participles, and Infinitives

Correct any errors in verbs in the sentences below. Write your corrections in the space above the line. Some sentences do not need any correcting.

1. My car was repaired at the same place where Andy always take *takes* his car.

2. In calculus class, I wanted to completed *complete* the homework, but I did not have enough time.

3. My parents were pleased with the gift Danielle gave them.

4. Once a week, Nathaniel cleans the bathroom and dusts the living room.

        looks
5. That rose bush look healthy, but it needs some plant food.

          boarded
6. By the time I got to the airport, the passengers had board the plane.

        is
7. One of the most beautiful streets in the city Lincoln Avenue.

         conquered
8. Today my son is a good swimmer because he has conquer his fear of water.

        is
9. Without a doubt, communication essential in a good marriage.

10. If my father manages to arrive home before dinner time, he
   collapses   *takes*
collapse into his armchair and take a nap.

Exercise 7

 Connect

Correcting a Paragraph with Errors in Necessary Verbs, Third Person Present Tense, Past Participles, and Infinitives

Correct the nine verb errors in the following paragraph. Write your corrections in the space above the errors.

                                          gives
      Eileen is the most popular person in her department because she give

so much to her fellow employees. Whenever she greets her office mates
                                  turn
with a smile or a silly joke, Eileen has the power to turned a dull day into a
                               she
happier one. Even when Eileen herself is feeling low, manages to make oth-
                        offers
ers laugh. She is also a good listener. She offer her total attention and does
                    has
not judge those who confide in her. She been known to spend hours on the
                            feels
phone with someone in trouble. Everyone feel comfortable talking to
              cares
Eileen, for she genuinely care about others. She is well-liked because she
        respond   *brighten*
knows how to responded to others and to brightened their lives.

Two-Word Verbs

Many verbs called **two-word verbs** contain a verb plus another word, a preposition or adverb. The meaning of each word by itself is different from the meaning the two words have when they are together. Look at this example:

I ran across an old friend at the ballgame.

You might check *run* in the dictionary and find that it means *to move quickly. Across* means *from one side to the other.* But *run across* means something different:

    not this: I ~~moved quickly from one side to the other of~~ an old friend at the ballgame.

    but this: I *encountered* an old friend at the ballgame.

Sometimes a word or words come between the words of a two-word verb:

Yesterday I *took* my brother *out* to dinner.

Here are some common two-word verbs:

ask out:	I hope Steve will *ask* me *out* tomorrow.
break down:	If you drive too far, the car will *break down*.
call off:	I *will call* the game *off*.
call on:	He may *call on* you for advice
call up:	Neil *calls* Marsha *up* on weekends.
come across:	Sometimes Joe *comes across* Nick at work.
drop in:	We can *drop in* on the neighbors.
drop off:	I can *drop* you *off* on my way to school.
fill in:	For this test, just *fill in* the blanks.
fill out:	You must *fill out* an application.
hand in:	Harry has to *hand in* his lab report.
hand out:	Marcy will *hand out* the tickets.
keep on:	We can *keep on* rehearsing our music.
look into:	The police want to *look into* the matter.
look over:	Tom intends to *look* the place *over*.
look up:	I can *look* the number *up* in the phone book.
pick up:	Tom went to *pick up* his dry cleaning.
quiet down:	The neighbors asked us to *quiet down*.
run into:	Maybe I will *run into* you at the park.
run out:	We have *run out* of coffee.
think over:	Thank you for the offer; I will *think* it *over*.
try on:	I like that dress; I will *try* it *on*.
try out:	Jack needs to *try* the drill *out*.
turn on:	*Turn* the radio *on*.
turn down:	Lucy wants to *turn* the proposal *down*.
turn up:	The lost keys will *turn up* somewhere.

Exercise 8

Practice

Writing Sentences with Two-Word Verbs

Write a sentence for each of the following two-word verbs. Use the examples above as a guide, but consult a dictionary if you are not sure what the verbs mean.

1. break down   I hope the air conditioner doesn't break down.

Answers Will Vary.

Possible answers shown at right.

2. look into   The Dean of Students will look into the incident.

3. fill out   Fabian has to fill out a police report.

4. run out   We have run out of ideas for the club.

5. come across   Let me know if you come across any old videos.

6. turn down   Mel turned down the job offer.

7. drop off   I can drop off the tools I borrowed.

8. think over   Melissa is thinking over her options.

9. call off   The band had to call off the concert.

10. try on   Alejandro is going to try on a blue suit.

Contractions and Verbs

Contractions often contain verbs you may not recognize in their shortened forms.

contraction: *I'm* making cookies.
long form: *I am* making cookies.

contraction: *He's* been out of town for two weeks.
long form: *He has* been out of town for two weeks.

contraction: *He's* studying German.
long form: *He is* studying German.

contraction: *They'll* meet us at the beach.
long form: *They will* meet us at the beach.

contraction: The *cat's* in the basement.
long form: The *cat is* in the basement.

Exercise 9

Practice

Contractions and Verbs

In the space above each contraction, write its long form. The first one is done for you.

She would
1. She'd make a fine manager of a large department store.

Sarah is
2. Sarah's calling a throat specialist.

Sarah has
3. Sarah's called a throat specialist.

We will
4. We'll follow your car.

song is
5. The song's better than the first one.

I am
6. At night, I'm too tired to go out.

You are
7. You're never home when I call.

you would
8. I knew you'd like this restaurant.

they will
9. Tomorrow they'll plan a birthday celebration.

will not
10. The child won't listen to the teacher.

TEXT CREDITS

PAGE 7: Edgar Allan Poe, "The Tell-Tale Heart," from *Great Tales and Poems of Edgar Allan Poe*. Reprinted with the permission of Pocket Books, an imprint of Simon & Schuster Adult Publishing Group. © 1960 by Washington Square Press; © renewed 1988 by Simon & Schuster. Reprinted with permission.

PAGE 76: From John F. Kennedy's Inaugural Address from *The Oxford History of the American People* by Samuel Eliot Morison. New York: Oxford University Press, 1965, p. 110.

PAGE 76: Martin Luther King, Jr., "I Have a Dream Speech." Reprinted by arrangement with the hiers to the Estate of Martin Luther King, Jr. c/o Writer's House, Inc. as agent for the proprietor. Copyright © 1963 by Martin Luther King, Jr. Copyright renewed 1991 by Coretta Scott King.

PAGE 91: James R. Miller, excerpt from "The Estimable Mr. Campbell" from *Tropic Magazine. The Miami Herald*, November 18th, 1990, p. 8. Permission conveyed through Copyright Clearance Center, Inc.

PAGE 149: Edna Buchanan, "The World's Most Dangerous Profession," from *The Corpse Had a Familiar Face*, © 1987 by Edna Buchanan. Used by permission of Random House, Inc.

PAGE 211: "Isidor and Ida Strauss: Inseparable in Life, Then in Death," excerpt from Sunken Dreams: Real Stories of the Titanic. *People Magazine*, March 16th, 1998, pg. 47. People Weekly. © 1998 Time, Inc. All rights reserved.

PAGE 248: Winston Churchill, excerpt from "Dunkirk" speech from *World's Greatest Speeches* by Lewis Copland and Lawrence Lamm, ed. Mineola: Dover Publications, 1973, p. 439.

PAGE 298: Daniel Meier, "One Man's Kids" from *The New York Times Magazine*, November 1st, 1987. Copyright © 1987 by the New York Times. Reprinted by permission.

PAGE 302: Athlone G. Clarke, "When Words Get in the Way." Originally appeared in *The Atlanta Journal/Constitution*, January 30th, 1995. Reprinted by permission of the author.

PAGE 337: Ved Mehta, "The Baby Myna," from *Vedi* by Ved Mehta. © 1981 by Ved Mehta. Reprinted by permission of George Borchardt Inc. on behalf of the author.

PAGE 344: Judith Ortiz Cofer, "I Fell in Love, Or My Hormones Awakened" from *The Looking Glass of Shame*. Reprinted by permission from the publisher of *Silent Dancing: A Partial Remembrance of a Puerto Rican Childhood*. (Houston: Arte Publico Press.)

PAGE 375: Lillian Gwin, "I Wish" from *Arrows Four: Poetry and Prose by Young American Indians* edited by T.D. Allen. © T.D. Allen. Reprinted by permission of the author.

PAGE 377: John Grisham, "Death Row" from *The Chamber*. Copyright © 1994 by John Grisham. Used by permission of Doubleday, a division of Random House, Inc.

PAGE 380: Al Roker, "My Childhood: Skips and Stoops, Sisters and Saturdays." Reprinted with the permission of Simon & Schuster from *The Games We Played* by Stephen A. Cohen. Copyright © 2001 by Stephen A. Cohen.

PAGE 403: Ronald Takaki, excerpt from *A Different Mirror*. © 1993 by Ronald Takaki. Reprinted by permission of Little, Brown and Company, Inc.

PAGE 406: Clifton L. Taulbert, "Brotherhood" from *Eight Habits of the Heart*, by Clifton L. Taulbert. Copyright © 1997 by Clifton L. Taulbert. Used by permission of Viking Penguin, a division of Penguin Group (USA) Inc.

PAGE 411: Ben Stein, "Why Not Real Awards for Real Achievements?" From *The American Enterprise Magazine*, Sept/Oct 1997. Reprinted by permission.www.taemag.com.

PAGE 434: Joseph Martorano/John P. Kildahl, "Say Yes to Yourself" from *Beyond Negative Thinking* Copyright © 1989 by Joseph Martorano and John Kildahl. Reprinted by permission of Perseus Books Publishers, a member of Perseus Books, LLC.

PAGE 438: Amy Dacyczyn, "How to Buy a Car" from *The Tightwad Gazette* by Amy Dacyczyn. Copyright © 1993 by Amy Dacyczyn. Reprinted by permission of Villard Books, a division of Random House, Inc.

PAGE 484, 487: Gary Klott, "Part-time Job May Do Teenagers More Harm Than Good" from *The South Florida Sun-Sentinel*, September 1st, 1996, section G, p. 6. Reprinted by permission of Knight Ridder/Tribune Media Services.

PAGE 504: Maya Angelou, "New Directions" from *Wouldn't Take Nothing For My Journey Now*, by Maya Angleou. Copyright © 1993 by Maya Angelou. Used by permission of Random House, Inc.

PAGE 508: Beth Nieman, "Home Away From Home" from My Turn column, *Newsweek*, November 11th, 1996. © 1996 Newsweek, Inc. All rights reserved. Reprinted by permission.

Page 295: Martial Colomb/ Getty Images, Inc.- Photodisc.; **page 296:** Simon McComb/ Getty Images Inc.–Stone Allstock; **page 334:** Arthur Tilley/ Getty Images, Inc.–Taxi; **page 335:** Haroldo De Faria Castro/ Getty Images, Inc.–Taxi; **page 372 A:** Jacques Copeau/ Getty Images, Inc.–Taxi; **page 372 B:** Anne-Marie Weber/ Getty Images, Inc.–Taxi; **page 373 C:** Bob Daemmrich/ Bob Daemmrich Photography/ The Image Works; page **400 A:** Barbara Reed, Michael Williams/ Animals Animals/Earth Scenes;

page 401 B: Tim Davis/ Photo Researchers, Inc.; **page 401 C:** Ryan McVay/ Getty Images, Inc.- Photodisc; **page 401 D:** Peter Vander Mark/ Stock Boston; **page 431:** Ryan McVay/ Getty Images, Inc.- Photodisc; **page 432:** Bill Bachmann/ PhotoEdit; **page 477 A:** Jade Albert Studios Inc./ Getty Images, Inc.–Taxi; **page 477 B:** Michael Krasowitz/Getty Images, Inc.–Taxi; **page 478:** G. K. & Vikki Hart/Getty Images Inc.–Image Bank.

Note: Itemized listings for **Florida Exit Test** competencies and **Texas Academic Skills Program** test objectives are on pages 524 and 528 respectively.